Muslim Networks
from Hajj to Hip Hop

ISLAMIC CIVILIZATION & MUSLIM NETWORKS

Carl W. Ernst and Bruce B. Lawrence, editors

edited by
miriam cooke & BRUCE B. LAWRENCE

Muslim Networks
from Hajj to Hip Hop

The University of North Carolina Press

Chapel Hill and London

© 2005 The University of North Carolina Press
All rights reserved
Manufactured in the United States of America
Designed by Eric M. Brooks
Set in Carter & Cone Galliard
by Tseng Information Systems, Inc.
Pattern on frontispiece and part titles
designed by Jay Bonner

The paper in this book meets the guidelines
for permanence and durability of the Committee
on Production Guidelines for Book Longevity
of the Council on Library Resources.

Library of Congress Cataloging-in-Publication Data
Muslim networks from Hajj to hip hop / edited by
miriam cooke and Bruce B. Lawrence.
    p. cm. — (Islamic civilization and Muslim
networks)
Includes bibliographical references and index.
ISBN 0-8078-2923-4 (cloth: alk. paper)
ISBN 0-8078-5588-X (pbk.: alk. paper)
1. Islam—21st century. 2. Ummah (Islam)
3. Panislamism. 4. Islam—Computer network
resources. I. cooke, miriam. II. Lawrence, Bruce B.
III. Title. IV. Islamic civilization & Muslim networks.
BP161.3.M85   2005
306.6'97—dc22   2004016548

cloth   09 08 07 06 05   5 4 3 2 1
paper   09 08 07 06 05   5 4 3 2 1

FOR RICH MARTIN

Friend, colleague, collaborator,

& inspired forger of multiple networks

at home and abroad

CONTENTS

PART III: TRACING MUSLIM NETWORKS

Muslim Networks from Hajj to Hip Hop is the second volume, following Carl W. Ernst's *Following Muhammad: Rethinking Islam in the Contemporary World* (2003), to be published in our series, Islamic Civilization and Muslim Networks.

Why make Islamic civilization and Muslim networks the theme of a new series? At present, the study of Islam and Muslim societies is marred by an overly fractured approach that frames Islam as the polar opposite of what "Westerners" are supposed to represent and advocate. Islam has been objectified as the obverse of the Euro-American societies that self-identify as "the West." Political and economic trends have reinforced a habit of localizing Islam in the "volatile" Middle Eastern region. Marked as dangerous foreigners, Muslims are also demonized as regressive outsiders who reject modernity. The negative accent in media headlines about Islam creates a common tendency to refer to Islam and Muslims as being somewhere "over there," in another space and another mind-set from the so-called rational, progressive, democratic West.

Ground-level facts tell another story. The social reality of Muslim cultures extends beyond the Middle East. It includes South and Southeast Asia, Africa, and China. It also includes the millennial presence of Islam in Europe and the increasingly significant American Muslim community. In different places and eras, it is Islam that has been the pioneer of reason, Muslims who have been the standard-bearers of progress. Muslims remain integral to "our" world; they are inseparable from the issues and conflicts of transregional, panoptic world history.

By itself, the concept of Islamic civilization serves as a useful counterweight to that of Western civilization, undermining the triumphalist framing of history that was reinforced first by colonial empires and then by the Cold War. Yet when the study of Islamic civilization is combined with that of Muslim networks, their very conjunction breaks the mold of both classical Orientalism and Cold War area studies. The combined rubric allows no discipline to stand by itself; all disciplines converge to make possible a refashioning of the Muslim past and a reimagining of the Muslim future.

Islam escapes the timeless warp of textual norms; the additional perspectives of social sciences and modern technology forge a new hermeneutical strategy that marks ruptures as well as continuities, local influences as well as cosmopolitan accents. The twin goals of the publication series in which this volume of essays appears are (1) to locate Islam in multiple pasts across several geo-linguistic, sociocultural frontiers, and (2) to open up a new kind of interaction between humanists and social scientists who engage contemporary Muslim societies. Networking between disciplines and breaking down discredited stereotypes will foster fresh interpretations of Islam that make possible research into uncharted subjects, including discrete regions, issues, and collectivities.

Because Muslim networks have been understudied, they have also been undervalued. Our accent is on the value to the study of Islamic civilization of understanding Muslim networks. Muslim networks inform the span of Islamic civilization, while Islamic civilization provides the frame that makes Muslim networks more than mere ethnic and linguistic subgroups of competing political and commercial empires. Through this broad-gauged book series, we propose to explore the dynamic past, but also to imagine an elusive future, both of them marked by Muslim networks. Muslim networks are like other networks: they count across time and place because they sustain all the mechanisms—economic and social, religious and political—that characterize civilization. Yet insofar as they are Muslim networks, they project and illumine the distinctive nature of Islamic civilization.

We want to make Muslim networks as visible as they are influential for the shaping and reshaping of Islamic civilization.

Carl W. Ernst
Bruce B. Lawrence
Series editors

Many people have contributed to the intellectual, financial, and material production of this book. While none of them is responsible for its final form, all made the book itself possible and better through their efforts.

We thank Manuel Castells and Janet Abu Lughod, whose written work and spoken words to two of our classes on Muslim networks helped provide some of the core ideas that have shaped our ways of thinking and also this book. We are also grateful to our students in the three classes that we taught together. Our lively discussions about concepts, categories, and issues informed both the tone and the content of this book. Our special thanks go to the contributors to this volume. Most lectured to our students while attending the several meetings we held at Duke University to discuss earlier versions of their papers. At every stage, in ways too many to document, they helped us to refine our approach and broaden our methodology.

Without the financial and moral assistance of Eula and Paul Hoff, this book would not have seen the light. They provided support from afar, in Colorado, but we are also indebted to others close to home in North Carolina. Both the Duke University Center for International Studies and the Duke University Offices of International and Interdisciplinary Studies helped us to hold meetings and to convene conferences that crystallized the content and design of the book. We want to acknowledge with special gratitude Rob Sikorski, Cathy Davidson, and Gil Merkx.

Finally, we want to thank Mindy Marcus, Kim Hawks, and Ginny Jones, from the Department of Asian and African Languages and Literatures. Together they collated and made sense of a jumble of widely disparate materials. Even as the publication deadline loomed large, they did their indispensable task with consistent good humor.

Muslim Networks
from Hajj to Hip Hop

miriam cooke & BRUCE B. LAWRENCE

Introduction

From Mecca to Medina, from Arabia to Senegal to Indonesia and always back to Arabia and to Mecca, this has been the spatial rhythm, the mobile trajectory of Islam over the past fifteen centuries. Mecca is the birthplace of the Prophet Muhammad. It is the capital city of Islam. And more. The organizing principle of Islamic ritual and imagination, Mecca has become the defining node for a worldwide community of believers who are linked to the Prophet Muhammad and to Mecca and to one another through networks of faith and family, trade and travel. To be Muslim is to be connected to coreligionists who each day turn toward Mecca five times. Each year, Mecca attracts millions of Muslims from all over the world who perform the great pilgrimage, or Hajj, one of the basic requirements of Islam. Daily and annually across time and space, the history of Islam flows from Mecca and back to Mecca. It flows through myriad networks. They connect individuals and institutions, at once affirming and transforming them.

"Muslim networks" is a key term with two parts. "Networks" refers to phenomena that are similar to institutionalized social relations, such as tribal affiliations and political dynasties, but also distinct from them, because to be networked entails making a choice to be connected across recognized boundaries. "Muslim" refers to a faith orientation, but also to a social world in which Muslims are not always dominant. Both the networked nature of Islam and the impact of Muslim networks on world history are pivotal. Yet neither has received its due from scholars. A correction is needed. This volume intends to provide it. The authors of the essays in this volume are humanists and social scientists, insiders and outsiders, Muslims and non-Muslims. In examining aspects of Islamic civilization, they highlight transnational interactions, they foreground exchanges, and they explore connections from Dakar in Senegal to Djakarta in Indonesia, from the seventh century to the twenty-first.

Muslim Networks as Medium and Method

Precisely because Islam is not homogeneous, it is only through the prism of Muslim networks—whether they be academic or aesthetic, historical or commercial—that one can gain a perspective on how diverse groups of Muslims contest and rearticulate what it means to be Muslim. Humanists and social scientists focus on different elements of the diversity intrinsic to Islam. Some concentrate on individual Muslims who live and work in far-flung parts of the globe yet are frequently in touch with one another. Others examine the multiple expressions of Muslim piety all over the world. Humanists tend to accent language and subjectivity; their goal is to understand and interpret the lives of individuals and communities and the specific histories and texts that shape identities. Social scientists, on the other hand, generally emphasize collective actors—Muslims versus non-Muslims. Their intent is to clarify, and if possible predict, social, cultural, political, and economic conflict and change. Only a networked approach puts humanists and social scientists into conversation with each other. What it reveals is the radical heterogeneity of Muslim cultural, linguistic, and political exchanges.

One key word frames the medium for constructing Muslim networks, even as it suggests a method for their analysis. That word is *umma*, commonly translated as "global Muslim community." *Umma* is flexible rather than static; it signifies all Islam, but does so within the broadest boundaries defining Muslim collective identity. Its history has no single trunk narrative, but its many strands stretch back to the seventh century. Mecca is their common node, and Arabia their focus. The first Muslim networks overlay the trading networks of pagan Arabia that linked a merchant named Muhammad to the metropolitan world of Mesopotamia and beyond. Networks of negotiations made possible the exchange of material goods, ideas, and people; they defined cultural practices in the earliest phases of Islamic civilization. Today, advances in microelectronics have produced new networks in cyberspace, and hip hop has become one of its Muslim idioms. While these new networks link formerly marginal or disenfranchised Muslims with one another, they also provide forums for new groups, whether in Arabia or America, to assert their understanding of Islam as normative.

Until the twentieth century, Muslim networks privileged men. Whether they were networks of travel, pilgrimage, or proselytizing, they were mainly networks of men on the move. The only network in which women's participation was traditionally acknowledged was the annual Hajj. It brought Muslims from Africa and Asia to the Red Sea and to the Hijaz region in western Arabia. Clad in the *ihram*, the plain cloth wound around their bodies, both male and female pilgrims worshipped together. The Hajj is limited to one month, yet pilgrimage routes function throughout the year. The Hajj routes overlay the multiple networks of traders, travelers, and seekers of knowledge that connect Muslims to each other. Other pilgrimages may take Muslims to places like Tanta, Ajmer, Touba, and Karbala, but each models itself on the Hajj network.

The most durable feature of the Hajj is travel. Through literature, we learn about the networked nature of Muslim mobility that accents the Hajj but also extends beyond it to privilege travel of all kinds to many places. Between the tenth and the fifteenth centuries, *adab al-rihla*, a genre of travel literature, emerged. Professional writers were commissioned to write *rihlas*. These became so popular that some of the later *rihlas* seem to have relied on earlier versions to fill in descriptions of places that their authors had not visited. Such *rihlas* were not so much fictions as recycled accounts. By the fourteenth century, the genre was so well established that the armchair travel writer could obtain narratives from far-flung corners of the Muslim world and adapt them to his purposes.

The travel writer often required a patron. For instance, the Moroccan sultan Abu 'Inan Faris (d. 1358) was so impressed with the peripatetic career of his countryman, the famous traveler Ibn Battuta (d. 1368), that he wanted to preserve its memory. He commissioned the belle-lettrist Ibn Juzayy to record and embellish Ibn Battuta's adventures. The resulting *Rihlat Ibn Battuta* tells of the legendary travels of a Moroccan religious scholar who journeyed throughout the fourteenth-century Muslim world. It was a Muslim world scarcely recognizable today. Ibn Battuta's journeys included a lengthy stay in Andalusia, as Muslim Spain was known from the eighth century to the sixteenth. His journeys also included an extended stopover in West Africa long before the Atlantic slave trade emerged and devastated that part of the sub-Saharan African *umma*.

Among Ibn Battuta's contemporaries and coreligionists was the celebrated North African historian Ibn Khaldun (d. 1406). Jurist, philosopher, litterateur, and historian, Ibn Khaldun circulated in the same regional network as Ibn Battuta, drawing on centuries-old connections that were moral as well as physical. His major work, *Introduction to History*, demonstrates how Arabic had become the lingua franca, and Mecca and Medina the geographic nodes, of a vast premodern Muslim network. The network was at once political and apolitical. In Albert Hourani's words, Islamic civilization rested on "a body of knowledge transmitted over the centuries by a known chain of teachers that preserved a moral community even when rulers changed" (1991, 4). The moral community persisted even when individuals were uprooted from their countries of origin; the sense of shared experience animated, indeed sustained, those like Leo Africanus who were compelled to move. An exile from Spain at the outset of the sixteenth century, the historical geographer Leo trod the paths of Ibn Battuta and Ibn Khaldun, traveling from southern Spain to northern Africa to Arabia, even enduring a "conversion" to Christianity while a slave in the Vatican.

Leo's case is instructive. An involuntary Muslim traveler who was not a trained jurist, Leo Africanus began his journeys when he was forced to leave his homeland by the *Reconquista* of Spain's King Ferdinand and Queen Isabella. A reluctant migrant, Leo was the victim of a turbulent history.[1] Ibn Battuta, by contrast, reveled in the opportunities that travel facilitated. Wherever he went, he found himself integrated more and more into *dar al-Islam* (the domain of Islam). To be Muslim and to be a Muslim judge opened up for him the full benefits offered by "a networked civilization," to use David Gilmartin's apt phrase.

Through Ibn Battuta's account, we are given a template for understanding Muslim networks. In this volume, Vincent Cornell and Muhammad Qasim Zaman examine aspects of his *rihla* to demonstrate how a religiously defined network can become a mirror reflecting premodern Muslim cosmopolitanism. The itinerant scholar revealed a world identified as Muslim that spanned continents and oceans. *Dar al-Islam* included non-Muslims as well as Muslims within its borders. It was an urban-based, cosmopolitan world, at once diverse and plural. It was connected from West Africa to China through waterways, port cities, and centers of political and religious power. Berbers, Arabs, Indians, and Sudanese could travel to the outer limits of *dar al-Islam*. Whatever obstacles they faced, they could rely on the hospitality of their coreligionists: everywhere, they found food and lodging simply because they were Muslims. From the caravanserais to the Sufi *zawiyas*, or lodges, to the generosity of local rulers, the traveler versed in Islamic sciences expected to find a welcome wherever he went. Often it was travel itself that conferred prestige and wealth. During his twenty-four years on the road and at sea, Ibn Battuta was honored with more than a maintenance allowance: as he moved further and further away from his North African home, he found himself materially rewarded and also encumbered. En route to India, he was surrounded by a large retinue of slaves, companions, and richly laden beasts of burden that he had acquired from his latest patron.

But how did this fourteenth-century network become so ubiquitous and so effective? There are several factors that distinguish the Muslim world, making its networks at once more interconnected and interactive than those of other contemporary communities. They include trade, language, Sufism, and scholarship, but above all they include common moral ideals and social codes.

Prior to the rise of Islam, trade networks had been widespread, extending across the Mediterranean to the Indian Ocean and the South China Sea. Muslim traders built on these networks and gave them added value. In China, for instance, there were trading links with the Arab world that could be traced back to the second century B.C.E. This commercial connection comprised overland networks cutting across the northern territories, also known as the Silk Road, and a southern sea route. Not long after Muhammad's death in 632 C.E., Muslim envoys crossed the Asian continent, using these established networks of trade and cultural exchange to carry the message of Islam. Well-armed and militarily trained but not aggressive toward the Chinese state, Muslim soldiers helped the emperors to quell local rebellions while they strengthened existing commercial and cultural ties. They and their young religion basked in imperial favor. Their experience anticipated that of later Muslim traders who made the perilous sea journey to the southern ports of China. These traders settled in major Chinese cities and, like their coreligionists in the north, benefited from the patronage of a state that recognized in them effective allies. The trust was transferable: the Mongols were enemies of Chinese royalty, yet during the thirteenth and fourteenth centuries they singled out local Muslims for their commercial experience and expertise. Mongol leaders appointed Muslim traders to administrative office. They consolidated Muslim networks throughout imperial China while also helping to incorporate them into a transregional system of Muslim networks (Yuan 2003). So prestigious were these trading networks that some people converted to Islam merely to benefit from the commercial security promised by their religious affiliation.

Communication was facilitated by the fact that Arabic and Persian were linguae francae used by most elites. Some command of one or both helped individuals to integrate easily and quickly into a local Muslim trading network. Yet as Cornell's essay makes clear, the linchpin for Muslim networks was not language per se but a double emphasis on reciprocity and hierarchy. Reciprocity, or *taskhir*, implied a mutual exploitation of the ruler and the ruled, the patron and the scholar, the divine and the human. Hierarchy was indispensable to reciprocity. In its most schematic form, Muslim society of the fourteenth century had four categories—men of the pen, men of the sword, men of negotiation, and men of husbandry—ranked from the highest, men of the pen, to the lowest, men of husbandry. Though justice itself was the paramount virtue, it was justice seen not as equality but rather as equity through the balance of reciprocal obligations. The ruler may have been privileged, but he was not exempt from the rules of society as a whole, being dependent on each of these four categories of men, just as they were on him. Nor did the ruled automatically support the ruler. Ibn Battuta, for instance, was expedient rather than subservient, linked to those like himself, men of the pen, rather than attached to those unlike him, men of the sword, or rulers.

Though the cohesiveness created by shared values was not limited to men of the pen, or 'ulama', they were its primary exemplars. Traveling throughout transnational networks, the 'ulama' disseminated Islamic knowledge; they also added value to the networks they inherited and developed. Muhammad Qasim Zaman explores how the cosmopolitan, scholarly language of Islamic religious discourse cuts across multiple frontiers, constructing a universe of reciprocal benefit to those who master it. This religious discourse is at once flexible and transferable across time and space. Not only did it span the known world of the fourteenth century, but it also persisted across the vicissitudes of political and economic change that separated the premodern from the modern world system. From Muhammad Shibli Nu'mani (d. 1914) to Abu'l-Hasan 'Ali Nadwi (d. 2000) to Yusuf al-Qaradawi, an Egyptian jurist currently preaching and issuing legal opinions out of Qatar, twentieth-century Islamic scholars were bound to their predecessors by a shared commitment that was and is also evidenced in a shared practice. Today's 'ulama', like their predecessors, Zaman argues, participate in "a historically articulated interpretive tradition" that legitimizes and gives meaning to authoritative interpretations of foundational texts. They form interpretive communities that may be mobilized against outside forces, whether twelfth-century crusaders or twenty-first-century neocolonialists.

Yet this mobile and enduring juridical authority comes at a price. Zaman notes that while their shared discourse has always allowed 'ulama' to communicate easily with each other wherever they happened to be, it has sometimes blocked their ability to communicate with other Muslims who were not in their social class. The majority of premodern Muslims were villagers or rural agriculturalists; they did not concern themselves with juridical values or the custodians of those values, the *'ulama'*. Premodern networks were expansive, but they were traveled by the elite.

During the fourteenth century, institutional Sufism was beginning to take hold. Sufis obeyed the same rules of reciprocity and hierarchical value that characterized other men of the pen. Brotherhoods supplemented and competed with juridical forms of Islamic loyalty. Sufi adepts traveled from one shaykh to another, acquiring esoteric knowledge and certificates of competency (*ijazas*) as evidence of their growing erudition. The shaykhs generally presided over *zawiyas* that offered accommodation and set no limit to how long visitors might stay. They facilitated a form of horizontal, or social, trust between believers that presupposed the existence of a vertical, or spiritual, trust between the individual believer and the transcendent other. At the core of this trust was the valuing of hospitality to "the son of the road" (*ibn al-sabil*). Hospitality was more than a cultural mandate; it was also an act of piety.

While pursuit of spiritual knowledge motivated travel, travel in itself could be—and often was—considered a religious act. A famous tradition exhorts Muslims to seek knowledge even in China. In most places, Muslim travelers could find lodging in a *madrasa* (religious school) or a *zawiya* or a more secular form of hostel. In Anatolia, for instance, *fityan* associations, or brotherhoods of young idealists, prided themselves on their generosity to learned strangers. Like the *madrasas* and *zawiyas*, they operated on an unspoken but resilient and dynamic notion of trust.

Trust was perhaps the most important factor in Muslim travel because it was at its core the key trait of Islamic spirituality. The basic meaning of Islam is submission to the One who is the Creator, the Guide, and the Arbiter of all human existence. Even when travelers were not in the vicinity of a *zawiya*, *madrasa*, or *fityan* association, they could rely on a pervasive code of trust.

Trust translated into hospitality that was religiously underwritten by *zakat*, or almsgiving, one of the five pillars of Islam. Trust in others, hospitality, and charity were measures of one's trust in God; they were vital elements of the pervasive social code of Muslim travel. So important was the practice of *zakat* that rulers competed with each other to show foreigners the greatest generosity. Wherever Ibn Battuta traveled, according to Ross Dunn, he was with hospitable people "who shared not merely his doctrinal beliefs and religious rituals, but his moral values, his social ideals, his everyday manners . . . his tastes and sensibilities" (1986, 7).

Ibn Battuta's experience was unexceptional for a man of his class and education.[2] By his own admission, he was not especially learned, yet he was able to find patronage wherever he went because of his training in Maliki jurisprudence. Even basic instruction in one of the four schools of Sunni jurisprudence qualified adventurers for employment. The farther they went beyond the heartlands of Islam, the more appreciated were their talents. *'Ulama'* traveled widely, especially to frontier kingdoms that were in need of jurists. Since the *'ulama'* were deemed to be the official guardians of Islamic law, practice, and morality, there was mutual benefit to be gained from peripatetic scholarship. The foreign *'ulama'* mediated between newly Islamized rulers and their people. As imported scholars, they gave prestige to rulers, whose appreciation of the scholars' learning proved their own credentials. Thus empowered, rulers could link themselves to the heartlands of Islam. The scholars, for their part, gained prestige and, more importantly, remuneration from generous patrons.

So it was with Ibn Battuta. When he left Tangiers in 1325, he was twenty-one years old. With the exception of a short stint as *qadi* of the Tunis Hajj caravan, Ibn Battuta was constantly on the move. He went wherever he could market his juridical skills. He benefited from the largesse of his fellow Muslims until he arrived eight years later in the court of the Delhi sultan Muhammad ibn Tughluq, who immediately appointed him *qadi*. By 1334, Ibn Battuta had acquired a profile for which his education alone would not have sufficed. His travels had included several extended visits to Mecca. He became a *mujawir*, that is, someone honored for having lived for long periods in the precincts of the Ka'ba. More than the ordinary pilgrim who came to Mecca for the annual pilgrimage, the *mujawir* was "credited with exemplary devotion to God and to His House." Dunn explains, "In a more practical light, a season or more in Mecca gave him the chance to make friends . . . , associations on which he might draw for hospitality over the ensuing two decades" (1986, 109). These titles were proofs of personal piety that added weight to his professional formation and allowed Ibn Battuta to move easily and comfortably throughout *dar al-Islam*.

Travel demonstrates how Muslim networks function as a medium; approaching Islamic civilization from a slightly different angle, it also underscores their function as a method of knowing. Networking through travel is not uniquely Muslim, yet it compels attention to key elements in a Muslim worldview that are otherwise ignored. Travel accents both mobility and place. It gives place, or location, an important role in the production of knowledge in a networked civilization.

Courtly patronage throughout the region facilitated the travel and residence of writers and artists in many nodes of the networked premodern

Muslim civilization. In other words, royal courts served as more or less secular loci for the articulation of the larger Muslim network of scholarship and creative production. And so in the tenth century we might follow the peregrinations of the poet al-Mutanabbi through sources of livelihood—now in Cairo praising his patron, now in Baghdad satirizing him—to reimagine the *umma* in his day. Through examining the urban-based networks of writers and artists, we begin to understand the world they inhabited and how that world is filtered through their writing and painting.

Intellectual history reflects both movement and place. Medieval history acquires a new life when we put dates, people, and places into conversation with each other. Ibn Battuta becomes the product as well as the subject of his far-flung travels. When we think about the materiality of the places he inhabited and their cultural and political climates, we can detect how his travel influenced him; the places he visited shaped his understanding of Islamic norms. We can ask: How did his interaction with patrons and also with Asian scholars affirm and extend the legal knowledge he had brought from Africa? How did he transform bits of information from his urban hosts into his own body of knowledge?

Ibn Battuta's *rihla*, like all premodern Muslim accounts, needs to be reread in such a way that the place of enunciation is highlighted rather than ignored or minimized. History will provide a series of signposts, each pointing to the zigzag process of connection and transition, each providing cultural translations, even if they are necessarily fragmentary and provisional. If orthodoxy remains a reflex of power, as Talal Asad has argued (1986, 15), then moments of exchange and conflict complicate a monolithic narrative of Islamic orthodoxy precisely to the extent that they specify and localize knowledge production. Individual actors and narrators need to be read in terms of an open-ended process. It is an exchange affecting actor and narrator as much as audience, revealing unpredictable outcomes linked to multiple strands of Muslim memory and imagination. Networked exchanges reinforce established norms and orthodoxies even as they submit them to constant scrutiny and challenge.

One of the aspects of this premodern itinerary that still challenges our imagination is the sequence of pilgrimages that the restless Ibn Battuta undertook after his twenty-year sojourn in the East. Not content to stay at home in Morocco, he undertook first of all a journey to Granada in southern Spain, where he enjoyed the hospitality of the last Muslim kingdom of al-Andalus. While there, he remarked upon the presence of Sufi dervishes: they seemed much the same as those he had seen in Persia and India. What he did not remark upon was the naturalized presence of a Muslim culture as part of Europe, something that has been denied vehemently by the official conservators of European culture (Menocal 1987). Ibn Battuta observed the continuity of life between Islamicate Spain and the regions of the East where he had spent much of his life. The current opposition between Islam and a Euro-American "West" would have been incomprehensible to this indefatigable voyager. After Granada, Ibn Battuta took another trip, this time to West Africa, a rich arena for the exploitation of both gold and slaves. Here Ibn Battuta observed the region that within a century would become the chief harvesting ground for the slave trade of North America, where Muslims would constitute one-sixth of the population of enslaved Africans. In other words, he was a witness both to the millennial presence of Islam in Europe and the prospective participation of Muslims in America.

In many exchanges, there are elements that do not translate well, yet they still provide opportunities for reflection. Breaks in communication reveal gaps in the seamless logic of the narrative (see Chakrabarty 2000). These silences or gaps in the historical record undermine the taken-for-granted. They inspire new questions that interrogate the dynamics of intellectual exchange. It is in the situated dialogue between scholars of very different backgrounds that we begin to detect how it is that networks allow for the ongoing adaptation and rearticulation of Islamic norms. How did Ibn Battuta's Moroccan-based knowledge impact the production of local knowledge in India or China? We do not know directly, but we can infer that adapting knowledge produced in one place to the exigencies of another will always involve compromises, reversals, and sacrifices, even as it also opens up exciting new ways of viewing the world.

Muslim Networks as Metaphor

The fourteenth-century North African Ibn Battuta foreshadows and informs the modus operandi of Muslim cybernauts in the twenty-first century. The Internet has enabled a new kind of Muslim network that is less elitist than its predecessors yet remains linked to earlier epochs of Islamic history in ways that often seem more metaphoric than material. Charles Kurzman argues in this volume that networks are nothing more than "a metaphor that privileges certain aspects of reality that are deemed to be of theoretical importance" while necessarily excluding others. For Kurzman, like Stuart Kaufman, the analyst of Boolean networks, exchanges are not predictable, nor can networks be reified (Mark

Taylor 2002, 147). Instead, argues Kurzman, networks should be viewed as metaphors of process, contingency, and variability.

The Internet reveals a paradoxical aspect of the metaphorical function of networks: they are de-territorialized and gender inclusive even while remaining socially restricted in other ways. Unlike in the time of Ibn Khaldun, Muslim women today can travel, physically and imaginatively, forming their own networks. The network linking a Saudi woman in her country's capital with an Afghan refugee woman and an American Muslim woman becomes a forum of virtual connections in which three women can imagine themselves together for various purposes—friendship, solidarity, security, and commercial exchange. At the same time, however, this network links three physical beings in real places: Riyadh, Peshawar, and Chicago. The cyber network is powerful precisely because it allows these two ways of connecting that are at once free of space and bound to place. It allows individuals—in this case, individual Muslim women—to think themselves elsewhere while remaining in situ; it opens up the possibility for actual movement that serves to reinforce virtual connections.

Muslim women's associations, such as Women Living Under Muslim Laws, or WLUML,[3] are proliferating across the globe. Daily, they bring new and previously marginalized actors into the *umma*. Established in 1986 by the Algerian Marie-Aimee Helie-Lucas, the WLUML network has brought together women from all over the world in an attempt to provide information and to support both Muslim women and women who are living in places governed by Muslim laws and who do not know where to turn for guidance. During the 1990s, WLUML undertook a "women and law" project, the goal of which was to counter the growing influence of Islamists. Like many other women's networks, its platform advocates peace, prevention of violence against women, opposition to religious fundamentalism, gender equity, and women's rights (Chatty and Rabo 1997, 33). It is concerned to "integrate theory and action around strategic gender interests and the practical needs of working class, peasant and urban poor women" (43). Such women's networks project a common pattern of fragmentation, dispersal, and reaggregation. They highlight women's emergent importance within the *umma*.

Three of the essays in this volume deal with women's networks that have come into prominence in the 1990s. At first glance, they may seem to be disparate cases, but they in fact share a preoccupation not just with women but with women in specific contexts that reflect universal Muslim values. Jamillah Karim's essay focuses on *Azizah*. The women who create and read this women's magazine are brought together through a radically feminist forum. *Azizah* is a fashion magazine unlike any other, not least because of its wide-ranging social agenda. Women's voices are heard here in a way that would have been unimaginable to Ibn Khaldun or even to mid-twentieth-century Muslim scholars. *Azizah* celebrates and caters to the radical diversity of American Muslim women. This diversity is expressed through their identities, their interests, and their agendas. The network is not merely a discursive space of connections; it is also premised on women's actual meetings. Above all, *Azizah* highlights race as a marker of Muslim identity. Previously, Muslim women of color in the United States lacked a community forum. Now they are networked with others like them, and not quite like them, on the glossy pages of a religiously defined magazine. Confident of the inherent pluralism of Islam, they collectively define what it means to be Muslim and woman; they challenge androcentric interpretations of Islam; they consider opportunities for American Muslim women that cross ethnic, class, and generational as well as gender boundaries. They experience a strong sense of both community and belonging. *Azizah* portrays—even as it expands—an Islamic feminist network.

Among the elite, Westernized women of Cairo depicted in Samia Serageldin's chapter, a new trend toward religious affirmation takes the form of Islamic salons. The women of these salons network around Islamic practices revived or reconfigured to adapt to the end of the twentieth century. Some of these practices, such as the Hajj, the *'Umra*, and participation in Islamic charities, are well established. But the recent phenomenon (for women, as opposed to men) of frequenting mosques or women's *zawias* and attending religious lectures and Quranic study circles presents an interesting anomaly. The traditional notion of the proper space for Muslim women is subverted in the name of religion and redirected from private to public. Networking for religious purposes creates a new spoke in a wheel of interconnectedness reinforced by multiple social and family relations.

After the 1991 Gulf War, Tayba Sharif interviewed Shiite women driven from their homes in southern Iraq to refugee camps in Saudi Arabia and thence to new homes in Holland. Her essay shows that in all their dislocations, the collective identity of these doubly marginalized women was preserved through vertical and horizontal networking. The vertical networking was constructed by their diachronic relationship to foremothers who had for the past fourteen centuries connected themselves to Zaynab, the granddaughter of the Prophet Muhammad. The horizontal network was constituted by groups of Shiite women who connected with each other in Iraq, Saudi Arabia, and Holland, primarily through ritual and spiritual observances learned and then carefully controlled by the *mullaya*, or woman religious leader. Sharif explains that the women's connections are established at special lamentation sessions to commemorate the heroism of Zaynab. The medium of networking is the telling of sacred narratives that connect history and ritual to the women's own stories of devastation. It is in the remembrance of their great warrior foremother, her grief for her murdered brother Husayn, and her defiance of the tyrant Yazid (who may stand in for any contemporary tyrant) that they link themselves with peers across time and space.

These modern networks, while far more inclusive than their precursors, still resemble those that have characterized the Muslim world in the past. Like Ibn Battuta, who could imagine himself anywhere in *dar al-Islam*, these women are at home in many places that little resemble each other except that they are marked Muslim. Trust is the moral and social glue holding them together, providing both meaning and direction to their lives. There is, however, a crucial difference. Whereas the ability to savor the benefits of *dar al-Islam* in the fourteenth century depended on material means, today's networks are less informed by economic or class indices. Ibn Battuta concerned himself only with those who made up the cosmopolitan class, a class that considered itself "guardian of high culture and its transmission within Dar al-Islam" (Dunn 1986, 116). It was only the elite who could afford the costs of travel and so avail themselves of the hospitality of the fourteenth-century *dar al-Islam*. In contrast, twenty-first-century Muslim networks require less physical mobility as they become more diffuse and accessible. Reduced costs make them increasingly available to anyone who has basic literacy, typing skills, and a little spare cash. (In 2002, the Tunis medina cybercafe charged one dollar per hour for the use of the Internet, while a Beijing Internet bar charged as little as five cents per hour; in the summer of 2003 in U.S.-occupied Baghdad, young Iraqis were flocking to the growing numbers of cybercafes to keep in contact with the world.)

To compare Muslim networks across time and space is not to erase difference from the social fabric of Islamic civilization. Even the key words we are using need to be interrogated. Judith Ernst urges readers to think carefully about the qualifier "Muslim." How is it to be applied to networks of artists? What is it that constitutes the Muslim-ness of a work of art, securing it as part of a larger whole called Islamic art? Is it the identity of the artist or the patron? Or is it the content of the work itself? Ernst challenges the reader to think critically about labels and the ways they are attached to people, institutions, and commodities. Islamic art itself remains a contested category invented by European scholars at the outset of the twentieth century. By drawing attention to the process by which Muslim identity is layered through art and its creation, Ernst opens up a critical dimension to the study of Muslim networks.

From the fourteenth-century world of Ibn Battuta to the twenty-first-century world of Muslim women cybernauts and warrior descendants of Zaynab, much has changed, nothing more so than the speed of communication over distance. Space itself seems to have been replaced by a distinctly non-geographic virtual space. Cyber networks challenge our constructions of space. They reveal a cosmopolitan imaginary realm that brings into question traditional orientations between East and West, based as they are on a zero-sum notion of cultural identity. Cyber networks blur the binary distinctions between *dar al-harb* (the abode of war) and *dar al-Islam*. Already in premodern times, Muslims had modified this rigid dyad to include two other subcategories: *dar al-aman* (the abode of safety) and *dar al-muʿahada* (the abode of covenant). In cyberspace, however, even these expansive categories are blurred by innumerable connections across space and time. The diachronic and transregional role of Muslim networks remains Muslim, but it does so largely because of an Islamic epistemology that links the seventh-century proselytizing and trading networks of the Prophet Muhammad with the fourteenth-century travel network of Ibn Battuta and the twenty-first-century networks of Sunni and Shiite women seeking legal counsel or religious community through cyberconnectivity.

Underlying the power of all networks is their instrumentality. If networks did not function as a medium, their benefit as a method or metaphor would be moot. The same is true for the Internet. More than a symbol, the Internet functions as an instrument facilitating exchange between widely different groups of consumers. The World Wide Web presents a framework for rethinking historical interaction in more fluid and contingent ways. Muslim history is no longer charted in complementary or divergent narratives; it now includes multiple strands braided together from past, present, and future elements. Marc Bloch was right: people are more the products of their times than of their ancestors (1953, 32), and because twenty-first-century Muslims live in the information age, they have become the new Ibn Battutas, each traveling via the Internet to new "ports" in search of information that can be transformed into knowledge. Ideas and people have continued to travel since the time of Ibn Battuta; twelfth-century equity, which stressed fairness, nevertheless accepted both slavery and sexism, while twenty-first-century equality, a norm for modern Muslims as for their non-Muslim contemporaries, affirms that race and gender must be inclusive.

Muslim Networks across Time

This volume does not aim to trace the history of networks that shaped, and were reshaped, by the diverse experiences of Muslims in what Marshall Hodgson calls the Afro-Eurasian *oikumene* (1974). Instead, it offers a new lens through which to view the formation and subsequent phases of Islamic civilization. From the eleventh to the sixteenth centuries, Muslims were at the forefront of global change. Muslim scientists and metaphysicians, such as Ibn Sina, al-Ghazali, and Mulla Sadra, were linked across polities and territories to other elites: their ideas and writings influenced not only their own but other networked societies. A major figure like al-Ghazali drew on Aristotle as well as Muhammad, then integrated their legacy with his own insights, which he in turn transmitted to European figures like Ramon Llull and Thomas Aquinas, with the result that David Hume's Enlightenment project in Scotland uncannily reflected ideas about causality that al-Ghazali had articulated in Baghdad several centuries earlier.

The process of transmission and transformation was materially assisted by the global extent of the *umma*. Until the sixteenth century, Islamic empires controlled large expanses of the world. Only with the European discovery and conquest of the New World did the axis of world power shift and networks become reconfigured. However, Muslim networks continued to be an important element of the capitalist world system. Under colonial rule, they proliferated from the Indian Ocean to the shores of the Atlantic. Despite political asymmetries, the colonial and precolonial periods are linked as phases in the networking of Muslim knowledge.

It was during the eighteenth and nineteenth centuries, while the Mughal and Safavid empires were experiencing internal revolt and foreign invasion, that a new strand of Twelver Shiite loyalty surfaced. From Karbala and Najaf in Shiite Iraq to commercial centers in Iran to princely courts in northern India, there emerged a major academic network of Shiite elites. The traffic was two-way, providing material as well as spiritual benefit to all: while juridical scholars of Iraq and Iran received large sums from their wealthy Indian coreligionists, the scholars of India benefited from the prestige of their northern neighbors. The scholars who participated in this network pursued the rational sciences along with the traditional religious sciences. They engaged European science as fellow consumers.

Sunni networks of learning also spread from the Arabian Peninsula to the east coast of Africa and to the Asian archipelago. Scholarly groups of Muslim reformers cooperated to expand the textual core of Islamic subjects. Several of these Sunni networks were motivated by loyalty to institutional Sufism, including the most socially active of Sufi orders, the Naqshbandiya. Naqshbandi leaders promoted Islamic revitalization and mobilized their followers for a double jihad. One form of jihad was directed militarily against European imperialism; the other was directed intellectually against imitative Westernization.

A vivid example of Sunni Sufi networking is the Senegalese Murid trade diaspora that Mamadou Diouf has analyzed in his essay on vernacular cosmopolitanism. Diouf aims to "elaborate a single explanation of both the process of globalization and the multiplicity of individual temporalities and local rationalities that are inserted into it" (2000, 679–80). Tracing the history of the West African Sufi Murid brotherhood from its foundation in the nineteenth century to the present, Diouf argues that the network grew "by offering a new religious form, a new memory, and new images to peasant communities that had been disrupted and severely disturbed by colonial military campaigns [and] epidemics connected with the Atlantic slave trade" (682). Concurrently engaged in exclusivist mystical practices that entailed specific social arrangements wherever they settled and in the international peanut business that the French prized so highly, the members of the Murid brotherhood were able to reconcile Islam and colonial modernity. Theirs was what Diouf calls "a unique cosmopolitanism consisting in participation but not assimilation, thus organizing the local not only to strengthen its position but also to establish the rules governing dialogue with the universal" (686). A major phase in the spread of the Murid network came in the 1970s, when drought drove peasants into the Senegalese cities and later out of the country. Members of the brotherhood wove an immense global network linked to their spiritual capital of Touba, with economic and distribution centers in Sandaga and Dakar. Wherever they went, they established a discipline and a "trust that [was] never broken" (694–95). Unbreakable trust is the key element of not only the Muridiya but all Muslim networks.

What took place in the Senegalese trade and spiritual network provides a model case of the integration of Muslims into the contemporary global economy. Muslims were able to turn to their advantage oppressive structures that colonial powers had put in place. Not only for African but also for Asian Muslims, a significant dimension of their history has been marked by European colonial expansion. One cannot talk about modern Islam or Muslim networks without taking into account the world-transforming activity of the eighteenth, nineteenth, and early twentieth centuries. It was in the colonial period that nationalist networks involving Muslims first emerged. David Gilmartin analyzes the complex ways in which Muslim networks formed in colonial India. Networked Muslims collaborated in the struggle for independence from the British and on behalf of the new Muslim state of Pakistan. Yet they also faced tensions, especially when the horizontal networks enabling the founding of Pakistan had to come to terms with the hierarchical structure of the new nation-state.

Not only in India but everywhere, the modern history of Islam became inseparable from both European and indigenous nationalisms that provided platforms for the performance of competing identities and the projection of specific images. European colonizers reinforced already negative images of Muslims (Carl Ernst 2003). Civilizations became symbolic envelopes for group solidarity: their hierarchical rankings, though touted as objective, in fact reinforced the Enlightenment bias that only western Europeans were the standard-bearers of modern-day reason and progress. The whole record of humankind was etched on a triadic model: the concepts of primitive, classical, and modern charted clearly differentiated temporalities. If Africa was primitive, Islam, like India and China, was classical. Its adherents had attained a certain level of reason, enough to move beyond the stage of primitive but no farther. Muslims could reach the stage of modernity only with the help of western Europeans. From such a perspective, the expansion of European colonial rule was not aggressive; it was simply the logic of progress.

Progress should have dictated that colonial rule would weaken and undercut Muslim networks. The opposite was the case. While colonial rule broke down connections between specific local Muslim groups (for example, Berbers and Arabs), it also fostered the revival of these same groups in resistance to European domination. Ironically, the very networks that opposed European rule also linked Muslims to the metropolitan capitals of France and England. Education, both secular and religious, became crucial in expanding Muslim networks throughout Africa and Asia. Education included more than curricular content; it also inscribed usage of European languages in new contexts. During the nineteenth century, French and English became regional linguae francae for Muslim communities, sometimes displacing local Muslim languages, whether Urdu, Persian, Pashto, or Bengali. Owing to its liturgical significance, Arabic was the only Muslim language to retain its prestige during the colonial period (Carl Ernst 2003).

Both anticolonial and subaltern networks were organized in secular terms, with mythical appeals and institutional mechanisms that reflected European nationalism. Ethnic nationalism became the primary organizing principle despite the deployment of religious symbols and the mobilization of religious movements. Albert Hourani notes that what had begun as an "attempt to protect Islam by reinterpreting it tended to end as a discussion of the possibility of creating a secular society with social action" (1991, 73). Ethnic and regional nationalisms provided alternatives not only to existing empires but also, more importantly, to the *umma*.

During the decade or so following World War II, most Muslim countries achieved political independence, but not under the banner of Islam. Despite their notable role in resistance struggles, Muslim activists and reformers took a backseat to the secular politicians who were building new nation-states. It was the circumstances of the late 1960s and early 1970s that returned Islamic rhetoric to the forefront of domestic, regional, and international issues. This was a period when Muslims contended not only with outsiders, primarily those in search of oil fortunes, but also with impure insiders, autocratic secularists. Islam was at once the goal and the method: Muslim networks claiming Islamic authority opposed secular networks that invoked national or republican loyalty. Islam became an empty symbol of freedom and solidarity. The ideal of the *umma* may have been invoked, but its reality was filled with ideological fury.

The degree of European influence on Muslim public life remains a subject of fierce debate. Did European occupiers repress Islam throughout the vast realm traversed by Ibn Battuta and his coreligionists? Yes and no. While colonial rule played a crucial mediating role in the emergence of present-day Muslim networks, state and society experienced different fates. Even though Muslim nation-states were often constructed through conciliar decrees, such as the 1919 Treaty of Versailles and the 1920 Treaty of Sèvres, few Muslim societies fully succumbed to European hegemony. Individual Muslims, and also collective Muslim networks, found a crucial third space, a breach between the past and the future that reflected indigenous norms and values. Nowhere is this clearer than in the case of Muslim Personal Law, or MPL. With the approval of colonial powers but on behalf of resistant Muslim elites, MPL flourished as a measure of Muslim collective life.[4] In other words, the advocacy of MPL served the elites and not the subalterns. Women rarely benefited in a context where the policing of their bodies was integral to the system. Since the 1980s, some women have organized in reaction to the imposition of MPL. They have banded together and formed associations like Maghreb Collectif, the Arab Women's Solidarity Association, and WLUML (Chatty and Rabo 1997, 24).

Exchanges between Europe and the Muslim world were reciprocal. European colonial powers found themselves shaped by their interactions with colonial subjects. Particularly in the postindependence period, mass migrations from former colonies flowed into European metropolises, leading to what Saskia Sassen calls the continuities and the "strategic discontinuities" in economic and political life of the late twentieth century. Before 1980, one could still speak of a world economy as though there were stable players who managed the world's resources for their own political ends. Since the Cold War, however, the global economy has been "characterized by a rapid growth of transactions and institutions that are outside the framework of interstate relations" (1999, 100). Above all, it is widely variable and adaptable networks that reflect new economic conditions even as they aggravate geopolitical asymmetry.

Information Revolution

During the second half of the twentieth century, technological innovation became the catalyst for wide-sweeping changes that relegated Muslim governments to the back of the global economic stage. Despite the fact that the Iranian Revolution (1978–79) coincided with a period of global restructuring, the Islamic Republic of Iran never acquired the minimal resources it needed to foster scientific or technological innovation. Instead, the regime's diplomatic isolation forced it to mobilize covert networks of cooperation in order to develop its technology, such as nuclear power, and to maintain technological assets, such as U.S. military equipment, left over from the shah's time. In that respect, it was like other postindependence Muslim nation-states. Some enjoyed huge oil wealth, yet they lacked the infrastructures that made possible scientific and technological developments elsewhere. This continues to be the case in the postindustrial era that has heralded the information revolution. To what extent do Muslims continue to be consumers rather than producers of a new knowledge, especially since that new knowledge is based in Euro-American and Asian nodes of cyberspace?

It is this query that Carl Ernst has engaged in his essay on contemporary Sufism. Ernst shows how the ideological as well as the technological aspects of the information revolution have influenced Sufi leaders and Sufi networks. From mass printing in the late nineteenth century to the information highway in the late twentieth, the "secret" has been disseminated in new ways to new Muslim consumers. The secret of knowing God lies at the heart of the Sufi quest, yet it has now become available to new communities from North America to Southeast Asia. They are so dispersed that, in Ernst's words, "the open secret of mysticism must be reconfigured in terms of what are basically advertising paradigms."

Nor was Sufism the sole dimension of Muslim collective life to be transformed by the information revolution. Until the mid-1990s, three forms of media defined the information age: print (newspapers), audio (radio, telephone, tape cassettes, and cell phones), and audiovisual (television and movies). Since then, satellite television, after overcoming local censorship barriers, has played the greatest role in Muslim countries. No initiative has succeeded or generated as much impact as has the satellite television station Al-Jazeera, established in the late 1990s. Its creators were BBC-trained reporters sponsored by the emir of Qatar. During the post–9/11 period, this satellite television station broadcasting from the Arabian Gulf became as familiar to American viewers as CNN. It provided the world with otherwise unavailable coverage; in a virtual theater, it brought together viewers from all over the Arab and the Muslim worlds. Programs like *The Opposite Direction* feature conflicting personalities who debate one another, often on subjects of religious interest. These programs have garnered huge audiences unused to such open expression of controversial views.

The most revolutionary potential of the information age, however, rests with the Internet. In Saudi Arabia, AwalNet was the first Internet service provider in the kingdom. On November 7, 1999, it published an article online in which it promised to "marry the Internet and Islam for the millennium." Linking people, places, and commodities with an immediacy that seems to conquer space, the Internet has engendered a new way of being in the world that the French philosopher Paul Virilio calls "tele-presence," or the technologically enhanced capacity to "be" in several places at the same time (2000). Consider the pious Muslim who would like to make the annual pilgrimage to Mecca but does not yet have the time or the money. She may have to content herself with a virtual Hajj for the time being.[5] She can perform the Hajj today via the World Wide Web in a way unimaginable even only twenty years ago. Networking provides a lifeline for Muslim immigrants trying to make a home far from home and to diversify their participation in various communities to reflect shared interests rather than shared place or shared ancestry.

Muslims may also form contingent virtual communities, like WLUML, at the collective and individual levels that provide safety, companionship, social support, and a sense of belonging. Tele-presence enables a new form of association that compels a reconsideration of the meaning of community. What is community when participants do not share place but can communicate as if they did? If shared physical place is not a necessary condition, is the notion of community as embodied contact but the romantic projection of an idealized past?

The Internet has compelled a rethinking of places; one must revisit and reimagine cities, states, and boundaries. Cybertheorists have projected cities in unanticipated ways. Virilio points to the new policy of trade globalization that has turned the "local city [into] a district, one borough among others of the invisible world meta-city"; he quotes Pascal to describe this place whose "centre is everywhere and whose circumference nowhere" (11). This transformation also projects a danger. The extraordinary acceleration in global connectivity has produced a phenomenon Virilio calls global "cyberoptics," which threaten to become a new panopticon (121). This state of affairs "brings with it the systemic risk of a chain reaction of damage that will occur as soon as globalization has become effective." It heralds the "tragedy of knowledge" when the information bomb explodes (107).

Less apocalyptic is the analysis of Saskia Sassen. She also points to the importance of meta-cities. Their emergence and growth has been enabled by the hypermobility of capital and the deregulation of multiple markets (1999, 88). If we expand her analysis to reflect the full tide of global change, we would include major Muslim cities such as Tehran, Dubai, Istanbul, Kuala Lumpur, and Djakarta, but also Los Angeles and Houston, London and Paris, where there are significant Muslim minorities. Indeed, no discussion of the polymorphous new global order of transterritorial communication is possible without attention to the growing role of Muslim migrant communities and their networks.

How new is this political and moral ferment? Sociologist Manuel Castells is unambiguous. The world, he argues, has witnessed only two major revolutions in information: first, Gutenberg and the printing press, and now the World Wide Web and cyberspace (1996). Jon Anderson and Gary Bunt agree. In their essays for this volume, they suggest that although the latest developments of the information age charted since the mid-1990s have links with the past, their technological wizardry, particularly the Internet, is unprecedented, even if its potential for social change is unclear.

Demurrals to the novelty of cyberspace also appear in this volume. In their respective essays, both David Gilmartin and Charles Kurzman argue that we need to look behind the current presentist rhetoric of globalization. When we do, they assert, we will find obvious antecedents that also suggest limits to the transformative potential of the information revolution that has occurred in the last decade. They point out that elements of trust have always been the cornerstone of connections among dispersed groups interacting through common needs and interests. For Gilmartin, moreover, the very proliferation of Muslim networks brings not only opportunity but rivalry. Muslim networks compete with each other in the new and enlarged public sphere of Pakistan, an unprecedented Muslim nation-state that was itself the product of the colonial period.

Pakistan raises acute questions about the proliferation of competing Muslim networks. Although Pakistan was created by Muslim networks, which networks defined its meaning? The meaning of Pakistan, argues Gilmartin, "was rooted in a vision of community defined not primarily by the structures supporting the colonial state but by the bonds of devotion and love linking individual Muslims to symbols of Islam" that were popularized through the networks of the press. Yet these print communities were far from uniform. Gilmartin demonstrates how the networks of the press in Pakistan both enabled and threatened—at precisely the same time— the effective imagining of a common Muslim community that embraced all Pakistanis. In other words, the top-down bureaucratic power inherent in the hieratic structure of the nation-state threatened the horizontal networks that had contributed to the formation of Pakistan.

Jon Anderson surveys the development of the information revolution in multiple Muslim contexts. Anderson showcases how well-suited the medium is for the modern Muslim struggling to come to terms with a world that does not share her values. Selim the Cybermuslim becomes for Anderson the virtual alter ego of the Muslim diaspora. He worships in a *Masjid* of the Ether, where he is provided "primers on Islam in a catchy, youthful idiom." Growing numbers of Muslims online are performing "pious acts of witness" for Islam in cyberspace. Even though the Internet may not be economically enabling, argues Anderson, it is socially, politically, and spiritually empowering.

Yet it is far from egalitarian. Afro-Asian Muslim students who came to the United States to be trained as engineers in the 1970s were the first to create Islamic websites (notably, through branches of the Muslim Student Association). They became catalysts for digitizing Islam. They put scripture online, making available many renditions of the Quran and Hadith that in turn facilitated the production of new *ijtihads*, or interpretations of foundational texts. But this initial stage in which individual Muslim engineers made texts available online has been followed by a stage in which officializing strategies have become dominant. National orthodoxies now control resources and project their view of Islam in cyberspace. What matters is not just who can read the Internet but who controls the webmasters and the websites that claim to speak on behalf of all Muslims.

One of the most frequented Muslim websites, IslamiCity, is an off-shoot of Human Assistance and Development International, or HADI, a Saudi overseas holding company based in California. In Arabic, *hadi* means guide, or leader, and it is toward Saudi norms and values that this site guides Muslim cybernauts. It reflects the effort of the Saudi government to project itself as the bastion of Islamic orthodoxy. The HADI-sponsored website contrasts with those created by a socially active but numerically small Shiite subcommunity, the Isma'ilis. Their sites are internally helter-skelter. Even within this demographically tiny subset of the Muslim community, there is huge diversity of ethnicity, faith, and practice. The Agha Khanis contrast with Bohras, who themselves are divided between progressives and conservatives (Blank 2001). The message in cyberspace is clear: there is no single Islamic orthodoxy to which all "true" Muslims must conform.

In short, authority is more diffuse now than it was two hundred, or even ten, years ago. *Ijtihad* used to be the purview of the *'ulama'*. The complex language of their religious discourse had blocked access to the amateur. However, the migrant engineer theologians changed all that by distributing authority among Muslim cybernauts. Gary Bunt details how e-*ijtihad* has opened up debates in cyberspace that had previously been limited or foreclosed. No student of contemporary Muslim expression can ignore Islam in cyberspace. Islamic interconnectivity on the Internet has huge implications for the ways in which interpretations and decisions are made and politics are conducted. Bunt connects this interpretive activity with the less benign phenomenon of e-jihad. E-jihad is holy war in cyberspace. It has accelerated since 9/11. Multiple competing groups offer their analyses and prescriptions for the appropriate response to U.S. actions in Afghanistan and Iraq and to the war on terror.

These religiously minded techies share the concerns of Muslims worldwide: they foster cyber Islamic environments that reinforce Muslim values no matter what dominant culture or vocational demands individual Muslims face. The most profound diversity is found in the global distribution of Muslims themselves. There remains a hierarchy of Muslim cybernauts. At its peak are Euro-American Muslim immigrants. With their heightened sense of diversity, their need for faith-based community, and the human and material resources to link themselves with other like-minded groups, they project themselves to be on the leading edge for change in the Muslim world as a whole. They may exaggerate the impact of their own role, but the scope of their imagined potential for change is itself noteworthy.

Central to the fostering of Muslim values is contestation of the notion of authority. The World Wide Web both enhances and threatens individual authority. On the one hand, individual authority is enhanced as the individual is given more options for the exchange of information and more ways to reach wide audiences and to elicit trust. On the other hand, the very proliferation of competing sites and the intrinsic democracy of the World Wide Web undermine any notion of consensual authority. New religious interpreters and online counselors have become Muslim netizens, advocating local versions of Islam.

Due to the freedom of expression made possible in cyberspace, both women's *ijtihad* and e-*ijtihad* have flourished. This new freedom of expression has produced a new audience for alternative interpretations. Consider the debate about women's rights. This debate can be closed in real space by a dogmatic male majority, but it remains open in virtual space. For example, there is a hadith, or tradition, attributed to the Prophet Muhammad that states, "Anyone who places his affairs in the hands of a woman shall never prosper." Traditionalists have used it to deny women any role in affairs of state, or even any access to professional employment and political power, yet Islamic feminists like the Moroccan sociologist Fatima Mernissi and the Nigerian jurist Sanusi Lamido Sanusi[6] have convincingly demonstrated its spuriousness.

Muslim Networks and Globalization

"Globalization," reckons Amin Maalouf, "draws us simultaneously toward two contrasting results, one welcome and the other not: i.e., universality and uniformity" (2001, 104). Scholars of twenty-first-century Islam must also learn how to steer a safe path between the Scylla of disconnected particularisms and the Charybdis of totalizing claims. How else can we find an appropriate way to speak about Muslims and their history in the world?

If the term "Muslim network" offers a more complex and advanced view of Islam and civilization, it also offers helpful epistemology in the post–9/11 context. Documenting a new paradigm for the study of Muslims and Islam, it poses a challenge to media mavens who want to homogenize Muslims and to Christian zealots who strive to demonize Islam. Muslim networks taken out of context or restricted to the post–9/11 context might seem to result in but one thing: acts of terror committed in the name of Islam (Varisco 2002). Yet "Muslim networks" can be an episteme as well as a shibboleth, and as episteme, "Muslim networks" compels us to examine the levels of learning and trust that have motivated so many Muslims across time and space. The Internet has been the medium empowering both mainstream Muslim groups and marginalized groups. For example, al-Qaeda is a network of hard-line Muslim guerrillas cofounded by Saudi dissident Osama bin Laden and the Egyptian doctor turned activist, Ayman Zawahiri, who have exploited the political and military potential of the Internet. These dissidents need to be understood in their own terms and not as emblems of Muslim networks. Structured around dispersed nodes that communicate with one another in nonlinear space, the al-Qaeda network relies on neither a hierarchical chain of command nor conventional rules of engagement. Rather, it mobilizes nimble, dispersed, and highly elusive units capable of penetrating and disrupting, or even destroying, massive structures. Its call for physical violence relies increasingly on what Gary Bunt calls e-jihad, "a digital sword striking at a broad selection of targets." E-jihad spans multiple operations, from the "mere" hacking of sites to the violent sanctioning of bloodshed.

In this volume, Quintan Wiktorowicz brings social movements theory to the study of a contemporary aspect of Islamic civilization: the origins, organization, and actions of the Salafi movement across the world. Though a minority of all Muslims, the conservative activists who make up the Salafis believe that Islam as text-bound faith has been eroded from within. They appoint themselves as free agents to rectify this situation. Though Salafis are united in their devotion to the Quran, they are divided among themselves between nonmilitant reformists and those who may sometimes be driven to extremes. Dissent from the current world order, from Muslim majority states, or from both links Salafi militants from Chechnya and Kosovo to Uzbekistan and Tajikistan, from Kashmir and Afghanistan to the Philippines, Indonesia, and West China. Wiktorowicz depicts a widespread phenomenon. Disgruntled religious activists are calling for a return to the fundamentals: when Muslim-majority nations stray from the straight path, these activists argue, they must be purified of the long-term legacy of European colonialism and the recent threat of American neocolonialism. Both the civil war in Algeria and Bin Laden's 1996 declaration of war on the United States demonstrate that the potential for violence is limitless for Salafis who condone its use.

While the case of al-Qaeda has become compelling in the aftermath of September 11, 2001, there is a complementary case that demonstrates how dissent can be peacefully channeled through Muslim networks. The women of Afghanistan were subjected to intense scrutiny after the U.S.-led invasion in October 2001. Most media and policy experts concluded that they had to be saved from the Taliban. Originally, no attention was paid to feminist networks like the Revolutionary Association of the Women of Afghanistan, or RAWA. Founded in 1977, two years before the Soviet invasion, RAWA worked to defeat the Soviets but also to provide help for Afghan refugees who had fled to Pakistan. Throughout the 1980s and 1990s, it functioned as a network of transnational cooperation and multitiered resistance. Since 9/11, its pivotal role on behalf of Afghan women at home and abroad has been dramatized through cyberspace. RAWA demonstrates the persistent resilience of Muslim networks. They can be read in a number of ways: as a major form of social and political organization, as a prism through which to read history, and as a symbol of hope for those who find themselves on the margins of our current world system.

Conclusion

Over the past fourteen hundred years, Muslim societies have been constantly networked. Networks are not new. What is new is the proliferation of *Muslim* networks through communications technology. Knowing that they are potentially in touch all the time provides Muslim cybernauts —and also their non-Muslim counterparts—with a new way of knowing and of being in the world, a new way of connecting across time and space. Nowhere is this more evident than in the global phenomenon of hip hop. Hip hop is a musical genre that has networked Muslims in many national and linguistic subcultures, and H. Samy Alim demonstrates both its versatility and its connectivity in the information age. If hip hoppers are the most recent Muslim cybernauts, they share a common challenge with all Muslim cybernauts: how to be hip and Muslim, how to be part of a transformative moment while retaining the sheet anchor of one's own identity. The information revolution emerges out of technological developments and organizational patterns dispersed throughout the world, yet to understand Muslim networks as a part of that revolution, one must explore both their historical antecedents and their adaptation to novel elements of the information age that have emerged since the mid-1990s.

A major goal of this volume is to relate the cyber *umma* to the historical *umma*. Only when we understand how they function together as twin trajectories of Muslim collective existence, or the straight path, can we grasp the enduring impact of a Muslim imaginary. Indeed, the straight path is one of the most fertile and recurrent metaphors from the Muslim imaginary. It is introduced in the opening chapter of the Quran. "Guide us on the straight path," Muslims ask of Allah each day, whenever they engage in canonical prayer. The straight path leads to peace and certainty, to trust and truth, in this world and the next.

The boundaries of digital Islam reflect the scriptural, creedal, and historical boundaries of Islamic thinking. There can be no Islam without limits or guideposts. You cannot have a straight path unless you know what is beyond or outside or against the straight path. Cyberspace, like social space, must be monitored to be effectively Muslim. As Gary Bunt has noted, "much is done by Muslims in the name of Islam that is dismissed as inappropriate, or worse, by other Muslims" (2000, 141). The horizontal, open-ended nature of the Internet makes the boundaries of digital Islam at once more porous and more subject to change than those of its predecessors. There are still the same guideposts: the scripture (the noble Quran), the person (the Last Prophet), and the law (the shari'a, or broad path, with the *'ulama'*, or religious specialists, as its custodians). Each term— the book, the prophet, the law—has to be defined historically and then redefined in cyberspace in order to reflect the diversity of resources and worldviews within the *umma*.

Contributors to this volume use a connective epistemology to understand the process of network formation. They ask not only how networks shape and reshape identities but also how they reinforce and undercut authority. How free are individuals to organize in states where authoritarian regimes mistrust all forms of uncontrolled association and will attempt to co-opt these organizations as part of their claim to support civil society? How free are women to organize within societies dominated by patriarchal kinship structures that adhere to strict hierarchies? Contributors are concerned to expose diversity of race, class, and authority within a frame of Islamic loyalty. Their interdisciplinary approaches combine the humanistic stress on continuity with social scientific attention to change. If the key concept for humanists is Islam across time, for social scientists it is Muslims in different times and places aggregating in networked structures that function as a metaphor for human relations. Each approach needs the other in order to make sense of the complexity that characterizes Muslim networks as expressions of the diversity of a worldwide community.

Muslim networks provide a theoretical approach to Muslims and to Islam highlighting transnational connections that are spatial yet not space bound. It thinks difference together in such a way that space both matters and does not matter. A networked epistemology pluralizes individuals. It allows them multiple contexts where no one identity predominates and none can be reified. Such an epistemology undermines all homogenized categories; it reveals beneath the apparently seamless whole the multiple strands that braid it together. Muslim networks mirror the relationship of Islam to world history. Muslim networks mark a series of creative responses to global systems, past and present. They both sustain and contest the systems of which they are a part. The work of Muslim netizens reveals the hope, and also the limits of hope, available to the twenty-first century *umma*. The *umma* will persist as a universal community bound by faith and ritual practices, yet the Muslim networks that define and sustain it will continue to create tensions and competing nodes of authority that confirm the synergizing diversity of both Islam and Islamic civilization.

NOTES

1. Amin Maalouf captures Leo's alienation in these words: "I come from no country, no city, no tribe. I am the son of the road, my country is the caravan, my life the most unexpected of voyages" (1992, 1).

2. Ross Dunn describes Ibn Battuta as belonging to a "large class of lettered but not accomplished men who, for want of serious career possibilities in the central cities, gravitated out to the expanding Islamic frontiers, where a Muslim name, a reasonable education, and a large ambition could see a man to a respectable job, even to riches and power" (1986, 312).

3. See ‹http://www.wluml.org› (accessed July 28, 2003).

4. See Kugle 2001.

5. See ‹http://islamicity.com/mosque/hajj/› (accessed July 28, 2003).

6. See ‹www.gamji.com/sanusi.htm› (accessed July 28, 2003).

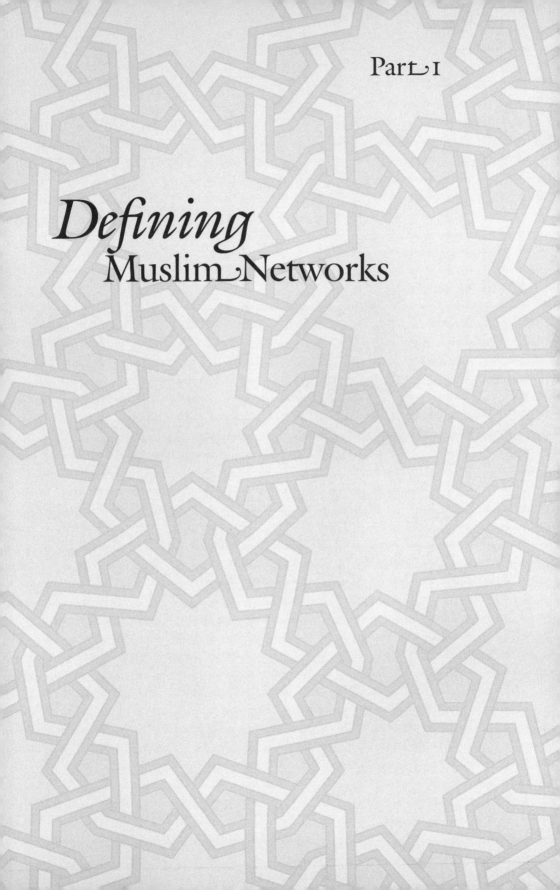

Part 1

Defining
Muslim Networks

VINCENT J. CORNELL

Chapter 1

Ibn Battuta's Opportunism

The Networks and Loyalties of a
Medieval Muslim Scholar

American university students, exposed for the first time to the travel memoir (*rihla*) of the fourteenth-century Moroccan scholar Ibn Battuta, typically have three reactions. First, they are amazed at the wanderlust of a man whose journeys occupied nearly half of his life and who did not rest until he had seen most of the known world from Morocco to China. Second, they disapprove of his apparent callousness toward women; he marries and divorces a series of spouses across Asia, leaving a string of children in his wake. The impression of callous machismo is reinforced by certain statements that Ibn Battuta himself makes in his narrative, as when he says of the women of the Maldives: "All of these products of the coco-palm and the fish which they live on have an amazing and unparalleled effect in sexual intercourse, and the people of these islands perform wonders in this respect. I had there myself four wives, and concubines as well, and I used to visit all of them every day and pass the night with the wife whose turn it was, and this I continued to do the whole year and a half that I was there" (Gibb 1958–2000, 4:823–24). Finally, students react negatively to Ibn Battuta's opportunism and self-promotion. Like a medieval carpetbagger, this scholar, whom Ibn Hajar al-ʿAsqalani (d. 1448) described as having only "a modest share of the sciences,"[1] marketed himself as a noted specialist in Maliki jurisprudence and attained important posts in the governments of several states without remaining for very long in any of them. Why, students ask, was Ibn Battuta so self-aggrandizing and cavalier toward his employers? Where was his sense of citizenship? Where was his sense of loyalty?

31

Few subjects better illustrate the conceptual gulf that separates the resident of a medieval Muslim state from the modern citizen of a nation-state than the issues of identity and loyalty. The citizen of a nation-state sees herself as belonging to an entity that transcends the most basic familial and social ties. Ideally, at least, the identity of a national citizen is bound up with shared notions of homeland in a territory defined by mutually recognized and contiguous borders, a common government, a common language, common customs, often a common religion, and a sense of social union that represents the norms and expectations of those who see themselves as sharing the same idea of "nationhood."[2] This sense of nationhood is reinforced by symbolic tokens such as a flag, diplomatic recognition, a national army, and membership in international organizations such as the United Nations.

By contrast, Ibn Battuta, like other intellectuals in medieval Europe and the Muslim world, had no such idea of citizenship. The imagined communities that he saw himself as part of were both more vast and more parochial than the modern concept of a nation. He was never a Moroccan, because there was no nation of Morocco during his lifetime. Apart from his Islamic identity, which was a complex construction in itself, Ibn Battuta's primary loyalties and identities could be understood almost entirely through his name: Abu 'Abdallah Muhammad ibn 'Abdallah ibn Muhammad ibn Ibrahim ibn Muhammad ibn Ibrahim ibn Yusuf al-Luwati al-Tanji. His civic identity was defined by the locale in which he was born (the city of Tangiers in the northern part of what was then called *al-Maghrib al-Aqsa*, "the Far West"), and his personal loyalties were defined almost exclusively by kinship. First, he was a member of the Luwata Berber tribe that had occupied the region of Tangiers since Roman times. More specifically, he was the descendant of an honorable line of local jurists, whose names would have been known to any native of Tangiers that he might have met in his travels. To the end of his life, he would have referred to himself primarily as a *Tanjawi* by origin, from an old and respected family, and tied by kinship to a lineage that confirmed his status as one of the notables (*'ayan*) of his native city. In a way that would be understood by residents of the American South, Ibn Battuta was an "original family" notable from a bloodline that had long counted in civic affairs, not unlike the inhabitants of the Greek polis for whom Aristotle's theories of government and ethics were formulated. Like Mario Puzo's Don Domenico Clericuzio in *The Last Don*, his loyalty was to "the creatures of his blood first; his God second . . . ; and third, his obligation to the subjects in the domain of [his] . . . family. . . . [The] government . . . never entered the equation" (1996, 59–60). His network was socially defined but politically anodyne.

"Our Thing" I: Racketeering and Instrumentalism in the Medieval Muslim State

The foregoing reference to a contemporary novel about the Mafia suggests ways in which Muslim networks are not unique in their function. Ibn Battuta, like Don Domenico Clericuzio, would have had good reasons not to let the government enter into the loyalty equation. With regard to the state and its functions, medieval Muslim notables resembled Mafia dons in the same way that governmental ethics paralleled Mafia-style instrumentalism. In an important article written about twenty years ago, the historical sociologist Charles Tilly remarked, "If protection rackets represent organized crime at its smoothest, then war making and state making—quintessential protection rackets with the advantage of legitimacy—qualify as our largest examples of organized crime" (1985, 169). The medieval state, whether in Europe or in the Muslim world, was a coercive enterprise that was based on the concept of protection as business. In the Muslim world, barely fifty years after the death of the Prophet Muhammad, social realities and the necessities of statecraft overrode the egalitarian principles of the Quran and the early Islamic community of Medina. By Ibn Battuta's time, the dominant form of government was the sultanate. The Arabic term *sultan* means "one who exercises power (*sulta*)," or, in more colloquial terms, "strongman" or "dictator." Sultans and their officials ruled over a populace that was designated as *al-ra'iya*, "the flock." The flock needed the sultan and his army for protection against local violence and external invasion. This army was not a professional army in the modern sense; it consisted of tribal warriors related by kinship or ethnicity to the sultan, a special class of slave-soldiers known as *mamluks* (individual strongmen and their retinues) who owed the sultan their personal loyalty. In return for being protected by these military forces, the flock paid taxes—assessed in land, money, or labor—that supported the sultan and his army and bestowed legitimacy upon them. This relationship was expressed in a formula known as the circle of equity, which owed its origins to the paradigmatic sultanate of the Seljuq Turks, who ruled over Central Asia, Iran, and Iraq in the eleventh century C.E. (r. 1038–1157). The formula reads as follows (Itzkowitz 1972, 88):

1. There can be no royal authority without the military.
2. There can be no military without wealth.
3. The flock produces the wealth.
4. The sultan cares for the flock by promoting justice.
5. Justice requires harmony in the world.
6. The world is a garden, and its walls are the state.
7. The support of the state is Islamic law (shariʿa).
8. There is no support for Islamic law without the military.

Apologists for this system, which remained dominant in the Muslim world until the nineteenth century, justified its existence in terms of the need for protection against external enemies. Sometimes, this argument was combined with the argument that the sultanate protected and extended the reach of Islamic law, so that the sultanate could pass itself off as a "jihad state" that represented the political and military interests of Islam in a particular region. But most of the time, the circle of equity was used as a convenient excuse for the state to create its own means of self-justification, and it obscured the fact that the greatest threat to the flock was often the state itself. The circle of equity was not a circle of equality, and those privileged within its network were those who benefited from its hierarchical structure. Muslim populations suffered as the result of overtaxation and other predatory practices on the part of the state and its officials even more than they did at the hands of external invaders. As Charles Tilly observed, "Someone who produces both the danger and, at a price, the shield against it is a racketeer" (1985, 170–71). Thus, according to Tilly's definition of racketeering, the medieval Islamic sultanate could legitimately be seen as a protection racket, and *la cosa nostra*, "our thing" for the sultan and his military commanders, was a Mafia-like enterprise with the sultan as *il padrone*, the chief patron or "godfather."

The key to running a successful protection racket is to strike a balance such that the extortionate demands of the racketeer are not so great as to drive his clients to seek "protection" from someone else. Patronage quickly loses its value if the cost of maintaining the patron drives one to ruin. There is an unspoken reciprocity in such arrangements, whereby the client expects the patron to provide a sufficient return of protection or other useful services as recompense for his investment. Just as the patron may make the client "an offer he can't refuse," so the client, in the long run, may maintain expectations that the wise patron cannot refuse either. To put it another way, a sultan, in his role as chief patron, must act as a husbandman over his flock. Even if he chooses to be an absentee patron who entrusts his flock to "shepherds" such as military governors and tax officials, he must see to it that the flock is cared for in such a way as to maximize long-term profitability over short-term gain. In actual practice, justice in the fourteenth-century Islamic world was a matter of perception and was negotiable, at least up to a point. Practical justice depended on a Hobbesian balance of competing self-interests in which the level of maintenance required for the sultan and his retinue plus the maintenance required by the military and local officials was not so great that the flock lost its means of livelihood. Intelligent sultans and their officials were aware that hopelessness could constitute a serious disincentive to the production of wealth. The failure of the state's enterprise could come quickly if the flock realized that its sheepdogs were really wolves.

Despite the fact that medieval Muslim reformers often decried the exploitative nature of state formation and state maintenance, the basic premises of the system were seldom challenged on the ground. Acknowledgement of the status quo is amply illustrated in books of Islamic jurisprudence, in which the issue of property expropriation (*ghasb*) by the state constitutes a major subcategory of legal practice.[3] Most of the time, however, the principle of the inalienability of property ownership was honored more in its breach than in its observance.

The reciprocal nature of the relationship between the sultan and his flock was also acknowledged in theological and moral writings. The Spanish Sufi Ibn al-ʿArabi (d. 1240), who was born to a family of notables from Murcia and who demonstrates upper-class values in his works, saw the reciprocity that characterized relations between patrons and clients as mirroring the reciprocity that pertained between God and the world. This reciprocity, which Ibn al-ʿArabi termed "mutual exploitation" (*taskhir*), meant that although a higher order of being or social status (such as God or the sultan) might exploit or subjugate the lower orders (humanity or the flock), a lower order might also "exploit" or constrain a higher order (Izutsu 1983, 182–86). According to Ibn al-ʿArabi, higher orders subjugate lower orders through an act of will (*taskhir bi-l-irada*); this is part of the nature of things. God exploits humans so that they serve him; humans exploit animals, plants, and minerals for shelter and sustenance; animals exploit plants for sustenance; and plants exploit minerals. But the divine economy of justice also imposes a "return" on this exploitation, for if exploitation were unrequited, the moral balance of the universe would be upset. Thus the lower orders have the right to exploit or constrain the higher orders by virtue of their subservient status (*taskhir bi-l-hal*). Ibn al-ʿArabi describes this type of reciprocal exploitation by using the example of a sultan and his subjects, thus demonstrating that he sees a congruence between the social hierarchies of human beings and the natural hierarchies of existence:

> The *taskhir* is of two kinds. The first is a *taskhir* which occurs by the will of the "exploiter" (*musakhkhir*) who subdues by force the "exploited" (*musakhkhar*). This is exemplified by the exploitation exercised by a master over his slave, though both are equal in their humanity. Likewise the exploitation exercised by a Sultan over his subjects in spite of the fact that the latter are equal to him as far as their humanity is concerned. The Sultan exploits them by virtue of his rank.
>
> The second kind is the *taskhir* by the "state" or "situation"; like the *taskhir* exercised by the subjects over their king who is charged with the task of taking care of them, e.g., defending and protecting them, fighting the enemies who attack them, and preserving their wealth and their lives, etc. In all these things, which are the *taskhir* by the state, the subjects "subjugate" their sovereign. In reality, however, this should be called the *taskhir* of the "position" (*martaba*), because it is the "position" that compels the king to act in that way. . . . Thus, in this sense, the whole world acts by its very "state" as a "constrainer" which constrains the One who is impossible (on the level of common sense) to be called "constrained."[4]

Justice in the medieval Muslim world was more about proportionality than equality. The root meaning of *'adl*, the Arabic word for justice, does not connote equality in the sense of sameness, but rather conveys the idea of equalizing, or restoring balance. As such, it has much in common with the Classical Greek word for justice, *dikaiosune*, which carries the connotation of fairness rather than equality (MacIntyre 1998, 11). This similarity of meaning was not lost on early Muslim philosophers and jurists, who saw in *'adl* and the related term *haqq* Aristotle's notion of distributive justice. Aristotle defined distributive justice in terms of the mean: "To do injustice is to have more than one ought, and to suffer it is to have less than one ought" (79). Thus to be just is to be fair, right, or in accordance with the law. Corrective justice entails restoring the fair balance that has been lost. The Arabic term *haqq* means, according to the context in which it is used, "law," "right" (in the sense of personal or legal rights), "truth," or "portion." To be a just man (*rajul 'adil*) in a medieval Islamic context meant to uphold the law (*haqq*), which is grounded in the divine truth (*haqq*), and to reestablish fairness by restoring things to their original nature (*haqiqa*); this is accomplished by regulating (*tahaqquq*) the distribution of goods such that everyone receives his rightful share (*haqq*). But receiving one's rightful share does not mean receiving the same share as everyone else. Since human society is naturally hierarchical, receiving the same would mean that some people would receive more than they ought, thus creating injustice. Medieval Muslim society was not a caste system, and it was possible for a peasant or one of the urban poor to become a scholar, a Sufi saint, or even a notable, but the typical peasant was not a scholar or a notable and was not to be treated like one. This Aristotelian notion of distributive justice and proportional ethics was often expressed in the hagiographies of Muslim saints, in which a common trait of the saints was their ability to understand intuitively what was due to each individual and class of person under the rules of distributive justice.

Ibn Battuta would probably have known of the Moroccan saint Abu al-'Abbas al-Sabti (d. 1204), the patron saint of the city of Marrakech, who was born and raised in Sabta (modern Ceuta), a short journey along the Mediterranean coast of the Far Maghrib from Ibn Battuta's home town of Tangiers. In his chosen role as patron and spokesman for the poor of Marrakech, Sabti based the entirety of his saintly career on Aristotelian notions of distributive justice and corrective justice. As for his approach to distributive justice, the rigorously systematic way in which Sabti distributed alms out of the donations that people gave him is one of the clearest expressions of proportional ethics to be found anywhere:

> I divide everything that comes to me into seven portions. I take one-seventh for myself and the second-seventh for that which I am required to spend on my wife and the small children under her care, as well as the slaves and slave-girls [in our household], all of whom number thirty-two individuals. Then I look after those who have lost their sustenance; they are the neglected orphans who have neither mother nor father. I take them in as my own family and see to it that not one of them lacks a [proper] marriage or a burial, unless someone else provides it for them. Then I look after my kinfolk, who number eighty-four individuals. They have two rights: their right as family members and their right as residents [in my household]. Then come those who have been deprived of their support as mentioned in the Book of God Most High. They are the poor who have fallen into hardship on the Way of God—those who are unable to work the land and are thought of as ignorant, but who are rich in patience and restraint; they are the ones unable to manage their own affairs. I take them in as if they are my own relatives, and when one of them dies, I replace him with another.[5]

Was Sabti consciously following Aristotle in his distribution of goods? Or was he simply following the Quranic admonition (16:90): "Verily Allah commands justice, the doing of good, and giving to one's near relatives"? Most likely, the Islamic notion of distributive justice had become so imbued with Aristotelian ethics by Sabti's time that Aristotle's "hidden hand" could no longer be discerned. Sabti's notion of corrective justice was equally Aristotelian. His way of restoring a just balance of goods through the redistribution of personal wealth was not aimed at social equalization but at the restoration of individual material rights, whether they consisted of money, property, food, or even children. Termed by Sabti "sharing in proportionate measure" (*mushatara*), this restitution of rights constituted a form of miraculous extortion whereby those who had "more than they ought" were compelled by threat of divine sanction to redistribute the excess among those who had "less than they ought." For the most part, excess personal wealth was redistributed to individuals, but at times the redistribution could be collective, as when Sabti convinced the daughter of the ruler of Marrakech to donate one thousand gold dinars to the city's poor. Sabti's saintly form of extortion was a very tangible application of Ibn al-ʿArabi's concept of *taskhir*, in that he restored the lost material rights of the subjugated poor by extorting excess (and thus unjust) wealth from the racketeers who ran the state. What ultimately protected him from persecution by the state was the fact that for Sabti, "excess" did not mean "surplus," so that he never demanded more than the just mean. Sabti's racket, if it can be called such, was to offer the power elites of Marrakech protection from God's corrective justice by indemnifying them through acts of social justice against debasement in the present life or the hereafter. "Who is it that will give to God a goodly loan, so that He may increase it many-fold?" asks the Quran (2:245). Using more philosophical language, Sabti stated, "Potential existence is actualized through generosity [*Al-wujud yanfaʿilu bi-l-jud*]."[6] If Robin Hood had been a saint who could perform Aristotelian ethical miracles like Sabti, Richard the Lion-Hearted might never have left his French prison and returned to England.

Even an upper-class Sufi such as Ibn al-ʿArabi had to acknowledge that "some kings act only for their own selfish purposes" (Izutsu 1998, 185). Not every capital city was lucky enough to have a divinely sanctioned moral censor like Sabti. Even the best of rulers had to act cruelly at times in order to keep their thrones. The conflicting claims of morality and the realities of power caused medieval Muslim jurists such as Ibn Battuta to maintain equivocal and often contradictory attitudes toward their royal patrons. The most successful of these rulers were, again, not unlike Godfather Don

Domenico Clericuzio in Mario Puzo's *The Last Don*: "Don Domenico led his family to the very heights of power. He did so with a Borgia-like cruelty and a Machiavellian subtleness, plus solid American business know-how. But above all, he did so with a patriarchal love for his followers. Virtue was rewarded. Injuries avenged. A livelihood guaranteed" (1996, 60). Compare this passage with Ibn Battuta's description of his most significant patron, Sultan Muhammad ibn Tughluq of Delhi (r. 1325–51), and the similarities are unmistakable: "This king is of all men the most addicted to the making of gifts and the shedding of blood. His gate is never without some poor man enriched or some living man executed, and there are current amongst the people [many] stories of his generosity and courage and of his cruelty and violence towards criminals. For all that, he is of all men the most humble and the readiest to show equity and to acknowledge the right. . . . He is one of those kings whose felicity is unimpaired and whose success in his affairs surpasses all ordinary experience, but his dominant quality is generosity" (Gibb 1958–2000, 3:657–58).

Like an extended Mafia family, the medieval Muslim state was more a network of personal loyalties than a formal bureaucratic institution. Its internal ethic consisted of a soulless instrumentalism in which royal patrons ranked their soldiers and other clients according to the value they could produce for the ruler. In the states of the Maghrib out of which Ibn Battuta came, governments were family enterprises in which the ruling groups maintained close ties with their kinsmen, whether on the personal, clan, or tribal level. In terms of the reciprocal rights held by clients against their patron, such kinsmen had a distinct advantage over non-kin, because their loyalty was more dependable. The downfall of a familial state could mean the downfall or even extermination of an entire kinship group. Officials of the state who were not related to the ruler had to try much harder to prove their value. The virtues of loyalty and service to one's patron were well rewarded. The lavish gifts given by Muhammad ibn Tughluq to his foreign visitors were designed to lure such outsiders into a web of personal obligations to him so that he could use them as instruments of his power. For all intents and purposes, officials without familial ties like Ibn Battuta were slaves of the sultan, and rulers such as Muhammad ibn Tughluq had no scruples about expropriating their officials' wealth and sacrificing their lives when their usefulness ended. Kinship by marriage might help extend one's life of service, but not always. In Ibn Battuta's long and chilling litany of Ibn Tughluq's extortions and persecutions of the servants of his realm, one senses that the greatest fear of those in government service was the seeming randomness of an official's rise and fall and the fact that an official's ultimate fate depended, in a moral sense, not on the sins that the official committed while in office but on the sin of government service itself.[7] Even the relatively enlightened Marinid sultan of Fez, Abu 'Inan Faris (d. 1358), who welcomed Ibn Battuta at the end of his travels and is eulogized lavishly in Ibn Battuta's *rihla*, was not free of the moral stain of state power. In 1356, when Abu 'Inan tried to visit the Sufi saint Ahmad ibn 'Ashir of Salé (d. 1362), the saint went to great lengths to avoid meeting the sultan because the sultan had attained power by deposing his father. After Ibn 'Ashir sent Abu 'Inan a letter reproaching him for his misdeeds and warning him of his imminent downfall, the sultan replied ruefully, "All Sultans are unjust and despotic, are deceived by their confidants, and allow their intimates to carry them away with their passions" (Cornell 1998, 144).

"Our Thing" II: The Guild of the 'Ulama', *Protectors of Islam*

The story of the failed encounter between the Marinid sultan Abu 'Inan and the Sufi saint Ibn 'Ashir, and the extent to which Ibn Battuta (or Ibn Juzayy, his ghostwriter) describes manifold examples of the generosity and cruelty of Muhammad ibn Tughluq, suggest that much more is at stake in these narratives than a mere description of events. Rather, such encounters between sultans and scholars suggest a morality play in which the *sultan*, the "possessor of power," and the *'alim*, the scholar or "possessor of knowledge," are the chief characters. What are important in these encounters are not only the personalities that take part in them but also the roles themselves. The philosopher Alasdair MacIntyre uses the term "character" to express a social role that links dramatic and moral associations in this way: "In the case of a *character* role and personality fuse in a more specific way than in general; in the case of a *character* the possibilities of action are defined in a more limited way than in general. One of the key differences between cultures is the extent to which roles are *characters*; but what is specific to each culture is in large and central part what is specific to its stock of *characters*." For MacIntyre, characters are moral representatives of their culture "because of the way in which moral and metaphysical ideas and theories assume through them an embodied existence in the social world." "*Characters*," he explains, "are the masks worn by moral philosophies" (1984, 28). Characters are useful to the historian of cultures because their unique embodiment of personality and role helps to reveal the moral fault lines that exist within societies. Because they are objects of regard for significant segments of the population, characters legitimate specific modes of social existence and provide a cultural and moral ideal (29). Just as "the culture of Victorian England was partially defined by the *characters* of the Public School Headmaster, the Explorer, and the Engineer, and that of Wilhelmine Germany was similarly defined by such *characters* as those of the Prussian Officer, the Professor and the Social Democrat" (28), so medieval Muslim society was partially defined by the characters of the Sultan and the Scholar.

"The worst of scholars is he who visits princes, and the best of princes is he who visits scholars," said the Persian Sufi Jalal al-Din Rumi (d. 1273).[8] This statement conveys a trope that has been a fundamental part of Islamic ethics since the era of the Umayyad caliphate (661–750). According to this trope, the state, by attempting to regulate the affairs of the material world, is unavoidably polluted by the world, and thus it pollutes anyone who comes into contact with it.[9] For Sunni Muslims, the only states that were free of this corruption were those established by the Prophet Muhammad in Medina (622–32) and the "Rightly-Guided" caliphate of his fist four successors, Abu Bakr, 'Umar, 'Uthman, and 'Ali (632–61). All other states, including the Umayyad caliphate of Damascus and its successor state, the Abbasid caliphate of Baghdad (750–1258), were touched by worldliness and were thus polluted to a greater or lesser degree.

Acting as a bulwark against the state and its corruption were the men of knowledge (*rijal al-'ilm*, or *'ulama'*), who upheld the moral values of Islam and protected the people from the excesses of rulers. Although the category of men of knowledge potentially included all of the religious, including jurists, theologians, philosophers, Sufis, and a variety of mystically minded and non–mystically minded ascetics, the jurists eventually came to dominate this category because of their specialized knowledge of Islamic law. Principle seven of the circle of equity, discussed at the beginning of this chapter, states: "The support of the state is Islamic law (shari'a)." Because of the importance of the shari'a to both the state and Islamic society in general, it was a foregone conclusion that those who interpreted the law (*fuqaha'*, sing. *faqih*) would be the men of knowledge (*'ulama'*) par excellence. True men of knowledge had to be independent. If they were not independent and sought royal favor or patronage, their judgment would become corrupted. Rumi said of such scholars, "Whether it is the prince who formally visits him or he who goes to visit the prince, he is in every case the visitor and it is the prince who is visited" (Arberry 1975, 13).

In the Far Maghrib of Ibn Battuta, the character of the scholar-jurist commanded enormous respect as a moral ideal in society. Those who were credited with establishing the rule of Islamic law in a particular locality were given the honorific "anchors of the earth" (*awtad al-ard*) and after death entered the ranks of local saints. They were given this honorific because they acted metaphorically as "tent-pegs" (the literal meaning of *awtad*), holding down through their teachings and moral example the great tent of divine justice that protected everyone within its shadow. By interpreting and defending the shariʿa, and by maintaining God's justice on earth, they were also regarded as representatives and defenders of the people, and they passed into folklore as a sort of North African Muslim equivalent to the minor prophets of Israel.[10] In a tradition frequently cited by the *ʿulama'* themselves, the Prophet Muhammad said, "The *ʿulama'* are heirs to the prophets."[11] Local histories in the Maghrib are replete with stories of scholarly "anchors of the earth" such as Darras ibn Ismaʿil (d. 968) and Sidi Bu Jida (d. 978), both of Fez, who defended the political and moral integrity of their city long after their deaths (Cornell 1998, 9–12).

By Ibn Battuta's time, the *ʿulama'* saw themselves as a network of corporately organized professionals, a quasi-class that occupied a position in the social hierarchy just below that of the rulers. Perhaps the clearest view of their self-image as characters in a morality play can be found in the Persian jurist Nasir al-Din at-Tusi's (d. 1273) description of the social hierarchy of the Muslim state. Each member of the classes depicted in this hierarchy constitutes a moral and metaphysical "character" in the sense that MacIntyre uses the term. By depicting each social category as a quasi-caste, Tusi reveals his debt to both Aristotle and the social system of pre-Islamic Sasanian Persia. Overall, this model gives an accurate picture of how Ibn Battuta would have conceived of himself at the court of Delhi, if not in his home country:

> First come the Men of the Pen such as the masters of the sciences and the branches of knowledge, the canon-lawyers, the judges, secretaries, accountants, geometers, astronomers, physicians, and poets, on whose existence depends the order of this world and the next; among the natural elements these correspond to Water. Secondly, the Men of the Sword; fighters, warriors, volunteers, skirmishers, frontier-guardians, sentries, valiant men, supporters of the realm and guardians of the state, by whose intermediacy the world's organization is effected; among the natural elements these correspond to Fire. Thirdly, the Men of Negotiation, merchants who carry goods from one region to another, tradesmen, masters of crafts, and tax-collectors, without whose cooperation

the daily life of the species would be impossible; among the natural elements, they are like Air. Fourthly the Men of Husbandry, such as sowers, farmers, ploughmen, and agriculturalists, who organize the feeding of all the communities, and without whose help the survival of individuals would be out of the question; among the natural elements they have the same rank as Earth. (Tusi 1964, 230; in Itzkowitz 1972, 39)

Three important points emerge from this description of social categories. First, although Tusi places the *ulama* below the rulers (who, not being mentioned as one of the elements, seem to be outside of the social order), he nonetheless praises them as those "on whose existence depends the order of this world and the next." Second, he places the *ulama* above the military, from whose ranks the sultan comes. The implication of this (at least to a perceptive military ruler) is that the *ulama* are more important to the functioning of the world—and hence the state—than the ruler himself. Third, a subtler message is conveyed by Tusi's pairing of each class with one of the four elements. According to the ranking of the four elements passed down since the time of the Greek mystical philosopher Empedocles, water was matched with earth, and air was matched with fire.[12] When translated into Tusi's schema, this means that the "fire" of the military cannot "burn" without the "air" of the merchants, whose taxes and tax-collection services provide the funds to support them; likewise, the agriculturalists' "earth" needs the "water" of the *ulama* so that the land may sustain life through God's grace. This is more than just a restatement of the circle of equity. Recent studies of premodern Muslim society have demonstrated that the majority of *ulama* came from the mercantile class.[13] Thus it might be argued that the *ulama* and the merchants constitute the most fundamental elements of society. Just as life on earth cannot exist without air and water, so the social life of Muslim society cannot exist without the *ulama* and the merchants.

The solidarity of the *ulama* was based in part on a common education and a common epistemology. The educational basis of this solidarity was the *madrasa*, a type of religious school that usually provided a legal education.[14] The *madrasa* system as an institution was created in the eleventh century by supporters of the Seljuq sultanate, who wished to promote a standardized version of Sunni Islam. The epistemological basis of *ulama* solidarity could be found in the content of the *madrasa* education, which relied on the *usul* (roots, or fundamentals) method of legal reasoning. This method, which is attributed to the jurist Muhammad ibn Idris al-Shafi'i (d. 820), stressed the use of written scriptural sources (primarily Quran and Hadith) as the basis of legal decisions. Under the *usul* method, "law-finding" consisted of the application of Aristotelian logic to scriptural sources. By the late eleventh century, the growing popularity of Shafi'i jurisprudence and the *usul* approach to knowledge had led to the "usulization" of intellectual life in the Islamic East. Because the *usul* approach was based on legal reasoning, training in the roots of jurisprudence (*usul al-fiqh*) was fundamental to all forms of higher education. Whether the graduates of *madrasas* were to become jurists, theologians, Sufis, government officials, historians, scientists, or mathematicians, all shared the same *usul*-based education.

This was particularly true in the Maghrib, where the *usul* method became dominant in the twelfth and thirteenth centuries. Under the Maliki school of jurisprudence, which predominated in this region, nearly all *madrasas* were endowed by officials of the state. The *qadi al-jama'a*, the chief justice of a city and a government appointee, was responsible for the hiring of all teaching faculty in a *madrasa*. If necessary, he could also determine the curriculum that was taught. Ibn Battuta's youth coincided with the period of the introduction of abridged texts for *madrasa* education, which stressed rote memorization over the dialectical disputations that had characterized advanced study sessions in earlier times. Sultan Abu al-Hasan al-Marini (r. 1331–48), whom Ibn Battuta's patron Abu 'Inan deposed in order to take power, was a great builder of *madrasas*. In the Far Maghrib alone, he constructed such schools in the cities of Marrakech, Meknes, Taza, Salé, Anfa (modern Casablanca), Asafi, Azemmour, and Ibn Battuta's home city of Tangiers. Compared with some of their counterparts in the East, who enjoyed a *madrasa* education that was less subject to standardization and governmental control, run-of-the-mill *'ulama'* such as Ibn Battuta must have appeared as cookie-cutter scholars, more striking for their adherence to common tradition than for their originality. On the other hand, they would have shared a remarkably strong sense of esprit de corps and loyalty to their own kind. When these *'ulama'* were far from home, their attachments would have been transferred to like-minded compatriots from other schools of jurisprudence.

The solidarity of the *'ulama'* often led them to pass moral judgments on the state. Nearly all of the formulators of premodern Islamic political theory were *'ulama'*. What is remarkable about their theories is how little they dealt with actual realities and how often they expressed ideals. All of these theorists bemoaned the emasculation and eventual elimination of the Islamic caliphate (called in their works the "imamate"), which they saw as providing the only truly legitimate form of Islamic government. Some, such as the theologian Abu Hamid al-Ghazali (d. 1111) and his teacher Abu al-Ma'ali al-Juwayni (d. 1085), who worked for the Seljuqs, were apologists for the sultanate system. But other scholars were more critical of military-dictatorial regimes and stressed the role of the *'ulama'* as guardians both of Islam and of the rights of the civilian population. One of the more pragmatic of these critics was Abu Bakr al-Baqillani (d. 1013), a Maliki jurist from Basra whose views were influential in the Maghrib. Baqillani's version of realpolitik posited the *'ulama'* as ethical watchdogs over the imam, who did not have to be a caliph and whose responsibilities in office were limited to protection, taxation, and the promotion of Islam (1987, 477–78). Along with the leaders of the major social groups within the realm, the *'ulama'* constituted "those who loosen and bind" (*ahl al-hall wa al-'aqd*). It was they who conferred legitimacy on the ruler by confirming a negotiated "contract" (*'aqd*), or set of understandings, by which the ruler governed. In principle, only one scholar was necessary to confirm the "contracted" (*ma'qud*) ruler in office. It was better, however, if the contract between the ruler and the scholar was witnessed (467–69). A ritual of formal witnessing, known as the *bay'a*, was held in Ibn Battuta's time at every change of ruler and continues to be practiced today in the Kingdom of Morocco. Ideally, the best-qualified (*afdal*) candidate would be chosen as the ruler. But when the realities of political life made it impossible to select the best candidate, a sufficiently qualified (*mafdul*) candidate would do (475).[15] In such cases, the *'ulama'* were responsible for watching over the ethical affairs of the state and advising the ruler on matters of religion and morality. When the ruler acted unjustly, it was their obligation to object, and in extreme cases they were even authorized to remove the ruler and replace him with another (478–80). Perhaps because of the widespread influence of Baqillani's writings, the Maghrib was one of the few places in the Muslim world where one could find states ruled by jurists prior to the creation of the Islamic Republic of Iran in 1979.[16]

When viewed in light of the solidarity that prevailed among the *'ulama'*, the low esteem in which most of them held the state, and their sense of entitlement as self-appointed guardians of Islam, Ibn Battuta's attitudes toward personal loyalty and government service begin to make more sense. Sometimes, the supercilious demeanor of the *'ulama'* could be downright irritating. How could anyone expect a sultan such as Muhammad ibn Tughluq not to react when a scholar such as Ibn Battuta's friend Jamal al-Din al-Maghribi—who was on the sultan's payroll—recited the following verses (Gibb 1958–2000, 3:685): "As for their Sultans, ask the clay about them / Those powerful heads are now but empty skulls"? Given the precariousness of their positions at court, it is amazing how many of these scholars seem to have disregarded the danger of scorning, if not actually biting, the hand that fed them.

The military commanders upon whom Muhammad ibn Tughluq's power depended were hard and brutal men, and they had to be kept under control by hard and brutal means. In order to keep the violence of these commanders in check, any infraction at court that involved physical harm to another was punishable by death. But even by resorting to such extreme measures, Ibn Tughluq was not able to quell all violence, nor was he able to protect all of the members of his family. In a short but poignant vignette, Ibn Battuta tells us that the sister of the sultan often complained to her brother about her mistreatment at the hands of her husband, a commander by the name of Mughith. Despite the fact that Mughith's wife was the sister of one of the most feared rulers in the Muslim world, Mughith's violent nature eventually led him to beat his spouse to death. However, because of Mughith's high rank as an ally, or "king," of the realm, the most that Ibn Tughluq could do was banish him for his crime (3:691).

Although brutal means were sometimes justified, Ibn Battuta's descriptions of Muhammad ibn Tughluq's sadistic punishments give a clear impression that some of his worst tortures and humiliations were reserved for the 'ulama', especially those who dared to defy him or whose popularity he deemed to have become too great. One of these unfortunate scholars was the Sufi master Shihab al-Din al-'Umari, whose eventual disgrace and execution almost cost Ibn Battuta his life as well. This shaykh, who was noted for his moral virtues and fasting and had received the favor of Ibn Tughluq's predecessors, took it upon himself to assert his moral authority and criticize the sultan for his oppression. He was eventually beheaded, but only after Ibn Tughluq mocked his highly vaunted purity by forcing him to consume more than four pounds of human excrement (3:697–700). Ibn Battuta also informs us of the executions of other Sufis and jurists whose only crime was daring to express their own opinions about matters of state. The trope of the corrupting influence of government service on otherwise upright officials is expressed in Ibn Battuta's account of two jurists from Sind who were tortured into confessing to a crime they did not commit. Before their execution, they were forced to write a statement acknowledging their crimes and absolving the sultan of responsibility for their deaths; they wrote in the document "that their confession had been made without compulsion or coercion, for if they had said that they had been forced to make a confession they would have been most severely tortured, and they held that a quick beheading was better for them than to die under painful torture" (3:701–2). To add insult to injury, and perhaps to demonstrate to the *'ulama'* the practical limit of their virtuousness, the sultan ordered the "qadi" (either the chief judge of the palace or the Hanafi *qadi* of Delhi) to be brought in to hear the confessions of these men and put his seal on the document as a testament to its veracity.

Clearly, Ibn Battuta had very good reasons to distrust the sultan whom Ross Dunn has described as "the odd duck of fourteenth-century rulers" (1986, 189). It is also clear that "to take service with Muhammad Tughluq was to live a life of reckless insecurity, to spin the wheel of chance with every word or action on which the sultan might choose to have an opinion" (192). But Ibn Tughluq, extreme as his actions may have been, was no lowbrow Turkish enforcer. Paradoxically, he was one of the best-educated rulers of Delhi, and he composed significant works of religious scholarship. Had he not been a sultan, he might have been one of the *'ulama'*. When Ibn Battuta arrived in India, he came on the scene at a time when the state was locked in a struggle for power with the *'ulama'*, who were in open revolt against Ibn Tughluq's policies of administrative centralization. This is why Ibn Tughluq spent such lavish sums trying to recruit foreign officials whose loyalty he could purchase and who had no local or regional ties that could be used against him. To return to the Mafia analogy used at the beginning of this chapter, he was like a don trying to recruit a new crew in the midst of a war of families after discovering that his own wiseguys had turned against him. This is an old story in the annals of power politics, and seen in this light, Ibn Tughluq was not as much of an "odd duck" as he might otherwise appear. Except for the level of his brutality, he was very similar to Ibn Battuta's final patron, the Marinid sultan Abu 'Inan, who was the most *'ulama'*-like of Marinid rulers, and like Ibn Tughluq, he was abandoned by many of the religious leaders whose support he sought.

It is important not to idealize the *'ulama'* just because their stated aim was to promote religion and virtue and their methods were less brutal than those of the sultans they served. When viewed institutionally, it is clear that they too had an enterprise—*la cosa nostra*, "our thing"—and acted corporately and politically in their self-interest to make their "thing" as successful as possible. Besides having an interest in promoting religion, education, and moral values, they also represented the interests of the mercantile class. Acting in ways that bring to mind the political attitudes of eighteenth-century Whigs, they promoted policies such as peace, limited taxation, fair dealing, property ownership, and individual and collective rights, all of which had the virtue of being both morally defensible and good for business. These men of knowledge, or intellectual wiseguys, constituted their own guild, if not a mafia, and could act every bit as instrumentally as did the agents of the state. They could also act ruthlessly against their rivals, as when ʿAbd al-ʿAziz al-Qayrawani (d. 1350), a jurist of Fez and a contemporary of Ibn Battuta, tried to outlaw the practice of Sufism by openly acknowledging in a fatwa that Sufis were a political threat to the *ʿulamaʾ* because they were popular among the masses.[17] Indeed, the very existence of the Marinid state in the Far Maghrib was a result of a bargain that was struck between the *ʿulamaʾ* and the Banu Marin ruling clan. Much as the *ʿulamaʾ* of Iran supported the Seljuqs in the eleventh century, the *ʿulamaʾ* of the Far Maghrib used the military power of the Banu Marin and their Zenata Berber allies to reestablish the hegemony of the Maliki school of law in their region after it had been threatened by the centripetal forces of tribalism and heterodoxy.[18] However, just as the *ʿulamaʾ* could help create a state, they could also bring it down. In May 1465, a jurist named ʿAbd al-ʿAziz al-Waryaghli (d. 1475 or 1476) incited the inhabitants of Fez against ʿAbd al-Haqq II, the last Marinid sultan, who was trussed up like a sheep and had his throat cut by his own soldiers.[19]

"People are people, and the days they are as one; / Time is but time, and the world is his who has won" (Ifrani [1970s?], 24). These verses were composed by Muhammad al-Sheikh al-Saʿdi, a subsequent dynasty builder of the Far Maghrib who, like Muhammad ibn Tughluq and Abu ʿInan al-Marini, tried to combine in himself the characters of scholar and sultan. Ibn Battuta would probably have agreed with him. The paradoxes and dilemmas of loyalty that Ibn Battuta faced in his travels were typical of those that every self-motivated and ambitious intellectual faced in both Europe and the Muslim world prior to the advent of the nation-state and the ideal of nationalism. Since there was as yet no nation to serve as a focus for his loyalties, and because the state was a coercive and exploitative enterprise, the only transcendent loyalty to which Ibn Battuta could appeal was that of religion. All other loyalties were self-serving, parochial, or both. As a Muslim scholar who enjoyed a greater level of physical and social mobility than his European counterparts, Ibn Battuta had the advantage of a wider range of options. But how could the loyalties that served him in Tangiers serve him in India? The support of family, tribe, and fellow *Tanjawiyyin* was left thousands of miles behind him; the state was likely to devour him, and personal friends might betray him; his wives might console him for a time, but they had the disadvantage of being foreigners whose primary loyalties were to their own kin. Furthermore, because most of his marriages were instrumental, he could not expect bonds of affection to form in the way they would have if he had married for love. The world of Muslim states and Islamic diaspora communities did provide him with a sort of homeland from North Africa to China, but whenever possible he still preferred to associate with fellow Maghribis. Even his fellow Suhrawardi Sufis could provide but limited solace and support for him. So what was left? What Ibn Battuta most relied on was his loyalty to himself and his own skills at network maintenance. These were qualities that he could share with others of his training and background. In the final analysis, loyalties such as these were the only loyalties that a stranger in a strange land like Ibn Battuta could afford. Ultimately, it is his attention to the motto "To thine own self be true" and his belief in individual autonomy that make him understandable to the contemporary reader, despite the vast gulf in time, culture, and morality that must be bridged between them.

NOTES

1. Ibn Hajar al-ʿAsqalani, *Al-Durar al-kamina*, quoted in Gibb 1958–2000, 1:ix.

2. The Enlightenment concept of social contract has been critiqued many times. John Rawls replaces this term with the related but more inclusive concept of social union, which I use in the above passage (1999, 456–62).

3. See, for example, Wansharisi 1981, 9:537–82. The section cited is entitled "Decisions Concerning Usurpation [*ghasb*], Compulsion [*ikrah*], and Proprietary Rights [*istihqaq*]." Issues of rape (*ightisab*) are also included in this section.

4. Translated in Izutsu 1983, 185. Where appropriate, I have replaced Izutsu's translation of *taskhir* as "constraint" with "exploitation" or "subjugation," which I believe more fully convey Ibn al-ʿArabi's sense of the term.

5. Translated in Cornell 1998, 85. The quotation comes from Tadili 1984, 459–61.

6. Translated in Cornell 1998, 91.

7. See, for example, Gibb 1958–2000, 3:695–708.

8. Arberry 1975, 13. This saying appears in the first sentence of the first discourse of Rumi's *Kitab fihi ma fihi*. Rumi attributes it to the Prophet Muhammad.

9. For a good overview of this trope in biographical literature on the ʿulama', see Cook 2000, 50–66.

10. In a tradition similar to that of the "anchors of the earth," Jewish tradition alludes to thirty-six righteous scholars who, usually unrecognized, sustain the world. See Gendler 2003, 25.

11. See, for example, Ghazali n.d., 1:5. See also Ibn Maja al-Qazwini n.d., 1:81.

12. See Wright 1995, 22–30. Equally relevant to the present discussion is the fact that Empedocles often opposed fire to all of the other three elements to-

gether (24). In Tusi's schema, this would put the military in opposition to the interests of the scholars, the merchants, and the agriculturalists alike, a situation that often paralleled actual fact.

13. For two of the best-known and most highly regarded examples of such studies, see Bulliet 1972 and Petry 1981.

14. The best introduction to the *madrasa* system in Islam remains that of Makdisi 1981.

15. This was justified by the need for defense against external enemies.

16. The city-state of Sabta (present-day Ceuta) was ruled by "the Greatest Jurist" (*al-Faqih al-Mu'azzam*), Abu al-Qasim al-'Azafi, from the year 1250. Rule of the city continued under the jurists of the Banu al-'Azafi family until 1320. See Ferhat 1993, 230–59.

17. Cornell 1998, 129. See also Cornell 1999.

18. Cornell 1998, 125–36. The use of educational institutions by the Marinid *'ulama'* to promote their political and social agendas is also detailed in Mediano 1995, 31–71.

19. For the details of this revolt, see García-Arenal 1978.

Chapter 2

A Networked Civilization?

Recent years have seen a dramatic increase in scholarly interest in networks. The modern revolution in information technology has given rise to new forms of social, political, and economic organization that are increasingly independent of state control. Emblematic of this transformation, of course, has been the rise of the Internet, which has called into existence a dense network of communication largely unconstrained by national boundaries. Interest in the Internet has spurred a new wave of social analysis focusing on networks and on their potential to transform the world's social organization in the new, global "information age."

Indeed, the network has become, for many, the central metaphor for understanding the contemporary age. This preoccupation with networks has only been accelerated by popular reactions to the dramatic events of September 11, 2001. As one newspaper columnist noted in the wake of September 11, the spread of "global terrorism" dramatized the critical need to understand networks and their importance in the modern world (Ignatius 2001). To help us in this, he directed our attention to a recent study from the Rand Corporation that argued that the "network form" of social organization is "on the rise in a big way," fueled by new forms of communication and "deeply affecting all realms of society." With networks, or "webs of dispersed, interconnected 'nodes,'" on the ascent, both "global civil society" and "uncivil society" have begun to gain increasing power "relative to state and market actors," a trend likely only to accelerate in the future. "Netwar," or conflict focused on the operation of networks, the study concludes, could well be the wave of the future (Arquilla and Ronfeldt 1996, 17–18, 23–24, 33–34, 53–54).

Given the events of September 11, such interest in the "network form" has particular resonance, of course, for writing and research on contemporary Islam. Worldwide Muslim networks, whose spread has been facilitated by migration, print, and most recently by the Internet, have been the subject of increasing scholarly investigation. But the use of the network as a metaphor for understanding the dynamics of Islamic history and Islamic civilization is hardly new, and it long predates September 11 and the development of the Internet. The pivotal importance of this metaphor for understanding Islamic societies was, in fact, clearly argued in the 1970s by Ira M. Lapidus, who noted how differing root metaphors seem to help us make sense of different world civilizations.

Lapidus underlined the importance of the network metaphor for understanding the Islamic world by contrasting it with the root metaphors that had been commonly used to analyze the civilization of China. The critical root metaphors for the analysis of Chinese civilization, Lapidus argued, were those of hierarchy and balance. The notion of society as defined by the "balanced tension" of opposites lay at the heart of the ways that historians and philosophers had long tried to make sense of the structure of Chinese civilization. This notion shaped standard analyses not only of the Chinese state but also of that central cultural figure of Chinese civilization, the Confucian sage, who, as Lapidus puts it, was seen by many to balance "both the tensions and the unity of state and society" in his own soul. Though China was marked by a variety of social organizations and considerable internal conflict, the dominant "image of Chinese society which emerges in the historiography," Lapidus suggested, was that of "a mobile," trembling in balance: "Though in constant movement, the mobile as a whole floats gracefully, a complete form, a harmonious totality, assuming innumerable variant configurations without loss of its inherent unity." Balance and ordered hierarchy provided the metaphorical frameworks, in other words, that in spite of China's internal divisions, tensions, and conflicts allowed scholars, Confucian and otherwise, to forge a civilizational image of China as a whole (1975, 27–31).

This image contrasted sharply with the dominant metaphorical image projected of Islamic civilization, an image that drew on the concept of networks. Like Chinese states, many Islamic states, such as the Abbasid or Ottoman caliphates, had no doubt balanced elite and local authority in the exercise of imperial power, and historians had thus at times also turned to the metaphors of hierarchy and balance to make sense of them.[1] But more frequently in Islamic history, state and society were only weakly integrated. The moral influence wielded by the religious establishment, with its sometimes extensive geographical connections, was often largely independent of the state, while in many Islamic polities, society was far more "segmented and inchoate" than was the case in China. "Coalitions, alliances, and social cooperation motivated by common interests and fortified by religious and sometimes political norms" were the critically defining features of medieval Islamic politics, and many historians thus made sense of these societies only by projecting "an image of society as a network of relationships between component groups." Far from being the linchpin of a balanced hierarchical order, as in China, then, the state in these Muslim societies was oftentimes best understood as simply one of "the dense knots where many network lines crossed." Networks, in preference to "an image of society as an architectural or hierarchal structure," had long provided the dominant metaphor shaping an overarching historical image of Islamic civilization (32–40).

Such differences in root civilizational metaphors were of course in part, as Lapidus recognized, a product of scholarly presumption. But these differences were also in many ways intrinsic to cultural self-perceptions among Muslims and Chinese themselves. "They correspond," Lapidus wrote, "to the cultural style and the world view of each civilization," embodied in art and philosophy as much as in political arrangements. In Islam, the network metaphor thus had roots in "orthodox Islamic philosophy and theology" and in Muslim views of the world. Islamic thinkers tended to see the universe as without "overall pattern," but rather as a product of God's continual creation and recreation. Islamic arts, he noted, also tended to subordinate inner meaning to form and decorative effect. History and even "human life itself" were thus, in Lapidus's argument, largely conceptualized not in terms of an Islamic structural order but rather in terms of "movements and actions correctly performed at each given moment in accord with God's will"; "in the same way," Lapidus explains, "society is an ever living, never completed network of actions" (42). The network metaphor for understanding Islamic societies, he thus argued, had powerful roots in Muslim self-perception.

But if Lapidus saw the network image of society as at least partly embedded in the fundamentals of Islamic belief, his argument about the importance of root metaphors was also clearly drawn from the particularities of history. The continuing power of the network to define an image of Islamic society was preeminently rooted in the distinctive, weakly integrated cultural relationship between state and society that he saw as one of the hallmarks of premodern Islamic history, whether in the Maghrib, the

Middle East, or India. The distinctive patterns of this history have been described by many historians, including Marshall Hodgson, who emphasized the counterpoint in the medieval Muslim world between the militarization of government and "the relative liberty of the individual, unwilling to subordinate his management of his own fate to superior social institutions or to corporate standards other than the minimum imposed by the Shari'ah law" (1974, 2:67). Vincent Cornell underscores this same tension, suggesting in his essay in this volume how the medieval 'ulama' developed a set of political ideals that crossed the boundaries of particular political systems—and particular structures of political authority—even as their ideas engaged little with the actual ways that medieval Muslim rulers operated. Not only the connections (and travels) of the 'ulama' but the persistence of an idealized political vision of Muslim community that transcended the realities of state power thus defined a historical vision of civilization for which the network metaphor was unusually apposite.

Yet Lapidus's argument focuses not simply on the premodern Muslim world but on Islamic civilization more broadly, as it has survived into more recent times. One might push Lapidus's argument further by suggesting that the network as a root metaphor for Islamic civilization gained more vitality in recent centuries due to the history of European colonialism, which encompassed the great majority of Muslim societies in the nineteenth and twentieth centuries and defined a cultural gulf between state and society far more profound than Muslim societies had witnessed in the medieval period. In such circumstances, the network metaphor gave coherence to an encompassing image of Islamic history rooted not just in medieval historical patterns but in more modern ones as well. The tension between a moral community—defined by networks and cutting across political systems and political boundaries—and the realities of state power became in modern times all the more marked.

And yet the persistence of a networked view of Islamic civilization in a postcolonial world dominated by nation-states raises far more difficult issues. As Vincent Cornell notes in his essay, a "conceptual gulf" separates in many respects the identities and loyalties of the citizens of nation-states from those of the denizens of the networked world inhabited by Ibn Battuta. Indeed, the bonds of loyalty and identity tying modern citizens to particular homelands and nations appear in certain respects to be antithetical to the bonds that shaped that world. In assessing the contemporary value and the political implications of using a network metaphor for the analysis of Muslim societies and politics, one must understand how this metaphor operates in relationship to the patterns of state-society relations that have characterized the more contemporary Muslim past.

This essay will explore the relationship between networks and the construction of one of the first of the postcolonial, national Muslim states of the twentieth century—Pakistan. In the process, I will speculate about the value of the network metaphor for making sense of the Pakistan movement, focusing in particular on the relationship between networks and modern imaginings of both state and community. What do such modern Islamic movements suggest about the value of maintaining an image of Islam in the modern world as a distinctly networked civilization?

The Pakistan Movement:
Networks, the State, and the Image of Community

The creation of Pakistan represented an important moment in the history of the Muslim world, for it was a moment that brought into clear focus the modern intersection between Islamic history and the history of the nation-state. Much has, of course, been written about the origins of the Pakistan demand and about the Muslim League campaign that led to India's partition. Pakistan was established in 1947 as a self-consciously Muslim state, a state created to give concrete expression to the political aspirations of British India's large Muslim population. But the Pakistan movement was laced with ambiguities. In order to assess Pakistan's relationship to the image of a networked civilization, this essay will examine the role of the images of Muslim civilization and Muslim nation that were mobilized in bringing Pakistan into existence and the contradictions that these images engendered.

The backdrop to Pakistan's creation was, of course, both the history of Islam on the Indian subcontinent and the history of British colonialism. Indeed, the particular image of the Indian Muslim community that lay behind the Pakistan movement was one that was powerfully shaped in many respects by the distinctive history of British rule in India. The power of the British colonial state, from which Pakistan emerged, rested firmly on a British vision of India as a starkly segmented society, a structure that in British eyes defined India's social essence. Indians were divided along multiple lines of social cleavage, a fact no less true of India's Muslims than it was of India's numerically preponderant population of Hindus. As Mushirul Hasan puts it, "Islam in India, past and present, unfolds a bewildering diversity of Muslim communities" (1997, 7). Muslims were organized according to caste and tribe, Sufi brotherhood and sect, occupation and neighborhood. Muslim elites of India, like those medieval elites described by Lapidus, were "not defined by position in an imperial hierarchy or by any uniform educational or cultural attainment" (1975, 33), but variously by family prestige and connection, wealth derived from trade or landholding, educational achievement, and sometimes by state office holding. These divisions were critical to the structure of colonial rule.

This is not to say that the British state, any more than most medieval Muslim states, was oblivious to hierarchy—far from it. Particularly in the decades after 1857, the British made significant efforts to organize their rule around a hierarchy of status gradations, seeking to incorporate the indigenous "natural leaders" of India's many segmented communities into a graded hierarchy of status at the pinnacle of which was the British queen and her Indian representative, the viceroy. Graded titles were thus distributed to many Indian notables, suggesting an ordered relationship to the sovereign. This vision was dramatized through the holding of imperial *darbars*, adapted from Mughal practice, in which India's princes and other notables—Hindu, Muslim, and Sikh alike—participated in grand spectacles of imperial incorporation and hierarchical ordering.[2]

But hierarchy hardly defined for the British, or for most Muslims themselves, an image of the Muslim community as an integrated unit defined and balanced by a rank ordering of status gradations. Proper gradations of status were, no doubt, critically important to the ordering of Muslim society in the localities, and most elite North Indian Muslims saw the maintenance of *sharafat*, or gentility linked to place, lineage, and cultural style, as central to the proper, normatively defined ordering of Islam. But whatever else the British state in India might have been, it was not Muslim, and it thus could play no role in integrating social hierarchies into a unified cultural whole. Quite to the contrary, the British sought self-consciously to separate their state from the cultural ordering of Indian society and from the Muslim community, seeing the colonial state as standing above a society defined by a multiplicity of parochial communities. The separation of the state from society was further reinforced by British attempts in the late nineteenth century to objectively define and fix indigenous communities through vast ethnographic surveys and through the Indian census. The image of the Muslim community that emerged from these efforts was one of a large social community defined independently both of the state and of structures of power. While this was a community bounded by census definitions of "Muslim-ness" (which were loosely based on ancestry and culture), it was one with no defining structure of power. Local structures of power, of course, there were—in abundance; but with no intrinsic relationship to the definition of the Muslim community as a whole, patterns of power based on wealth, kinship, alliance, and patronage defined the workings of Muslim politics under the umbrella of British bureaucratic and military power.

This situation echoed in many respects premodern Muslim patterns, as did the images of Muslim community that this structure evoked. With the power of the state structured by non-Islamic principles, local hierarchies of power among Muslims operated in counterpoint to the idealized image of a Muslim community that transcended state power, a community defined by pilgrimage, Islamic practice, and imagined genealogical connections to the Middle East and to the time of the Prophet Muhammad. But there was also a crucial difference separating the British colonial state from its medieval Muslim forebears. While the British created a power structure in which lineage and patronage connections were central to local Muslim influence, just as they were in many medieval Muslim societies, the British bureaucracy, and particularly the census, also defined the Muslim community in a new and powerful way—as a reified, bureaucratically defined entity bounded by the administrative reach of the state. Shaped by administrative definitions, the Muslim community in India was a distinctively Indian entity. Perhaps even more important, the census defined an image of the Muslim community as a homogeneous entity in which elite and common Muslims counted equally. This image represented a sharp break from the networked model that had shaped medieval thinking, and it is little wonder that it generated considerable ferment in Muslim thinking in India.

Among the most noteworthy of those who sought to negotiate the meaning of Muslim community in this new political terrain were the reformist 'ulama' associated with the new religious seminary founded at Deoband in the 1860s. The history of Deoband has drawn considerable attention in recent years, not least because of its links to the late-twentieth-century emergence of the Taliban in Afghanistan. But the Deoband movement was in fact complex and varied in its manifestations in British India. On one level, the reformist 'ulama' operated within an intellectual tradition dating back to medieval times. They saw reliance on and commitment to the shari'a as the foundation for the imagining of an idealized political community that transcended the structures of political power supporting the state. But at the same time, they also disclosed a heightened concern with the actions and behavior of common Muslims as part of an imagined Muslim community that was shaped at least in part by the colonial state's definition of an enumerated and administratively bounded Indian Muslim community. It was not enough for the *ulama* to imagine themselves as part of elite moral networks cutting across worldly structures of political power, as had been the case with many of the medieval *ulama*. Given the structure of the colonial state, with its ability to bureaucratically conjure the existence of religious communities encompassing elite and common people alike, the Deobandi *ulama* also developed an important commitment to spreading a sense of moral community—and of commitment to shari‘a—among the common people.[3]

But just as important as their change in attitude was a new commitment by the *ulama* to participation in—and increasing reliance on—the new public realm of publication and print, itself a product of changes brought to India by British colonialism. Although connections of personal allegiance and discipleship no doubt continued to be important in shaping their influence, the *ulama* relied increasingly on published tracts, treatises, and printed fatwas in Urdu to draw their dispersed nodes of teaching and influence into a larger framework of common imaginings. In using an indigenous language, Urdu, to spread their message, the *ulama* demonstrated their concern with a distinctively Indian Muslim community, a community now encompassing the entire Muslim public of British India.[4] This was a community that was imagined as morally independent of the state and yet at the same time defined by the colonial boundaries of India.

Perhaps equally important, the public realm of print also created an arena in which the voices of the *ulama* were thrown together with those of many other Indian Muslims, who in the late nineteenth and early twentieth centuries joined with and sometimes challenged the *ulama* in debating the changing meanings of Muslim community under the umbrella of British colonial rule. Urban newspaper editors played increasingly important roles as spokesmen and publicists for networks of elite Muslims. The elites, in turn, used the press to establish increasingly broad sets of linkages that drew together local networks and patronage structures, even as they joined in debates about the social and political meaning of Muslim community. Some editors also developed their own independent followings, relying not simply on elite patronage but on emerging commercial publication markets as well. All these leaders, including *ulama* and lay Muslims alike, joined in debating publicly the relationship between social life and changing definitions of community in colonial India. They focused their attention not just on elite Muslims but also on the behavior and commitments of nonelite Muslims—including women.[5] This was, of course, only an incipient process in colonial India, where the spread of literacy and of markets for publication were still limited. But the realm of printing nevertheless provided a new, public arena in which the cultural meaning of Muslim community in India was widely reimagined.[6] Indeed, the dissemination of printing in nineteenth-century India prefigured the more dramatic changes in technologies of communication that have marked the more recent information age.

But the emerging realm of print and publication proved in the end to also have an ambiguous relationship to the development of a new image of a moral Muslim community within the colonial context. On the one hand, the realm of print proved critical in knitting together disparate local networks as never before, thus strengthening for many Muslims the image of a Muslim community in India, defined by the census, that was firmly grounded in the Indian environment and encompassed all India's Muslims even as it remained morally independent of the state. But on the other hand, debate in the public sphere also encouraged the assertion of a range of competing and crosscutting identities and interests. Some in the Indian National Congress held out the image of an Indian nation that incorporated Indian Muslims as part of a larger nation, transcending religious communities; others stressed the power of regional identities, whether Tamil, Punjabi, or Bengali, to politically trump Muslim solidarity. If the public realm of print and publication was an arena for the imagining of national communities, as Benedict Anderson argues (1991), it was a venue for the imagining of many other forms of community as well. While print and publication thus strengthened a vision of Muslim society as held together by connections independent of the structure of the state, the press also opened up a new arena in which divisions and competing interests within the Indian Muslim community were paraded publicly for all to see.

It was in this context that an old language of moral solidarity, embodied in normative concepts such as *millat* and *umma* and in the image of Islam as a networked civilization, took on new public significance.[7] This was a language with deep historical roots that suggested a community defined by the moral standing and commitments of individual Muslims, commitments that not only transcended structures of state power but also transcended other earthbound and potentially divisive identities as well. It was an image of community that transcended local cultural ties. But for that very reason, it also created significant tensions as it was injected into ongoing social and political debates that gave to the Indian public sphere its distinctive Indian flavor.

Nowhere were the tensions more clear than in public debate among the *'ulama'* themselves. Through their reforms and their public writings, the Deobandis had conjured an image of a unified community defined by the spread of adherence to the shari'a among common Muslims. In a world of European colonial domination, they saw the spread of shari'a-based standards of personal behavior among the common people as critical to the setting of community boundaries. But in the very act of disseminating such standards, they stirred up fierce opposition, particularly in public debate with those who saw such reforms as a challenge to the distinctive features of Indian culture and Indian Islam. Among the most effective opponents of the Deobandis were the Barelvi *'ulama'*, who coalesced under the influence of Maulana Ahmad Raza Khan of Bareilly in the early twentieth century. The Barelvis, no less than the Deobandis, relied on the realm of press and publication to define themselves and their image of community. Indeed, they too saw themselves as reformers inspired by the image of a Muslim community composed of moral individuals guided by networks of *'ulama'*. But they bitterly rejected the Deobandis' universalist attacks on popular customs associated with Sufi shrines and on the popular veneration of the Prophet, customs which the Barelvis saw as foundational features of Indian Muslim belief and life (Sanyal 1996). Nor were the Deobandis and Barelvis alone in engaging in increasingly polemical debate in the early twentieth century as the realm of print expanded. Sufis too engaged in the active use of printing to disseminate their own arguments and views, in the process shaping a distinctively Indian Islam.[8]

Such controversies gave rise to considerable tension in Muslim politics and to considerable commentary and soul-searching as well. But they also pointed the way toward a distinctive form of public rhetoric that sought to transcend such sectarian debates in the quest for images of Muslim unity. If debates about the nuances of the shari'a often led the *'ulama'* into bitter controversy, then the key to the assertion of unity in the public realm was public action that transcended such controversy. And nothing focused such action more powerfully in the early twentieth century than the public defense of Islamic symbols. Threats to Islamic symbols, such as the Prophet, the Quran, the mosque, generated a form of highly charged rhetoric in the early-twentieth-century press that gained a central place in the public sphere. Calls to public sacrifice in the name of those symbols had universal resonance, evoking the participation of Indian Muslims in a universal *umma*. Yet at the same time, the process of publicizing such calls to sacrifice was firmly embedded in the politics of the Indian public sphere.

If society was defined, as Lapidus puts it, by a "never completed network of actions," then public acts of sacrifice and devotion—publicized by the press—defined a Muslim community that was simultaneously both universal and grounded in India's particularities.

In the early twentieth century, a symbolic vision of Muslim community was thus enacted in numerous public campaigns, all of which extended well beyond the *'ulama'* and depended critically on the networks of publicity associated with the press. One of the earliest examples of these campaigns was the Kanpur mosque affair of 1913, an attempt to turn a small neighborhood mosque in Kanpur (which was "martyred" by British officials to make way for a new road) into a symbol of popular commitment to the Muslim community. This was a mosque of no historical or regional significance, but it came to be a symbol of Islam and of community unity precisely because its cause was taken up publicly by politicians, poets, and newspaper editors as the symbolic cause of the Muslim community as a whole. So important were these protests that they significantly roiled North Indian politics for some time (Freitag 1988, 119–22). Such also was the case in a later agitation in the Punjab surrounding the publication in the mid-1920s of a Hindu-authored pamphlet entitled *Rangila Rasul* that defamed the Prophet Muhammad. Muslim leaders used the press and the platform to call on Muslims to make their commitment to the Prophet's honor public. By protesting the pamphlet's defamation in public meetings and in the press, some Muslims defined an image of community whose touchstone was the individual Muslim's love and sacrifice for the Prophet, demonstrated through publicized action in the streets of Lahore.[9]

Devotion and sacrifice in the name of Islamic symbols also served to imaginatively link the Indian Muslim community to Islam's worldwide cause. Networks of connections had, of course, long linked South Asian Muslims to the Middle East and Southeast Asia through pilgrimage, networks of traveling *'ulama'*, Sufi orders, and the flow of religious ideas. But now Muslims used the networks of the press and publications in India itself—and Islamic symbols—to shape an image of the Indian Muslim community as a key player in the worldwide *umma*. Perhaps the most dramatic example of this was the Khilafat movement following World War I. This movement projected the defense of the Ottoman *khalifa* (caliph) against encroaching European power as a focus for the devotion and sacrifice of all Muslims, but preeminently for those of India, who had witnessed European colonialism firsthand. The fact that the Turkish sultan had no direct political influence or authority in India only rendered the institution of the *khilafat* more powerful as a pure symbol for Indian Muslim sacrifice (Minault 1982). It suggested the presence of a community defined outside structures of politics and residing within individual hearts. If interactions among Muslims were defined not by an architecture of power but by a "never completed network of actions," then the symbolic center of the community lay, in this imagining, in the symbols that were the focus for individual Muslim loyalty and sacrifice, even if those symbols were situated thousands of miles away.

Still, the translation of such symbolic commitment into effective political action within colonial India proved in all these movements to be highly problematic. Though these movements depended critically on the new Muslim networks centered on the press, they in fact appealed to a moral image of community standing outside the structure of society altogether, an image defined neither by the state nor by local political structures, but by personal attachment to symbols. Attempts to translate these movements into concrete political organization thus produced widespread frustration. Cooperation by Khilafat movement leaders with anti–British Congress nationalists in the early 1920s, for example, created considerable short-term enthusiasm but little in the way of effective organization among Indian Muslims. Indeed, the model of a networked moral community transcending territorial structures and earthbound identities meshed uneasily with the Congress vision of a territorial Indian nation-state that could ultimately replace the British. Similar problems plagued the organizational efforts arising from other such symbolic campaigns.

Nevertheless, the enthusiasm generated by these campaigns was critically significant in that it provided the backdrop to the emergence of the Pakistan demand in the 1930s. This was a demand that sought to reconcile the tension between moral community and practical politics that had marked earlier campaigns, a demand that grew out of the tensions these earlier movements provoked. And the key to this effort was the reimagining of the state. The colonial state, with its hierarchal and bureaucratic structure, was on one level the very antithesis of the vision of community defined by individual devotion to Islamic symbols. But some Muslim leaders increasingly held out in the press and on the public platform in the 1930s and 1940s the image of a newly imagined Muslim state—Pakistan—that might be capable of reconciling the tensions between the various imagined states. Muhammad Ali Jinnah, who took over the leadership of the All-India Muslim League in the mid-1930s, embraced Pakistan in 1940 as the birthright of India's Muslims, who, he said, constituted a nation. Pakistan thus represented the rightful claim of India's Muslims to gain power over their own lives by rejecting colonialism and taking their place as a territorial nation in the modern world. But at the same time, he went out of his way to leave Pakistan as vaguely defined as possible, emphasizing its power as a symbol of moral community quite apart from its potential grounding as a territorial nation. Pakistan was thus presented in the press both as the vehicle for India's Muslims to take their place in a world of nation-states and as a symbol of Islamic community like the Prophet or a mosque, sacrifice for which would underscore every Indian Muslim's personal place in the larger *umma*.[10]

In practice, of course, the creation of such a state was marked by sharp contradictions. If Pakistan was a symbol, it meant different things to different people. Tensions in its meaning were heightened by the very vagueness of its territorial definition in the 1940s. Perhaps most critically, the translation of the Pakistan demand into a political reality required that the Muslim League win elections in India's provinces, and this meant trolling for political support within provinces (such as Bengal and Punjab) that had long been influenced by powerful regional Muslim political parties. If the image of Pakistan was the antithesis of colonial political power, winning support nevertheless meant coming to terms with the local structures of faction and hierarchy that had long defined the structure of power under British colonialism. In the end, such efforts in fact proved central to the success of the Muslim League, bringing it victory in India's critical 1946 provincial elections.[11]

But the very success of the league in winning such support highlighted the Pakistan demand's contradictions. The willingness of the Muslim League to rely on the local power structures of the colonial state threatened for some to compromise fundamentally Pakistan's meaning as an Islamic symbol. None in fact attacked Jinnah and the Pakistan movement more forcefully for this than the leading Deobandi *'ulama'*. Many Deobandi *'ulama'* reviled Jinnah and the leaders of the Muslim League as hypocrites who were only too willing to compromise principle for expedience. Using language that echoed the mistrust of the state that characterized the medieval *'ulama'*, they attacked the movement's leaders as men so deeply enmeshed in the political structures of the colonial system and in the quest for state power that they had lost any real commitment to Islam. The vision of community held by these *'ulama'* had been generated independently of British colonial authority, and they now feared the implications of a corrupt state that had little regard for the *'ulama'*'s networks of influence or for the shariʿa and yet claimed as a Muslim nation the direct cultural loyalties of its citizens.[12]

Such ideas suggested the continuing tension between a vision of moral community defined by commitment to the shariʿa and a nation defined by the relationship of citizens to the state. Yet even among these *ʿulama*' there were many who could not resist Pakistan's distinctive symbolic appeal given the pressures facing India's Muslim community at this critical juncture. Whatever the political compromises it involved, the Pakistan movement promised to define symbolically the presence in India of an imagined community rooted in the devotion of individual Muslims to a powerful symbol of Islam. Though the demand was for a Muslim state, the image of moral community embodied by Pakistan as a symbol was in fact one imagined by many as transcending all structures of authority. The fact that Pakistan's creation involved the Muslim League's maneuvering within the everyday networks of colonial politics only dramatized the importance of giving such a vision of community a symbolic reality that stood above— and indeed was defined in opposition to—these earthbound networks. In this sense, the meaning of Pakistan was rooted in a vision of community defined not primarily by the structures supporting the colonial state but by the bonds of devotion and love linking individual Muslims to symbols of Islam.[13] In this, even for many of the *ʿulama*', the *umma* and the nation were brought together, whatever worldly contradictions their joining entailed.

But it should hardly be a surprise given these circumstances that the Pakistan movement provided little in the way of a concrete blueprint for how the state of Pakistan should exercise its power. If the state was a stage on which the unity of the community was symbolically displayed, the new Pakistan state's power rested inevitably on the tools of political control left to it by the British. For this reason, many of the supporters of the Pakistan movement were, from the very beginning, deeply conflicted about the relationship of the state to the society that it purported to rule. Reflecting the symbolic, unitary moral foundations on which Jinnah had based his claim for Pakistan, many of Pakistan's early leaders, particularly those who were migrants from North India, were highly suspicious of local and regional identities in Pakistan, which they saw as a threat to the new state. Though the press had proved critical in creating the image of Pakistan as both a national and an Islamic state, many state elites came to view the press with suspicion, seeing it as an arena for publicizing and crystallizing potentially divisive and threatening regional loyalties. Political elites in Pakistan thus sought repeatedly to isolate the Pakistani state from the political pressures of Pakistani society in the ensuing decades by turning to the army to protect the state, by appealing to textual Islam as a state-manipulated fount of legitimacy, or both. Though the mobilization of local support had in fact been critical to Pakistan's creation, the state largely sought over the years to separate itself from such structures—and thus from society itself.[14]

With the state only weakly integrated with society, Pakistani society thus took on after partition many features resembling the quintessential networked Muslim societies described by Lapidus. On one level, of course, the state ruled Pakistan in accord with the nation-state model and gained a considerable amount of foreign aid and legitimacy in the process. But Pakistani society remained weakly integrated; it was, to use Lapidus's phrase, defined by "coalitions, alliances, and social cooperation motivated by common interests and fortified by religious and sometimes political norms," but it was without a culturally integrative architecture of power. There were local structures of power, but the framework of political integration was provided by a state—in fact, a bureaucracy and an army—that relied on support largely external to society itself.

Meanwhile, many *'ulama'* and Islamists looked to independent Islamic networks extending beyond the boundaries of Pakistan to define their own sense of identity. But like many medieval rulers, Pakistan's rulers responded only by attempting to co-opt such networks in the interests of their own legitimacy. This was perhaps most dramatically the case when General Zia-ul-Haq manipulated networks of *'ulama'* and Islamists in the 1980s in an effort to cement the army's hold on the state, at the same time casting Pakistan as a frontline state in the Islamic world's struggle against the Soviet Union in Afghanistan. But if this effort helped to legitimize the regime, which is questionable, it served also to separate the state yet further from the everyday structures of social order in Pakistani society, encouraging, in fact, an increasingly bitter spiral of armed sectarian conflict to grow as Islamists vied for moral supremacy (Zaman 1998b). In such conditions, relations between state and society (even in the decade of civilian rule after Zia's death in 1988) showed an ever-increasing tendency to diverge. Indeed, even as Pakistan's leaders tried to justify their actions both in the language of Islamic unity and in the geopolitical language of national interest, Pakistan came increasingly to resemble the predatory, militarized states of the medieval Maghrib described by Vincent Cornell.

Conclusion

The history of Pakistan thus points us back to the continuing power in the modern world of the medieval models of state-society relations that defined Islam as a networked civilization. And yet it also suggests the critical importance of grounding such metaphors in historical processes. If the continuing weak integration of state and society in Pakistan today links the history of Muslim community in South Asia to a networked past, the story of Pakistan's creation also suggests the complex interaction between modern images of state, society, and community that shaped Pakistan's emergence. If the historical image of Islam as a networked civilization provides us with a backdrop for understanding much in the dynamics of Pakistan's creation, so do the histories of colonial rule in India, of the emergence of a public sphere of print and publication, and of the normative model of the modern nation-state. The value for us of a networked metaphor for Islamic civilization thus lies not in its descriptive power to capture the essence of Muslim politics and Muslim societies but rather in its ability to direct us toward an understanding of the interaction between essentialized moral images and shifting historical forces that the imagining of Islamic civilization has entailed.

This is no less true in today's information age than it was in the middle of the twentieth century. The Internet, like the world of print and publication, is a realm that supports newly imagined moral unities, but also bitter competition and multiple identities. While it has opened the arenas of public debate to increasingly large numbers of people, it has hardly resolved tensions between moral community and structures of authority. Such tensions continue to be played out through appeals to symbols. Public criticism by some Muslims of Salman Rushdie's *Satanic Verses*, for example, mirrored in certain respects, though on a far larger scale, the public devotion to the Prophet visible in criticism of the publication of *Rangila Rasul* in the Punjab over a half century earlier. Publicized acts of sacrifice, such as the 9/11 massacre, still evoke images of a community rooted in networks and actions that transcend territorial politics, even as they spark revulsion among vast numbers of Muslims who reject the politics and values on which they are based. In all these cases, the public protection (or destruction) of symbols as acts of political devotion is played off against the conflict and debates that inevitably mark the public sphere. Indeed, the analysis of the network as a metaphor for understanding Muslim civilization cannot be separated from the larger conflicts and debates that have long shaped the imagining of civilization itself.

1. Such a metaphorical vision was in fact embodied in the "circle of equity," a justification for state authority discussed by Vincent Cornell in the previous essay. Interestingly, Cornell finds the metaphor of the Mafia more appropriate for creating an image of Muslim state making.

2. For a discussion of *darbars*, see Cohn 1983. David Cannadine has also written of this structure, suggesting its importance to the image of empire held by the British themselves (2001, 46–54).

3. For a description of the development of the Deobandi *'ulama'*, see Metcalf 1982. I do not mean to argue that the Deobandi *'ulama'* were entirely incapable of imagining a structure of power that would serve their vision. In fact, when the British regime began to be challenged, some proposed the need for a leader like Amiri Hind from among their own ranks who would provide stable leadership to aid them in bringing their vision to fruition. But even this was hardly based on an integrated vision of a *structure* of power. For some discussion, see Hardy 1971.

4. For a discussion of the relationship between the public development of vernacular languages and changing conceptions of religious community, see the essays in Jones 1992. I do not mean to say that the *'ulama'* did not also publish in Arabic and attempt to engage with an extra-Indian Muslim community, but publishing in Arabic was swamped by the volume of publishing by the *'ulama'* in Urdu. See Zaman 1998a.

5. For a good introduction to many of these concerns, see Metcalf 1990.

6. For a general discussion, see Robinson 1996.

7. For a discussion of the important role of normative ideas about community in shaping twentieth-century Muslim politics, see Shaikh 1989.

8. See, for example, Buehler 1998, 190–223.

9. For a brief discussion of the *Rangila Rasul* case, see Thursby 1975, 40–47. Another similar campaign was that in defense of the Shahidganj mosque in the 1930s. See Gilmartin 1988.

10. Jinnah was himself more concerned with Pakistan as a nation than as a symbol of the *umma*, but his vagueness in defining Pakistan made it readily available as a symbol of personal Islamic commitment. For an excellent discussion of Jinnah's political strategy (though with little attention to the religious meanings attributed to Pakistan), see Jalal 1985.

11. For a good account of these critical elections in the Punjab, see Talbot 1980.

12. See, for example, Hardy 1971. Interestingly, Muhammad Iqbal and some of his followers had attacked Jinnah on similar grounds a decade earlier, criticizing his willingness to compromise with the regional Unionist Party in the Punjab for political expedience. See Batalvi 1969.

13. Such conceptions of a community defined by love had, of course, important Sufi roots, but they also drew heavily in the Pakistan movement on the European-influenced thinking of Muhammad Iqbal. The actual creation of

Pakistan also involved a complex set of negotiations between the British, the Muslim League, and the Congress Party, which it is impossible to detail here. For a good account, see Jalal 1985.

14. For a discussion of the early emergence of a state dominated by the army in Pakistan, see Jalal 1990.

Chapter 3

The Network Metaphor & the Mosque Network in Iran, 1978–1979

Over the past generation, even before the World Wide Web popularized imagery of the Net, the network metaphor made strong inroads into social science. "Society as network" joined "society as living organism," "society as war," "society as market," and other images in providing master metaphors for social scientific research. Network, in social science, is a metaphor representing human relations as a structure of nodes connected by spokes (see Figure 3.1).

Nodes are the social units that make up the network; they can be of any scale—individuals, groups, institutions, nations, and so on. Nodes have occupied the cross-disciplinary literatures on social movements and social capital, each of which focuses on the embeddedness of individuals within social networks (see Oberschall 1973 and Tilly 1978 for paradigm-founding works on social movements; see Putnam 1993, 2000 for influential statements of the social capital thesis).

Spokes are the relations that connect the nodes; they can be of any dimension—economic exchange, friendship, information flow, war, migration, and so on. Spokes have occupied the literature on globalization, which focuses on the proliferation and acceleration of international exchange along paths of least resistance (see Castells 2000 for an explicitly network-based approach to globalization).

Structure is the pattern formed by the nodes and spokes; it is centralized or decentralized, dense or diffuse, homogeneous or riddled with structural holes and bridges, and so on. Structure has occupied the specialized field of "network analysis," which has developed sophisticated statistical tech-

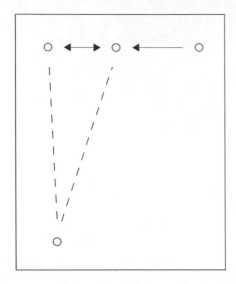

FIGURE 3.1.
Network metaphor

niques to describe and analyze different patterns (see Wasserman and Faust 1994 for the definitive introduction to the field).

Before going any further, we can already identify several things that networks are *not*, in the social-science perspective. Networks are not reality; rather, they are a metaphor that privileges certain aspects of reality that are deemed to be of theoretical importance. Networks are not limited: one cannot say that one human institution is a network and another is not. Networks are not new: ancient institutions can be studied through the network lens as easily as contemporary ones. And networks are not inherently egalitarian or liberatory: they may have any structure, including hierarchy, and any ideological content.

This essay will examine the network metaphor as it applies to a particular Islamic setting, the mobilization of the "mosque network" during the Iranian Revolution of 1978–79. All three social-science images work for this network. The nodes—whether buildings or personnel—were clearly embedded in a network of comparable nodes, and indeed were constituted by their membership in the network: that is, a mosque or a mullah only came to be considered a mosque or a mullah, as distinct from other buildings and professions, when the network bestowed accreditation. The relations linking the nodes involved time-honored practices such as training, communication, financial donations, and pilgrimage, including ritualized formulas for the expression of respect, condolence, congratulation, and other routinized interactions. The structure of the network was expressed in hierarchies of master-pupil relationships, formalized through the granting of *ijazat* (licenses), the collection and distribution of *zakat* (religious taxes), and the recognition of *maraji'-i taqlid*, the handful of religious scholars deemed by laypersons and other scholars to be "sources of imitation."

Numerous observers of the revolution have attributed the outbreak and the outcome of the Iranian Revolution to the existence and strength of the mosque network. As a physical resource, mosques provided spatially and culturally central locations for public meetings. They were the starting point for countless demonstrations and the distribution point for information, leaflets, and funds raised privately from the faithful. As a human resource, the *ruhaniyat*, or religious scholars, had lines of communication that allowed them to coordinate actions around the country and a traditional position of legitimacy and solidarity in Iranian society. As an ideological resource, Shii Islam spoke out for revolution in a voice understood by the Iranian populace.

But this picture of the mosque network is a snapshot taken at the end of the revolutionary movement, not at the beginning. In 1977, as the revolution began, the mosque network was not the unified, autonomous, powerful institution that it appeared to be two years later. Its nodes were contested, its spokes were disrupted, and its structure was about to be overturned; these three points form the outline for the rest of this essay. I wish to conclude from this study that the network metaphor can be seriously misleading if it is permitted to reify the network in question. The politically active Iranian mosque network was not a cause of the revolution, but rather its by-product.

Contested Nodes

Iran had 9,015 mosques in the mid-1970s, according to the Iranian Ministry of Endowments (Akhavi 1980, 208). These buildings, along with tens of thousands of other religious sites, formed a network that reached into every neighborhood and village in the country. Yet this network was not nearly as strong as its size might suggest. The actual religious sites were under state surveillance, and many religious leaders sought to protect their mosques from state retaliation by banning expressions of political dissent. One leading religious scholar in Qum, for example, told a visiting anthropologist "that he allowed no political discussions in his schools, his classes, his mosques, and even among his followers" (Braswell 1975, 113). As a result, the Islamic revolutionaries found themselves frozen out of the very sites that later came to be called the basis of their mobilization.

In one of the first protests of the revolution, in January 1978, radical seminary students tried to start a demonstration at a mosque in Qum in protest against a newspaper article that had slandered Ayatullah (later Imam) Ruhollah Khomeini. Shaykh Murtaza Ha'iri, a moderate religious leader, told them to stop. According to a SAVAK (security police) report later published by the revolutionaries, Ha'iri explained that he felt responsible for the mosque: "My view is that steps must be taken in this matter [the newspaper article], but the fear is that if such a matter is spoken of here, they [government forces] will shut this place down like the Fayziya Seminary" (SAVAK *va ruhaniyat* 1992, 207). The Fayziya Seminary in Qum had been the site of student protests in June 1975 and was still shut in early 1978, a vivid reminder of state power.

The fact that SAVAK agents reported Ha'iri's comments verbatim is an indication that his concerns were not unfounded. Indeed, the monarchy's security forces attacked numerous religious sites over the years and jailed and killed many religious scholars. (I have compiled lists of such incidents in the appendices to Kurzman 1994). A flood of SAVAK documents published over the past decade suggests that surveillance of religious sites was extensive. Even dissident activities at religious sites were infiltrated, such as the "roving Monday evening Quranic study class" led by Ayatullah Muhammad Bihishti in Tehran: "Approximately 100 people attended this session," one SAVAK memorandum reported. "After the evening prayer and supper, Dr. Bihishti translated and analyzed verses 70 to 77 of chapter 3 of the Quran. During his discussion, he explained in Quranic terms the characteristics of hypocrites and how to breach the opposing lines and break their spirit" (*Yaran-i imam* 1998–99, 3:244).

Moderates were not the only ones to fear state surveillance. Some of Khomeini's seminary student followers referred to him by his initial, "khe," an Iranian seminary student recalled (Shirkhani 1998, 222). A teenager from Tabriz stated that he and other oppositionists went to the mosque because they "could talk there." But asked if that meant there was no fear of the security forces inside the mosque, he continued: "Sure we were afraid. We only talked with people we knew. If someone was in the mosque who we didn't know, we didn't talk" (Respondent 34, interview by the author, Istanbul, November 15, 1989).

The revolutionary mobilization may be read in part as an attempt by the radicals to wrest nodes of the mosque network from the control of moderates. On several occasions, senior religious scholars all but shooed demonstrators out of their mosques. In March, Hujjat al-Islam Murtaza Aba'i told participants in a mourning ceremony at the 'Azam Mosque in

Qum: "Considering that the mischief-making agents [of the government] are planning to take advantage of demonstrations [and] slogan-shouting, it is requested of the respected gentlemen that they give the enemy no excuse and refrain from any sort of demonstration, either during the ceremony or afterwards. Given this advice, anyone who takes such steps is not one of us" (*Khabar-namah*, April 6, 1978, 4). In July 1978, Ayatullah Hussein Khadami of Isfahan urged relatives of political prisoners to leave his house: "Dear respected sisters, I implore you to end your sit-in and hunger strike and return to your homes. Rest assured that if, God forbid, the aforementioned acceptance of your demands proves illusory, you can come back to me" (*Zamimah-yi Khabar-namah*, September–October 1978, 29).

Ultimately, the moderates lost control of the mosques. Khadami, for example, fell into despair, according to the U.S. consul in Isfahan, and stopped attending mosque services (National Security Archive 1989, docs. 1870–71). Khomeini's representative in Tehran, Ayatullah Muhammad Bihishti, told activists in Isfahan to "use Khadami as a symbol, but organize a leadership office yourselves," according to a SAVAK wiretap (*Yaran-i imam* 1998–99, 3:374).

Disrupted Spokes

The spokes of the mosque network were built through the rhythmic and ritual passages from mosque to mosque and from shrine to shrine. Travelers on pilgrimage carried messages from religious scholars in their hometowns to colleagues in distant cities and back. Couriers brought donations to senior scholars and subsidies from senior scholars to the institutions they supported. Postal services delivered a constant flow of correspondence on matters trivial and profound, as witnessed by the many volumes devoted to Khomeini's correspondence. In the modern era, this network was reinforced by telegraph and telephone lines—these were employed most famously in the international telephone calls from France that brought Khomeini's message to his followers throughout Iran in the final months of the revolution.

The power of these spokes has often been noted in the literature on the Iranian Revolution. For example, one scholar has argued that there was "no way to cut" the religious activists' "lines of communication" and that "their organization was, therefore, uncrushable" (Salehi 1988, 137). But these spokes were more vulnerable than the common image suggests. The state monitored pilgrimages, maintained surveillance over religious scholars, and frequently disrupted the spokes of their networks.

Religious scholars were aware that their relations were under surveillance. One ayatullah in Tehran requested that American embassy visitors park several blocks away and that they not identify themselves over the phone on the assumption that SAVAK had him under surveillance (National Security Archive 1989, doc. 713). A religious scholar in Qum feared a government trap and stopped going to women's houses to perform "temporary marriages," a legitimate contractual relationship in Shii Islam (Haeri 1989, 159). In addition, suspicion of spies was widespread among the religious opposition. A follower of Ayatullah Murtaza Mutahhari in Tehran told me that he did not share oppositionist tracts with many of his friends because he was not sure he could trust them (Respondent 15, interview by the author, Istanbul, October 31, 1989). Several interview respondents told me of a recurrent anecdote in Iran that describes a class of religious students with undercover agents in its midst. The cleric tells his students to untie their turbans and then to tie them up again. The agents are unable to retie their turbans and are thus identified (the story also appears in Pliskin 1980, 64, and Mossavar-Rahmani 1987, 228–29).

This paranoia was to some extent justified, since the state routinely used information about religious networks to disrupt them. Khomeini's exile in 1964 was one of the most dramatic of these interventions: from the center of Islamic activism in Qum, Khomeini was removed, first to Turkey and later to Iraq, where he was geographically marginal to Iranian clerical life. Visitors to the Shii shrines in Iraq could smuggle messages to and from Iran, but the time and danger involved were sufficient to reduce Khomeini's centrality in the mosque network. Other activist clerics were sidelined in other ways. Ayatullahs Mahmud Taliqani and Hussein-ʿAli Muntaziri were put in jail; Ayatullah Muhammad Bihishti eventually stopped teaching because of his repeated arrests (*Pishtazan-i shahadat* 1981, 16).

Moreover, each act of protest resulted in further disruptions of the network. One religious scholar in Tehran noted in the mid-1970s: "It was his opinion that it was better to be vague in relationships between mosques because of the difficulty which existed between Islam and the government. The less organization there is, the more difficulty the government has in its coercive powers upon Shiʿites" (Braswell 1975, 118). After the activism of December 1977, for example, five of the most militant midlevel scholars in Qum were exiled to small towns in distant provinces, according to SAVAK records (*Inqilab-i Islami* 1997–99, 1:225–26). The exiles were virtually lost to the movement; activists in Qum knew what cities they had been sent to but had no contact with them and did not even have their addresses, according to a seminary student who was sent from Qum to locate several exiles and get their signatures on a petition (Shirkhani 1998, 229). When Islamists convened the Society of Qum Seminary Instructors in early January 1978 in an attempt to mobilize the mosque network, they could gather only eight participants, and one of them, Nasir Makarim, "was a friend of Mr. [Kazim] Shariʿat-Madari [a non-revolutionary ayatullah] and could not be counted as an activist," an organizer later recalled (176). At least thirty-seven more midlevel scholars were sent into internal exile in the first half of 1978, including Makarim, according to a list published by the liberal opposition (*Zamimah-yi Khabar-namih*, July–August 1978, 27–28).

Thus the spokes of the mosque network, like the nodes, were quite tenuous at first. They only emerged as potent resources through months of revolutionary mobilization.

Overturned Structure

The hierarchical structure of the Shii mosque network has always been somewhat loose. Junior scholars and lay folk could choose among multiple "sources of imitation," each of whom ran separate though often interrelated systems of instruction, guidance, and financial support. For a time in the mid-twentieth century, one scholar gained such stature that he was commonly recognized as the sole source of imitation of his era. From this position, Ayatullah Husayn Burujirdi was able to reorganize the clerical establishment along slightly more hierarchical lines. But after his death in 1961, no single scholar was able to step into his shoes, and the establishment reverted to the more usual pattern of multiple authorities, each of whom was considered to be the ultimate arbiter on religious matters for his followers (Akhavi 1980).

All of the half-dozen sources of imitation except Khomeini were nonrevolutionary. This is not to say that they were entirely pleased with the monarchy. They and other nonrevolutionary religious scholars had numerous grievances about secularization, foreign influence, state control of religious institutions, and other trends, according to social scientists who conducted interviews in the mid-1970s (Braswell 1975, 132; Tehranian 1980, 21, 28). But the scholars framed their grievances in reformist, not revolutionary, terms. As a result, Khomeini's revolutionary supporters found the multiheaded structure of the mosque network to be a significant hindrance to their mobilization, and they set out to change it.

One aspect of the radicals' attempt to restructure the mosque network was the use of the title "imam" for Khomeini, probably spoken publicly for the first time in the fall of 1977 at a commemorative service for Mustafa Khomeini in Tehran (*Shahidi digar* 1978, 113; *Inqilab-i Islami* 1997–99, 1:52; Shirkhani 1998, 32, 141). This was a highly charged term that alluded to the twelve imams, male descendants of the Messenger Muhammad, who are held by Shii Muslims to have been divinely selected for leadership of the Muslims. Twelver Shiis—the dominant branch in Iran—believe that the twelfth imam, Abu'l-Qasim Muhammad, went into a state of "occultation," or hiddenness, in the ninth century and will return one day as a messiah to establish the reign of Islam under his just rule. Calling Khomeini "imam" introduced connotations of messianic deliverance, though his followers did not go so far as to suggest that he was in fact the messiah.

The novel title upended the traditional hierarchy of Shii religious authority. For the past several centuries, religious authority had followed from scholarship. A scholar gained titles and authority through recognition of his (rarely her) intellectual achievements—first by his teachers, who granted permission to teach; then by his peers, who granted a certain title (for example, in the twentieth century, ayatullah); then by his followers, who adopted him as a source of imitation out of respect for his great erudition (Moussavi 1985). Khomeini had passed through these phases by the mid-1970s. But the title "imam" placed Khomeini above the other sources of imitation, and it did so more for his political leadership than for his scholarship.

The other sources of imitation resented this inversion of the hierarchy. Several of them refused to attend a series of mourning ceremonies for Khomeini's son Mustafa in Qum in the fall of 1977, according to a SAVAK report, because "the religious speakers were going to call Ruhollah Khomeini the undisputed source [of imitation] for the Shii world and the abovementioned ayatullahs construed this as an insult to themselves" (SAVAK *va ruhaniyat* 1992, 202). The following week, the Tehran bazaar commemorated Mustafa's death by going on strike, ignoring a recommendation by Tehran's senior ayatullah, Sayyid Ahmad Khansari, to open their shops (*Dar-barah-yi qiyam* 1978, 1:138–39). This was an omen of changes to come in the structure of clerical authority.

In the first months of 1978, as the revolutionary movement emerged, militants first tried to convince the senior scholars to join the movement before they turned to harsher methods. They recognized that they needed the moderate clerics on their side. "Everybody has got to strike," one militant religious scholar told another in Mashhad in February; "We can't just strike by ourselves" (*Yaran-i imam* 1998–99, 5:716). The primary tactic was to challenge the moderates publicly, in effect embarrassing them into a more revolutionary position (see also Bakhash 1984, 177–86). Khomeini spoke repeatedly on this theme; in 1971, he said: "I consider it my duty to cry out with all the strength at my command and to write and publish with whatever power my pen may have. Let my colleagues do the same—if they consider it proper, if they regard themselves as belonging to the nation of Islam, if they consider themselves to be Shi'a—let them give some thought to what needs to be done" (Khomeini 1981, 206).

One of the first religious street protests of the revolutionary period was also played out on this theme. On January 7, 1978, a national newspaper ran an article insulting Khomeini as a romantic poet and a British agent and arguing that he was alone among the religious scholars in opposing the government (*Ittila'at*, January 7, 1979, 7). The next day, some of the seminary students in Qum "called off classes, and then, on the advice of their instructors [two midlevel followers of Khomeini], they said, 'Let's go and ask the "sources of imitation," the theology teachers of the religious circles, what their view is on this article'" (Respondent 7, formerly a seminary student in Qum, interview by the author, New Jersey, 1989). But this query was no neutral appeal to the expertise of seniority. The radical students knew what response they wanted and were hoping to pressure the senior scholars into publicly denouncing the offending article and expressing sympathy with Khomeini. Several hundred strong, the students marched from house to house, clashing several times along the way with police, beating two men accused of being government agents, and breaking several bank windows. When they reached each destination, they sat in the courtyard and waited for the ayatullah to come out and address them (*Zamimah-yi Khabar-namah*, March-April 1978, 16–18; Shirkhani 1998, 86–91).

The senior scholars were hesitant to support open protest. Shari'at-Madari kept the crowd waiting for more than an hour (Shirkhani 1998, 38, 201–3), then told them: "Before your arrival, I was busy working on this, and I am continuing to telephone, write, send messengers to Tehran, and so on. I continue to work on this, I hope that they [regime officials] will refrain from this sort of insult, and ones like it, but I can do no more than this" (*Zamimah-yi Khabar-namah*, March–April 1978, 16). Ayatullah Muhammad-Riza Gulpayigani sounded considerably more sympathetic to the protesters: "Maintain your unity and solidarity and continue your peaceful demonstration. You will undoubtedly find success" (15; Shirkhani 1998, 37, 86, 143). However, he also sounded a plaintive note of impotence: "I telegraphed members of parliament [several years ago on another matter], but they didn't pay any attention" (*Nabard-i Tudah'ha*

1978, 2). Only Ayatullah Shihabuddin Najafi-Mar'ashi, so moved that he cried during his speech, was an unqualified success with the student activists (Shirkhani 1998, 88, 110, 144, 152, 174, 204). He too said he had written to Tehran in protest and, pleading old age and heart trouble, asked to be excused from further efforts. But he stated his support for the demonstrators several times in no uncertain terms, according to a transcribed recording of his speech: "I hope that, God willing, God . . . will add daily to your successes. . . . May God grant your wishes, which shall, God willing, strengthen Islam, strengthen the Quran, and strengthen religion, God willing" (242).

On the second day of the students' rounds, January 9, the police opened fire on the crowd, killing five youths (283–91). Rumors spread of far greater casualties (*Inqilab-i Islami* 1997–99, 2:17; Shirkhani 1998, 74, 226; Stempel 1981, 91), with religious oppositionists' estimates ranging up to 300 dead (Davani 1998, 7:48; Khomeini 1982, 285, 297, 299). Now the sources of imitation made more pointed statements. Still, however, they focused on the tragedy and not on the legitimacy of the state; they called for mourning ceremonies, but not for political protests (*Dar-barah-yi Qiyam* 1:83–89). Khomeini responded from exile with a somewhat backhanded compliment: "The great *maraji'* of Islam in Qum have expressed themselves courageously both in their speeches and in their [written] declarations, including the one they issued two or three days ago on the occasion of the fortieth day after the massacre and the general strike ordained for that day, and they have stated who is responsible for the crime—not explicitly, it is true, but by implication, which is more effective. May God keep them steadfast" (1981, 212–13). This dynamic continued throughout the year of revolution: radical Islamists challenged reformists and pressured them with public invitations to join the revolutionary movement, and the reformists were pulled somewhat reluctantly along.

A second tactic of the revolutionaries was to subject themselves to state repression, thereby radicalizing the moderates. For example, almost all of the senior religious scholars called for restraint in the fortieth-day mourning ceremonies for the January killings in Qum. As Shari'at-Madari said in an open letter, "It is our expectation that the Muslim public will maintain complete dignity and calm in the observation of the aforementioned ceremonies" (*Dar-barah-yi Qiyam* 1:88).

In the northwestern city of Tabriz, however, radical Islamists refused to remain calm. As mourners arrived for a memorial service at the central mosque, they found it locked and guarded by police (*Faraz'ha'i* 1989, 28–35; Nahavandi 1981, 120–21). A crowd gathered, quickly turned hostile, overran the police, and then set about trashing banks, liquor stores, and government buildings. Many opposition sources admit that the crowd—more specifically, radicals within the crowd—initiated the violence (Murad'hasali-Khamanah 2001, 11; Patriotic Muslim Students 1978, 62–64; *Ruz-shumar-i Inqilab* 1997–99, 2:603–4; Shirkhani 1999, 27, 42; Union des Étudiants 1978, 11–12). The identity of these radicals, like much else about the events of this day, is unclear. It is likely, though, that they were followers of Khomeini, since the only other consistently confrontational group in Tabriz—university students—was busy with separate protests of its own that day at the Tabriz University campus (*Inqilab-i Islami* 1997–99, 3:33; Raja'i-Khurasani 1984, tape 1, p. 21). The state reacted with a massive application of force, bringing in troops and tanks from nearby bases. As in Qum in January, official and opposition casualty counts differed widely: the government admitted to fewer than 10 deaths (*Inqilab-i Islami* 1997–99, 3:37; *Ruz-shumar-i Inqilab* 1997–99, 2:601), while the opposition claimed 500 (Algar 1983, 103; Fidirasiyun-i Muhasilin va Danishjuyan-i Irani dar Faransih 1978, 78). Recent prorevolutionary reviews of the event, however, have stated definitively that the total was 13 dead (*Inqilab-i Islami* 1997–99, 3:37; Shirkhani 1999, 143–76).

On the afternoon of the Tabriz riot, Shari'at-Madari heard that his call for calm had been undermined and repeated his instructions for a stay-at-home strike: "No sort of convulsive expressions and destructive demonstrations are permissible" (SAVAK *va ruhaniyat* 1992, 217). Yet as a result of the act of provocation and the ensuing repression, Shari'at-Madari felt compelled to come out with a statement defending the radicals, whose methods he condemned. "When the government, itself, does not respect the law, and discriminates in its application, what can it expect of others?" he asked (Davani 1998, 7:99). This was not good enough for the radicals. They denounced and defrocked Shari'at-Madari after the revolutionary movement came to power. Among their charges was that he had criticized the heroic uprising in Tabriz as destructive (Parsa 1989, 202).

The radicals' third tactic was to threaten moderate religious scholars with hardball lobbying, reminding them in terms that were sometimes less than respectful that a public image of acquiescence would do little for their popularity. Ayatullah Muhammad Saduqi, a close associate of Khomeini's from his days as a seminary student in Qum in the 1930s (Khalkhali 1982–83, 2:577), specialized in this form of pressure. After the January massacre, Saduqi traveled to Qum from his home in Yazd to ask the senior scholars' permission to mobilize protest against the regime. They told him to wait for their say-so (*Yaran-i imam* 1998–99, 2:93). In late March 1978, he apparently decided he had waited long enough and arranged protests in honor of the martyrs of the previous month (2:105; Khalkhali 1982–83, 2:582; *Dar-barah-yi Qiyam* 3:20–24). Security forces opened fire on the demonstrators who poured out of Saduqi's mosque, killing 27 by official count, or more than 100, according to the opposition (*Dar-barah-yi Qiyam* 3:26). Thereafter Saduqi was uncompromising. In a letter to Ayatullah Abu al-Qasim al-Khui, a relatively apolitical source of imitation in Najaf, he wrote: "Not a single sentence has been heard from your direction expressing your disgust and hatred of these terrible actions [of the state]. Silence in the face of these inhuman acts might be a sign of approval of such treason" (*Zamimah-yi Khabar-namah*, July–August 1978, 16–17). In a letter to Ayatullah Khadami of Isfahan: "People, especially the young, expect the clergy to lead, and the silence of the clergy in response to the people is contrary to their expectation. The recent silence of the clergy has been extremely costly to the clerical community" (Parsa 1989, 204). In a telegram to the three leading sources of imitation in Qum: "The cruelties of this oppressive regime are beyond what words can say and pens can write. . . . The Muslim people of Iran have been awaiting the promulgation of the orders of the great religious leaders, and have been counting the days impatiently" (Saduqi 1983, 68).

The aggressive tone of such messages constituted a departure from the niceties of clerical communication and a rejection of the established clerical hierarchy. For a midranking scholar to use such language toward more senior scholars suggested that the structure of the mosque network was shifting. By the fall of 1978, the structure had shifted so far, according to a SAVAK report, that "middle-of-the-road religious scholars" were "expressing their solidarity with the radical religious scholars in order to protect their own position among the devout" (SAVAK *va ruhaniyat* 1992, 245).

The Iranian Revolution was remarkably nonviolent compared to other revolutionary movements, but verbal attacks sometimes shaded into threats and even physical attacks on nonrevolutionary religious scholars. In May, radicals may have threatened Khansari and other religious scholars in Tehran who had opposed the revolutionary mobilization, though this information is suspect, as the source is a royal official who wished to discredit the opposition (National Security Archive 1989, docs. 1397–98). In August, the security police in Mashhad reported, "Progovernment religious scholars are opting not to take sides out of fear of persecution by religious fanatics or are being forced to participate in their [oppositional] meetings" (*Yaran-i imam* 1998–99, 5:758). In September, when Shari'at-Madari met with regime officials (Ruhani 1982, 146–57) and tried to start a campaign for political moderation, "the negative reaction to Shariat-Madari's tentative first efforts was so great and so threatening that he . . . lapsed into piqued and official silence" (Binder 1979, 53). Months later, radicals attacked the homes of two progovernment religious scholars in Dezful, and a third was beaten in the streets of Tehran (Parsa 1989, 201; *New York Times*, January 29, 1979, A4).

By early 1979, when the Pahlavi dynasty fell, nonrevolutionary Shii leaders had been silenced or persuaded to join the revolutionary movement. In city after city, learned elderly scholars found themselves losing popularity to brasher young ones: Ayatullah Muhammad-Taqi 'Alami, more learned but less revolutionary, lost out to Ayatullah Asadullah Madani in Hamadan (Khosrokhavar 1979, 87). Ayatullahs 'Abdallah Shirazi and Hasan Qumi in Mashhad found themselves under the influence of lower-ranking *hujjat al-Islams* (*Yaran-i imam* 1998–99, 5:838). Khadami in Isfahan gave way to Ayatullah Jalaluddin Tahari and others. As for the three senior sources of imitation in Qum, Khomeini's chief representative, Ayatullah Muhammad Bihishti, bragged in a conversation in December 1978, according to a SAVAK wiretap, "They are being cooperative. But nobody listens to them" (3:388). The shift in structure must be deemed to have been completed when three of the most authoritative figures in Shii Islam were reduced to the status of clerics ignored by their coreligionists.

Lessons about Muslim Networks

The Iranian context is distinctive because Iran is the largest Shii society in a predominantly Sunni *umma*. Developments in Iran should not be translated automatically into generalizations about Islam. Indeed, the Iranian Revolution itself, despite many predictions and its own best efforts, failed to have much of a domino effect on other Muslim societies. Aside from ideological differences, the Shii mosque network had an organizational distinctiveness in that these mosques were considerably more autonomous from the state than most Sunni mosque networks have been in recent times. The Pahlavi monarchy's surveillance and repression of the mosque network was not nearly as extensive as, say, the Egyptian state's virtually total control of Islamic institutions. Leading Iranian Shii religious scholars may have been timid, but they were not, at least, appointed by the government. In addition, Shii religious scholars raised a good portion of their funds directly from the faithful, rather than indirectly via state dispensation. Indeed, one of the lessons that radical Islamic movements drew from the Iranian Revolution was the need to create self-funded religious institutions. Radical groups in Egypt and elsewhere started their own illegal mosques in empty apartments and basements, which the security forces shut down as fast as they could locate them.

Despite the uniqueness of the Iranian context, I propose that the mosque network's involvement in the Iranian Revolution can teach us three lessons about Muslim networks in general—indeed, about all social networks.

(1) Networks must constantly be built and rebuilt. Nodes, spokes, and structures only form a network so long as people maintain them through ongoing interaction. Yet this interaction is always vulnerable. It may decay over time as people explore new patterns of interaction, such as the secularized styles of life that so worried the religious scholars of Iran. It may implode through internal dissension, as happened when Islamic leftists in Iran broke into factions in the 1970s, with some groups adopting secular Marxism. Or it may be subject to external pressures such as those described in this essay: the surveillance and repression that the Iranian monarchy applied to the Shii mosque network. These pressures made it difficult for the mosque network to reproduce itself over time—or rather, its reproduction was channeled into patterns that the state found less threatening.

(2) Networks may have a variety of purposes that are not easily transferable to other goals. Even where networks are able to maintain themselves, their patterns of social relations may be geared to serve particular interests—to serve the state, to build community, to make money, or simply to maintain themselves. When insurgents in the network try to mobilize it for different interests—to conquer the state, for example—the network structure may be as much a hindrance as a help (Kurzman 1998b). Radical Islamic scholars in Iran had to build a counternetwork, reactivating the Society of Qum Seminary Instructors, which had been dormant, and founding new groups such as the Society of Struggling Religious Scholars of Tehran and the Revolutionary Council, which directed the final months of the revolution from Tehran. It took a new network to commandeer the old network.

(3) Networks should not be reified; rather, the process of reification should itself be an object of study. It can be misleading to think of networks as "things" with independent existence. It was such thinking that led observers of the Iranian Revolution to take the finish-line snapshot of the mosque network and presume that it had existed in this form all along. Yet social actors themselves sometimes treat networks as having independent existence and adjust their own behavior accordingly. During the Iranian Revolution, for example, the presumption that Khomeini

commanded widespread allegiance through the mosque network led Iranians of various political persuasions to see him as the only viable alternative to the shah and therefore to give him their support (Kurzman 2004). Networks can have real effects aside from their actual characteristics if they come to be perceived as real.

NOTE

I thank my fellow participants in the Muslim Networks Conference at Duke University in March 2001 for their comments and suggestions. Portions of this essay build on Kurzman 1994.

Chapter 4

The Scope & Limits of Islamic Cosmopolitanism & the Discursive Language of the 'Ulama'

Sometime after the fourteenth-century North African traveler Ibn Battuta (1304–68) arrived in Delhi, the capital of the Muslim state in India, the sultan appointed him as a judge (*qadi*) of the imperial capital.[1] This appointment, Ibn Battuta tells us in his *Travels*, came despite the fact that he did not speak the native languages. Furthermore, as he pointed out to the sultan, Muhammad ibn Tughluq (r. 1324–51), he belonged to the Maliki school of Sunni law, dominant in his native North Africa, whereas most Muslims of northern India adhered to the Hanafi school (Ibn Battuta, 513; Gibb, 3:747). And yet the sultan did not want to reconsider his decision.

Ibn Battuta's appointment as a judge in Delhi is an illustration of what scholars have often characterized as the "cosmopolitanism" of premodern Muslim societies.[2] This example is by no means typical, of course, of how a foreign visitor might have been treated in a distant land. Yet it suggests, as does Ibn Battuta's career as a whole, the existence and efficacy of a shared and longstanding language of discourse and learning, of shared ideas about what constituted valuable knowledge and how such knowledge was articulated, preserved, and transmitted.[3] By the end of his journeys, Ibn Battuta had "visited territories equivalent to about 44 modern countries" and traveled about 73,000 miles (Dunn 1986, 3, 12 n. 2). And while much of this remarkable achievement must surely be attributed to his energy and to a good fortune whose effects he experienced repeatedly, a language of discourse also facilitated his journey and his reception in otherwise unfamiliar places. It was this "language" that enabled Ibn Battuta to be appointed a judge in a land thousands of miles away from his native home even when he did not actually speak the local languages in which the people communicated with one another in their day-to-day lives.[4]

This chapter seeks to examine some facets of this language of religious discourse as well as some of its limits. We shall take Ibn Battuta as our initial guide here, but my primary focus is on modern rather than medieval Islam. Though not himself a religious scholar of any distinction (Gibb, 1:ix–x; Dunn 1986, 312), Ibn Battuta partook of a tradition of religious learning, a tradition that was among the crucial bases of the patronage he enjoyed in Delhi as well as of his own persistent interest (on display throughout his *Travels*) in the careers and fortunes of those who likewise shared in that tradition. From long before Ibn Battuta's time to the present day, it has been in terms of a language imbued with the ethos of this tradition that Muslim religious scholars, the *'ulama'*, have typically asserted their identity, their authority, and their aspirations to converse with one another and with earlier generations of scholars. What does it mean for such traditionally educated Muslim religious scholars to want, or to be able, to speak this language in the often radically altered and continually changing contexts of modernity? What are the limits of this language? And what light can some understanding of both its scope and its limits shed on how religious discourses are articulated in the contemporary Muslim world? These are among the questions I wish to address in this essay. But a sense of Ibn Battuta's own world may provide something of a context in which to consider them.

The Limits of Ibn Battuta's Cosmopolitanism

Delhi was not the only place where Ibn Battuta was well received or even where he served as a judge. In 1341, Muhammad ibn Tughluq, the Delhi sultan, had decided to send him as an ambassador to the ruler of China, launching him on what turned out to be a long, dangerous, but always eventful journey. The journey took him to Malabar, the Maldives, Sumatra, and eventually to southern China, and it was during this part of his travels that he officiated for eighteen months or so as a *qadi* in the Maldives.[5] However leisurely the pace of his journey, the fact that he was traveling as the ambassador of the sultan of Delhi, and that he had served as a *qadi* of the imperial city, made him very attractive as a choice for this position in the Maldives (Ibn Battuta, 582, 590; Gibb, 4:834, 843; Dunn 1986, 232). Ibn Battuta professes to have been reluctant to serve in this capacity. But he was clearly aware of the great influence the *qadi* wielded among the people of the Maldives, and if he was keen not to draw the attention of the grand vizier to his own talents, his severe rebuke of the incumbent judge as someone who "did nothing right" scarcely helped his anonymity (Ibn Battuta, 581–82, 588; Gibb, 4:833–34, 840). Here is what he tells us about how he acted once he had been "compelled" to become the *qadi*:

> When I was appointed, I strove my utmost to establish the prescriptions of the Sacred Law [*rusum al-shar'*]. Lawsuits there are not like those in our land. The first bad custom I changed was the practice of divorced wives of staying in the houses of their former husbands, for they all do so till they marry another husband. I put a stop to that. About twenty-five men who had acted thus were brought before me; I had them beaten and paraded in the bazaars, and the women put away from them. Afterwards I gave strict injunctions that the prayers were to be observed, and ordered men to go swiftly to the streets and bazaars after the Friday service; anyone whom they found not having prayed I had beaten and paraded. I compelled the salaried prayer-leaders and muezzins to be assiduous in their duties and sent letters to all the islands to the same effect. I tried also to determine how women dressed, but I could not manage this. (Ibn Battuta, 588; Gibb, 4:840–41)

The inhabitants of the Maldives, Ibn Battuta tells us, were Muslims of correct belief, good intention, and righteousness (Ibn Battuta, 594; Gibb, 4:824). And unlike the inhabitants of Delhi, but like Ibn Battuta himself, they adhered to the Maliki school of law (Ibn Battuta, 579; Gibb, 4:830). This fact should have facilitated his functioning as a *qadi* among them. Yet for all its self-congratulatory tone, the foregoing account of how he conducted himself might already point to the limits of people's endurance of the shari'a as Ibn Battuta understood it. Elsewhere, in speaking of the "physical weakness" of the local inhabitants, Ibn Battuta tells us of people in his presence fainting when he once ordered the hand of a thief to be cut off (Ibn Battuta, 574; Gibb, 4:824). Though he does not dwell on this episode—and he certainly did not see it this way—it is conceivable that what we have here is an instance of local custom defining the scope of shari'a norms even among people who, on Ibn Battuta's own testimony, were otherwise "good" Muslims. If someone who could be seen as authentically representing an Islamic scholarly tradition would be attractive *for that reason* in a particular locale, his zealous upholding of what he saw as the norms or imperatives of that tradition may nevertheless have been hard to accept for the local people. His predecessor as the *qadi*, who, as Ibn Battuta saw it, "did nothing right," may yet have been rather more apt at reconciling shari'a norms with—or translating them into—local custom. As it turned out, Ibn Battuta did not stay long in the Maldives. And though his departure was primarily occasioned by the political rivalries in which he found himself embroiled, he may also have come up against the limits of the cosmopolitan scholarly language that had initially facilitated his reception.

The same may well be true of his experience in Delhi itself, where he served as *qadi* for nearly eight years (Dunn 1986, 3). In an otherwise rich account of his observations and experiences in India, it is remarkable that he tells us very little about his conduct as a judge. Knowing that he did not speak the local languages, the sultan had assigned two deputies to assist him in his judicial business (Ibn Battuta, 513; Gibb, 3:747). He did, on occasion, pass legal judgments, and he carried out other functions that may have been assigned to *qudat* at that time (Ibn Battuta, 526, 544; Gibb, 3:762–63, 4:789; Dunn 1986, 205). As would again have been true of other *qudat*, he was expected to refer cases that did not, or were not allowed to, fall within shari'a jurisdiction to "secular" legal authorities, and he was present when the latter ruled or when their sentences were carried out.[6] But, on at least one occasion, he did complain to the sultan that he had not had much to do as a *qadi* (Ibn Battuta, 522; Gibb, 3:759), and it is possible that his position in Delhi was more ceremonial than real. Even with his two deputies, then, there may have been severe limits on the ability of a foreign, Maliki judge to effectively function in an imperial, North Indian, Hanafi environment.

While we have so far seen the North African Ibn Battuta's appointment to judicial office in Delhi as an illustration of premodern Islamic cosmopolitanism (in which context we have noted certain limits to this cosmopolitanism), this is scarcely the only way to interpret it. Ibn Battuta was not the only foreigner honored with the sultan's patronage in Delhi at the time. Yet Muhammad ibn Tughluq, the sultan who bestowed his patronage on Ibn Battuta and others, was far from representing the norm in this as in many other respects. As Peter Jackson notes, this sultan "made greater efforts than any other Delhi ruler to attract into his service Muslims from every part of the Islamic world" (1999, 294). But many Hindus were equally the recipients of his patronage, and, as Jackson argues, these facets of patronage were "two arms of a policy which aimed at creating a counterweight to the Indian Muslim nobility, since the Tughluqid dynasty had come to power only a few years previously in the teeth of determined Indian Muslim opposition" (294). Ibn Battuta's reception at Delhi is thus not an expression of a timeless, reified Islamic cosmopolitanism but something that is better situated at the meeting point of his own ambitions and a sultan's political agenda. As we have observed, furthermore, there may have been constraints on how much the cosmopolitanism of the Moroccan judge would have been acceptable to those affected by his presence among them.

Yet, if we should not exaggerate the appeal of this cosmopolitanism, we ought not to neglect its significance either. Even if Ibn Battuta's accomplishments could fit well into a sultan's specific political goals, the fact that a language of scholarly discourse *was* intelligible enough across Muslim societies to make this possible is worth underscoring. Nor, of course, were Delhi or the Maldives the only places where this language opened doors for Ibn Battuta. His travel accounts are replete with similar instances. Among Muslim communities on the Malabar Coast, for instance, he found himself in the presence of local Muslim rulers but also of Sufis and scholars from far off places. People like the "pious jurist from Mogadishu . . . who had studied at Mecca for fourteen years and for the same length of time at Medina . . . and had traveled in India and China" mirrored some of his own cosmopolitanism, his own ability to find a home and forge ties in distant places (Ibn Battuta, 561; Gibb, 4:809). He speaks of attending discussions on Shafi'i law—another widespread school of Sunni law, predominant in Southeast Asia—in a local sultan's presence in Sumatra, and he describes communities of Muslims, their scholars, and their judges in China (Ibn Battuta, 619, 627–46; Gibb, 4:878, 888–910), all while providing striking portraits of just how interconnected his world was:

> One day [while in Fou-chou in China,] . . . a big ship arrived belonging to one of the jurists most highly regarded by [the local Muslims]. . . . I was asked if I would receive him. . . . I was surprised at his name but when we conversed . . . it occurred to me that I knew him. . . . I said: "Which country are you from?" He said: "From Ceuta." I said: "I am from Tangier." He greeted me again and wept and I wept too. I said: "Have you been to India?" He said: "Yes, I have been to the capital Delhi." When he said that to me, I remembered him and said: "Are you al-Bushri!" He said: "Yes." He had come to Delhi with his maternal uncle Abu'l Qasim of Murcia. He was then young and beardless but one of the ablest students; he had memorized the *Muwatta* [a founda-

tional text of Maliki law]. . . . Later on I met his brother in the country of the Blacks. How far apart they were! (Ibn Battuta, 637–38; Gibb, 4:899–900; see also Dunn 1986, 260, 281, 296)

The Scope and Limits of a Traditional Language in the Modern World

The scholarly language that Ibn Battuta shared in some measure with the countless saints and scholars he encountered throughout his journeys and, indeed, with numerous others had many limitations. Yet it has been a durable language, as the travels of many others attest.[7] When Muhammad Shibli Nuʿmani (d. 1914), a traditionally educated North Indian scholar who was at the forefront of efforts to reform institutions of Islamic education in the British colonial milieu, visited Constantinople and Cairo in 1892, it was a similar language that he spoke, and he expected, not unreasonably, to be understood in its terms.[8]

At the same time, however, Shibli was acutely aware that times had drastically changed. Indeed, unlike Ibn Battuta, this was precisely the reason why he had set out on his travels: at a time when Muslims were facing the unprecedented challenges that their subjugation to colonial rule posed for them, Shibli had wanted to understand how institutions of Islamic learning were faring in certain other major centers of Islamic culture in order to devise ways to reform them at home. In the course of his travels, he came to feel that, for all its faults, the system of traditional education in India was in fact superior to what he had seen of it in Constantinople and Cairo—an unedifying realization that suggested to him the hard times on which such education had fallen everywhere. Even so, there was still a world of traditional learning to relate to, and he describes both this world and his own ability to be recognized in it with undisguised satisfaction. On his way to Constantinople, Shibli had briefly stopped at Izmir, where he met some of the local religious scholars at a bookstore adjacent to the mosque:

After the [Friday] prayers, most ʿulamaʾ and authors gather here. When I got there . . . and after I had been introduced, someone said, "We were just discussing a [legal] issue; let us revisit it, if you wish." I accepted this gladly. The matter under discussion was mutʿa [a controversial Shii practice that allows "marriage" on a temporary basis in exchange for monetary compensation]. . . . I spoke at some length about it, and everyone agreed with my views. These people could not converse in [literally: could not understand] the Arabic language; therefore, I spoke in Persian. Such discussion and debate usually takes place in a very polite manner, a style that is common in these lands. There is no better way than this for a stranger to meet and develop ties with the *'ulama'* [here]. . . . This sort of intellectual session was to prove a major cause of my success during these travels; indeed, on some occasions, they provided me a way out of difficulties which I had no other means to deal with. (Shibli Nu'mani n.d., 24)

Such interactions—and the shared language of discourse they exemplify—have often continued to characterize the culture of the contemporary *'ulama'*, but especially that of the more prominent among them. Few religious scholars illustrate the power and reach of this language better, perhaps, than Sayyid Abu'l-Hasan 'Ali Nadwi (d. 2000), the longtime rector of the Nadwat al-'Ulama' of Lucknow in India. Nadwi was one of the founders of the Nadwat al-'Ulama', a movement that had sought to bring together the *'ulama'* of South Asia on a shared platform from which to promote a new vision of Muslim unity and a "reformed" Islamic education. The Nadwa was also self-consciously oriented toward the Islamic and especially the Arab world, and the graduates of its Dar al-'Ulum have often taken great pride in their facility in the Arabic language. It is this orientation that helped make Abu'l-Hasan 'Ali Nadwi one of the most prominent *'ulama'* on the global Muslim scene during the latter half of the twentieth century.[9]

Nadwi wrote on a broad range of things, including history, politics, Islamic religious thought, biographies of holy men, and an extended autobiography, and he did so in both his native Urdu, the language spoken by the Muslims of North India and Pakistan, and in Arabic. Among his writings best known outside South Asia are extensive diatribes against the "materialism" of Western modernity as well as denunciations of the type of secular pan-Arab nationalism, or "Nasserism," articulated most forcefully, as the latter appellation suggests, by the Egyptian president Nasser (Jamal 'Abd al-Nasir [r. 1954–70]). Some of Nadwi's polemics, often self-consciously addressed to the Arabs, found a comfortable and, indeed, rewarding niche in the international Muslim politics of the 1950s and 1960s. The Saudis saw Nasserist ideas of pan-Arabism and Arab socialism as a grave threat to their own Wahhabi ideology, and Nadwi and his colleagues at the Nadwat al-'Ulama' came to enjoy considerable Saudi favor and patronage. For the last several decades of his life, Nadwi held positions of some influence with several international Islamic organizations sponsored by the Saudis. In 1980, he was the recipient of the prestigious Faisal Award, named after King Faisal (d. 1975) of Saudi Arabia, and the Nadwat al-'Ulama' flourished under his rectorship, bringing in financial patronage from abroad and new openings for its graduates in many Arab countries.

Tempting as it is, we should not, however, reduce Nadwi's recognition in the Arab and Muslim world to his Saudi sponsorship. It is better seen in the context of a lifetime of sustained engagement with the challenges confronting the Arabs and Islam, an engagement that itself derives from the orientation of the Nadwat al-'Ulama' toward the Arab world, but also, and more specifically, from Nadwi's conviction that the preservation of Muslim cultural and religious identity in India could only be anchored in a sense of belonging to the greater Muslim world. With this conviction, Nadwi became, in the words of the Qatar-based Egyptian scholar Yusuf al-Qaradawi (on whom more later), a veritable "ambassador, not just of the people of India but of all non-Arab Muslims, representing them in Arab countries and among Arab scholars, preachers, and thinkers . . . , at their academic and proselytizing institutions, and at their cultural and religious associations" (2001b, 145).

But Nadwi's recognition in the Arab and Muslim world also meant a new kind of influence in India, a new political stature at home. It is not surprising, therefore, that in the mid-1980s he should have been the obvious choice to lead the All India Muslim Personal Law Board in its effort to reverse a highly controversial decision of the Indian Supreme Court. The case involved the appeal of an indigent Muslim woman, Shah Bano, to be financially supported by her former husband. The standard interpretations of the shari'a made no allowance for such support beyond the expiry of the three-month "waiting period" following a divorce. But the high court of the state of Madhya Pradesh, and then the Indian Supreme Court, ruled in favor of Shah Bano, and the Hindu chief justice of the Supreme Court went so far as to offer a fresh interpretation of the Quran in arguing against the long-established Muslim legal tradition on this matter. Many Muslim modernists hailed this decision as a much-needed reform of Islamic law, but the *'ulama'* and other conservative segments of the Muslim population in India saw it as an intolerable interference by a Hindu-dominated state, through its judicial arm, into their sacred law and legal tradition.[10] To the *'ulama'*, the issue here was not, in the first instance, the amelioration of the position and rights of Muslim women but rather the religious identity of the Muslim community. At stake was also the question of who represented Islam and of how persuasively the claim to so represent it might be made. As those broadly recognized (even in popular caricatures) to be the representatives and custodians of the Islamic religious tradition, the *'ulama'* arguably had an advantage in this respect over their modernist opponents. And with his stature not just in India but also abroad—of which, as he acknowledges in his autobiography, he did not hesitate to remind the prime minister, Rajiv Gandhi (Nadwi 1983–97, 3:113–34)—Nadwi had a considerable advantage over other Indian Muslim leaders. In the end, it was to the *'ulama'* and their followers that the government listened more intently than it did to anyone else. The ruling of the Supreme Court was set aside through parliamentary legislation in 1986, and the authority of those who claimed to speak the language of the Islamic discursive tradition was affirmed.

If this episode illustrated the Indian state's recognition of the authority of the *'ulama'*, however, it equally underscored the limits on the ability of the *'ulama'* and the Muslim modernists to successfully communicate with each other. It is striking that the religious leaders of even the Daudi Bohras, a sect of the Isma'ili Shia who are usually viewed with grave misgivings by the Sunni *'ulama'*, were in accord with the *'ulama'* in their opposition to the Indian Supreme Court's verdict in the Shah Bano case.[11] But it is equally significant that the *'ulama'* and the modernists were ranged on opposite sides in this controversy, with the modernists accusing the Indian government of nothing less than "pandering" to the *'ulama'*. As the "secular modernist" historian Mushirul Hasan lamented, "The Indian state . . . [had] bolstered the religio-political leadership . . . [and had] ignored liberal Muslim opinion over the Shah Bano case to negotiate with Muslim priests."[12]

In speaking of the difficulties inherent in representing or translating the ideas and beliefs of one "linguistic community" into those of another, the moral philosopher Alasdair MacIntyre has argued that "the outcome in each case of rendering those beliefs sufficiently intelligible to be evaluated by a member of the other community involves characterizing those beliefs in such a way that they are bound to be rejected."[13] For it is different traditions that such linguistic communities represent:

> Conceptions of courage and of justice, of authority, sovereignty, and property, of what understanding is and what failure to understand is, all these . . . [are] elaborated from exemplars to be found in the socially recognized canonical texts. . . . [W]hen two . . . distinct linguistic communities confront one another, each with its own body of canonical texts, its own exemplary images, and its own tradition of elaborating concepts in terms of these, but each also lacking a knowledge of, let

alone linguistic capacities informed by, the tradition of the other community, each will represent the beliefs of the other within its own discourse in abstraction from the relevant tradition and so in a way that ensures misunderstanding. (1987, 392)

Elsewhere, I have argued that, despite the massive transformations that modernity has forced onto their institutions and their discourses, the 'ulama' continue to define their identity and authority in terms of a highly rich and complex Islamic discursive tradition. While Muslim modernists, Islamists, and other "'new' religious intellectuals" obviously also recognize the authority of Islam's foundational texts, the 'ulama' are typically committed to a historically articulated interpretive tradition with reference to which any particular reading of the foundational or other texts finds meaning or legitimacy in their discourses.[14] Even when they share texts with others (and in many instances, as with the texts that are part of the *madrasa* curriculum, they do not), there is a way of approaching them that is often distinctive to the culture of the 'ulama'. Conversely, as Roxanne Euben has argued, even as the college and university-educated Islamists articulate their Islamic norms—which they then seek to see publicly implemented— on the basis of a radically new reading of the Quran, theirs is typically an "anti-hermeneutical stance" whose very authority depends on the denial that their reading is peculiar or new or, indeed, "a" reading at all (1999, 86). There is a sense, then, in which Muslim modernists and the 'ulama' are members of distinct linguistic communities, a fact that is reinforced by, but goes far beyond, the actual languages from which each community primarily draws its intellectual sustenance and in which its members often prefer to express themselves.[15] The Shah Bano controversy is, perhaps, as good an illustration as any of the difficulty for members of one linguistic community of being able to justify their reasoning to the other community in terms that would not immediately seem to the latter to be shallow, even dishonest, and in any case would be, as MacIntyre puts it, "bound to be rejected."

I do not, of course, wish to suggest that the existence of distinct linguistic communities is anything new to Islam. Distinctions between those who have a privileged understanding of things as they "really" are and all the rest are widely attested to in premodern Muslim philosophical, theological, mystical, and other discourses. For instance, while Muslim philosophers typically insisted that they spoke of the same truths, albeit differently arrived at and differently expressed, as those the Prophet Muhammad had preached,[16] they were often also convinced that any effort to communicate with people outside their privileged ranks in their own, philosophical language was not just doomed to failure but also extremely perilous. *Hayy ibn Yaqzan*, a philosophical tale by the Andalusian philosopher Ibn Tufayl (d. 1185) that recounts how a child growing up alone on an uninhabited island is able to discover metaphysical truths through his own unaided intellect, can be read not only as evocative of how many Muslim philosophers viewed the path to the attainment of such truths but also as an argument about the limits of language itself.[17] Hayy, the protagonist of this story, does not take long to learn the language of the community inhabiting a neighboring island when he finally encounters a person who has abandoned that community after long having been part of it (Goodman 1972, 160). But when the two make their way back to the city to teach people how to behold truths without the veil of images, metaphors, and externalities, Hayy quickly discovers his limits even in communicating with the most gifted, albeit nonphilosophical, minds. Though Ibn Tufayl describes Hayy's failure as the refusal of his audience to go beyond the externals of the law, at issue here is clearly also a failure of one sort of language to make any inroads into another linguistic community. Realizing this failure, Hayy "apologized, dissociating himself from what he had said." The tale continues: "He told them that he had seen the light and realized that they were right. He urged them to hold fast to their observance of all the statutes regulating outward behavior and not delve into things that did not concern them, submissively to accept all the most problematical elements of the tradition and shun originality and innovation" (164).

This cautionary tale should suffice here to show that the problem of different linguistic communities is scarcely a modern problem. If, despite the limits of his own cosmopolitanism, Ibn Battuta could still act as a judge half a world away from his native land, there was nevertheless very little Hayy could do to make himself intelligible to the inhabitants of a neighboring island. It might be argued that the onset of colonial rule—in India, for instance—helped forge a new uniformity of discourse that transcended the earlier particularisms of the local languages. In varying degrees and at different levels, this new uniformity might be seen in the effort of British colonial officials to develop and standardize some of the Indian languages they encountered and eventually in the emergence of English as the "language of the empire."[18] But this is also true in the sense, as anthropologist Bernard Cohn has shown, of early British Indian colonialism's "invasion of an epistemological space occupied by a great number of a diverse variety of Indian scholars, intellectuals, teachers, scribes, priests, lawyers, officials, merchants and bankers, whose knowledge, as well as they themselves, were to be converted into instruments of colonial rule" (1985, 283). A new language of discourse began to evolve in this process. But if, in melding different forms of knowledge and modes of discourse into shared frameworks, colonial and postcolonial regimes have bridged some earlier gulfs, they have equally contributed to new ruptures within what may previously have been coherent traditions.

Communities of discourse, new as well as old, have continued to evolve. But just as we should not imagine that such communities are necessarily or exclusively a product of modernity, we should also not overdraw the firmness of boundaries between them—for instance, in case of Islam, between the modernists, the Islamists, and the *'ulama'*. Indeed, Nadwi's own career suggests some of the ways in which Islamists and the *'ulama'* sometimes came together in the course of the twentieth century. Nadwi is often credited, for instance, with introducing into Arab-Islamist circles the idea of a new *jahiliyya*, a highly evocative term that refers to the "age of ignorance" that the advent of Islam had brought to a close but that had reemerged in the "pagan ignorance" of the modern world, with its secular nationalism, its materialism, and its sundry other false gods. This way of characterizing the world seems to have originated with Abu'l-A'la Mawdudi (d. 1979) of Pakistan, one of the foremost Islamist ideologues of the twentieth century, with whose Jama'at-i Islami Nadwi was briefly associated. The idea was given a radical reformulation by the Egyptian Islamist Sayyid Qutb (d. 1966), in whose later writings it became the cornerstone of a justification for the overthrow of the established political order in such tyrannical and ungodly Muslim societies as his native Egypt (Zaman 1998a, 71 n. 62). Qutb had written a foreword to one of Nadwi's best-known books, *What Did the World Lose with the Decline of the Muslims?*, and throughout his career, Nadwi maintained cordial relations with many Arab Islamists.

Part of Nadwi's success in the Arab world surely owed itself to such ties, which were reinforced by Saudi patronage of causes and concerns shared by Nadwi and all of his associates. But part of it was also due to his ability to write in an accessible idiom not common among the more traditional *'ulama'*. One of the ways in which the Dar al-'Ulum of the Nadwat al-'Ulama', where he was educated, was different from other Indian *madrasas* was, of course, precisely its concern to inculcate a solid competence among its students in the modern Arabic language with the expectation that this linguistic facility would become the basis of a sustained intellectual engagement with the contemporary Arab and Muslim world. There was some interest in the teaching of the English language as well, though there was notably less enthusiasm for it than for modern Arabic. In his extensive writings, Nadwi sometimes draws on works in the English language in a way that serves, despite the polemical uses to which he put his familiarity with English as well as his other knowledge of Western societies, to indicate to his readers that he does have some firsthand acquaintance with those societies (Qaradawi 2001b, 146). And this, together with his ability to write for a broad, literate audience rather than only for fellow *'ulama'*, has contributed to the wide dissemination of his works in Muslim South Asia and in the Arabic world.

Nadwi is not unique among the modern *'ulama'* in his concern with addressing, and his ability to address, a broad and diverse Muslim audience. In some ways, the career of Yusuf al-Qaradawi, himself the author of an admiring biography of Nadwi and arguably the most influential of the *'ulama'* in the contemporary Muslim world, is even more illustrative. Qaradawi, who holds a doctorate (1973) from Egypt's al-Azhar, the millennium-old seat of higher Islamic learning, has written extensively on Islamic law, Islamic rituals, contemporary Muslim politics, facets of Islamic thought, and, not least, globalization. In many of his works, he has sought to promote his vision of a "moderate" Islam that steers clear of a rigid attachment to past authorities just as it refuses to follow the modern world in all its paths, an Islam that aspires to be as moderate in its politics as in any other arena.[19] Unlike Nadwi, he writes only in the Arabic language, but he has used not only print but also electronic and information technologies to disseminate his views, and his writings are widely accessible in many Muslim societies.

As a graduate of the Azhar, Qaradawi is the product of a time when this premier institution of Islamic learning was undergoing major government-sponsored reforms. While the long history of reforms at the Azhar goes back to the early nineteenth century, the most dramatic of governmental initiatives to restructure the institution was undertaken under President Nasser in 1961. The goal was not only to better regulate the affairs of the Azhar but also to ensure that its graduates had some grounding in the modern, secular sciences. As political scientist Malika Zeghal has shown, an unexpected result of this initiative was to produce *'ulama'* who have been able to relate to college and university-based Islamist trends in ways that may not have been possible earlier: governmental reforms of the Azhar have served to equip the *'ulama'* with a new language with which to understand the world around them and to try to make themselves understood in it. New alliances between Islamists and the *'ulama'* of the Azhar have thereby become possible, as has a new prominence of the role of the Azhar in public affairs in Egypt (1995, 1999). It is in this new language that Qaradawi has been able to articulate his views with considerable effectiveness. And he has done so while remaining closely allied with the Muslim Brotherhood, Egypt's oldest and most influential Islamist party, thereby becoming one of the preeminent examples of a traditionally educated scholar who bridges the distance between the contemporary Islamists and the *'ulama'*.

Among Qaradawi's many writings is a relatively recent book series that seeks to offer a detailed exposition of some of the teachings of Hasan al-Banna (d. 1949), the founder of the Muslim Brotherhood. Taking Banna's "Twenty Principles," a brief statement of his reformist goals and guidelines, as a point of departure, Qaradawi plans to devote several volumes to "treating diverse intellectual issues—of law and legal theory, faith and practice—where the [true] path might have become obscured."[20] Only a few volumes have been published so far, but the project indicates clearly the degree of Qaradawi's devotion to Banna and his Islamist ideals. But this project can also be read as something more ambitious and significant, namely, as an *'alim*'s effort to appropriate an Islamist text and reinscribe it in the discursive tradition of the *'ulama'*. Consider this example. One of Banna's twenty principles states:

> The opinion of the leader [*imam*], or of his deputy, is to be followed in matters where nothing else is available from the foundational texts, or in cases where what is available [in those texts] can be interpreted in various ways, or in matters that relate to public interest. [The leader's opinion is to be followed] as long as it does not conflict with a [specific] principle enunciated by the shari'a. And [as for the leader's opinion itself,] it may vary with varying circumstances, and as custom and customary practices change. The basic principle in the matter of liturgical practices is worship [as prescribed], without taking any account of what it "means"; but in customary practices, [the basic principle] is to take account of their underlying rationale, the rules governing them, and their purposes. (quoted in Qaradawi 2000b, 7–8)

This principle serves as the basis of Qaradawi's book, *Al-siyasa al-shar'iyya fi daw' nusus al-shari'a wa maqasidiha* (Governance according to shari'a norms in light of the sacred legal texts and their purposes), a work that runs to over three hundred pages and offers an extensive discussion of the juristic concepts of *maslaha* (public interest) and, as the work's title suggests, of *siyasa shar'iyya* (governance according to shari'a norms). Writing extensive commentaries on the basis of sometimes highly concise, even cryptic, texts is, of course, nothing new in the scholarly tradition of the *'ulama'*,[21] though it has been, at best, uncommon for modern *'ulama'* to treat Islamist texts as the basis of their own exegetical efforts. But then this book series is best seen not so much as a commentary on Banna's "Twenty Principles"—though that is precisely what it purports to be—but rather as a properly credentialed religious scholar's full and proper explication of what any given Islamic principle entails and where it is to be situated in the juristic tradition. Even as Qaradawi continues to profess his own devotion to Banna's sagacity (and there is no reason to doubt the sincerity of such professions), Qaradawi here provides us with a remarkable instance of the different languages that the Islamists and the *'ulama'* speak even when they seem to be on the same side.

The difference is at its most benign in the foregoing instance, though it is far from being insignificant, but Islamists and the *'ulama'* have often also differed in ways that are both more conspicuous and less civil (Zaman 2002, 102–8). The differences in question are often more fully on display in the attitudes of the *'ulama'* toward, and the relations of the *'ulama'* with, the Muslim modernists. But even here, sharp distinctions are not always sustainable. Such founding fathers of Islamic modernism as Muhammad 'Abduh of Egypt had a traditional religious training, after all, and both Mahmud Shaltut and 'Abd al-Halim Mahmud, the rectors of the Azhar during the 1960s and the 1970s respectively, had affinities with many Muslim modernists.[22] Likewise, Qaradawi's "traditional" Islamic training at the Azhar is itself a product of a time when this institution was undergoing some radical modernizing reforms, as already noted. At the same time, his own commitments sometimes make it hard (and not always useful) to sharply distinguish him from the Islamists over whom he has exerted a large influence. These caveats remind us that categories like the "*'ulama'*," the "Islamists," and the "modernists" are far from being monolithic and that particular "traditionally" trained religious scholars might have some significant commonalities with a modernist or an Islamist worldview or both, just as modernists and Islamists may themselves encompass a range of positions. Yet despite these caveats, the foregoing illustration of Qaradawi's appropriation of Banna's "Twenty Principles," as well as the Shah Bano controversy, also suggests that there are, indeed, different languages of discourse in contemporary Muslim societies.[23] If we are not to draw our boundaries too firmly between them, we should also be wary of collapsing them into the illusion of a shared discourse.

How far are *'ulama'* like Qaradawi conscious of, and to what extent do they acknowledge, the barriers of language of which I have been speaking in this chapter? As noted earlier, Qaradawi has repeatedly insisted in his writings on a path of moderation. Insofar as the claims of contending traditions are concerned, Qaradawi views moderation as a rejection of two extremes: a rigid adherence to the medieval Islamic intellectual and religious heritage on the one hand and an unquestioning embrace of contemporary Western norms and ideas on the other (2001a, 44). Both of these extremes, he suggests, get in the way of leading a good Muslim life in the present. Qaradawi thus clearly parts company with those (especially among the *'ulama'*) who see adherence to the historically articulated Islamic tradition as a good in itself, that is, as the surest means of securing Islam's welfare at any given time, irrespective of the particular demands of that day and age. To Qaradawi, it is Islam's foundational texts, not the tradition of debate and scholarship about them, that are sacrosanct in and of themselves (41–60). This position once again brings him close to many Islamists in their critique of the Islamic tradition, though, as we have seen, Qaradawi has remained insistent on working through, rather than outside of, the traditional resources in responding to what he sees as Islam's contemporary challenges.

So far as the two extremes between which he wants to navigate are concerned, however, Qaradawi is not at an equal distance from each:

> If we disapprove of imitating [*taqlid*] the great jurists and leaders of the community from among our ancestors because their thought and their creative solutions were for their own times rather than for ours . . . , we undoubtedly disapprove even more of another sort of imitation that is pervasive today. This imitation, that of the West—which seeks to govern our intellects and orient our lives . . . , to bow our heads to Western thought . . . , to divest us of the roots of our faith and culture, our civilizational identity, our religious and intellectual characteristics . . . is, without question, to be refused, for it represents foreignness [*ighti-rab*] for us today just as does the imitation of our own ancestors. The imitation of our ancestors is foreignness in terms of time, and that of the West is foreignness in terms of space. What is required is for us to live in our own time and space; we want to think for ourselves with our own minds, not with those of others. . . . However, our ancestors— even when temporally distant—are closer to us in terms of thought and sensibility: their points of departure are the same as ours, their goals are the same as ours, their methods are ours. And yet they do not live our lives . . . and cannot confront our challenges [for us]. . . . But as for the Westerners, they are farther removed from us [than our temporally

distant ancestors], for their points of departure are not ours, their goals are not ours, and their methods are not ours. Their imitation is thus all the more reprehensible. (7–8)

For Qaradawi, the distance that separates Muslims today from their premodern forebears is of a very different sort, then, than the distance between Islam and the West today or, more specifically, between those beholden to "Western" ways of thinking and the more "moderate" people in contemporary Muslim societies. But even as Qaradawi considers the Westernizers to be immoderate and thus misguided, there is no sense here that differences of background and orientation impose any particularly severe barriers to mutual communication or intelligibility.

Indeed, Qaradawi speaks repeatedly of the need to address people in their own "language." In a book on Islam and globalization (*Al-Muslimun wa'l-'awlama*), he argues that "globalization" has come to signify the domination of the United States over the rest of the world and that globalization in this sense of neocolonialism (*isti'mar jadid*) represents a danger to Islam and Muslim societies (2000a, 9–86). Yet a clash of civilizations (*sidam al-hadarat*) is not an inevitable outcome of globalization, he says with specific reference to the work of Harvard political scientist Samuel Huntington.[24] Muslims and everyone else threatened by this neocolonialist globalization ought to close ranks against the challenge and strengthen their own identities and their potentialities, Qaradawi argues, but they should also be willing to accept the best of what globalization has to offer them (132–33). Indeed, if globalization is a form of neocolonialism, it also creates unprecedented opportunities for Muslims to present their religion to the world with the help of modern media and in "the language of the age" (143–44, 6, 137, 149).

But what does it mean to speak to people today in their language? Qaradawi's conception of what this requires centers on the use of new media to reach new, global audiences, and as his own discussion of the challenges of globalization suggests, it involves an engagement with contemporary problems and an ability to articulate an "Islamic" response to them in something of a conversation with other Arab and Western scholars who have written on these issues. But how much of a rethinking or reformulation of Islam does this ability to speak the language of the day require in this globalized world? Though not specifically in response to this question, Qaradawi does note the need for what he calls "internal reform" (*islah al-dakhil*). By this, he means ridding oneself of a mind-set that wishes to live only in the past or one that imputes all ills to the machinations of others; such reform also means learning to rely not on "the myth of the inspired, infallible leader" but rather on the people themselves, "for they are the ones who make history" (135–37, quotation on 136). Such internal reform need not, by any means, be inconsequential. And yet it is unclear just how far-reaching Qaradawi really means it to be. He often writes in the conviction that of all the religious and moral systems Islam alone has the message with which to address and resolve the various problems that he sees as afflicting the world: "It is the message of moderation and balance, one which combines the . . . spiritual and the material, the ideal and the real . . . , the individual and the collective, science and faith . . . , and such other opposites whose union people have thought to be impossible. Under the shadow of Islam, they all come together in harmony" (143–44). Such grand but extremely vague formulations, coupled with his insistence that "the content of the message is stable, while the means for disseminating it vary" (147) seem, in the end, to reveal a rather limited view of what being able to speak a new, modern language might entail.

A New Cosmopolitan Islamic Language?

If *'ulama'* like Qaradawi may have only an uncertain grasp of the constraints imposed by different languages of discourse on mutual comprehension between and among linguistic communities, the significance of his insistence on speaking in a modern idiom is nevertheless worth underscoring. For even as an unattained goal, its importance lies in the effort to make the discursive language of the *'ulama'* relevant to the contemporary world or, to put it differently, to express contemporary issues and concerns in that language. The effort is predicated on a commitment, of course, to the continuation of the scholarly tradition of which this language is the medium, but it is also guided by the desire to enhance the reach of that tradition without yet abandoning its language.

In an earlier work, I have argued that the modern *'ulama'* have often been able to write both for specialized audiences of fellow scholars as well as for ordinary believers, competing with "'new' religious intellectuals" in seeking popular audiences while striving to also maintain their longstanding scholarly culture (2002, 38–59). While the impact of new media and mass education has no doubt been momentous almost everywhere in the Muslim world (Eickelman 1992; Eickelman and Piscatori 1996, 37–79, 131–35), neither these nor other facets of modernity have necessarily marginalized the *ulama* or eroded their authority. They have, however, challenged the *ulama* to adapt their discourses to new contexts and new media, and *ulama* in several contemporary societies have often done so with considerable dexterity. As should be clear from the foregoing, I have tried to go beyond that argument in this essay to show that the effort to speak to different audiences does not *necessarily* take the form of writing in different, even if simultaneous or parallel, registers. *'Ulama'* like Nadwi, Qaradawi, and, from an earlier generation, Shibli Nu'mani have written primarily for a nonspecialist Muslim audience, but they have written in a way that is fully at home in the Islamic religious tradition. What we have here is a language that seeks multiple audiences, an intelligibility across local cultures. It remains a language of the *ulama*, and it does so not only because those using it are themselves trained as such or because of the commitment to the Islamic tradition that this language expresses but also because the claims of the *ulama* to religious authority are best articulated in its terms. This language as the medium of authority is the basis of the ties and the networks that *ulama* have often been able to forge among themselves across particular cultures.

Yet the appeal of this language in the public sphere obviously depends not simply on claims to authority meant to resonate with its use but also on its broader intelligibility, and such broader intelligibility also threatens to dilute the authority this language is supposed to carry. If this dilemma is not simply the failure to grasp some of the challenges modernity represents to religious traditions, then the rather limited sense we have detected in Qaradawi of what it means to speak a new language may well be a precise expression of it. But what is more grave than even this dilemma is the fact that important parts of the language of the *ulama* still remain unintelligible to many others—for example, to those lamenting the Indian state's willingness to "negotiate with Muslim priests" during the Shah Bano controversy. Ultimately, Qaradawi and Nadwi can speak much more intelligibly to each other and to other *ulama* across Muslim societies than perhaps either can to many modernists in their own societies. And yet if the language of *ulama* like Nadwi and Qaradawi is not the language that many Muslim modernists can, or even want to, hear or comprehend, it is also not simply the language of the premodern *ulama*. It *is* a new language, one which, if it is far from transcending its many limitations, does nevertheless aspire to become the basis of a new Islamic cosmopolitanism. Some of the broader appeal of this language may lie precisely in this aspiration.

NOTES

1. Ibn Battuta 1997, 512–13; Gibb 1958–2000, 3:747. These works will hereafter be cited "Ibn Battuta" and "Gibb," respectively.

2. On Ibn Battuta as a preeminent example of premodern Islamic cosmopolitanism, see Dunn 1986 and Hourani 1991, 128–29. By far the most insightful interpretive history of premodern Islamic cosmopolitanism remains Hodgson 1974. For one especially evocative discussion, see 2:329–68.

3. For a later period, see Robinson 1997.

4. I use the term "language" in this essay primarily, but not exclusively, in the sense of a mode of discourse that draws on a particular cultural and religious tradition. In this sense, the Muslim jurists and, indeed, the traditionally trained Muslim religious scholars in general may be said to have had a distinct language. It should be noted, however, that this view of language overlaps to some degree with medieval juristic views of language in a more conventional sense. Language (*lugha*) was the focus of considerable attention on the part of medieval jurists, given that the constraints and possibilities of discerning the intent of the divine Lawgiver depended on how language itself was viewed. (For an illuminating discussion of the medieval juristic conceptions of language, see Weiss 1992, 117–50.) As Bernard Weiss notes, "The Lugha was essentially a body of conventionally established correlations between vocal sounds and meanings that remained constant over time—in other words, a firmly fixed and stable lexical code" (117). As a "code," it was assumed to have been handed down from generation to generation, and in this and certain other ways it was not unlike the knowledge of the normative example of the Prophet Muhammad (124–30). This way of viewing the language assured the jurists that even from a distance of centuries from the formative years of Islam the linguistic subtleties of the foundational texts remained accessible to them, but it also enabled the scholars to see themselves as possessing a shared language of discourse across time and geographical distance.

5. This was the duration of his tenure as *qadi* as suggested by Gibb (1:xii); Dunn says it was eight months, but that seems less likely (1986, 3).

6. See Ibn Battuta, 544; Gibb, 4:789. On sultan Muhammad ibn Tughluq's revival of the practice of the ruler making himself available for the "redressing of wrong" (*al-nazar fi'l-mazalim*), a kind of secular justice often counted by medieval theorists among the attributes of a good ruler, see Ibn Battuta, 470; Gibb, 3:694–95.

7. See, for instance, Fattah 1998. Also see Robinson 1997.

8. Shibli Nuʿmani n.d. On this work, see Troll 1997, esp. 150–52.

9. On Nadwi and his career, see Zaman 1998a and 2002, 160–70. I draw on both of these earlier discussions in this essay.

10. By "modernists," I mean, broadly speaking, those who have been educated in modern Western (or Westernized) institutions and have sought to rethink Muslim practices, institutions, and discourses in light both of what they take to be "true" Islam—as opposed to how the Islamic tradition has evolved

in history—and of how they see the challenges and opportunities of modernity. On the Shah Bano controversy, see Engineer 1987; Lawrence 1998, 131–56; Mushirul Hasan 1997, 263–69; Nadwi 1983–97, 3:111–57; Zaman 2002, 167–70.

11. See Blank 2001, 279–82.

12. Mushirul Hasan 1997, 323. The characterization of the *'ulama'* as "priests" is obviously intended to be derogatory. On the "secular modernists," a category in which Hasan seems to count himself, see 319–27.

13. MacIntyre 1987, 390. Also see 1988, esp. 370–88.

14. On "'new' religious intellectuals," see Eickelman and Piscatori 1996, 13, 43–44, 77, 180. On the Islamic discursive tradition as the framework in which the modern *'ulama'* typically define their claims to authority, see Zaman 2002, esp. 3–11.

15. In South Asia, for instance, leading Muslim modernists have usually written in English, whereas until recently most *'ulama'* have had only very limited or no acquaintance with this or any other European language; some of the leading *'ulama'*, for their part, have continued to produce works not just in Urdu, the cultural and literary language of the Muslims of North India, but also in Arabic.

16. See Marmura 1983.

17. Goodman 1972. On this classic, see the various articles in Conrad 1996b and, in particular, the chapter by Lawrence I. Conrad, 1996a.

18. On efforts to develop and standardize Indian languages, see Cohn 1985. The Mughals had already sought to promote Persian as "the language of the empire." See Alam 1998, 317–49, esp. 325–35. Alam writes, "The nonsectarian and liberal features of Persian made it an ideal forum through which the Mughals could effectively negotiate the diversities of the Indian society. The culture and ethos of the language matched with their vision of an overarching empire" (348).

19. On Qaradawi, see Zaman [2004], 129–55. For a pioneering discussion of Qaradawi's thought, see Salvatore 1997, 197–209.

20. Works published so far in the series include Qaradawi 2000b, 2001a. While the former is an exposition of a single principle out of Banna's twenty, the latter expounds on four of the principles. For a brief description of this series, see Qaradawi 2000b, 5–9 (quotation on 5); also see Zaman [2004].

21. See Messick 1993.

22. On Shaltut, see Zebiri 1993; on 'Abd al-Halim Mahmud, see Zeghal 1995, 143–61.

23. For other illustrations, see Zaman 2002, esp. 60–110.

24. Qaradawi is here referring, of course, to the highly controversial Huntington 1996. For Qaradawi's discussion and critique of this work, see 2000a, 4, 5, 110–20.

Part II

Imagining
Muslim Networks

Chapter 5

The Problem of Islamic Art

When we look at Muslims and Muslim cultures in the modern context, we confront the concept of Islamic art. The phrase suggests that the item or artifact in question is Islamic—in origin, in expression, and in usage. Yet how can we sustain such a religious definition of the artifacts and artistic creations that are classified in museums as "Islamic art"? To accommodate an understanding of religion that includes culture, scholars have adapted the term "Islamicate,"[1] suggesting that "Islamic" may be related to actors or interests but is expressed either by or for a non-Islamic audience or an audience for which the fine line between Islamic loyalty and other loyalties is shaded. Both "Islamic" and "Islamicate" have served to describe the aesthetic realm, but do they help us understand what is Muslim about Muslim networks? Do such networks become Muslim because of their authors, their audience, or their content?

In this essay, I will present a few illustrative examples of artists whose work engages on some level with Islam. I will ask how our usual ways of defining their work become problematic in the context of a networked contemporary global culture. When we look at Islam through the lens of art and artists, we bring into sharp focus questions about how interests and identities help to shape and redefine what is Islamic art in the modern context. If art is a vehicle for self-expression, how does the tangential aspect of religion affect notions of what constitutes Islamic art? Have advances in communications technology and travel influenced contemporary networks of art and artists identified as Muslim? It is my contention that by framing questions of medium and technique, of style and content, and by pursuing issues of patronage and heritage, we can begin to unravel some of the complicated ways in which the Islamic/Islamicate tension plays out in the networked world of the twenty-first century.

Artists and skilled craftsmen, both Muslim and non-Muslim, have always been in demand. Subject to patronage expectations and rewards,
they have moved from place to place. At times, they were spoils of war;
sometimes, they were prerogatives of empire; at other times, they simply
went where the work was. Even when artists stayed in place, the arrival
of new patrons, especially new rulers, changed the artistic landscape. In
twelfth-century India, for example, the artisans responsible for the Qutb
Minar outside of Delhi were Hindu workmen from that area who were engaged to build monuments reflecting the power and cultural antecedents
of their new Muslim rulers. Because of their mobility, artists and craftsmen have tended to be at the edges where cultures meet and mix. Yet at
the same time, their very mobility and malleability have put them at the
very center of new networks—reformulated workshops and schools with
new mixes of techniques, styles, and subjects—resulting in new synthesized arts, crafts, and architecture.[2]

The scale of our mobility in the information age has radically changed.
Communications technologies have made virtual travel a viable alternative
to actually going from place to place. Theoretically we all—or at least those
of us with access to modern libraries, the Internet, television, telephones,
movies, and other accoutrements of modernity—have access to the history and culture of every time and place. Having this access, of course,
presumes an elite status. In fact, what we think of as contemporary "art,"
whether it is visual art, music, literature, dance, theater, or movies, presupposes a cosmopolitan elite engaged in creating it. What are the consequences for Muslim networks of the fact that artists can now move freely
through much of the world and can in one way or another imaginatively
engage with the visual and literary traditions of any of them?

One result of this heightened accessibility and unprecedented mobility
is a person like Jay Bonner, one of the world's expert designers of Islamic
architectural ornament. Jay Bonner's biography redefines what is meant
by Islamic/Islamicate art. During his childhood in Menlo Park, California, Bonner doodled complex geometric patterns. In his teenage years, he
discovered Islamic geometrical design and then studied at the Royal College of Art in London, where he earned his master's degree in 1982. Spe-
cializing in both geometrical design and arabesque, he has collaborated
with an architectural calligrapher from Pakistan, wood-carvers in Pakistani
Kashmir and Morocco, ceramicists in Turkey, marble workers from India,
tile makers from Morocco, and modern architects from the Middle East
and Europe. Elements of his design work are now installed in the Great
Mosque in Mecca, the Prophet's Mosque in Medina, and the mosque at

the Data Darbar Shrine in Lahore, Pakistan. In a forthcoming book, he outlines his theories on the practical methods used in the past by skilled craftsmen to derive original ornate and complex Islamic geometric patterns.

Because modern buildings are all designed and built with high-tech procedures and materials, their construction is difficult for those attuned to Islamic or Islamicate values. As Jay Bonner has noted, it is a constant and delicate challenge to balance the complex technological factors of construction with the traditional techniques still adhered to by the craftsmen essential to Bonner's complex designs. Consider Bonner's account of networked design and construction on the Sliding Domes project for the Prophet's Mosque in Medina:

This project was undertaken by the architectural firm Sonderkonstrutionen und Leichbau, headed by Dr. Bodo Rasch, in Stuttgart, Germany. The Sliding Domes project took several years to complete, and the team that worked on this project was made up of many Europeans, several people from England and the United States, a group of highly skilled woodcarvers from Morocco, as well as individuals from Venezuela, Egypt, Saudi Arabia, Uzbekistan, China, and India. I have no idea as to the religious makeup of all these people, but I assume the team was mostly Muslim and Christian. I do know that there was at least one Buddhist in the group.

The actual fabrication process also balanced traditional craftsmanship with state-of-the-art manufacturing. All of the floral ornament on the interior of the domes was hand carved in Morocco by highly skilled and experienced traditional woodcarvers. Over a hundred carvers were employed for over a year while carving these floral elements. The wood was Atlantic cedar from the Atlas Mountains. The beauty of these domes would not have been possible without the skill of these woodcarvers. Conversely, the use of these traditional craftsmen would never have been possible were it not for the high tech engineering and manufacturing of the other components of these domes. There are very real difficulties in incorporating craft-based production into modern architecture. Concerning design, traditional craftsmen have not generally been trained to work outside their regional style, and often find it difficult to create works that use designs that are unfamiliar to them. Production also poses a problem when involving traditional craftsmen in large modern projects. Without training and experience, it is difficult to scale up to the production requirements needed for a large project, or to incorporate fittings and fixtures that are compatible with modern construction standards. Likewise, the lack of computer skills will often make it difficult to transfer information. Until more craft studios in countries like Morocco are experienced with larger projects and production requirements, the answer to these concerns is significant onsite supervision.

The modern age has made such diversity among design teams more possible than ever before. However, with the rapid spread in the use of the Internet for sending and receiving digital information, I have found that as a consultant, I travel to the offices of my clients less, and work more from my own studio. While this is good for my family life, it is not always ideal in facilitating the cross-cultural exchange of ideas that I advocate. (unpublished paper)

Particularly challenging to Bonner in the context of the Sliding Domes project was the charge given to him to design ornament that was "pan-Islamic," in other words, design ornament that could be universally recognizable as Islamic but was not specific to any geographical region or historical period. This was especially difficult, since historically there has never been anything that could be called "pan-Islamic" art. Specific styles and forms have always been associated with particular places, empires, and times. Here is how Bonner describes the dilemma he faced:

By far the most difficult aspect of my own involvement in this project was the initial design of a pan-Islamic floral style [see Figure 5.1]. The design brief, given to me in 1988, required the creation of a floral ornamental style that would be, at once, recognizably Islamic to Muslims from all parts of the world, but would not be identifiable to any period or region of the Islamic world. Considering the location—the Prophet's Mosque being a place of pilgrimage for millions of Muslims from all quarters of the world—I felt that this design brief was immensely appropriate. The idea from the client was that the ornament should include all Muslims, and exclude none. The completion of the concept for the design was intensely difficult, but very successful.

In designing this motif, I tried first to pinpoint those elements that recur throughout the tradition in the floral idiom, and then to use those common elements in such a way that an essential quality was created. I felt that certain qualities of the overall structure of Mamluk floral ornament fulfill those notions of essentiality, so that was a starting point. But then the floral and leaf forms, and other connecting details had to be added in order to bring the design to life. Scale was also very impor-

FIGURE 5.1. Sliding Domes: M'tawa floral panel, Prophet's Mosque, Medina, Saudi Arabia; design by Jay Bonner for SL-Rasch GmbH. (Photograph by Jay Bonner; reprinted by permission of Jay Bonner)

tant, since the details had to be simple enough to be seen from a great distance—15 meters—yet the overall design had to have enough visual character to be recognizably Islamic.

Both residents and pilgrims alike have accepted the completed Medinan domes and their ornamental style. It is said that to copy is the greatest form of flattery. I am told that similar floral motifs created in this pan-Islamic style, by designers other than myself, are being used in various projects in the Medina area. (unpublished paper)

The journey of Jay Bonner is itself a dramatization of the networked nature of both modern society and Islamic/Islamicate art. An artist originally from California who studied Islamic ornamentation styles and techniques in London and who now lives in New Mexico, Bonner designs on a computer in collaboration with architects in Europe and the Middle East (with help, of course, from FedEx, telephones, and e-mail). He has developed designs in partnership with Pakistani calligrapher Rasheed Butt, and these designs, some of which are considered "pan-Islamic," are executed in tile, marble, wood, and metal by traditional craftsmen from all over the world; included among their clients are contractors whose patrons are the foundations that support the holiest Muslim shrines.[3]

Historically, the kind of networking exemplified by Bonner's work has always been possible, though the geographical dissonances were not so dramatic in the past as they are today. There are many other examples of people who have been able to become authentic, complete participants in some part of a "foreign," formerly inaccessible tradition. Consider the sensational ballerina Altynai Asylmuratova from Alma-Ata in Kazakhstan, who has performed with the Russian Kirov Ballet in Los Angeles in the title role of Juliet. Consider too the American poet Christopher Lee, who writes in Urdu and participates in poetry readings in India under the pen name of Firang Newyorkavi (Foreigner from New York). Such committed, engaged people turn upside down our notions of who's an insider and who's an outsider, especially when they move between cultures, in both directions.

Not everyone, however, has either the inclination or the vocation to become a skilled practitioner of some aspect of a secondary culture. There can be many purposes and many different intentions. Some of my own artwork has illuminated literature from South Asia.[4] My intention with this work has been to give to a Western audience a taste of aspects of these traditions that are not popularly accessible in the United States. With my illumination, I try to provide a visual translation to people not acquainted with much of the art or literature from South Asia. While evoking the feel of a particular form of Indian painting appropriate to the subject—the illustration to a Sufi story set in Mughal India, for example (see Figure 5.2)—I nevertheless work with gouache and Italian watercolor paper, media that are different than those used by Mughal and Rajput painters. I avoid identifying a particular style from the outside and then slavishly reproducing it. Instead, I try to work from the "inside out," focusing on the content of the narrative and using principles adhered to by early Indian miniature painters. (I stress, for example, their emphasis on line and two-dimensional composition instead of on depth and perspective.) The result is a hybrid; it is something neither entirely Western nor like the traditional Indian paintings of similar subjects, though my paintings do clearly acknowledge their historical models. A similar hybridization can be seen in the delicate botanical and bird paintings that were commissioned by Europeans in India in the eighteenth and nineteenth centuries and executed by indigenous Indian artists. While they met the scientific requirements of their patrons, these paintings still exhibit a distinctly Indian sensibility in their stylistic refinement.[5]

Whether in total immersion in a foreign artistic tradition by individual artists or in varying degrees of mixing of content, culture, style, and method, one can detect artistic ferment all over the world. There are Asian painters, including Muslims, who use strictly modern, Western modes of abstract painting, as well as Americans and Europeans who utilize forms associated with traditional Asian art, including those associated historically with Islam. There are artists in Asia employing media and styles of modern abstract painting to express traditional subjects and artists using traditional styles and media to express modern, more "Western" subjects.

While the well-known Iranian artist Hossein Zenderoudi uses modern media and styles, he incorporates more traditional motifs, for example in his strikingly graphic use of Arabic and Persian calligraphy to project what one critic calls "the interplay of modernism and Islam" (Holland Cotter, *New York Times*, September 27, 2002). In the book *Hafez: Dance of Life* (1988), Zenderoudi has placed Persian calligraphic versions of Hafiz' poetry on colorful backgrounds inspired by modern abstract styles of painting. The visual results are reminiscent of both traditional, formal calligraphic compositions and vibrant, modern graphic pieces. Yet what dramatizes this book is the interplay between the translator's focus and Zenderoudi's art. While Michael Boylan's translations focus mostly on the earthly, more romantic elements in Hafiz' poetry, the artist uses modern graphic forms to highlight and reinvigorate traditional metaphysical principles inherent in the poetry of Hafiz. Michael Craig Hillmann explains in the book's afterword: "For example, [Zenderoudi's] illustration for 'Morning Light' . . . spiritualizes a courtly love poem through the repetitive clusters of the written word Allah, together with the superimposed, upward moving triangles on the vertical axis reminiscent of Zenderoudi's Sufi painting called 'Keramat' (1983)" (104).

Perhaps Zenderoudi's most renowned work is an illustrated Quran. It won the international UNESCO prize in 1972 as the most beautiful book of the year, even though it is graphically very different from a traditionally calligraphed and illuminated Quran. As in the example of his *Hafez: Dance of Life*, Zenderoudi presents the holiest of Islamic books with a modern graphic sensibility that embodies for the modern viewer the sense of gravity and beauty associated with much earlier versions of the Quran.

As a young man, Zenderoudi studied with the Armenian Iranian teacher and gallery owner Marcos Gregorian, who had studied in Rome.

FIGURE 5.2. Illustration from "The Awakening," by Judith Ernst; gouache on paper, 10 x 16 inches. (Reprinted by permission of the artist)

Zenderoudi was encouraged to take seriously the art of local popular culture, including "coffee house painting." At that time, this genre, which pictures religious and popular literary themes, was considered primitive and marginalized as a sort of outsider art. Yet in 1960, Zenderoudi produced his own linocut version of the martyrdom of Imam Husayn. Featuring the centerpiece of Shiite spirituality dating back to 680, the work was titled *Who Is This Hossein the World is Crazy About?* (Art critics did not miss

the fact that the artist's name is also Hossein.) Gradually, however, Zenderoudi inspired a new artistic movement called "Sagha-Khaneh." It refers to a ceremonial public structure that holds water for travelers passing by, constructed in memory of the Shiite martyrs who were denied water in the hot desert of Karbala. Fereshteh Deftari observes:

> Exterior and interior decoration of these structures—which are often located in bazaars—may range from a simple brass hand (symbolizing the severed hand of Hazrat Abbas, who attempted to bring back water

from the Euphrates) and a drinking bowl, to religious prints and objects such as padlocks or pieces of cloth knotted around the grillwork in acts of private devotion. In addition to functioning as a fountain, the whole complex constitutes a kind of mnemonic installation, a quotidian affirmation of faith, an intermediary between believers and their aspirations.[6]

Using this as a symbol of indigenous cultural and religious iconography, the Sagha-Khaneh movement became the umbrella under which several Iranian artists of Zenderoudi's generation formulated a distinctively modern national art. Since 1961, Zenderoudi has lived in Paris, where he has developed his more calligraphic style. In it, "he navigates back and forth through the millennia, from cuneiform to Arabic script, and through cultures, both indigenous and foreign. Divorcing text from meaning, from literature, from religion, and from language itself, he turns word into image and function into form."[7] His work continues to be exhibited in museums in Europe and the United States and in Iran and other countries in the Middle East.[8]

While Zenderoudi took modern, abstract styles and used them to express traditional subjects and content, the young Pakistani artist Shahzia Sikander, at least in her early work, used a very rigorous and traditional training in miniature painting to express modern and very personal themes.[9] Sikander studied miniature painting at the National College of Art in Lahore under Bashir Ahmed, whose teachers were the last of a line of traditional painters going back to the wellsprings of Mughal painting. Ahmed taught his students to make fine brushes using baby squirrel fur and to use pigments ground from semiprecious stones. At the time Sikander entered the program, miniature painting was thought of as an anachronism. According to a paper by Vishakha N. Desai based on interviews with Sikander and others, "Sikander's attraction to the miniature was actually a form of resistance to the prevailing fashion of working with oil on canvas." Desai explains: "It was almost as if turning to miniature painting, with its labor-intensive technique and its demand for solitude, was the ultimate subversive or avant-garde act" (2001a, 14). Interestingly, it was two of Sikander's other teachers in Lahore, Zahoor ul Akhlaq and Salima Hashmi, whose influence led to the integration of the miniature painting program into the curriculum of the National College in Lahore, even though they themselves favored techniques and styles considered more modern. Yet "modern" for them was also a catalyst for reengagement with the traditional: once both ul Akhlaq and Hashmi gained fellowships to study abroad, they found that the cultural distance afforded by travel made them intellectually engaged with the tradition of miniature painting and attracted to its possibilities as a modern medium (14).

In her gouache painting *The Scroll*, finished in 1992 as a final project for her degree in Lahore, Sikander employed her finely developed traditional miniature painting technique, with its use of continuous narration, or multiple images from different times shown in the same frame. Not only did she expand the width of her "miniature" painting to sixty-four inches, however, she also used traditional stylistic tools to show her various activities as she moved through a day in the life of her family, a subject very modern in its sensibility.

In 1993, Sikander continued her graduate art training at the Rhode Island School of Design. Still a resident of New York, she has expanded far beyond the technical boundaries of miniature painting into installation and much larger digital images. Even in these forms, however, her references to figures and decorative motifs associated with traditional miniature painting are unmistakable. She has also started to mix in images associated with Hindu India, which was not considered acceptable in Lahore during her undergraduate years despite the fact that her teacher, Bashir Ahmed, encouraged his students to go beyond the traditional Mughal subjects and was himself interested in Kangra painting (Desai 2001b, 70).

Sikander's cultural interests could not be contained in narrowly religious categories. As Dana Shelf, curator of Sikander's exhibit at the Kemper Museum of Contemporary Art in Kansas City, writes, "Her mixed Muslim and Hindu iconography and hybrid painting style suggest that in her world experience, all mythologies, geographical borders, and cultural codes can and should be called into question" (1998). With this kind of expansive borrowing and mixing taking place in every direction, who can claim any cultural ownership? Whose heritage is genuine, whose spurious? In an interview with Vishakha Desai, Sikander talked about her engagement with subjects of Rajput painting as a Pakistani Muslim: "When you're focusing on miniature painting and you come across a Mewar painting from Rajasthan, do you ignore it because it is from a Hindu court or do you embrace it because your family is Rajput?" she asked (Desai 2001b, 67–68). A Rajput Muslim, she is at the same time a student of modern art who forthrightly acknowledges the influence on her work of artists like David Hockney, Frida Kahlo, Anselm Kiefer, and Eva Hesse.

These are larger issues that go beyond Hindu/Muslim conflict in South Asia and the associated struggles for national identity, or even questions of ethnicity. These issues of cultural identity and ownership are not new; it is only because geographical and cultural distances have collapsed that they seem more dramatic today. A cosmopolitan example from medieval Georgia is instructive. Shota Rustaveli wrote the Georgian national epic *The Knight in the Panther's Skin* in the late twelfth or early thirteenth century (1986). He claimed to have written it in the style of the Persian epic, which, while not Islamic in content, by this time was certainly connected to an Islamicate empire. Rustaveli dedicated his work to his Christian queen (and perhaps his paramour), Tamar. To this day, the models of ideal Georgian manhood and womanhood are the four main heroes and heroines in the story. Two of them are Arab, while two are Indian. Since my grandfather was Georgian, I have a claim to this heritage. But does my mere ethnicity allow me to claim a special empathy with the cosmopolitan, Georgian connections exemplified by this great epic? Or does deep engagement with a country and affinity for its culture and language become a valid foundation for a claim on its heritage?

To further our understanding of the complex influences on a modern South Asian Muslim artist such as Shahzia Sikander, we must also consider some of her cultural antecedents, like the famous twentieth-century painter Abdul Rahman Chughtai. Until his death in the 1970s, Chughtai worked in India and Pakistan. While he was an iconic artist in Muslim Pakistan, his work elegantly synthesized multiple styles of Indian painting, from the Buddhist images at Ajanta to the work of the Mughal painters to the Hindu-themed paintings of the Rajput miniaturists. Some of Chughtai's subjects were associated with culturally Islamic themes, and he seemed to be keenly aware of the need to create a distinctively Mughal-inspired sensibility in his art, yet his synthesis of painting styles from the entire Indian subcontinent is clearly related to his early association in Calcutta with members of the New Bengal Movement led by Rabindranath Tagore's nephew, Abanindranath Tagore.[10] Tagore was associated with Ananda Coomaraswamy, who in turn had been inspired by the revivalist Arts and Crafts Movement in England of William Morris and his colleagues. Tagore, together with other artists of the New Bengal Movement, wished to revitalize Indian art by looking to traditional Indian models and subjects, including Hindu and Buddhist literature, for inspiration. Attracted by this movement, European and Japanese artists came to study in Calcutta, with the unintended consequence that Indian artists started to use a Japanese technique of watercolor that, by washing off color from the paper surface, resulted in a delicate, suffuse glow (Husain 1994, 28). Though Chughtai was known to prefer working on his own and in fact split off from the New Bengal Movement quite early, this Japanese technique remained fundamental to the style that he developed throughout his career.[11]

The question posed by this imported Japanese technique involves the extent to which cultural mixing of artistic forms is necessarily based on the existential decision of the artist. What may seem to the outsider like aesthetic revolutions may in fact be incidental effects dictated by the inherent physical qualities of new materials. Think about the very different stylistic parameters that one sees in mosaic, fresco, watercolor, and oil painting on canvas. Work by a Western-trained artist using Chinese brushes, paints, and papers can look much like a Chinese painting simply because of the unique characteristics that Chinese brushes and paints produce on rice paper. Think of the stylistic changes in Persian and Indian painting that occurred when artists started to use oil paints as they did in Qajar Iran. Did these changes occur because of artistic intention, influenced by Western painting, or were they simply brought about by a change in medium?

As a more recent example of the same process, consider the Iranian films *Gabbeh* and *The Color of Paradise*. Both represent a real departure from American and European filmmaking. Both are composed of dialogic vignettes that dynamically play off of the visuals, creating a subtle poetic structure rather than a narrative one. They are not based so much on the models of John Huston or Ingmar Bergman as they are visual evocations of traditional poetry like that of Hafiz and Rumi. However, since the medium is so familiar to us, we see them as part of a continuous tradition of modern cinema, even though their informing spirit is quite different.

But if Bengal was the locus of the New Bengal Movement, which seems to have influenced Chughtai and other artists in Pakistan, contemporary painters in present-day Bengal (substantially Bangladesh) have sometimes departed from those local traditions. Muhammad Kibria, a pioneer of the modernist movement in Dhaka, graduated from the Calcutta Art School in the 1950s, just at the time that several painters were coming back to Bengal after having studied art in Europe. Kibria's work was at first influenced by these painters, but then in the early 1960s he went to Japan in order to study graphic art. There, he radically changed his style. His paintings became purely abstract, using the interplay of texture and color to create quite beautiful visual harmony. Today he is regarded as one of the most prominent painters in Bangladesh, even though there is nothing visually inherent in his work that suggests the cultural location of the artist. His paintings, while extraordinary, could have been created by an abstract painter residing anywhere in the world. The same could be said of his student, Muhammad Eunus (see Figure 5.3). Following the lead

FIGURE 5.3. Untitled (1999), by Muhammad Eunus; oil on canvas, 21 x 21 inches. (From the collection of Tony Stewart)

of his teacher, Eunus studied in Japan, receiving his M.F.A. degree from Tama Art University in Tokyo. Another contemporary Bangladeshi artist is Muhammad Fokhrul Islam, who is equally abstract in his painting style (see Figure 5.4). Fokhrul, though his work is visually connected to modern, Western styles, nevertheless uses media not usually associated with modern art, including mustard oil, printer's ink, and leatherworking tools, which he uses to inscribe paper. He also makes it very clear that he considers himself both a Muslim and an artist, and so he has made a conscious choice to use only abstract forms in his artwork. To the casual viewer, this is a surprising twist, since his work would appear to be informed not by Islamic principles but rather by modern abstract sensibilities.[12]

Until now, implicit in the cases I have discussed has been the notion of the artist as an autonomous agent making individual creative decisions based on his or her own notions of artistic integrity. But one cannot ignore

FIGURE 5.4. Untitled (2003), by Muhammad Fokhrul Islam; printer's ink and mustard oil on paper, 14 x 11 inches. (From the collection of Tony Stewart)

the question of patronage. Jay Bonner, after all, is working in the context of a patronage system not unlike that represented by the builders of the great Islamicate monuments of the past; the resemblance extends to the guilds of traditional craftsmen who create his designs in stone, wood, and tile. Working within a particular set of traditional design parameters, he creates original work that he probably would not characterize as self-expressive, even though he considers it to be individually challenging and artistically fulfilling. His patrons see themselves as the modern preservers of an Islamic aesthetic, which they now conceptualize as "pan-Islamic."

Do use by the patron or the patron's intentions for the work determine whether or not a work can be called Islamic? Certainly the patron's wishes and the viewer's purposes are significant. Much of the European, especially French, Orientalist painting done in the nineteenth century seems peculiarly voyeuristic and theatrical; it projected colonialist fantasies on subject peoples for an eager European public with a taste for the exotic. But what about the images of the Madonna and the Christ child painted by Mughal artists and collected in folio volumes with other curiosities for the entertainment of the Mughal court? Certainly these "Occidentalist" paintings were not considered sacred, since they were not used ritually, but does their subject make them religious? What about the intent of these artists and the purposes of their patrons? Christ appears in the Quran, and according to Hadith, the Prophet protected an image of the Madonna and child while ordering the destruction of the idols in the Ka'ba. Assuming these Mughal artists were Muslim, as were their patrons, does that make these paintings Islamic, even though the images seem to have been used for entertainment by the court? What if the painters were Hindu, working for Muslim patrons? Or does it really matter? Perhaps these questions reflect more about our modern preoccupation with religious identity than they do about the thinking of the Mughal painters and the wishes of their royal clients.[13]

When we consider the patronage issue in the context of today's corporate patrons, the picture becomes even murkier. When editors become essentially marketers; when most movies are made for a mass market; when cultural icons of other countries, like the Taj Mahal, are used to sell Coke and Nike products, then all of our idealistic notions of individual intent, integrity, and cultural engagement become muddled. With corporate sponsorship, the bottom line is profit, and the individual artist does not necessarily have much creative control. Even the viewer's engagement comes into question. Should an artwork commissioned by a large American bank to go with the decor in its branch office in Riyadh, even if done by an artist native to that country, be considered Islamic/Islamicate?

So what is Islamic art in this modern, networked context? We began with Jay Bonner, who works in some ways within a very traditional model of style, technique, and patronage, though his work is networked in new ways. Most would probably agree that his work is Islamic, especially since it has been commissioned for monuments central to Islamic loyalty and piety. Some of my work has been with nominally Islamic subjects, though aimed at a Western, non-Muslim audience. Is it Islamic? Perhaps Islamicate, but not Islamic. In Hossein Zenderoudi, himself originally from a majority Muslim country, we see an artist who uses symbols and texts traditionally associated with Shiite Islam, albeit with a very modern and personal graphic style. Shahzia Sikander has taken a very traditional style associated culturally with Islam and used it to connect all of the varied and multicultural elements of her personal universe, including some (but not all) associated with Islam. The Pakistani painter Abdul Rahman Chughtai synthesized several traditional styles of Indian painting while creating work emblematic of Mughal culture for modern Pakistanis. And then we have to appraise the three Muslim artists from Bangladesh: despite their country of origin and the professed creedal and ritual practice of at least one, all of them paint in abstract styles that could have been used by artists anywhere in the world.

The list of hybrid artists could be extended. What of the work by the Malaysian artist and social activist Sharifah Zuriah Aljeffri, who did a series to commemorate the atrocities in Bosnia (see Figure 5.5)? Using Chinese brush technique, she painted lines suggesting Arabic calligraphy punctuated by bold brushstrokes of red that are emblematic of the violence aimed at Bosnian Muslims, especially women. Inspiration for the series came from the highly apocalyptic *surahs* (chapters) 40–46 in the Quran, which highlight the letters "ha" and "mim" as evocations of Judgment Day and the separation of good from evil. She calligraphs these letters in her Bosnian series, as well as the word *rahim* (the compassionate), which comes from a root meaning "womb." Focusing on Yusof 'Ali's interpretation of this series of *surahs*, she meditates on the relation of faith to unfaith, revelation to rejection, goodness to evil, and truth to falsehood. Aljeffri says of the Bosnian series, "*Ar-Rahim* is one of the attributes of Allah meaning The Compassionate. There is a connection between *Rahim* and *Ha Mim*. *Rahim* symbolizes the completion and healing of *Ha Mim*. It is with the Compassion of Allah, that we can prevail over the heinous acts and atrocities taking place in Bosnia" (1993). The overall visual effect of her work is evocative of Chinese or Japanese free-form calligraphy, but her social commentary, in combination with the Arabic letters, adds a drama and immediacy to what is usually a much more rarefied medium.

The book *Manifestation of Feeling: A Selection of Painting by Iranian Female Artists* was published in 1995 by the Center for Visual Arts, part of the Iranian Ministry of Culture and Islamic Guidance. It includes a tremendous variety of painting, from traditional miniature styles to completely abstract works, with every imaginable visual permutation in be-

FIGURE 5.5.
Bosnia 9 (1992),
by Sharifah
Zuriah Aljeffri;
48 x 106
centimeters.
(Reprinted by
permission of
the artist)

tween those two extremes. One painting, *Palestine*, by Badri Alaie, is a bold, obviously political graphic statement showing the Star of David serving as a nailed-on gate over a door behind which, the viewer is led to assume, the Palestinian people are held hostage (see Figure 5.6). Interestingly, she signs this painting in roman letters, suggesting, perhaps, that she envisioned a foreign market for the work.

Another artist featured in the same book is Feeroozeh Golmohammadi, who, in her watercolor *Ascension*, has included details reminiscent of Persian themes—costumes, headgear, prayer beads, and a phoenix-like bird at the bottom (see Figure 5.7). Her imagery and mystical theme are similar in style and content to the work of the twentieth-century German artist Sulamith Wülfing as well as to the contemporary, popular new age artist Susan Seddon Boulet.[14] Another colorful painting is *Tile Pond* by Narges Rasoulzadeh Nameen, a sort of "miniature painter meets Matisse" that recalls Matisse's famous 1912 painting popularly known as *The Goldfish (Red Fish)* from the Pushkin Museum in Moscow (see Figure 5.8).[15] Nameen combines the flat, one-dimensional composition of miniature painting, the beautiful tile work of the pond, and a traditional use of a painted frame with the loose oil technique and bold imagery of Matisse and his followers to produce this lively painting of goldfish in a pond.

These comparisons are not made to suggest that Golmohammadi's or Nameen's paintings, or any paintings that may have similarities to the work of European or American artists, are necessarily derivative. Instead, this similarity of styles exemplifies how images, as well as ideas, are now globally available and reflect an increasingly shared medium. Hybridity expands rather than contracts the world of art and the human imagination.

Perhaps the liveliest portrait of artistic diversity and hybrid rearticulation of multiple motifs is found in the artwork (and writing) of Durre Ahmed. A teacher at the National College of Art in Lahore, Pakistan, Ahmed attempts with her work "to forge a new episteme for Muslim society's encounter with globalization" (Irfani 1997, 245). In her "reconstruction," *One and a Half*, she uses a simple three-dimensional form based on the Urdu saying *dairh eenth ki masjid* (a mosque of one-and-a-half-bricks) to evoke the possibility of the traditional makeshift mosque used by travelers, laborers, and others unable to perform their prayers in a more well-established place of worship (see Figure 5.9). The phrase is also used to describe those who are nonconformist, those who go their own way and do not need the formality of the mosque for prayer. This adds a political dimension to her piece: on display in Pakistan, it mirrors that country's checkered history of political freedoms. While using the language of post-

FIGURE 5.6. *Palestine*, by Badri Alaie; oil on canvas, 100 x 80 centimeters. (From Rahimi 1995)

FIGURE 5.7. *Ascension*, by Feeroozeh Golmohammadi; watercolor, 62 x 42 centimeters. (From Rahimi 1995)

modernism in her treatise explaining her work, she also points the way to a post-postmodern art that conceptually is able to assert an Islamic sensibility, even a local Islamic spirituality, while engaging in a many-faceted modern intellectual discourse (Durre Ahmed n.d.).

Can we decide, or at least articulate, how we might use the term "Islamic art" in our globalized world? Is it the artists' faith that makes the difference, even though we have no way of knowing how faithful they are? Is it their ethnicity, whether or not their homeland is a majority Muslim country? Does their location of residence make a difference, whether or not they are expatriates? What if an artist is a minority in a majority Muslim community, say a Zoroastrian in Iran? Is the subject matter the defining aspect? Is the style the key, in which case we would presumably only include work done in a style traditionally associated with Islam? Is the patron the defining factor, or is it important to consider what use the work will be put to? Does that mean no commercial work would be allowed, even though we do consider caravansaries, palaces, and many other secular buildings from the past to be characteristically Islamic?

Even without considering the vast changes that the world has under-

FIGURE 5.8. *Tile Pond*, by Narges Rasoulzadeh Nameen; oil on canvas, 67 x 48 centimeters. (From Rahimi 1995)

gone in the last fifty years—increased immigration, worldwide media penetration, and the spread of global communications systems, including the Internet—that have resulted in our present globalized environment, the term "Islamic art" (coined by European art historians barely a century ago) remains slippery and elusive. Part of the problem is the absence of a single, monolithic Islamic culture. As we saw with Jay Bonner, a modern-day Muslim country had to invent "pan-Islamic" art. Even the notion of "pan-Islamic" conceptually leaves out the many non-Muslims who were always part of Islamicate cultures. As Jonathan Bloom and Sheila Blair point out in the introduction to their book, *Islamic Arts*, "It is easier to say what Islamic art is not than what it is. . . . Islamic art refers neither to art of a specific era nor to that of a particular place or people. . . . Islamic art is neither a style nor a movement, and the people who made it were not necessarily Muslims. . . . Whereas some Islamic art was undoubtedly made by Christians and Jews for Muslim patrons, some 'Islamic' art made by Muslims was intended for Christians or Jews" (1997, 1). The term "Islamicate" might give us a larger umbrella under which to rethink these issues, yet it

FIGURE 5.9. *One and a Half* (1996), by Durre Ahmed; "reconstruction" in terra cotta. (Photograph by Durre Ahmed; reprinted by permission of Durre Ahmed)

too presupposes a cultural and regional cohesiveness that is undermined by the global influences and cross-fertilization of artistic options brought about by our increasingly networked world.

Artists are defined by mobility and malleability. They have always moved and been moved around from place to place. Perhaps because of this mobility, they have tended to be on the fringes, at the edges where cultures meet and mix, forming new networks—reformulated workshops, schools, styles, and forms. If our project to study Muslim networks means anything, it is that we should not overly define or try to separate this from that, Muslim from Muslim, Muslim from Christian, this region from that region, this ethnic group from that one. Instead, we must try to find, in all of their complexity, the points at which people inhabiting Muslim cultures interact, have always interacted, and will always continue to interact with people elsewhere. Rather than defining or tracing or shoring up identities, we should try to recognize the multiple levels on which Muslims and Muslim cultures have nourished and engaged both insiders and outsiders. This is not only an academic imperative. When we reduce art and artists to a one-dimensional identity—for example, a religious identity—we dehumanize. It becomes easy to assume that the defining element in "their" art, unlike ours, is only that of religion, without reference to any of the many other dimensions of life and culture that fill us out as people and give us reality as human beings. Perhaps the more nuanced approach afforded by our network methodology can help us to overcome some of the dehumanizing stereotypes that are so much a part of most Americans' notion of Islam and Muslims.

NOTES

1. Marshall Hodgson (1974) coined the term "Islamicate."

2. For a wonderfully lively, fictional account of the effects of such forces on artists and craftsmen in the seventeenth-century Ottoman Empire, see Pamuk 2002.

3. To see more of Bonner's work, go to ‹http://www.bonner-design.com›.

4. See Ernst 1995.

5. For examples, see *Festival of India* 1985, 57, or Bautze 1998, 331.

6. Deftari 2002, 74. Deftari's excellent article gives a full account of Iranian modernism from its beginnings at the turn of the twentieth century through the 1970s and situates examples of artwork in terms of the international influences on various artists (through travel, study, and foreign and foreign-trained teachers) as well as the ongoing debate about "How to be Persian and modern? Which direction to take: the West or the past, or both?" Deftari explains: "This other modernism, like many of the culturally specific modernisms that emerged around the globe, was neither synchronous nor synonymous with the one constructed in the West. Its impulse being at the same time nationalistic and internationalist, it looked inward as well as outward. In art, its languages included both realism and abstraction, but formal issues were not its primary

problems: the fundamental questions of Iranian modernism addressed the notion of identity" (81–82).

7. Ibid., 78. This description is of course not quite applicable to the above examples of his Hafiz illustrations or his Quran, which are both intimately tied to language, meaning, literature, and religion (or in the case of Hafiz, at least to metaphysics).

8. You can see examples of Zenderoudi's work at ‹http://www.zenderoudi .com/›.

9. You can see examples of Sikander's more recent work at ‹http://www .bombsite.com/sikander/sikander.html› (accessed May 26, 2004).

10. For examples of work by this school of painters, see Nivedita and Coomaraswamy 1914.

11. You can see some of his paintings at ‹http://megaeast.com/default.asp? section=art%20and%20culture&page=chughtai.com› (accessed May 26, 2004).

12. You can see a sample of contemporary paintings by artists from Bangladesh at ‹http://www.chayamachigaro.com/exhibition/bangladesh/bangladesh .htm› (accessed May 26, 2004).

13. For a discussion of Islamic religious identity as a creation of census and population figures, see Carl Ernst 2003, chapter 2.

14. For Wülfing's work, see ‹http://www.lightworks.com/gallery/wulfing .html› (accessed May 26, 2004). For Boulet's, see ‹http://mystic-caravan.com/ boulet.htm› (accessed May 26, 2004).

15. See ‹http://www.artnet.com/magazine/features/tuchman/tuchman1-16-7 .asp› (accessed May 26, 2004).

Chapter 6

Sacred Narratives Linking Iraqi Shiite Women across Time & Space

> He who remembers us [the family of the Prophet Muhammad] or
> he from whose eyes a tear as small as the wing of a gnat will fall at our
> mention, God will forgive all his sins, be they endless as the foam of
> the sea. JAFAR AL-SIDDIQ (the sixth imam)

In March 1991, thousands of Iraqi Shiites fled their homes to American-held lines in southern Iraq after the betrayal of the Shiite Uprising and were transported to a Saudi refugee camp in the desert not far from the Iraqi border. Throughout the year 1993, small groups of these refugees were resettled in the Netherlands. Three years after they were resettled, I had become acquainted with many of them. I decided to make the lives of fifty of these women the subject of my doctoral dissertation.

The most significant interviews I recorded were with older women, especially with Fatima, Habiba, Nabila, Amina, Jamilah, Umm Ahmad, Umm Faris, and Solima, the *mullaya* (religious leader). At first, the women were afraid to tell their personal histories, preferring to resort to Quranic modes of narrative and to poetry, but as they reestablished themselves in their new environment and became comfortable with me, they gained the confidence to use their traditional frames of narrative.

These Iraqi Shiite women have lost family, history, and culture. Yet one essential aspect of their identity has remained and in fact deepened during the refugee process: the art and tradition of interspersing personal with religious narratives. Above all, the narratives of these women relate to time-sanctioned rituals of mourning. These rituals become a narrative thread tying together those who share a memory of the sacred histories and

132

symbols of Shiism. They function as a means of connection, commemoration, and therapy. They create a diasporic network that projects female actors as the custodians of hope in the face of what to many would be unspeakable horrors, unbearable traumas.

This chapter explores a ritual specific to women that is called *majlis al-qiraya*, or gathering for remembrance and mourning for members of *ahl al-bait* (the Prophet's family). These rituals involve women and children, and they usually take place in the home. The *majlis al-qiraya* is the setting for the recitation of laments and for ritual acts of weeping and mourning. The aim of the poetic laments is to describe and share the sufferings of *ahl al-bait*, who fought in order to bring justice to their Islamic nation.[1] The stories and poems provide insight into the ways in which ordinary Shiites from different communities establish and maintain links horizontally to each other and vertically back through time to the wellsprings of their religion.[2]

Since the seventh century, Shiites have performed the rituals of the *majlis*, thereby creating strong relationships with previous generations (Haydari 1999). When the refugee women who are the subject of this study come to the *majlis* to remember the pain and suffering of *ahl al-bait*, they bring with them individual and collective traumas from two wars and political oppression, traumas they are not supposed to express publicly. These traumatic events vary from the most personal—torture, rape, and witnessing the torture or death of loved ones—to collective sharing in the trauma of a persecuted community. Some women have firsthand experience with all of these traumas, while others shared in traumatic events by listening to stories told by other women, frequently at the *majlis*.

The women I interviewed have been victims of persecution in Iraq since the 1970s, refuge seekers in Saudi Arabia, and alienated resettled people in the Netherlands. The accumulated traumas they lived through were heightened by a sense of multiple betrayals that has haunted them from the moment their 1991 uprising was crushed by Saddam Hussein and the United States abandoned them. More betrayals by the United States and its allies in the Gulf War followed as the Iraqi refugees were promised immediate relocation in the United States when they crossed over into American-held Iraqi territory. Instead, they were sent to the Saudi Rafha Refugee Camp in the desert. Though they were told it would be a "temporary refuge," they spent three years (1991–93) of harsh isolation in this place, the equivalent of a prison camp. The indifference and hostility of Saudi Arabia, a nation which was instrumental in the American decision to betray the uprising and which refused to allow the refugees to integrate within Saudi society, exacerbated the sense of betrayal. These numerous traumas were aggravated by the acute sense of guilt the women felt about abandoning members of their families when they chose to flee Iraq and for their complicity (however passive) in the breakup of what remained of their extended families at the time of resettlement. The women believe that their show of devotion within the *majlis* can transform their suffering into something good—the collective, religious communing and remembering. For the rite to serve its religious purpose, the women have to interact with their history, remember and relive it, and then show their piety by weeping.

In the essay that follows, I examine the women's use of religious symbols and sacred narratives to overcome their own suffering, fear, sense of loss and betrayal, and emotional collapse. Since the seventh century, Shiite women have utilized the narratives of the *majlis* with the familiarity of close relatives, layering their own stories with ancient stories. I am less interested in the objective truth of their stories than in the meaning these women give to the events they have experienced. How does the story unfold? How does the narrator address her subjects? What language does she use? Is the story linear or circular? What do the pauses signify? What role do these narratives play in perpetuating Iraqi culture in the Netherlands and informing a collective identity?

I argue that the narration of sacred stories helps to heal the psychological and emotional wounds of wars and exile. Women find comfort in collective crying during the ritual narration of the seventh-century betrayal and death of members of the Prophet's family by venting their own pain through that of others. What interests me is how the women I met connect the history of the Shiites with their present in the Netherlands.

Shiite Narratives and the Framework of Religion

One of the crucial differences between the Shiite and the Sunni communities is reflected most clearly in their respective attitudes toward the relationship between "the man" and "the book." For the Sunnis, the Quran is its own proof by virtue of its *i'jaz* (miraculous uniqueness). Thus, in Sunni Islam "the book" takes precedence over "the man" (Schubel 1993, 15). For the Shiites, the proof of the verity of the Quran lies with the Prophet, hence *ahl al-bait* is central to Shiite belief and devotion. The emphasis on individual and communal allegiance to the Prophet has important consequences for Shiite thinking, practices, and rituals.

Shiism takes its name from the Arabic word *shi'a*, meaning "partisan of" or "supporter of" ʿAli, the cousin and son-in-law of the Prophet Muhammad. The Shiites believe that God and Muhammad designated ʿAli as the rightful first successor to the political and spiritual authority of the Prophet. The Sunnis, on the other hand, believe that ʿAli is the fourth legitimate caliph in Islam, having followed the three caliphs Abu Bakr, ʿUmar, and ʿUthman, and that together their rule makes up the epoch of the four Righteous Caliphs. The Shiites resent the Sunni Muslim community's rejection of ʿAli's sole right to inherit the caliphate. For them, the imamate, or Islamic leadership, is more than political, it is an office of miraculous, mystical, and soteriological power. Their belief is based on a Quranic verse (2:124) in which God promises to make Ibrahim and his descendants imams. According to religious history, the Prophet Muhammad and ʿAli, his cousin, were descendants of Prophet Ibrahim through his son Ismaʿil. Muhammad was last in the line of prophets, but ʿAli, as the verse says, was promised by God to become imam.[3]

Like the prophets, ʿAli and the imams are thought to be *maʿsum* (immune from error), capable of guiding the community because they have esoteric knowledge from the Prophet (Hoffman-Ladd 1992, 626). For the Shiites, the Prophet and his family are more than simply human beings. They are prophetic wisdom incarnate, and they represent the prophetic light in the world. Thus the denial of ʿAli's right to the caliphate constituted a sacrilegious betrayal. Shiite teachings are based on the Quran and Hadith, which affirm for Shiites that their beliefs have firm textual authority.

The love of *ahl al-bait* is accepted by both the Sunnis and Shiites, and it unites them. Most Sunnis and all Shiites express their love for the Prophet's family by visiting and taking care of their tombs, composing love poems for them, holding celebrations, and giving charity in their names. What distinguishes the Shiites is that they hold mourning rituals that serve as a platform for expressing their love for *ahl al-bait*. The life histories of each family member and the events of their lives are important sources for the *majlis al-qiraya*.

The importance of the history of the holy family for Shiite piety is reflected in the ritual calendar, which contains more than forty-eight death and birth celebrations for the Prophet, the twelve imams, and the women of *ahl al-bait*—Sayyida Fatima in particular. Fatima was the daughter of the Prophet, the source of the imams, and the mother of Sayyida Zaynab, the granddaughter of the Prophet and the sister of Hasan and Husayn. Each anniversary gives Shiites the opportunity to reaffirm their allegiance through emotional acts of devotion. Their devotion and love for *ahl al-bait* determine the forgiveness of their sins. It is this devotion to *ahl al-bait*, and the hope of salvation through this love, that allegedly distinguishes Shiite from Sunni Islam at the level of popular piety (628).

Personal contact with *ahl al-bait* is established during the rituals of mourning and remembrance. This contact can be seen in its most striking and visible form during the public remembrance and mourning of the martyrdom of the third imam, Husayn. The revival of his memory takes place in the month of Muharram, the first month in the Islamic calendar. The rites of remembrance of and mourning for Husayn are intense, and they reach their climax on the tenth of Muharram, the day Husayn was martyred in the battle of Karbala in 680.[4] Karbala, a city in southern Iraq by the Euphrates, was the home of some of the women who were interviewed for this study.

Although the battle of Karbala was small in terms of the number of troops and casualties, the impact it had on Shiism is staggering (Richard 1995, 29). It represents for all Shiites the prototypical struggle between the persecutor and the oppressed. The martyrdom of Husayn is emblematic of every struggle for justice. This belief explains why many of the women interviewed for this study would say: "History is repeating itself. We are oppressed by Saddam as Husayn was oppressed by Yazid."[5] In their poetry, these women invoke Husayn and Yazid to refer to their own suffering and oppression.

In 680, the people of Kufa, another city in the south of Iraq that was home to many of the women interviewed for this study, begged Husayn to come to Iraq and lead them in revolt against the tyrant Yazid. Husayn and his small entourage left Medina for the south of Iraq, but before they reached Kufa, Yazid and his army stopped them. No relief came from Kufa, and Husayn was martyred in Karbala along with nearly all of his family. The people of Kufa were so terrified of Yazid that they did not dare rise up against him. In other words, the very people Husayn had come to rescue betrayed him. Ibrahim al-Haydari explains the effects of Husayn's martyrdom on the Iraqi Shiites: "There is no land that has been as bloodied as the land of Karbala and no nation that has mourned its hero as the Iraqi Shi'ites have mourned al-Husayn. To some extent, that sadness and mourning for al-Husayn has become part of the character of the Iraqi Shi'ite selfhood" (1999, 35).

The massacre at Karbala remains alive through the *majalis al-qiraya*. Unlike the Muharram rites, which are carried out only during the first ten days of the month and are known as *majalis al-azza al-Husayniya*, the *majalis al-qiraya* are practiced throughout the year, and they mourn all the members of the Prophet's family, not only Husayn. The rituals of remembrance always involve weeping, a practice much critiqued by Sunnis. To the Shiites, weeping for *ahl al-bait*, and in particular for Husayn, is not only legitimate but also redemptive. Inability to weep may prove that one is spiritually lost. The sixth imam, Jafar al-Siddiq, asked the Shiites to compose poetry about Husayn and his uprising in order to keep Husayn's memory alive. He also said, "There is no servant [of God] whose eyes shed tears for us, whom God will not grant the reward of countless ages in Paradise" (Shams Al-Din 1985, 217–18).

Healing at the Shrines

The women I interviewed believe that every Muslim who is a true lover of *ahl al-bait* should visit the sacred shrines, especially those in Najaf,[6] Karbala, al-Kazimiya,[7] and Samara,[8] at least once in his or her lifetime. "Visitors" acquire special religious and social status as true lovers of the Prophet's family. Almost all the women I interviewed had gained the title of "visitor," some because they lived far away and yet made the holy visit, others because they were residents in sacred cities and always enjoyed the blessings of visiting the shrines.

The women visited the shrines most often during difficult times like the first and second Gulf wars. Women who could not afford to visit sent letters of complaint, request, and supplication to the imams. Such letters included requests for peace, health, protection, and the safe return of loved ones. Many women mentioned to me that the tomb of Imam 'Ali in Najaf was filled with hundreds of such letters, pasted in layers on the windows and doors of the tomb. The letters may have been the only means available to their authors to express and to relieve their suffering. The women I interviewed suffered the most from anxiety and social pressure. Their visits and prayers in shrines to the holy family had a psychological function in addition to their religious functions, because such visits helped them experience peace and comfort and thus cope with their anxiety. Amina explained how she would tie a green thread in the tomb's window. When God answered her request, she would keep her vow and throw money or gold through the window, give offerings to one of the keepers of the shrine, or distribute money for the poor in the name of the imam. Jamilah claimed that the imams cure illness.

Habiba mentioned that the Baath regime forbade the Shiite rituals of mourning and remembrance in 1977. The police locked the big gate that led to the shrines of Husayn and 'Abbas. They stood by the locked gate with guns to prevent people from entering the shrine. People stood by the gate, praying and chanting, and suddenly she and the other members of the crowd saw the gate open on its own. The police, frightened, ran away, and the Shiites entered with joy. Fatima recalled that when the government forbade the rituals of remembrance, it also prohibited pilgrimage to the holy shrines, but to no avail.

It runs in our blood to worship this holy family! I remember once after this banning decree in 1980, a rich man from our neighborhood brought many buses at midnight and invited people to travel free of charge to Karbala. At 3 A.M., we drove down to the area of the Ma'amil, and from there we went on foot to Karbala to reach the holy shrines and visit Imam Husayn, 'Abbas, and Qassim. After this, we went back to spend the night in a tent! We were a group of girls and we were laughing, weeping, and talking! We stayed in the tent until noon the next day, when we were told that there would be "jogging" in memory of Husayn. Even kids of only four years were involved in this rite, all dressed in green. People were reciting for 'Abbas during the jogging, but never to Zaynab. We believe that 'Abbas would get nervous if she were mentioned. It happened that during the "harder" jogging, some people mentioned her. I was washing my face when I saw smoke from the top of 'Abbas's tomb! We were amazed, and people were scared. Then we were ordered not to mention her again! When I started jogging, I nearly fainted. A man met me and gave me a sweet, milky drink. When I drank it, I felt refreshed and jogged for three hours, and I was ready for more. An old man riding a horse was leading the caravel, and we repeated after him. He was reciting poetry, and we responded. In our area, the Communist Party was very active amongst the Shiites, while the religious Islamic parties were not. Although the Communists were heretics, they still observed the Shiite rituals. They served the funerals and did the Husayn readings. They believed. That was the society they had entered, and they could not change its practices!

Such narratives attest to the centrality of collective remembrance in Shiite culture. Although the Iraqi government had worked to prohibit such gatherings, the Shiite community persevered.

The Setting of Remembrance

The sacred narratives that tell the stories of the bravery and sacrifice of the heroes and heroines of Karbala are called *khitab Karbala*, or

Karbala discourse. The miraculous narratives of Karbala help to heal suffering and trauma. As the women I studied attempt to rebuild their lives in the Netherlands, they attend *majalis al-qiraya* and make them a part of everyday conversation, thereby serving their religion and releasing their own personal pain.

In what follows, I shall describe the *majlis* of Sayyida Zaynab. She is the heroine of Karbala, the one who kept the memory of the holy family alive when she said to Yazid, "By God, you will never take from us our memory" (Shams Al-Din 1985, 218). One of the women said to me that without Zaynab, the history of *ahl al-bait* would have been long forgotten. Zaynab is the spokesperson and the protector of *ahl al-bait*. Defiant while helpless, she rescued Islam and kept alive the memory of *ahl al-bait*. Shiites credit her with being the first to hold a *majlis* to mourn Husayn when she was a captive in Damascus. Even more important was her rescue of ʿAli, the only son of Husayn to survive Karbala. She ensured the survival of her nephew and thus of the line of imams.

Majalis al-qiraya are held in private homes, where an invited congregation may range in size from a dozen to a hundred women but averages around fifty. The *mullaya*, an Iraqi colloquialism for a female mullah, serves as the leader of women's *majlis*. *Mullayat* are usually local women who have had traditional training. Only women are allowed to attend *majalis al-qiraya*, and there must be no men within earshot. The *majlis* hostess is very aware of the range of choices open to her in terms of which *mullaya* to choose, the types of performance to sponsor, the hospitality to offer, and the ambience to create.

The first step in the process is the preparation of the location. The performance I will recount took place at the home of one of the interviewees, who happened to be a *mullaya*. I arrived at three o'clock in the afternoon on September 17, 1999, to attend a *majlis al-qiraya* for Sayyida Zaynab that would be held at seven in the evening. I came early to observe and help prepare the house, as participation in preparation is part of piety. Two other women had already arrived to help with the cooking and moving furniture out of the sitting room. The room was then empty apart from a big, colorful Persian carpet and a few pictures on the wall. There were three pictures in the *mullaya*'s sitting room. One of them was a picture of the first imam, ʿAli, the second was of the third imam, Husayn, and the third image was a wall-size poster of palm trees, which symbolize divine grace and are an icon of nostalgia for the homeland of Iraq. Most of the houses of the Iraqi women in the Netherlands have these pictures on the wall. Some houses also have verses of the Quran or a saying of one of the imams in calligraphic

Arabic. The aim of such visual presentations is to remind the women of their country, their history, and their religion.

These visual presentations provide a window onto the rituals. Alan Radley explains that people who are forced from their homes establish a special form of remembering, which he calls "grieving." Objects may repair a biographical disruption the individual has suffered and evoke memories even while they remain embedded in the material world. The artifacts sustain remembrance and shape the recounting of history (1990, 50, 51, 57). Thus the pictures of imams and palm trees represent the Iraqi women's past, present, and future, providing a setting within which to tell their own stories.

By six thirty, most of the women had arrived, and it was time for the *maghrib* (sunset) prayer. Before the prayer, I was given a *turba*, a small, fine, round stone. To create *turba*, pieces of clay from Karbala are dried and burnished into square, rectangular, or oval shapes; they are placed on prayer mats, and the person who is praying places his or her forehead on the *turba* instead of the ground. Each of the women had one. The woman sitting next to me said to me, "This piece of *turba* was made from the earth of Karbala, and it is our tradition to use this earth, which was purified by the blood of Husayn, for prayers, to represent the land where Husayn was martyred for us." This stone, representing the first step in the ritual of remembrance, serves as the gateway into the history of Karbala and *ahl al-bait*. Individuals are reminded of their unique, Shiite-specific history five times a day when they pray and use the *turba*.

Since remembrance is at the core of Shiite belief, the deployment of such objects is particularly important. It is for this reason that the artifacts of place are as important to the Shiite rites as are the sacred texts they recite. Objects establish a connection with the past that helps to sustain identity (47–48). Thus, with the *turba*, the familiar images on the wall, and the nostalgic smells of Iraqi food in the air, we all began the *maghrib* prayer together.

The Remembrance and Mourning Rites of Zaynab

The aim of the stories that unfolded in this *majlis* was to draw inspiration from the lives of the female members of *ahl al-bait*, who set examples of female heroism. The women who participate in the ritual also gather strength from the stories of the lives of the twelve imams, who suffered persecution and martyrdom, and of the Shiites who, in the centuries of persecution that followed, met similar fates with apparent equanimity or even enthusiasm. These stories blend the fantastic with the historic; the events recounted are not simply historical, but metahistorical. Their content and recitation are archetypal, outside of, yet parallel to, real time and place.

Here, I am going to concentrate on the "constructed" poetic stories about Sayyida Zaynab. In this ceremony, the retelling of the story only begins after visual and spiritual preparation for the emotional part of the rituals has been made. The women, dressed in black, sat on the floor in four lines in a square, facing each other, with their backs against the walls. When the first square was completed, the latecomers started new lines inside the square, eventually forming a second square. The small children[9] up to three years of age sat next to their mothers or on their mothers' laps. The older children sat together, forming another square. The women conversed quietly with each other.

The ceremony began the moment the *mullaya* entered the room. She was at the very center of the last square, so that all the women and children could see what she was doing and hear what she was saying. The *majlis* began calmly with the first *qaʿda* (sitting). The women remained seated, listening to the *mullaya* and reciting verses of the Quran for blessings. When she invoked the prayer for the Prophet and his family, especially Zaynab, the women joined in the "Amen" to close the prayer. Next, she addressed Imam Husayn in her own words: "O my Imam Husayn, often I visited your tomb and touched the earth in which you lay. Now I long to return to you. Years have passed in which I missed the joy of being in your garden. I have tried to visit you, but the flashing sword of Yazid [Saddam Hussein] prevented me. When it became so difficult to see you, I visited Syria to taste and smell the earth of Sayyida Zaynab's tomb. Your presence in Sayyida Zaynab let me commune with you. Sayyida Zaynab and you are with us in spirit although far away."

The *mullaya* apologized for not being able to do her duty and visit Husayn's tomb in Karbala because Saddam Hussein, whom she called Yazid, would not allow her to visit. Unable to resist her longing for *ahl al-bait*, however, she traveled to Syria, one of the places Sayyida Zaynab is believed to be buried. Zaynab was very close to her brother Husayn, and thus through her the *mullaya* was able to regain Husayn's blessings. The *mullaya* continued, saying that she felt the presence of Husayn and Zaynab with her in the Netherlands. Then she recited prayers and blessings for Sayyida Zaynab. Next she recounted Sayyida Zaynab's role in the historic events of Karbala. Husayn knew that he was going to be martyred. This is why he took the women of his family with him. He wanted Sayyida Zaynab to complete his message after his death. She survived the battle and became the protector of the Prophet's family. Taken as a captive to Kufa, she spoke to its governor in defense of her brother and his family. Then she was taken to Yazid at his court in Damascus. She again spoke out in defense of her sisters and saved her nephew from being killed. Although she was powerless before the caliph, her strength carried the message.

Then the *mullaya* addressed a special prayer to Sayyida Zaynab in the name of all those assembled at the *majlis*: "O Sayyida Zaynab, woman of faith and light, granddaughter of our Prophet Muhammad, we ask you to brighten our life with your wonderful light and to give us the strength to face the difficulties of our time. May God help us to meet with you in your high place in Paradise. O our great Sayyida Zaynab, bless our gathering in your name and thousands of prayers and peace be upon you." Then, the *mullaya* stood up and began to recite an elegy from the perspective of Sayyida Zaynab witnessing the martyring of her brother. She started the recitation in a peculiar, deliberately quivering voice, reminiscent of a lute. The strings of lament flowed from one theme to another.

Shiite women have used therapeutic poetic narrative since the time of Zaynab. Their narrative is not in the form of testimony but rather takes the form of poetry that laments the suffering of *ahl al-bait*, with which Shiite women can empathize. They mix classical poetry of the sixth and seventh centuries with poetry the women write themselves concerning *ahl al-bait*. When Solima, the *mullaya*, described her feelings at Rafha Refugee Camp, she slipped into sorrow when describing how she heard of the death of Sayyid Abu al-Qasim al-Khui, the head of the Shiite community and a descendant of the Prophet's family. She recited a long poem, at the end of which she substituted herself for the departed scholar and leader:

> I wish that my body had rested
> In earth before his
> And my eyes had not seen that morning
> My loving heart was broken by his departure
> Everyone would have sacrificed herself for him
> Had it been possible.

According to a Shiite hadith, members of the Prophet's family and the sixth imam, Jafar al-Siddiq, said, "God has built a house [*bait*] in heaven for whomever recites a line [*bait*] of poetry about us." In another hadith, Imam Jafar al-Siddiq said, "Whoever recites poetry about Husayn and makes thirty others weep will have heaven as the reward." During my interviews with the refugee women, these hadiths were mentioned many times.

I was often taken aback by the spontaneous poems that women recited during pauses in their telling of their life stories. Without introduction or explanation, each poem would answer a question. In describing a terrible moment, the language of the story would become lyrical. The use of lyricism is not a conscious decision on the part of these women, but rather a consequence of their deeply embedded sense of rhythm. Poetry in storytelling ensures the preservation of the stories through mnemonic devices of rhyme and rhythm. Metaphor also serves memory. The stronger the images, the longer the story will live in the personal—and thus the collective—memory. When I asked Solima how she felt about the fact that the mourning ceremonies were forbidden by the Baath regime, she said:

The tyrant [Saddam] forbids us to walk in your path
Alas, he accepts no mourning ceremonies!
He says, "I am the Ruler.
I want to destroy them and rest.
Why do you not rise up, ʿAli,
And put an end to this?"

When I asked Habiba why she came to Holland, she replied:

We will ask why Zaynab was taken hostage
The people of Umayya will be erased forever.
Everyone in the world must witness what we do.

In the passage Habiba recited, she is Zaynab, and the people of the Baath regime are Umayyads. Recalling the day the Americans struck Iraq on January 17, 1991, and the explosions in Basra, Habiba quoted a Quranic verse from the "Earthquake" (99:1): "It felt like the day 'when the earth was shaken to her utmost.'" The women's vocabulary is intense. Even when describing everyday occurrences, they will use words like "destruction," "persecution," "failure," "killing," and "collapse." When describing an especially bitter food, a woman might exclaim that the food "harmed" her mouth. A four-year-old girl complained that her mother had "fled" the room, a verb usually used to describe the forced exile of a refugee. Everyone regularly used the words "justice," "injustice," "extortion," "unfairness," "iniquity," "oppression," "disaster," and "pain."

The *majlis* is a space of intensive group therapy that allows the women to escape their houses and realities and to share in a carefully constructed commemoration. They can listen and relate to their history while fulfilling their religious duty. They comfort each other in the conversations that follow weeping.

Repetition and simplicity of phrasing characterize the poetry of the *majlis*. The laments vary considerably in length, structure, and content. The first verse of the poem is an invocation and hymn to God's oneness and power. The second verse is a brief introduction to Zaynab's story. The poem ends with the poet speaking as Sayyida Zaynab, asking the listeners to recite the first verse of the Quran. The laments ritually invoke a relationship of individual kinship, beginning with phrases like "O my brother" or "O my mother." In the first line of the first lament, Sayyida Zaynab calls her brother "son of my mother." She wishes to die so that she can be with him:

> O son of my mother,
> My soul has left me
> But what is the use of my soul without you
> Your pain is my pain
> Ya Husaynnah, Ya Husaynnah!

After each episode in the lament, the women join with the *mullaya* in chanting the one-line refrain, "Ya Husaynnah, Ya Husaynnah!" (O my Husayn!). This ritual remembrance continues until the *waqfa*.

The women now loosen their scarves, stand up, and form one circle around the *mullaya*, who chants an especially powerful lament in a strong, grief-stricken voice. Its dirgelike rhythms evoke deep pain that echoes the anguished rhythms of Shiite funerals. The women's voices become stronger and louder as they join the *mullaya*, chanting in unison the refrain, "Ya Husaynnah, Ya Husaynnah!"

The *waqfa* is the emotional climax. The crying is more intense, and the women's love and remembrance of *ahl al-bait* is at its most passionate. This stage is called *ma'tam*, a term that signifies acts of lamentation for the dead. The thudding sound of the *ma'tam*, during which participants slap their chests in unison, percussively accompanies the chanted laments. The human chest becomes a musical instrument, filling the room with a steady, rhythmic beating. By achieving this state and encouraging others to weep as well, one ensures one's own salvation and that of others.

When the *mullaya* observes that the women are at a height of emotion, she beats her breast and her face with her hands to make them cry until they all achieve a state of unity in their sorrow. The chant continues as the women rock back and forth in unison, following the rhythm with the beating of their chests. All are weeping[10] by this point, and some are even crying out in sudden bursts, "O Husayn, O Victim of Tyranny!" or "We wish we were with you, Husayn!" or "O Husayn, God curse Yazid!"

The *majlis* itself is a passing on of history and of identity in the face of the enemy who drove these women into exile, whether they call him Yazid or Saddam. In another verse, one sees again the parallel between Zaynab's heroic message and that of the Shiite women themselves. She has not yet realized that she has been chosen by God. By implication, the women present have also been chosen:

Zaynab calling out,
Who will carry my message?
Who will preserve the legacy of my past?
Ya Husaynnah, Ya Husaynnah!

When the *mullaya* is satisfied that the women have reached the peak of pain and grief, she ends the *waqfa* by leading them in a Quranic recitation. Then the *mullaya* and the women sit for a brief rest, drink water, and wipe away their tears. After two further historical narratives, one from Syria and the other from Karbala, the women stand up and listen to the *mullaya* recite a personal supplication. She asks, on behalf of all of the assembled women, for Imam Husayn and Sayyida Zaynab to mediate God's forgiveness for all of them. In a message of hope for all participants, she ends the *majlis* with a direct petition to God, asking him for the forgiveness of sins and the acceptance of the *majlis*. The women recite this prayer with her.

Though the *majlis* has formally ended at this point, in another form it continues. While sandwiches, drinks, and Arabic coffee are served, the women can now talk to each other about their personal problems in the presence of the *mullaya*. They talk about their children's problems at school, life in Holland, and their personal feelings about resettlement. A statement Fatima made during the *majlis* reflected the feelings of many women at the gathering: "When I was ill, I could not blame anybody for not visiting me, since I knew that everybody's circumstances were governed by family and household. I could not go to America and join my brothers, since my husband and children were here. I have no plans to return to Iraq, since my children [who were born in Holland] have grown up here. I told the social worker that I needed Dutch citizenship since I could not return to Iraq, and she promised to think about it."

After a silence, she continued.

I would have learned the language if my mind were not so overloaded. I always think about the future of my children in Holland, my other kids in Iraq. I always dreamed of them. Always I saw the police chasing me during my sleep. A couple of days ago, I dreamed that my child in Iraq was in the hold of a big snake, and I was fighting to release him. I really do not know what would happen to my children if I were dead! I could not explain all my fears and nightmares to my women friends, since they might have their own fears—even more than mine! We gather to have fun, and nobody would be ready to deal with those miserable stories of Iraq. In our last gathering, while we were having fun, a lady spoke about Iraq, and all requested her to stop it, since it would take us into pain and mourning. So she changed the topic!

A prolonged silence followed the anecdote about a woman who had been chastised for mentioning painful histories.

Fatima's story touched upon numerous issues that face Iraqi Shiite refugee women and their families in the Netherlands, including marital, economic, social, and psychological hardships. Constant worry about the safety of their children, both in Iraq and in Holland, compounds their sense of alienation. Though Fatima described the pleasure she has in the company of her friends, she hesitates to burden them with her pains. Her narrative illustrates how important talking is to healing troubles.

Fatima's story encapsulates what most of the women present have undergone and thus can relate to. The expectation that sooner or later there will be a disaster is so much a part of Shiite collective consciousness and identity that there are even those who define peace as traumatic. Nevertheless, the women struggle to establish a sense of stability and familiarity within the labyrinth of new problems.

Solima shared a story of a traumatic moment with the group. Her story concerns the act of gathering for *majlis* itself and how a *majlis* in Iraq led to her torture.

The mourning ceremony was supposed to be secretly held, but a neighbor came without an invitation. I did not know who opened the door for her. The next morning at 8 A.M., a police officer came to my house and took me to his office. They brought me back at 6 P.M. and dropped me at our door, unconscious. I regained consciousness at 11 P.M. During the interrogation, the man asked me what we had been doing last night. I told him that we had some guests. He turned on a recorder, and to my astonishment it was my voice talking during the mourning ceremony. All the stories I told and all the poems I recited. The man behind me during the interrogation got very angry when he heard the tape and poured a cold liquid on my foot. That liquid fried my foot like eggs in boiling oil. I went into a coma, and when I awoke I found my father, mother, brothers, and sisters all around my bed with pale faces. When I looked at my foot, I saw the flesh was gone and only the bones were left, hurting like hell. It was sulfuric acid. During the interrogation, they asked whether I was not afraid of them when I conducted the *'ashura* ceremony. I said to him I fear only God and my imams. But I was really afraid of them.

The horror of Solima's story added another dimension to the gathering. The women need the connection of fellow Shiites in the familiar setting of the *majlis*. Moreover, they derive courage from the ceremonies themselves. At this point in the evening, the women could discuss their difficulties with their husbands and with life in Holland in general. Some of the women had already phoned the *mullaya*, seeking her advice prior to the *majlis*. The *mullaya* could now refer to those problems and provide her advice both for the benefit of the woman who had called her and for the benefit of the other women, who could also join in offering advice. After this session, the women gathered their belongings, embraced, and returned to their own homes. One woman explained, "The *majlis* became our secret place for sharing pain and suffering and discussing problems we face in Iraq, and now in exile." The *majlis* had also been the safest place for speaking of forbidden subjects in authoritarian Iraq.

The *mullaya* is both a facilitator and a religious leader. It is critical that the *mullaya* fully comprehend the women's own stories and experiences as well as the telling of these life stories in the sessions of dialogue that follow the rituals. She must also be able to recreate the essence of these stories so that she can invoke them in her talk after the *majlis* rituals. She absorbs the nature and the rhythms of the women's experiences and needs, and she passes them on in her presentation. It is a complete process. She commemorates the ordeals of the group by lamenting them in her own adept, musical wording. Her rehearsal of the narration has to be effective to make the audience listen. The *mullaya* retells, reconstructs, and relives history as sacred narrative.[11] In retelling historical events, she compels the Shiites to remember their history, connecting them with shared origins. In reconstructing historical events as poetry and reciting the sacred narrative in a way that evokes emotion, she facilitates the grief and weeping. By providing a performance so intense that it unlocks repressed emotions, she allows the women to reconnect with the deepest levels of their consciousness. She draws other participants into the stories by means of her skillful use of symbolic details and dramatic presentation.

Solima recalled how she became a *mullaya*, and in her story we can read how a network of Shiite piety is constructed:

Since childhood, I used to gather my family and speak to them. I would only allow them to go to the toilet after I had finished my speech. Later I began to observe my grandmother speaking in *majalis* and dreamed of the day that I would be like her. I imitated her hand movements and the expressions of her face. I used to attend all of the ceremonies at the age of fifteen years, although I was married in a whole other city than mine! I used to leave my daughter with her grandmother. My in-laws discouraged me, but I insisted. During my attendance, I used to ask for the permission to speak in front of the "Grand Mullah." After a while, people began to ask me to do the *majalis* for them. This happened also in Rafha and Holland. The tradition of reciting and telling stories is an important part of our lives, since it had connotations to our cause in Iraq. Now, unfortunately, the youth are no longer interested in this type of art. Here my daughters are no longer interested, and I am afraid that this sort of art and religious act will vanish from our house after my death! Now our children could not feel our suffering and our cause in Iraq, and they looked at it simply as backwardness. Now I receive calls from women above fifty years of age requesting me to train them in reciting in spite of the fact that they were not interested in this art while they were in Iraq! I memorize many speeches, poetry, and stories. I am a living book. The way one recites the story may be more important than the story itself! I became a *mullaya* at the age of fifteen years. This title was not easy to attain. It requires courage, eloquence, and historical knowledge! Now people try to learn through cassette recordings. I used to do the memorization by myself alone. Some *mullayat* prefer to do it in a group. But to serve the meanings of Imam Husayn, I preferred to practice the *majlis* alone, since sharing the recitations with others when they are not ready would give me the impression that my reward from God would be less and decreased!

Shiite rituals take the participant to a point of intense suffering in order to help him or her reconnect—either symbolically or mystically—with those who embody the root paradigms of Shiite Islam (Schubel 1993, 5). The women remember their own histories when listening to the *mullaya*. They reexperience them as they recite with her, and they take their place in the great lineage of Shiite history. The women are lifted out of their own era and their own sufferings. The notion of the saving quality of pain is translated into real life as continued sacrifice and martyrdom by analogy with Husayn, who chose the path of martyrdom on behalf of his family and his fellow Muslims. The women identify with the greater struggles of the holy family, and only then are they able to reveal their own stories.

The participants share their pain together with the utmost intimacy. Sitting close together in a square or standing close together in a circle also enables the women to respond to each other's body language. While chanting, the women rock back and forth and slap their chests and their thighs to the rhythm of the chant. The chants, reinforced by movement and gestures, enable the women to become one with the suffering of *ahl al-bait*. Physically, emotionally, and spiritually connected to the stories of the Prophet's family, the women's own histories naturally come to the surface. Speaking out secures recognition of their suffering, which is usually enveloped in silence. The *majlis* provides these women with a historical explanation for their trauma, victimization, helplessness, and betrayals. They are able to construct, from the telling of historical traumas and of their own traumas, connections between their religious culture and their lives.

The ceremony provides women who have accepted traditional gender roles with a rare and valued opportunity for self-expression and leadership outside the home. For many women, the *majlis* provides one of few occasions to meet and chat with other women in a communal space. The freedom this ceremony affords is a crucial gift of hope and healing for many of these women, who are otherwise isolated in a foreign society.

Therapeutic Narratives

Psychologists and historians have long analyzed the personal narratives of trauma survivors to comprehend how meaning is attached to experiences of annihilation and destruction (Herman 1992). In my interviews with the Iraqi Shiite women, I found numerous instances of survival methods. When women and men were talking about their life stories, many were reserved in their feelings and expressions, as though they had nothing to tell.

The women never broke into tears when telling me their stories. Their life stories are not told from self-pity, and crying is seen as inappropriate in their telling. Tears are saved for the memorized, collective stories of Husayn and his family, in whose tragedy the women recognize their own tragedies (Lila Abu-Lughod 1985). Abu Hamza al-Thumali reported that Imam al-Siddiq once said, "Weeping and grief are reprehensible for men in all occasions for grief except weeping and showing grief for Husayn ibn 'Ali. Only this brings reward." Weeping for members of *ahl al-bait* is legitimate because it is not of a personal nature. Upon finding a parallel story with Husayn's martyrdom and Zaynab's epic sadness, women can find solace in the knowledge that they are not alone.

Such encounters with sacred history through the drama of Karbala allow participants to manifest loyalty to and solidarity with the Prophet and his family and thus with the Shiite community at large—for them, the "true Islam." The participants are transformed. The invocation of grief through its enactment in the company of others who are also grieving is therapeutic. Although I was an observer, it is important to note that I was in no way detached from the *majlis* experience. I chose to engage in it. My mother passed away in February 2000, and during the *majlis* of 2001 I felt a special interaction between the *majlis* participants and myself. I experienced the process of sharing my pain through remembering the pain of others. This experience of listening to the eloquent lamentations that describe the pain of a daughter losing her father or a sister losing her brother led me to relate to my own grief and to weep. And the experience was therapeutic.

Within the stories that I collected, a seemingly simple narrative of a battle in the Iran-Iraq War could turn quite suddenly into a narrative of the Prophet's grandson dying at the Battle of Karbala. While describing the hardships that led up to the 1991 uprising, the narrator would transform the story into a historical homage to a Shiite uprising in the twelfth century. The women I interviewed were very knowledgeable about the history of the Shiite religion. Although they were not well read and some were illiterate, their religious history was sound because it has traditionally been passed down orally.

Many women I interviewed spoke in the collective "we" when referring to their own experiences. When a woman told me her life story, I was struck by the fact that invariably her story would be framed within the context of the story of her family and community. The personal narrative was in fact simultaneously a social narrative. This was a recurring pattern in the fifty narratives I gathered. Rather than refer to herself as an individual, each woman nearly always utilized the first person plural "we" and "us" to tell what would otherwise be considered a personal history. Each felt connected, as an individual and as a member of the Shiite community, to the holy family of the Prophet. The women's sense of belonging strengthened their sense of blood connection to their own families and, through the Shiite faith, to the holy family. However, the collective articulation did not erase the individual voice. The women talked about their own parts in the two Gulf wars and their active roles in the March 1991 uprising. Their war tales explored the hidden and the unknown story of Arab women in times of war. Their "history-telling" of war contradicts the stereotype of Arab women as subordinated. Their war tales differ from "the war story," in which, according to miriam cooke and Alessandro Portelli, men are at war and women are at home (cooke 1997, 15; Portelli 1991, 27). The women I interviewed were on the front, traveling to the Iran border to provide food, hide soldiers, and assure the safety of their loved ones. The theme of their war stories is bravery and action.[12]

Their stories are woven with memories from disparate parts of their lives. In the middle of a story about Holland, they break away to tell a tale of prewar Iraq. They will skip ahead to Rafha Refugee Camp and then back to Holland and then to Husayn and his family, whose pain is theirs. When they begin a story describing the horror of a son executed by Saddam, they will end the story with Zaynab's feelings when Husayn was killed. They may also incorporate other people's memories into theirs, but they are encouraged to create narratives that make sense to the group. When talking about their lives, the women were conscious of injustice and its root causes. Before, during, and after the Iran-Iraq War, the Baath Party was using intensive surveillance upon the Iraqi people. To protect themselves and yet continue to communicate, the Shiites developed a language of codes and symbols. They used proverbs and poetry, sayings of their imams, or even Quranic verses to respond to questions. Outsiders will find such responses enigmatic.

Their histories are not marked by dates but rather by events, as in "the year of the poisoned wheat crop." (That year, I found through outside research, was 1974.) As I initially lacked the ability to decipher their chronology, the stories unfolded outside time. Only when the women spoke of moving to new locations did I realize that time had passed in their narratives. There is, however, a chronology of place—which is in fact of central importance in the telling of stories—in all of their tales. Establishing the landscape of a story is paramount in its recounting. Umm Ahmad described how her house was destroyed in March 1991: "Streets were full of people; children were screaming; we were running . . . planes filled the sky and the sky rained red fire. . . . the house fell off. . . . smoke—. . . very dark smoke filled the air. . . . We ran. . . . And here we came [to Holland]; we live here. . . . the plane dug a big hole in the roof. . . . We fled. We live here now. . . . The house is well furnished with big carpets that filled the rooms. . . . the big windows in the guest room bring in the smell of fruit trees. O Husayn, I will tell you. Our loss is great!" Umm Ahmad's memories of the fires weave into descriptions of her Dutch home and back to her home in Iraq and then into an invocation of Husayn. As she talks, the fluidity of her remembrances creates a network that links her with other Shiites across time and space.

The narratives of these women are also filled with nonverbal communication. They utilized their hands and heads to say what the words could not touch. One especially poignant nonverbal indication is the slight shaking of the head when someone brings up a particularly painful or unjust happening. Slowly, the women will all move their heads from side to side in collective, mourning unison. It is a noble head gesture that does not affect the rest of the body and is usually accompanied by a deep, guttural sigh of sad solidarity.

The women were often silent. Silence is a tool of resistance that also marks fearfulness. Why should they share their stories when they have experienced nothing but betrayals? When faced with a journalist's questions, a refugee authority's questionnaires, an outsider's curiosity, these Shiite women would often remain silent, thus empowering themselves by keeping control over their histories. The persecution that these women have endured compounded their sense of secrecy and sensitivity.

The narratives were full of cryptic allusions to such genres as classical poetry and to sayings from the imams. Narratives were not straightforward, and people used genres to express a situation instead of simply reporting a story. The women's form of speech may be viewed as a folk art form. The judgment of what is a "good" narrative often rests within the community itself. A "good narrative," as defined by the Shiite refugees, would be one that was effective in creating an emotional mood, communicating a moral insight, and moving the listeners to a new level of understanding or action. The eloquence of the speaker is as important as the narrative itself.

Habiba described life in Iraq before Saddam as "a good life, but 'the world is like a snake, smooth and soft, but with a fatal poison.'" She was quoting Imam 'Ali's words to give meaning to the end of her happiness, the end of a good life in a good land. By making such recitations during the course of telling their life stories, the women added a collective wisdom, a layer of beauty and truth, to their accounts.

Conclusion

The stories that took place in Iraq were distinctly different from those that took place at Rafha and in Holland. Situated within the complexity of the battleground-homeland, the Iraq narratives are marked by pride and sorrow. There is a sense of loss that permeates the telling of any history that took place in Iraq. Stories of Saudi Arabia, however, are distinguished by a tone of betrayal. More angry than sad, the accounts of Rafha reveal the women's sense of frustration and their longing for their homeland. Because the climate, Islamic culture, and Arabic language were all familiar and the border was nearby, Iraq still felt close. Thus in narratives about Rafha, the women spoke of home urgently, many of them believing they would soon return. In Holland, however, the tone and language of the narratives changed drastically. There is a deep sense of collective identity-seeking. The theme of religious freedom arises again and again. The women are consciously proud of their language, culture, and religion. Their view of Iraq, though, has altered. It is no longer just across the border. Now that the women are resettled, their narratives of their homeland evolve into stories of nostalgia. Iraq continues to be their origin, but it is no longer their home.

Because they are religious, the women's testimonies also create an intense solidarity among the members of the Shiite community. They help to exorcise a destructive, violent past, turning pain into a religiously legitimate motivation for thriving and working in pursuit of social ideals even in exile. To give testimony is to bear witness; it is to tell the unofficial, subaltern story and to construct a history of a people whose history will not be told otherwise.

NOTES

1. On the suffering of the holy family, see Amili 1992, Aqaad 1997, and Arjomand 1996.

2. On maintaining links with the religious symbols, see Muzafar 1999, Waili 1997, and Fadlallah 1997.

3. *Imam* in Arabic means "leader." In Islamic terminology, this refers to any person who leads others in prayers. However, in Shiite theology, the term "imam" also refers to each of the twelve successors of the Prophet.

4. Since the tenth century, Karbala has been a religious and scholarly center. The shrine of Husayn, covered with ivory, gold, silver, and precious stones, is there. In his shrine are Husayn's two sons ('Ali and the infant Abdullahi). Close to Husayn's tomb, there is that of his brother 'Abbas. To the east is the tomb of the son of Imam Hasan (the second imam). See Haydari 1999, 257–72.

5. Yazid was the son of Mu'awiya, the first Umayyad ruler, who, from the Shiite perspective, usurped the dynasty. Mu'awiya came to power following the death of Imam 'Ali, who had fought against Mu'awiya during his brief stint as

Sunni caliph and first Shiite imam. Yazid inherited the Umayyad caliphate from his father.

6. Najaf is considered one of the most sacred cities in Iraq. In the center of Najaf is the Imam 'Ali mosque and shrine, which is among the most important places of worship in Iraq. Its dome is covered with gold. Shiites' ultimate wish is to be buried in this shrine to claim the advocacy and protection of Imam 'Ali on the Day of Judgment (Haydari 1999, 240–56).

7. Al-Kazimiya is geographically and historically connected to Baghdad. Just north of Baghdad, it is affected by the development of the latter. In the center of al-Kazimiya lies the shrine of the two Jawad imams, Imam al-Kazim and his grandson Imam Muhammad al-Jawad (Haydari 1999, 268–74).

8. Samara is north of Baghdad and east of the Tigris. Imam 'Ali al-Hadi (d. 868) is buried there with his son Imam Hassan al-'Askari (d. 873). Samara also has the Ghaiba Tunnel, from which Imam al-Mahdi disappeared; the Shiites expect his return to bring back justice to the earth (Haydari 1999, 278).

9. Children are brought to *majalis* to experience the ritual. They are taught the ritual by experience only, not by verbal teachings.

10. As every woman was weeping, I found myself in tears, too.

11. See Fadlallah 1997, 46–49, and Haydari 1999, 35–44.

12. On the theme of war stories, see cooke 1988, which reflects the voices of Arab women writers who wrote about the Lebanese Civil War. See also cooke 1997, which discusses Arab women writers and Gulf War stories.

Chapter 7

The Islamic Salon

Elite Women's Religious Networks in Egypt

This essay has three goals: (1) to describe how the Islamic practices of elite Egyptian women evolved during the late twentieth century, (2) to place that evolution in the context of the religious revival of the society at large, and (3) to examine it from the perspective of Muslim networks. Though many have studied the "Islamization" of Egyptian society over the past quarter century, most tend to explain it in terms of disenfranchisement and exclusion. This approach fails to account for the upward creep of Islamization among the traditionally secular elite, and in particular among women. Islamization at the top defies the law of social gravity that dictates that the masses take their social cue from the elite and not vice versa.

Historically, elite women were at the forefront of social, cultural, and political movements in Egyptian society. The Egyptian women's feminist and nationalist movement was launched after the First World War. Its leaders were upper-class women who had access to education, the prerogative of a very narrow elite in a society where it was denied to the masses in general and to women in particular. Eventually, upper-middle-class women launched their own parallel movement, marking the beginning of a split along class lines (see Badran 1995; Lawrence 1989, 1998).

Although elite women, with their educational, economic, and social advantages, provided the model for other urban women, both middle- and lower-middle-class, during most of the twentieth century, the last two decades of the twentieth century changed the trend: the culturally modernist, Europeanized mores associated with the elite have been yielding to the more conservative, openly Islamic, "authentic" posture associated with less advantaged classes. It is this creeping Islamization of the elite that must be explored in depth and detail. The new trend toward religious affirmation takes the form of networking in various forums around Islamic practices, some innovative, some revived and reconfigured to adapt to new pressures.

My perspective is that of an outsider/insider. Born Egyptian and educated abroad, I now live in the United States but visit Egypt regularly and for extended periods of time. I have been able to take stock of the evolution of Cairene social norms, but more particularly of the milieu of the landed bourgeoisie who are the subject of this essay. In the late nineties, I began the systematic study of increased Islamization among elite Cairene women. I sought out opportunities to attend the various gatherings of a religious nature that were frequented by this group. I then conducted interviews with several members between 1999 and 2000 for extended sessions.

The Islamization of Egyptian Society

When I was on the campus of Cairo University in 1970, I knew exactly two Egyptian students who wore head scarves and mid-calf skirts. They were two sisters from a distinguished family. Their Islamic attire singled them out on a campus where female students of all backgrounds made the effort to dress and to style their hair according to the prevalent Western fashion. Today, the overwhelming majority of female students at Cairo University, and a sizable minority at the American University, are *muhaggabat*, or "veiled," which in the Egyptian context means wearing a head scarf or some more formal head covering but does not mean veiling the face.[1]

The Islamization of Egyptian society over the past quarter century is no longer in dispute. Most analysts proclaim it a fait accompli: in the struggle between the secularists and the Islamists, the latter have won. Even though observers do differentiate between radical Islamists and a more moderate, more traditional Islamic movement, they are prone to see the appeal of Islam as a constant.[2] They explain the appeal of Islam to the disadvantaged and disenfranchised in social or economic terms or both. A more nuanced approach is needed to understand the parallel evolution, or Islamization, among the religious elite.

An unmistakable trend is the increase in public manifestation of Islamic practice among the traditionally secular, Westernized classes and the concomitant creation of networks in a religious forum. This is particularly striking in the case of elite Cairene women, who have begun to frequent mosques; attend *zawias*, or prayer spaces set aside for women; and participate in Quranic study circles, including *tajwid* classes to learn the correct reading and pronunciation of the Quran. This trend, while asserting an Islamic posture, conversely also reflects the adoption of a Western model of networking around church or synagogue activities. The current shift from private to public space is significant in that it subverts the traditional notion of women's space in the name of religion.

Attending Friday and feast day prayers was a custom observed by men rather than women; it is now common among women. Although congregating in some sort of mosque or Islamic center is routine among Muslim women in diaspora communities in the West, this practice was uncommon in Egypt until the last decade of the twentieth century. As far back as 1911, Egyptian feminist Malak Hifni Nassef had petitioned Parliament for the right for women to attend the mosque, but her request was denied.

Women today are much more likely than ever before to attend Friday sermons in mosques, sitting in a separate area from the men. They may listen to the same sermon as the men over the loudspeaker or have their own woman preacher. For the feast day prayers, major mosques in Cairo are set aside for women's use, and still the overflow fills the surrounding squares. During Ramadan, evening prayers draw large crowds of women.

Zawias are a new phenomenon in Egypt. The term refers to spaces, such as the ground floor of a building, that are set aside for women's exclusive use. New centers are appearing in upscale neighborhoods all over Cairo. Another new phenomenon is women preachers. Sermons at the *zawias*, as at mosques, are delivered by women who have studied religion formally for at least two years and have received a certificate to preach from the Azhar or another authority.

Islamic Salons

Some of the new networks revolve around traditional Islamic practices—charity, pilgrimage, and Ramadan observances—reclaimed and reimagined over the past decade to emphasize both the devotional and the social component. Other new practices, such as attending religious lectures and Quran study circles, provide spaces for networking that might be called "Islamic salons." Like earlier salons, they function as women-specific gatherings, but unlike them Islamic salons focus on Islamic practices.

The oldest and most consistent form of "Islamic" networking revolves around support for charitable organizations. Elite women are active on the boards of orphanages, in the women's arms of political parties, in organizing Ramadan soup kitchens, and in Rotary and Lion's Club fund-raisers. Some of the established charities are run by the daughters and granddaughters of the women who founded these institutions.

Charitable institutions require considerable commitments of time and money. Fund-raising includes organizing galas and cultural events such as fashion shows. Typically, a member of an orphanage "adopts" a group of about ten orphans. She visits the orphanage at least twice a week, spending several hours with her charges and acting as mentor, teacher, and surrogate parent. Several times a year, and particularly during Islamic holidays such as Ramadan, the Greater and Lesser feasts, and the Prophet's birthday, she takes her charges for an outing of their choice. Together they shop for clothes and school supplies. When one of the girls in her "adopted" group becomes engaged, the mentor contributes to the expenses of her bridal dowry.

If the role of philanthropy in the lives of the Cairene elite involves intensive social networking, so too do other specifically Islamic rituals like the 'Umra. Once a rare practice, this out-of-season pilgrimage to Mecca and Medina[3] has become almost an annual event for many. Although the preferred month is Ramadan, many women choose to go in the preceding months, Ragab or Sha'ban, to avoid the large crowds that Ramadan attracts. 'Umra entails a strong social network, since the women on 'Umra tours maintain contact after their return; pre-'Umra and post-'Umra parties cement the bonds created during the trip. The post-'Umra celebration echoes the Islamic tradition of welcoming the returning Hajj caravan.

Ramadan observances have also evolved to emphasize both the social and the devotional aspects of the holiest season of the year. Even otherwise nonpracticing Muslims observe Ramadan and participate. More than a social custom, visiting family and friends during Ramadan is understood to be an obligation enjoined on Muslims during the holy month.[4] Over the past decade, this tradition has grown noticeably in importance and has increasingly moved into the public sphere. Socializing around Ramadan meals was always a given, but what once took place overwhelmingly in private is now increasingly a public and commercial phenomenon.

Publicity for Ramadan events reveals a conscious effort to commercialize Ramadan on a par with Christmas and New Year's Day in the West. A secular symbol, the lantern, or *fanous*, has come to replace the traditional religious symbol, the mosque, as a code for Ramadan in the media and in commercial advertisements. *Iftar* and *suhur* are now big business for hotels and restaurants. Upscale commercial establishments capitalize on the nostalgia of their elite patrons for "authentic" Ramadan atmosphere, or a "Naguib Mahfouz Ramadan," by attempting to recreate the ambiance of the Old Cairo neighborhoods in the ersatz "tents." In the seventies and eighties, these same patrons used to venture into the genuine, hookah-smoking cafés in the alleys around the Hussein Mosque and Khan Khalili to satisfy their nostalgia for the Ramadan atmosphere they lacked in their own neighborhoods of Zamalek or Garden City. Today, the "atmosphere" is brought to them.

If socializing during Ramadan has become more emphatic and more public, the devotional aspects have also assumed greater importance and have made a parallel shift from private to public space. A practice that is playing an increasingly prominent role for elite women is mosque attendance for the daily *tarawih*—optional prayers between sunset and night prayers. These women now regularly make time between *iftar* and *suhur* engagements to attend *tarawih* prayers in a *zawia* or in a mosque, in a separate space for women.

Whereas *tarawih* prayers are open to anyone walking off the street, other religious gatherings for women of a more private sort seem to serve a networking function. These are the Islamic salons frequented by socio-economically homogeneous groups of women. One recent phenomenon is the "lessons," which are given on specific days of the week in a specific *zawia* by women with formal Azharite training and certification. These classes, although they are held in a public space, are in fact attended only by women who are referred to them. Each lesson runs for one to two hours and focuses on a specific topic, which can be as banal as the proper way to wash before prayer or as controversial as whether mothers should allow their daughters to wear a head scarf if they so wish.

Another sort of lesson in these Islamic salons is *tajwid*, or improvement in Quran reading, taught by formally trained teachers on specific days of the week. Some of the women teachers are from the same milieu as their acolytes. The classes are a year-round phenomenon, and some women attend them for years. These sessions are often held in a home rather than in a public place, and they can be attended by invitation only.

One function of Islamic salons is as a sort of clearinghouse for religious literature, in particular for literature dealing with the role of women in Islam. A popular book in these circles was T. A. Ismail's *The Status of Women in Islam* (2000), available in both English and Arabic and, like most such books, distributed free of charge courtesy of the author. The book affirms the dignity and rights of women under Islam, hence its popularity among this set of readers. It asserts that since women went to the

Prophet to pledge allegiance (*bay'a*) just as men did, it may be inferred that women's right to vote is entrenched in Islam. It also claims that a woman has every right to ask for a divorce if she is mistreated, since the Quranic injunction is to "live with a woman in kindness or release her with kindness."[5]

If Islamic salons are women-only gatherings (*mugtama'at sayyidat*) in Egypt, they are partly inspired by the proliferation of this model in segregated countries such as Saudi Arabia and the United Arab Emirates. In such societies, religious conservatism favors the sex-segregated Quranic study circle. Returning Egyptian expatriates were familiar with this model and helped promulgate it in Egypt.

Islamic salons represent a new spoke in a wheel of interconnectedness. Since the same women network extensively among themselves in other social forums, why do they feel the need to network in a religious context as well?

The only valid answer to this central query must come from the women themselves. The elite Cairene women I interviewed, in their forties and early fifties, represented a bridge generation in more than one sense. Less conservative than their mothers in the 1970s, they were in the 1990s likely to be less conservative than their daughters. Yet it is this generation that has shifted the most toward conservatism over the past two decades. The same women who wore short skirts in the 1970s now attend Islamic salons; a few have even adopted the head scarf. Since Cairene elite women come into their prime as arbiters of society in their forties and fifties, my interlocutors are among those who currently set the tone of social discourse. The insights they provide into the evolution of their religious mores and practices suggest that part of the explanation must be sought in terms of a genuine quest for a spiritual balance to overwhelmingly worldly lives.

When asked why they attend Islamic salons, most cite the need to compensate for what they consider to have been a relatively secular upbringing and education that left them without a proper grounding in Islamic scripture. Some, having been raised in nonobservant homes, feel the need for instruction in ritual practices; they wish to know, for example, the proper way to perform ablutions before prayer. Some admit that as they get older there is less preoccupation with the realm of the senses and of the emotions, and they look to intellectual pursuits or to religion to provide an alternative.

It is important to keep in mind that the Islamization trend is relative and continues to be in conflict with worldly or class imperatives and also with male prerogatives. The role of husbands and fathers is not to be underestimated in a male-dominated society. The early feminist movement in Egypt certainly would have had no chance of success, indeed of survival, without the tacit or explicit support of modernist husbands and fathers. Today's movement toward a more emphatically religious posture among elite women elicits various responses from the men of their milieu. The most obvious issue, predictably, is the wearing of the *hijab*. Most husbands claim to leave the decision entirely up to their wives, but some, particularly those whose business affairs require an active social life and interaction with Westerners, flatly forbid their wives to cover their hair. A very few go as far as to prohibit their wives from attending Quranic circles on the basis that they might be unduly influenced by the teachings. Perhaps the most interesting aspect to an outside observer is the anomalies that can coexist within a single family. In one socially prominent family, the husband insisted that he would forbid his wife to cover even if she showed a serious inclination to do so, but he allows his college-age daughter to do so over his objections; to complicate the picture, this same husband and father has a sister who is not only *muhaggaba* but also a licensed preacher, and a sister-in-law who leads the life of an international jet-setter.

Social mobility, or the reaction to it, is an important factor in understanding the posture of the women interviewed. Coming from the old landed bourgeoisie, they set themselves apart from the overnight millionaires of Anwar Sadat's open door policy. Their more conservative stance distances them from what they see as the excesses of prominent members of this group. No longer the elite in purely economic terms, they deplore the "immodest" behavior of some of these nouveaux riches as inappropriate to a traditional society.

Among women from the traditional elite, there is also a trend toward reclaiming traditional culture in general, not simply religion, especially among the younger set. One example is the revival of "Henna Night" among young brides today, a custom that their mothers and grandmothers disdained. The custom has been reinvented along the lines of a bachelorette party with a token observance of tradition: hand painting is done with water-soluble henna instead of the original indelible kind. On a par with the revival of selective non-Western cultural traditions, the assumption of an Islamic posture may be interpreted as a way of laying claim to a more fully realized cultural identity free of what used to be called "the complex of the *Khawaga*," an inferiority complex relative to the West.

There is strong evidence to support a link between turning away from the Western model on the part of the traditional elite and the increasing politicization of this historically Westernized group in response to political developments in the Middle East over the past decade. The designation "internal diaspora"[6] is particularly apt for many members of this class—transnationally oriented professionals who form a sort of alumni club of former expatriates who have spent years studying and working in Europe or the United States.[7] The Internet has become their medium for sustained connection to the Western world, with which they continue to have strong ties, often through children who are studying or working abroad. Typically, members of the internal diaspora devote time every day to catching up on the latest news and editorials from a variety of international media available online; networking with family and friends abroad; and recirculating news, opinion pieces, and call-to-action petitions among various listservs to which they subscribe. The Islamic salon network extends beyond the physical limitations of location. A node in a larger transnational network, it connects to the Muslim diaspora in Europe and the United States.

The educated and privileged in Egypt are more likely than the average Egyptian to have access to satellite television and to be avid watchers of Al-Jazeera and the new Arab-language television stations as well as the BBC and CNN. They are far more likely to have Internet access at home and to subscribe to the online editions of international newspapers and newsmagazines. They have the access and the leisure to instantly circulate opinions and commentary to their extensive e-mail network, both at home and abroad. To fully appreciate the revolution that the current information free-for-all represents in a society where information has historically been tightly controlled, one need only recall that listening to shortwave radio could lead to arrest during the news blackout years of the Nasser era.

But information globalization has unpredictable and unintended consequences. Access to Internet information and satellite programming is leading to consolidation of public opinion across class lines in support for the Palestinian intifada, protest against the war against Iraq that began in 2003, and hostility toward the American role in the region in general. In the wake of the events of September 11, it is important to keep in mind that the support of a group that should have been the natural constituency for the Mubarak regime's pro-Western stance has been palpably alienated by Western—specifically American—policies in the Middle East.

Disenchantment with Western policy in the region and increased religious conservatism should not be interpreted, however, as erasing the fundamental differences in outlook and interests between the elite and radical Islamism. The elite remains wary of the Islamists, even though its members believe the government is succeeding in containing the Islamist threat.

Taking the long view of the trend toward Islamization among the Egyptian elite, one should note that if members of the younger generation are more assertive in their Islamic identity than their parents, this piety takes a new form: disinterest in political Islam and alienation from the religious establishment. The trendy new preachers who appeal to the young and privileged of both sexes today are the deliberate antithesis of the traditional Azharite shaykh and are independent of any religious establishment or political party.

A case in point is the most successful of these new televangelists, ʿAmr Khaled: thirtysomething, clean-cut, well-dressed, middle-class, and secularly educated, he took his message directly to the children of the upper classes where they congregated, in the Shams Club in Heliopolis or the Shooting Club in Mohandesseen and on satellite channels and Internet websites. Addressing his overwhelmingly young audience in their own idiom, colloquial Egyptian interspersed with references to exclusive resorts like Marina and trendy restaurants in Zamalek, he appealed to them with a message of divine love rather than retribution, individual morality rather than collective conformity. In spite of his moderation and deliberate distance from political Islam, Khaled's increasing popularity led the authorities to order him to cease his *daʿwa* entirely. Shortly afterward, he was sent into exile in England, sharing the fate of other trendy gurus who have been vaguely charged with preaching to the upper classes and convincing well-known actresses and singers to take the veil.

The Discourse of the Veil

Where do the women of the Islamic salons set stand on the question of *hijab*, a standard trope of Islamic discourse today? If veiling confers or jeopardizes membership in a club, according to milieu, what is the significance of this membership for religious networking?

The term "veiling" needs to be clarified. Neither religious piety nor even modesty is automatically to be inferred from any particular form of dress. Instead, veiling is inextricably linked to a complicated set of historical and cultural factors. Leila Ahmed (1992) traces the origin of veiling to the sophisticated court cultures of Persia and Byzantium, as well as to Jewish dress codes that were adopted in the first century of the Muslim conquests. Recent literature has extensively examined the significance of the veiling trend among lower-middle-class working women in Egypt (Macleod 1991) and across a broad spectrum of socioeconomic strata (Rugh 1986; Zuhur 1992). Our discussion will focus on the trend among the traditional elite.

Before the 1952 revolution that overthrew the Egyptian monarchy, aristocratic women wore the small, transparent veil called a *yashmak* when they were formally presented at court, long after they had abandoned any kind of veil in their everyday lives. There have always been class and regional variations in dress. The tightly knotted kerchief of the peasant woman differed from the black cloak (*milayya*) worn by women in the back alleys of the cities. Neither had much to do with modesty or anything to do with religion. Only Bedouin in the most remote oases covered their faces. Educated city women did not wear a head covering of any sort for most of the twentieth century. In fact, Palestinian refugee students on Cairo University's campus in the late sixties and early seventies were recognizable by the large scarves they wore knotted under the chin.

Today, the majority of female students on the campus of Cairo University and a significant number on the campus of the American University wear scarves over their heads. Most of them wear what I term "*hijab* lite," typical of certain modern young women: a coquettish scarf that covers most of the hair, worn with stylish jeans or pants, boots, sweaters, and makeup.

Islamic dress (*ziyy Islami*), on the other hand, involves a more complete head covering, rather like a nun's wimple and veil, as well as long, loose, coatlike clothing. This form of dress is interpreted as indicative of a more austere, religious orientation and is more common among the lower middle class and older women. Finally there is *niqab*, or face covering, which is still rare enough in Egypt to cause heads to turn.

During the past two decades, there has been a gradual erosion of the social stigma attached to wearing a head scarf. As the head scarf gained symbolic significance as *hijab*, it began to lose its class connotations; among elite women who profess to aspire to greater piety, however, the lingering social stigma continues to be the factor most often referred to as the reason for abstaining from wearing a head scarf. The next most commonly cited excuse is the disapproval of their husbands. Still others experiment, often wearing a head scarf for a while after their first Hajj, or perhaps wearing it only during Ramadan, the month of devotion. Older women sometimes wear a kind of token *hijab*, a sort of snood or turban.

The spread of *hijab* among the affluent classes has been attributed by some observers to the greater mobility of Egyptian social classes since the 1952 revolution (Ibrahim 1996). Some members of the new middle class who acquired sudden wealth as a result of Sadat's open door policy brought with them their own, more conservative mores. This, however, does not account for the gradual diffusion of the *hijab* among members of the old regime set. According to one study, considerable intermarriage and overlapping between the old and new elites in the seventies and eighties could shed some light on this phenomenon (124, 132 n. 6). The new socio-economic-political coalition that emerged in the Sadat years included elements of the partly rehabilitated old landed bourgeoisie along with the former managers and technocrats of the public sector, entrepreneurs from the public sector, and new capitalists who accumulated their wealth by working at high-level positions in the Gulf states. There was a marked incidence of intermarriage among the offspring of these various groups and between members of this new coalition and the revolutionary ruling elite. The latter is largely composed of military officers of lower-middle-class background who have been elevated to the ranks of the ruling class by virtue of their political power and economic opportunism. It is this mixture of new and old elites, goes the argument, that has facilitated scarf wearing as both acceptable and desirable in contemporary Cairo.

What is crucial to bear in mind is that the discourse of the veil, like the veil itself, has evolved. Once a marker of class rather than religious piety, it has become a more ambiguous symbol of conservatism that is not today a reliable marker of either class or religious piety. In many ways, the discourse of the veil distracts observers from more fundamental issues, such as family law reform.

The Issue of Family Law Reform Factored for Class

Family law reform has been slow to come to Egypt, at least partly due to the failure of networking among disparate socioeconomic classes of women. Given that the women's liberation movement started in Egypt in the early 1920s, reform of Islamic Personal Status Law regarding marriage, divorce, and child custody was long overdue by 2000. Some of the more notorious abuses of family law included polygamy and inequality of access to divorce.

Yet women have not been able to network effectively on behalf of causes that would benefit all equally. Mirroring the specifically Egyptian stratification of society, the feminist movement has always been split along class lines. Women with independent financial means and with strong family support are less vulnerable to the abuses of family law and consequently are less motivated to lobby for change. Disenfranchised and poorly educated women are in no position to work for reform.

Reform, when it does come, tends to come from the executive branch of government. The most significant changes in family law in Egypt were passed by presidential or ministerial decree, rather than ratified by Parliament, and have been vulnerable to reversal. In 1979, amendments to the Personal Status Law were dubbed "Jihan's Law," acknowledging President Sadat's wife's role in passing them. A mere six years later, they were repealed for "reasons of unconstitutionality." In February 2000, significant amendments to Personal Status Law were passed, again under the aegis of Egypt's first lady, now Susan Mubarak. The Ministry of Justice issued the amendments after a protracted and acrimonious debate in Parliament and in the media, but it had failed to muster the necessary votes in Parliament. As the United Nations Development Programme's Human Development Report for 2000 notes, the Personal Status Law was the "product of a dynamic and persistent alliance of civil court judges, women's groups, lawyers and progressive Muslim clerics. They won in part because they argued their case in the context of their culture, emphasizing aspects of Islam that confer equal rights on women."

The contractual nature of marriage in Islamic law makes it possible to introduce legislation restoring some measure of equilibrium to women's rights within marriage and in case of divorce. The resistance to such reform is, and has always been, more cultural than religious (Sullivan 1986). For instance, 'isma, a stipulation that can be included in the marriage contract to grant a woman the same right to divorce unilaterally as the man, has always been legal and provided for in the Islamic shari'a. However, it was only when elite women, backed by their fathers, asked for this provision in their contracts that 'isma began to gain social acceptance. The new marriage contract (as opposed to the version in force since 1931) contains a blank space in which future spouses may stipulate conditions, the violation of which become acceptable grounds for divorce. Even without the foresight of a 'isma provision, divorce is made easier for women to obtain under the newly revived khul', by which a wife can initiate divorce proceedings on the condition that she abandon all her rights to financial support and return any dowry she received.

One amendment to the new law is clearly more likely to be pertinent to elite women: it grants a married woman the right to apply for a passport and to travel without her husband's consent. This ruling came under so much attack that it is now under revision and might be repealed, an indication that the lack of cohesion and networking between elite women's movements and the masses of their countrywomen makes reforms targeted at elite women particularly vulnerable.

A poll conducted a year after the amendments were passed and reported in the English-language *Al-Ahram Weekly* is instructive (March 1–7, 2001). The respondents, preponderantly urban and nearly 40 percent university educated, were asked their opinions about discrete amendments to the Personal Status Law. While respondents generally felt unfavorably toward the issues that concern elite women most, they were overwhelmingly supportive of reforms that benefit the less privileged. Clearly, the majority does not support issues pertaining to women's personal emancipation, such as traveling without a husband's permission, whereas there is clear support for issues pertaining to material support as part of the traditional responsibility of the husband. The *Al-Ahram* survey highlights a basic problem with the advancement of women's rights in Egypt: the failure to bring the majority of women on board. There is inadequate networking between the minority of educated women who advocate both women's rights and reform of the Personal Status Law and the majority of Egyptian women, including the estimated 50 percent who are illiterate.

Conclusion

The turn to Islamic practice among elite Egyptian women has produced networking in public forums and the embrace of conservative mores. It cannot be explained as merely a reflection of zeitgeist or a conscious attempt to co-opt the more extreme Islamic discourse. Public religious practice is as much a spiritual imperative as a form of social networking. Both the assumption of an Islamic posture and the return to selective non-Western cultural traditions project a claim to a more authentic cultural identity. The erosion of the social stigma associated with *hijab* is both a cause and an effect of this process.

Islamic salons allow women to distance themselves from twin un-Islamic excesses, including (1) the rampant consumerist lifestyle of the nouveaux riches, and (2) the political extremism of Islamist elements. Yet the Islamic salon remains an elite abode, and its practices have not translated into networking between the elite and the masses for the reform of Islamic Personal Status Law. As Charles Kurzman notes in his study of the Iranian Revolution in this volume, "networks may have a variety of purposes that are not easily transferable to other goals." Nonetheless, alienation from the Western model of social and cultural modernity does link the elite and the masses in a radical politicization against Western policy in the Middle East.

NOTES

1. "Veiling" as it is understood in the Egyptian context will be discussed at greater length later in this essay.

2. See the arguments in Abdo 2000 and Weaver 1999.

3. Pilgrimage during the month of Zu El-Hijja is called Hajj and is required at least once in a lifetime of Muslims who are physically and financially able to undertake it. ʿUmra is a purely elective pilgrimage that may be undertaken at any time of year and does not count toward fulfillment of the Hajj requirement.

4. During this month, Muslims are enjoined to observe *silat al-rahm*, meaning literally "the connection of the womb."

5. As in many such religious publications, the author makes statements rather than offering arguments; sources are not systematically cited, not even the Quran. The implication seems to be that the events and quotations referred to are common knowledge.

6. I am indebted to Jon Anderson (2002) for this concept.

7. Many members of the traditional elite returned to Egypt in response to the new economic climate created by Sadat's reforms.

Chapter 8

Voices of Faith, Faces of Beauty

Connecting American Muslim Women
through *Azizah*

While the rest of the world launches into cyberspace, Muslim
women in the United States are celebrating themselves in print as they re-
assert their intellects, reclaim their bodies, and renew their spirit through
Azizah. *Azizah* describes itself as the magazine for "the contemporary
Muslim woman."[1] *Newsweek* called it "the first and only American magazine for Muslim women," explaining, "the glossy quarterly caters to a
multiethnic readership . . . and offers smart stories on everything from
birth control to surviving 9-11 backlash" (Lorraine Ali 2002). In this chapter, I will show how *Azizah* provides a critical medium for the creation of
Muslim women's networks. *Azizah* connects women beyond differences
in ethnicity, class, generation, professional interests, and Islamic practice
and perspective. A major site of cultural production where ideas are transmitted and contested, *Azizah* shapes an American Islamic feminist discourse while creating the beauty and gloss of *Vogue*.

Azizah challenges conventional representations of Muslim women like
the one on the cover of the December 2001 issue of *Time*. A woman wearing *hijab* (head covering)[2] looks dull and sullen, as if her smile had been
stolen. The caption reads, "Lifting the Veil: The shocking story of how the
Taliban brutalized women of Afghanistan." Inside, photos of women in
burqa appear as snapshots of ghosts, courtesy of the Taliban. There are also
pictures of Muslim women without *hijab*, smiling, appearing strong, but
the caption below these photos reads, "A Secular Model: Turkish women,
the most liberated in the Muslim world," as if liberation and *hijab* do not

mix. Where are the images of happy and strong Muslim women in colorful *hijab*?

Azizah hopes to challenge both American mainstream media and Muslim extremists. From opposite worldviews, they have misrepresented Muslim women as uniformly veiled, subordinate, uneducated, and passive. Such static images have been maintained only by silencing the voices of Muslim women. *Azizah* presents Muslim women—along with their faith and dress—with beauty and diversity. Instead of *Time*, the Taliban, or *Cosmopolitan*, American Muslim women can turn to *Azizah*.

Azizah *Confronts the Third-World Image*

In *Women Claim Islam*, miriam cooke shows how the revolution in information technology has been coupled with both an upsurge in the formation of religious groups and increased attention to women in Islamic society. As women become "more vocal and more visible," religious groups place them "at the symbolic center of their concerns and debates" (2001, viii). But the end result of these concerns and debates is to grant men political and ideological gains rather than to secure the rights of women (Zoya Hasan 1998). As a result, Muslim women have been imagined and portrayed more than they have been heard. However, cooke shows how Muslim women are tapping into patriarchal Islamist discourse. They are gaining mastery over its language, law, and metaphor while setting their own pro-woman agenda.

One gateway through which Muslim women enter into and transform patriarchal dialogue is a mode of communication that cooke calls "'imageness,' a visual reality that shapes consciousness" (128). Since the nineteenth century, imageness has served to create a static, homogenous image of Muslim women "as passive and oppressed . . . , more or less exotic, more or less veiled, more or less available, more or less oppressed" (130). Leila Ahmed (1992) and miriam cooke both show how Western imperialism and Western feminism played the foremost roles in imagining an essentialized Muslim woman: "Arab women's images were first filtered through Orientalist lenses—mysterious, alluring, secluded," cooke argues (126). Through an imperialist lens, Arab culture came to signify Islamic faith, Arab women came to signify Muslim women, and the Arab veil came to symbolize Arab and Muslim patriarchy. Chandra Mohanty theorizes about this form of reduced signification: a "monolithic notion of patriarchy or male dominance leads to the construction of a similarly reductive and homogeneous notion of what I call the 'third-world difference,'" she explains (1988, 63).

A hegemonic discursive strategy in Western feminist writing, the "third-world difference" produces the image of an "average third-world woman" as "sexually constrained . . . , ignorant, poor, uneducated, tradition-bound, religious, domesticated, family-oriented, victimized," and veiled (65).

The Islamist backlash against Orientalist notions of the "third-world difference" has led to further objectification of Muslim women. Islamists counter Western cultural hegemony by imposing the veil. Its public visibility has become the fundamental measure of "the Islamic state." Only by establishing a pure Islamic state can one defeat the West, Islamists argue, and the veiled woman signifies for them both loyalty to the Islamic state and allegiance to Islamic values over Western values. In effect, Islamists use the myth of the essential Muslim woman to complement and support the myth of a rigid, timeless Islamic state. Islamist discourses, entangled in "strident claims and counterclaims over who is the only true mantle-bearer of Islam," proclaim an immutable, standard Islamic society, ignoring "the actual diversities in structures, norms, and cultures visible in the Muslim world" (Shaheed 1995, 79). Above all, they neglect the differing realities and needs of Muslim women, shrouding their voices in the shadows of a snapshot. For cooke, however, the manipulation of image is not restricted to those in power: "To name and mark otherness is not the exclusive privilege of power; rather it is part of the contestation of power," she writes (2001, 129). Just as imageness has served to objectify and silence Muslim women, so it may paradoxically become the crucial doorway through which Muslim women can reverse its effect and claim their own Islamic agenda to empower themselves.

Azizah women have opened this door. They create their own images of Muslim women, and they write their own perspectives on faith and practice. Unveiling the multiple shades of Muslim women, *Azizah* women are "re-imaging" themselves in the "third space." Shahnaz Khan portrays the reality of Muslim women in North America as a "third space." It is a third space because here women can resist both Islamism and Orientalism, ideologies that objectify women through static, homogenizing symbols that do not account for their multiple, overlapping identities (2000). In the third space, U.S. Muslim women can negotiate traditional Muslim norms and North American ideals. While identifying with their Muslim communities, they can resist the racism and ethnic discrimination that they experience from the broader non-Muslim society. Ironically, they may at the same time identify with non-Muslim gender ideals to fight against the gender oppression within their Muslim communities. Muslim women are constantly negotiating as they imagine what it means to be a Muslim woman in North America. *Azizah* women inhabit the third space, contesting, claiming, and creating voices in the public realm. They inhabit the third space in order to tear down the "third-world" image.

"We Were Considered Quite Radical": The Women behind Azizah

As I trace how *Azizah* began to take shape and discuss some of the women who have forged its network, I highlight the ethnic spectrum of women in the *Azizah* network. They are African, American Arab, Asian, and European American Muslim women. Their ethnic diversity challenges essentialist representations and demonstrates the unique power of *Azizah* in the American *umma*, or Muslim community. The American *umma* consists of multiple ethnic groups positing membership on a nonethnic basis.[3] Creating bonds of "brotherhood and sisterhood" across these groups is among the highest ideals of Muslim solidarity. Ethnic segregation in American mosque communities indicates that this ideal is far from a reality.[4] *Azizah* illustrates how an Islamic feminist network creates bonds of sisterhood in an otherwise divided *umma*.

A Muslim woman in *hijab* appears on every cover of *Azizah*, even though inside *Azizah* there are pictures of women who wear the *hijab* and those who do not. Tayyibah Taylor, the founder and editor-in-chief of the magazine, embraces this image, using it on the cover to distinguish her magazine as one that is by and for Muslim women. The faces on *Azizah*'s cover are beautiful and happy.

On June 8, 2001, Tayyibah Taylor told me the story of *Azizah*. Born in Trinidad to a Christian family, she was a rebel from an early age. It was her inquisitiveness, passion, and diverse interests that led her to Islam, to Seattle's Islamic Sisterhood (SIS), and ultimately to *Azizah*. Tayyibah converted to Islam in 1971. She developed an interest in women's issues while studying in Saudi Arabia from 1979 to 1985. The gender segregation there was debilitating but also empowering, because Tayyibah had access to so many learned women. Tayyibah stated, "Not having to compete with men, not being compared to men, not having to deal with a male teacher's gender expectations, and not having the distraction of a sexually-charged atmosphere are all factors that can positively affect women when segregated." However, Tayyibah noted that this type of segregation works "only when everything is equal and it is a choice." And in Saudi Arabia, Tayyibah saw neither equality nor choice in the strict segregation. She considers the gender asymmetry forced upon women in Saudi Arabia to be indefensible: "There, I couldn't drive. My husband had to drive me everywhere or hire a driver for me or I had to take the bus. Taxis would not take a lone woman as a fare. I saw women's ankles being caned because they were showing as they walked through the *suq* [market]. All of the shops were run by men, so if you wanted to purchase underwear, you dealt with men" (e-mail interview by the author, June 27, 2002).

Upon her return to the United States, Tayyibah became more aware of gender inequalities in the American *umma*. She saw them as extensions of practices in Muslim countries. "*Masajid* [mosques] here put the women's entrances in the back alley," she stated, and "the women's *masalla* [prayer spaces] in the basement. Imams begin the *khutba* [sermon] with '*as salaamu alaikum* [peace be upon you], my dear brothers.' The 'role of the women in Islam' is often addressed, but seldom are the responsibilities of males addressed. Instead, polygyny is propounded as a right of males." Tayyibah objects particularly to the partition between men and women during Jum'a (Friday) service.[5] With a partition, women cannot see the imam, but men can. Some mosques accommodate women's spaces with television monitors. But Tayyibah stated, "I don't want to watch a T.V. screen." Some women say the partition affords them privacy. Others feel estranged from the *jama'a* (congregation). She explains: "I have always wondered about following an imam that you can't see or one who is leading a *jama'a* that you are not part of. Some women in Jeddah used to watch the Friday prayer and *khutbah* on T.V., then get up and follow the imam in Makkah from their living rooms in Jeddah. This never seemed right to me" (e-mail interview by the author, June 25, 2002). During my interview with Tayyibah on June 8, 2001, she asserted that gender segregation denies women equal and full participation and influence in the mosque. Such experiences led Tayyibah to organize the sisters' group, Seattle's Islamic Sisterhood (SIS), in the 1980s. Recalling the work she did with SIS for eight years, Tayyibah said, "We were considered quite radical!"

About her current Islamic feminist project, Tayyibah stated, "*Azizah*'s a perfect blend of my passions for Islam and reading and writing. It's just something that came out of me." *Azizah* was first conceived during a Muslim women's conference in Chicago in the early 1990s. A woman spoke about an existing magazine for Muslim women. The idea excited Tayyibah; she could not wait to see it. "But," Tayyibah explained, "when I went to her booth, it was just very small, kind of like a newsletter, so I was really disappointed." All the way home on the plane, she kept asking the two

Muslim women traveling with her, "Why can't we have a magazine?" And her friends finally said, "Tayyibah, why won't you just go ahead and do it?" "Okay, I will," she said.

Tayyibah knew that she could not publish a magazine alone, so she thought about whom she could enlist for help. She recalled, "I thought about Nadia, who's Arab American. Her father's Palestinian, and her mother's European American." However, Tayyibah did not choose Nadia because of her ethnicity, but rather "because she was a writer" and because of "her expertise in literature." Tayyibah knew Nadia through an Islamic school in Seattle where both were teachers. Nadia liked Tayyibah's proposition; "Oh! I wanted to do something like this too," she responded.

Tayyibah began her venture by thinking about the scope of the magazine she wanted to create and about publishing costs. But family matters intervened. A year later, she accepted an offer from a Muslim, male publisher to work on a magazine for Muslim children. After two issues, he proposed a Muslim women's magazine. Tayyibah commented, "Instead of me declaring it my intellectual property at that point and saying, 'This is mine,' we kind of segued into it, and it ended up being his." They named the magazine *Sisters*.

At a SIS event, an Indonesian American Muslim woman, Marlina Soerakoesoemah, introduced herself to Tayyibah. Marlina had seen the magazine and had read about Tayyibah in a Muslim newspaper article featuring Tayyibah's work on *Sisters*. Marlina told Tayyibah, "I've seen this and I so much want to work on this." Marlina became a freelance writer for *Sisters*.

After four issues, the publisher of *Sisters* lost interest in the magazine. "Because I hadn't written a contract," Tayyibah explained, "all the rights were legally his, and he offered to sell it to me, but I thought, 'Well, why would I buy my own creation?'" Soon *Sisters* stopped running. Tayyibah took a break from publishing and moved to Atlanta. "After I moved here, I said, 'No! I have to do this magazine.' And so I called Nadia and Nina [Marlina,] because they had worked with me on *Sisters*" (interview by the author, June 8, 2001).[6]

Tayyibah's goal was to publish the stories and ideas of American Muslim women. Because these women are ethnically diverse, the articles and pictures in *Azizah* are also wide-ranging. The stories featured in *Azizah*'s premiere issue highlighted women whom the three editors knew, women from a wide social and ethnic spectrum. Subsequently, the network has expanded to bring in more women to write about their visions for *Azizah*'s future.

Building the Network through Connected Communities

Azizah is the first magazine to target American Muslim women. This requires giving *Azizah* the chic look and the glossy feel of *Cosmopolitan* and *Vogue*, which all American women expect in a magazine. But it also requires establishing a dialogue with Muslim women to discover what they want in their own magazine. Tayyibah drew on the resources and input of longtime friends and new contacts. While *Cosmopolitan* engages its readers from the top down, defining image and discourse for a vast market of unconnected people, *Azizah* has built on the real friendships and encounters made at Muslim women's conferences, Quranic study circles, fashion shows, and parties. While attractive models pose on the cover of *Vogue*, the beautiful women who model for *Azizah* stand as models of heart, soul, and intellect in real Muslim communities.[7]

The primary way that *Azizah* builds its network is through a marketing tool called "celebrations." Open any issue, and you will find a page that reads "celebrating *Azizah*" or "*Azizah* celebrates." This page overflows with snapshots of colorfully dressed women of diverse ethnic backgrounds. They are embracing, smiling, laughing, speaking into microphones, brandishing copies of the magazine, and cutting cake. "Celebrations is a reflection of the spirit of the magazine," wrote Tayyibah. "We are doing in person what we do in print—celebrating the voice of the Muslim woman" (e-mail interview by the author, April 26, 2002). Whenever *Azizah* plans a celebration, Tayyibah sends notices to all her subscribers in the area, the local press, and potential advertisers.[8]

At every celebration, appetizers and drinks are served. They begin with Quranic recitation by a woman.[9] There are cultural presentations, including poetry, singing, and drumming. Women present inspiring speeches about what the magazine means to them. Subscriptions are sold. Tayyibah speaks about the vision of *Azizah* and asks the audience members what they would like to read. On April 26, 2002, she told me: "Celebrations are how we market *Azizah*. Word of mouth is essential in a niche market. We haven't advertised anywhere, so this is how people learn about us. It helps me keep my finger on the pulse of the sisterhood—what we are doing and thinking."

Outside of celebrations, readers connect with other women in the network through their stories. Some women, however, go beyond reading. Writers contribute to "Conversations," a two-page section devoted to readers' feedback. For example, Ayesha Lorenz Al-Saeed writes, "I would love to see an article about childbirth . . . because Muslim women have little privacy in Western hospitals."[10] Writing letters to the editor is not novel; people write letters to the *New York Times*. But with *Azizah*, the letters emerge from connected communities of people. In this way, *Azizah* develops as a space of trust, fortifying the network in turn as women grow increasingly comfortable sharing their life stories.

More than a magazine, *Azizah* provides through its network a sense of spirit and ownership that women carry into other parts of their lives. I write about *Azizah* because, as an American Muslim woman, I carry this spirit. I became a part of the *Azizah* network when I met Tayyibah at an interfaith health symposium sponsored by a local Muslim women's group. A week later, Tayyibah asked if I would write an article about Islamic spirituality for *Azizah*'s first issue. Since then, I have traveled to Muslim conferences across the nation meeting Muslim women who already know me from my picture and article in *Azizah*. Traveling to a Muslim conference in Canada, I saw a Muslim woman board my plane in Toronto. Admiring her grace and elegance as she walked down the aisle in her *hijab*, it dawned on me that she was Manal Omar, an activist who was on one of *Azizah*'s covers. Every time I open *Azizah*, I see names and faces of women I know from Atlanta, Washington, D.C., Chicago, Oakland, Houston, and New York.

Inside Azizah

It is the images inside *Azizah* that tell us who the women in the *Azizah* network are. Cream, caramel, and coffee complexions. Black, blonde, and brown hair that is straightened, curled, and twisted. Women in canary yellow silk caftans, burgundy jackets and black pants, and royal blue *shalwar khamiz*. Noble faces framed in embroidered chiffon and silk scarves, some wrapped lofty as if to meet the sky, others draped gently across shoulders and bosoms. An African American woman in a black robe—"America's First Muslimah Judge"—wearing a yellow head covering (Sabir 2001). A picture of the globe parted into four corners, in each corner a Muslim woman: "Different faces. Different perspectives. One faith. One magazine. *Azizah*" (Summer 2001).

African, Arab, Cambodian, European, Indonesian, Latina, Native, and South Asian American. Mothers, wives, daughters, sisters, artists, professors, film directors, lawyers, medical doctors, financial analysts, and community activists. As young as fourteen and as old as ninety-two, they write about topics ranging from Muslim women in the media to buying a home without interest to Arabic calligraphy to Mediterranean cooking to law.

Asifa Quraishi writes on Islamic law, pointing out "that several different legal opinions are valid and authoritative" (2001). Beth Howell-Mahmoud speaks about art, stating: "I don't mind when people are uncomfortable. Allah can open us up through that discomfort. My art has a political purpose and I want to make people think" (quoted in Khalid and Yamini 2001). Zainab Kahera writes on sports, arguing, "In some Muslim countries and communities, women and girls . . . may be discouraged from participation in sports. However, we know that in the first community of Islam, women excelled in archery and equestrian skills . . . , so we can deduce that the Prophet did not discourage sport" (2001). Tayyibah Taylor writes on female scholars in America, recounting how a man once asked Dr. Amina Wadud-Muhsin, an African American scholar, after a lecture, "Are you saying that a man can't interpret the *Qur'an* for a woman?" Tayyibah writes: "Dr. Wadud-Muhsin's reply was short, but courteous: 'What I am saying,' she said, 'is that a woman can interpret the *Qur'an* for a man'" (2001). Sharifa Alkhateeb writes about Muslim safe houses, explaining that a "good shelter is about transforming women from their shattered state to a self-affirming, positive lifestyle" (quoted in Majeed 2001). Manal Omar writes about global sisterhood, asserting: "It can only be celebrated if we move beyond one monolithic definition of sisterhood, and develop a sisterhood based on women's experiences across the globe. One fixed prescription to empower women cannot be enforced on everyone" (2002).

Azizah: *Breaking Ground in the American* Umma

What explains *Azizah*'s unprecedented inclusiveness? Tayyibah attributes *Azizah*'s diversity to the diversity that characterizes the global *umma*. She recognizes that "you can't have a magazine and say this is for Muslim women and then only have one ethnicity or one school of thought." If you did, she says, "it would be something else." Another important factor in ensuring *Azizah*'s diversity is its location in the United States. No other nation includes as many representatives of the *umma*'s various ethnicities as does the United States, and that means that no single ethnic group dominates.[11]

While the American factor is important, in most cases it has not translated into diversity in American Muslim media. *Azizah* contributor Sara Flynn stated, "My impression of the other big Muslim magazines is that they are really either by Arabs for English-speaking Arabs or they are by subcontinentals or English-speaking subcontinentals, and then the rest of us are just kind of there" (phone interview by the author, September 26, 2001). The other magazines to which Sara refers are *Islamic Horizons* and *Al-Jumuah*. *Al-Jumuah* shows no sign of ethnic diversity, because it prohibits pictures. It is published by Al-Muntada Al-Islami, a British Muslim group with offices in the United Kingdom, the United States, and Saudi Arabia. *Islamic Horizons* is published by the Islamic Society of North America (ISNA). Though ISNA primarily serves immigrant Muslims, it does make efforts to diversify leadership and membership. These efforts are reflected in pictures in *Islamic Horizons*, but the small African American presence almost appears as tokenism. *Azizah*'s exceptional representation of African Americans, who constitute at least 33 percent of the American *umma*, distinguishes it from other American Muslim magazines. For *Azizah* contributor Catherine England, *Azizah* reflects more than just ethnic diversity: "Diversity is not just about ethnicity. It's about age, about disability, or differing abilities. It's about children who don't have a voice" (phone interview by the author, September 25, 2001). By including these types of concerns, *Azizah* broadens standard conceptions of diversity to include class, profession, Islamic practice and perspective, and subject matter.

Would a magazine for Muslim men by Muslim men be as inclusive? Rather than asking if the identity "Muslim woman" creates an inclusive network, we should ask: What are the politics that bring together a group of women from diverse backgrounds within a common network that advocates the cause of "the contemporary Muslim woman"? What are the experiences that motivate women to form such a network? Posed this way, the questions emphasize the agency and individual experiences of *Azizah* women. They point to feminist strategies that build an effective Muslim women's network like *Azizah*. Muslim women are not being acted upon. Rather, they act. By accounting for the multiple circumstances and experiences of *Azizah* women, "Muslim woman" becomes a symbol of power that brings forth a range of voices previously hidden behind a symbol— behind the veil.

Creating Voice, Changing Image: From Individual to Collective Expression

The concept of a strategic feminist network implies that women use their individual experiences to create and support a common cause. It implies various motives that take on a shared aim. In June 2001, I asked Tayyibah what led her to reclaim the symbol of Muslim women in *hijab* and to use it in a revolutionary way that gives voice to countless Muslim women. Tayyibah has the exceptional ability to connect diverse women in a common network because she can speak from multiple perspectives that have been shaped by the different regions of the world in which she has lived. She was born in Trinidad but raised in the cultural traditions of Barbados, where her parents were from. She became a Canadian and later an American citizen. She studied extensively in Saudi Arabia. Reflecting on her range of cultural exposure, she stated, "I very easily relate to other people, so I can very easily slip in and out of a person's perspective, because I have different perspectives myself."

Azizah grew out of Tayyibah's multiple consciousness and her desire to give Muslim women a medium through which to express their love for Islam, their diversity, their intellect, and their style. To be an advocate for women, Tayyibah had to totally free herself from male control. Working under a male publisher on *Sisters* taught Tayyibah why it was so important for Muslim women to publish their own magazine. She wanted to do a story on breast cancer, but the male publisher responded, "No, don't do breast cancer. Do all the cancers, and don't use the word breast." Recalling this experience, Tayyibah stated, "So you see the limitations came from a very androcentric view."

Tayyibah refuses to compromise the voices of women in her "own creation." Some men have asked to write for the magazine, and her reply has been: "You will have to excuse us, but we're so thrilled to have our own magazine, we don't want to give it to anybody else." *Azizah* is a magazine for the Muslima by the Muslima. This position is not *against* men. Rather it is *for* women. Tayyibah stated: "It has nothing to do with men. It has to do with us, and where we are, and what we are thinking."

The politics behind the *Azizah* network is the politics of voice. Arguing that Islam is polycentric, made up of varied voices, Muslim women redefine their piety. "So often the pious Muslim woman has been defined as the quiet, silent one," Tayyibah commented, "but by providing a vehicle by which she can speak and express her opinions and concerns, . . . we are undoing that definition."[12]

If image has been the primary challenge to Muslim women's ability to express their true voices,[13] it has now become their primary opportunity to do so. *Azizah* gives Muslim women the opportunity to replace conventional, murky photos of veiled women with radiant photos of smiling faces. Consider the cover of *Azizah*'s third issue. Against a white background, the word "Azizah" appears in bold red. Under the word, a Muslim woman poses in a red and black *hijab*. Red lipstick, a touch of eye shadow, and painted nails bring color to the photo. Tayyibah strategically draws on conventional images of covered Muslim women and transforms them with light and color.

Tayyibah and her editors recognize the high value that American society places on a glossy photo. The magazine industry has an almost unrivaled role, outside of television and film, perhaps, in defining standards of femininity in a society that esteems women on the basis of physical beauty. The "model" woman must be beautiful enough to appear on the cover of a magazine. Tayyibah told me that she deploys popular magazine layout design but transforms it to create for Muslim women the "model" that they see in themselves. Tayyibah explained that Muslim women "see beauty in a righteous manner." She continued, "We're beautiful . . . but not in a provocative way" (interview by the author, June 8, 2001). Women in the network have responded favorably to how *Azizah* presents them. Reader Khadijah Sharif-Drinkard stated, "*Azizah* is very dear to me because the magazine represents Muslim women in their most beautiful form. I see my beauty, my intellect and my spirit" (e-mail interview by the author, September 24, 2001).

But not everyone in the *Azizah* network is happy. Dress conservatives object to the fact that some of the women do not cover. Others oppose displaying a Muslim woman on a magazine cover. One outraged reader, Sarah Sabo, protested the promotion of a "westernized version of Islam."[14] Another reader explained such objections in terms of male control: "It's because of what they're hearing men say. They seem to be more persuaded by their male family members" (phone interview by the author, October 10, 2001). Muslim women's disapproval of a Muslim woman cover model indicates their agreement with notions that women are best suited for private spaces, that they are not to be placed front and center in public spaces. Tayyibah is not surprised by these reactions. During her work with *Sisters*, her male publisher did not allow her to include photos of women without *hijab*. What she said to me was that "some of us cover and some of us don't." At the other end of the spectrum are Muslimas who call for discussion in the magazine of homosexual Muslims. Steering clear of this topic, Tayyibah explained, "It is not a very central part right now [of what] most of our readers are interested in reading about."[15] Thus, for Tayyibah, *Azizah*'s beginnings reflected her personal ambitions, but her end product must reflect collective interests and commercial viability.

From Image to Attitude: Contemporary and Feminist

Azizah uses image to project voice, to present Muslim women beyond the images. Tayyibah described "the contemporary Muslim woman" to me as someone who "contributes actively to her community, has confidence in her faith, believes in the inherent pluralism of Islam, and does not apologize for being Muslim or for being a woman." Target readers are contemporary Muslim women, whose alliance is grounded in common circumstances in Muslim communities across the United States. Although American lifestyle and Islamic ideals often constrain them, Muslim women use both worldviews to assist them in their expression and activity.

Such a form of expression as *Azizah*, arising simultaneously from opportunity and limitation, is characteristic of Islamic feminism. Scholar miriam cooke defines Islamic feminism as a form of positioning. Muslim women position themselves in their faith communities, believing them to be the primary sources of their empowerment. At the same time, patriarchal structures in their communities limit Muslim women's speech and power. "Do they accept their communities' reactionary norms or do they appropriate and in the process subvert them?" cooke asks (2001, 55). She argues that Muslim women claim these norms and at the same time challenge them by creating "contingent subject positions" (60). While establishing themselves as committed members of their faith communities, they may provisionally move outside them to align themselves when necessary with other members of the broader society, with non-Muslim women, for example. In the process, they gain knowledge and resources that enable them to resist patriarchal norms in their Muslim communities.

Islamic feminism involves a "multiple critique" (107). Muslim women may critique their faith communities by contingently networking outside of them when they feel under threat or without support. However, by remaining inside their faith communities, they intimate that outside networks are not adequate for them as venues for their personal expression. Islamic feminism, therefore, challenges the notion that by appropriating symbols that are esteemed in their faith communities, such as *hijab*, Muslim women surrender their power to stand against gender oppression. Conversely, since Muslim women interpret Islamic law to validate movement beyond their faith communities, Islamic feminism also defies notions that Islam inherently restricts women. As cooke theorizes, "They are claiming their right to be strong women within this tradition, namely to be feminists without fear that they [will] be accused of being Westernized and imitative" (60). Tayyibah affirmed that the *Azizah* woman "does not apologize for being Muslim or for being a woman."

Appropriating the principles of activity in community, confidence in faith, and certainty of Islam's pluralism that define Muslim feminism, *Azizah* offers a forum for conducting a multiple critique. Activism corrects the image painted by non-Muslims of Muslim women as anti-Western. Fawzia As-Sultan wrote: "Muslim women should become real citizens . . . involved with a variety of activities. . . . Let people see your humanity and complexity. That's the way to promote a good image of Muslim women" (quoted in Muhammad and Taylor 2001). Confidence in faith allows Muslim women to be "real citizens" and to fully contribute to American society within an Islamic framework, challenging notions arising from families and communities that suggest that their participation represents a betrayal of Islam. To make their challenge, Muslim women must believe in the inherent pluralism of shari'a, Islamic law. Often, pressures within their communities stifle Muslim women's expression more than images authored by non-Muslims. Rhonda Roumani argues that Muslim women must discuss controversial issues in their communities before they critique the media. She writes, "Then we will be able to honestly correct the image of Muslim women [in the media,] because we will be doing that in our own communities" (quoted in Muhammad and Taylor 2001).

For the Muslima and by the Muslima, *Azizah* creates an Islamic feminist network because it acts "with and/or on behalf of all Muslim women and their right to enjoy with men full participation in a just community" (cooke 2001, 61). *Azizah* critiques other magazines that claim to act as a mouthpiece for American Muslims. *Azizah* women assert that these magazines limit discussion of women's issues to a women's page and that they focus on ideals. As Sara Flynn stated, "They don't actually write it from the perspective of someone who goes to the supermarket in a hijab everyday" (phone interview by the author, September 26, 2001). *Al-Jumuah* magazine, for example, has an editorial staff and advisory board made up of men only. *Islamic Horizons* has an editorial advisory board of seven that includes only one woman. Tayyibah argues that this tendency to neglect women's views reflects the historical status of men as "the gatekeepers and interpreters of the primary sources of Islam" (interview by the author, June 8, 2001). Ignoring women's experiences, gatekeepers present Muslim women only as an ideal, static and silent. In the process, Muslim men reinforce images of themselves as tyrannical, unwittingly contributing to the paradigm of the "third-world difference."

Tayyibah takes the symbols "Muslim" and "woman," and, instead of presenting the combination "Muslim woman" as static, she associates it with a range of experience. But more than that, she asserts that it signifies an "extra experience," implying that Muslim women have an edge over Muslim men and over non-Muslim women.[16] "Unlike mainstream American women," *Azizah* reader Maha Alkhateeb states, "being *Muslim* is more important than anything else to us" (e-mail interview by the author, September 17, 2001). American Muslim women identify faith as their strongest commonality. They are more than feminists; they are Islamic feminists. They reference Islamic texts and confront the ideologies and practices within their tradition. The outcome is revolution where it matters most: at home and in their communities. Islamic feminism allows them to put their faith and communities first without renouncing their rights and responsibilities.

Muslim Women Scholars and Activists

Azizah brings together radically diverse women, providing a forum for many different voices. When I inquired about the importance of projecting diversity, Tayyibah responded, "I think it's more that I'm going for the stories and going for the profiles, and they are diverse" (interview by the author, June 8, 2001). They are stories that have not been told, like the story about breast cancer that Tayyibah had wanted to write for *Sisters* or articles questioning male-only leadership in the *masjid*. By including previously disregarded stories, *Azizah* has portrayed the broad spectrum of women's concerns. Among the content of *Azizah* that distinguishes it from any other American Muslim publication are articles that highlight women's scholarship and activism.

Azizah contributor Nadirah Sabir stated: "It was great to see the article on Muslim women scholars. So many people think women don't/ shouldn't study the religion" (e-mail interview by the author, September 24, 2001). Promoting scholarship is critical for *Azizah* as an Islamic feminist network. Situating itself within the Islamic tradition and American Muslim communities that esteem the traditional texts, *Azizah* provides a forum for the scholarship of Muslim women scholars and for readers who are learning how to read Islamic texts in a way that will empower them. This scholarship validates *Azizah*'s commitment to women's voices and to presenting them with all their diversity of perspective.

A special report in *Azizah*'s second issue was titled "Female Scholars in America: Changing the Patriarchal Shape of Islamic Thought." It featured four American Muslim women scholars: Dr. Amina Wadud-Muhsin,

Dr. Azizah Al-Hibri, Dr. Riffat Hassan, and Dr. Aminah McCloud. The introduction of the report, which was written by Tayyibah Taylor, explains: "Prophet Muhammad, peace be upon him, encouraged all his followers, female as well as male, to learn and seek knowledge. . . . thus, there is no reason to believe that the women in early Muslim society denied themselves the joy and privilege of Islamic scholarship." It continues, "As Islam spread to cultures that were rigidly monarchical or patriarchal . . . , the interpretation and practice of Islam assumed an androcentric perspective." However, the scholars featured in *Azizah* show how "the beautiful *Qur'an*ic ideals [do not support] the oppressive treatment of women in many Muslim societies, [thereby] inventing a feminism that is neither conventionally Eurocentric nor secular in its nature." In other words, they are shaping an *Islamic* feminist discourse. These scholars encourage other women to enter the dialogue, and they advise budding female scholars "to learn Arabic, and until they have achieved fluency, to team up with others who speak the language fluently" (Taylor 2001).

Each issue features a "Deen" section that focuses on an aspect of Islamic doctrine.[17] Writers use traditional Islamic texts to inform readers that they have a right to interpret Islamic texts and carry out Islamic legal reasoning. Hina Azam refutes assumptions that only "qualified teachers" with training in "the classical commentaries" have the religious sanction to interpret Quranic verses (2001). Asifa Quraishi encourages her readers to engage in *ijtihad*, legal reasoning, and to do so with confidence because there is not a single correct interpretation but many possible answers on any given point of Islamic law. She writes: "[Our] responsibility is to engage in the processes of inquiry and analysis. It is the effort and sincerity of the deliberation that counts, not the correctness of the conclusion" (2001).

These women are scholars but also activists. They are concerned with change that will make communities more inclusive. An interesting case concerns an influential article about disability, in which Basimah Legander-Mourcy gives voice to the invisible: "Sometimes I feel invisible in my wheelchair," comments Majeeda Harris. "I get looks in the mosque that say, 'Why are you here? What are you doing here?' . . . Muslims have a long way to go in gaining awareness of the needs of the disabled" (2001). In "Hajj in a Wheelchair," Betty Hasan Amin describes how a bus attendant on a shuttle to the Jeddah airport placed her in an unsafe space and she "quietly" wheeled herself to a safer spot. She writes: "The attendant came back . . . to rudely fling me back to where he thought I should be. . . . With defiance born of my human dignity, I moved back to the safer place, locked my chair into position and stared the bus attendant straight in the eye. There I stayed" (2001, 43). Women whom I interviewed praised *Azizah* for including the voices of the "invisible" in its very first issue.

Azizah: *Connecting across Differences*

Diversity can be divisive. Catherine England describes her local community as divided by ethnicity: "We have an Arab mosque, and a Pakistani mosque, and an African American mosque. . . . The mosque just becomes a social club for different ethnic groups. Those of us who don't really fit into any of these different groups often feel excluded" (phone interview by the author, September 25, 2001). European American converts often feel alienated in the American *umma* because they represent one of the smallest Muslim ethnicities.

Nadirah Sabir, an African American, considers *Azizah* to be a platform for the voices of white women that often go unnoticed in Muslim communities. She imagines *Azizah*'s abundant representation of white women as "probably surprising to many black American Muslims." *Azizah* not only raises awareness of these Muslim minorities but presents them in a way that makes other Muslim women proud to share sisterhood with them. Beth Howell-Mahmoud, a European American, wrote about artists in *Azizah*. Concerned that Americans knew much about the Holocaust but very little about the plight of Palestinians, Beth set up a mock Palestinian camp near an Israeli celebration at her local community center. *Azizah* reader Amidah Salahuddin, an African American, admired Beth's stand (interview by the author, September 4, 2001). Khadijah Sharif-Drinkard, also African American, was amazed by an article on Latina Muslims, another ethnic Muslim minority. She commented, "I do not think that most people realize that there are over 40,000 Latino Muslims in America and the number is growing by leaps and bounds every year" (e-mail interview by the author, September 24, 2001).

Nevertheless, the representation of ethnic diversity in *Azizah* has required some fine-tuning. While *Azizah*'s first issue featured women from diverse ethnic groups, including Arab Americans, European Americans, and Indonesian Americans, pictures of African American and South Asian women predominated.[18] Some readers pick up the magazine looking for women who share their faith, regardless of ethnicity. Others, however, are looking for women who share both their religion and their ethnicity, and such women have complained when their ethnic group has been underrepresented.[19] The editors now make a "concentrated effort" to even out the ethnicities of women represented in both the photos and the text. The covers of *Azizah*'s first five issues featured an African American, an Indonesian American, a Latino American, another African American, and an Arab American, in that order.

Muslim Women Envision the Future

Women in the *Azizah* network believe that they are the ones who will contribute most to creating an American *umma* that is sensitive and inclusive. Catherine England noted, "Maybe because we've been in the position of not having the power, women often can look at the other side, and can empathize more" (phone interview by the author, September 25, 2001). Sabirah Muhammad added, "We are learning from each other that women can take the lead . . . without the necessary validation of men" (phone interview by the author, October 6, 2001). Gail Madyun similarly commented: "The magazine may bring about a unity that at this time has not yet matured into the fullness that it should. Simply put, *Azizah* is dear to me because in it I see the future" (*Azizah*, Winter 2001).

Azizah is about equality, justice, dignity, and liberty for everyone. Reflecting American Muslim women's richness and diversity of voice, it enables recasting the face of Islam in America into multiple shades and complexions.

NOTES

1. *Azizah* magazine's logo is "For the Contemporary Muslim Woman." During the period that I wrote this essay, *Azizah* had published its first five issues.

2. The *hijab* should not be confused with a face veil, or burqa. When I use the term "veil," I mean a face covering.

3. A study of American mosques shows that the ethnicities found in American mosques include but are not limited to South Asian (Pakistani, Indian, Bangladeshi, Afghan), African American, Arab, African (sub-Saharan), European (Bosnian, Tartar, Kosovar, and others), white American, Southeast Asian (Malaysian, Indonesian, Filipino), Caribbean, Turkish, Iranian, and Latino Muslims. However, only 5 percent of American mosques are composed of multiple ethnic groups with evenly balanced presences. The other 95 percent of mosques have one dominant ethnic group, usually either African American or South Asian (Bagby, Perl, and Froehle 2001).

4. The concept of the "ethnic mosque" was theorized in Yvonne Yazbeck Haddad and Adair T. Lummis's seminal work in the field of American Muslim studies (1987). Since this publication, a number of others have portrayed ethnic

diversity and separation in the American *umma*. Among the more recent are Badr 2000, Denny 1998, Lincoln 1997, Smith 1999, and Turner 1997.

5. "In nearly two-thirds of mosques (66 percent), women make salah behind a curtain or partition or in another room. In 1994, 52% of the mosques said that women prayed behind a curtain. The practice of having women pray behind a curtain or in another room is becoming more wide spread" (Bagby, Perl, and Froehle 2001, 11).

6. Since *Azizah*'s premiere issue, Nadia is no longer an *Azizah* editor.

7. *Azizah* requires that cover models be photogenic, but they must also have a story behind the face. In other words, beauty is not enough to make it onto *Azizah*'s cover.

8. Aspiring to include women from all communities with a range of voices, *Azizah* celebrations take place in neutral locations in cities so that the network remains unassociated with a particular *masjid*, community, or *madhhab* (school of Islamic law).

9. Tayyibah noted that sometimes it is difficult to find women reciters because some women will not recite Quran if men are present.

10. Ayesha's ethnicity is unidentified. However, she writes to "Conversations" from Jeddah, Saudi Arabia (Spring 2001).

11. For this reason, *Azizah* is one of a kind in comparison to magazines for Muslim women in regions outside the United States, which "usually [reflect] only the women of the ethnicity in that country" (Tayyibah Taylor, interview by the author, June 8, 2001).

12. Ibid. Here, Tayyibah is critiquing the abundance of literature on "how to be an ideal Muslima," most of it authored by Muslim men. Rather than give Muslim women the opportunity to speak and reflect who they are, such literature instructs Muslim women to be passive.

13. "Women are easily turned by outsiders into images that then become emblems of their culture, for within the culture itself women serve that same function. No matter how many chaste, modest American women an Asian Muslim may meet, no matter how many assertive, independent, unveiled Asian Muslim women an American may meet, the basic image may not change as these individuals are seen as exceptions to a rule that they thereby serve to reinforce" (cooke 2001, 126).

14. Sarah Sabo's ethnicity is unidentified. However, she writes to "Conversations" from Santa Rosa, California (Summer 2001).

15. Tayyibah Taylor, interview by the author, June 8, 2001. *Azizah* did review Shahnaz Khan's *Muslim Women: Crafting a North American Identity*, which features Muslim women who identify themselves as feminists and broaches controversial issues such as homosexuality.

16. Tayyibah's conception of an "extra experience" is akin to W. E. B. Du Bois's "double consciousness" (1989). In its first sense, double consciousness represents a negative conflict that African Americans experience. The descendants of African slaves, African Americans live in "a world which yields [them]

no true self-consciousness, but only lets [them] see [themselves] through the revelation of the other world" (5). They struggle to attain their full humanity in the face of white eyes that see African Americans as less than human. However, their extra experience, or other consciousness, which whites do not have, is a value and love for their blackness that potentially gives them the power to recreate themselves in their eyes and the eyes of others.

17. In the first five issues, all of the "Deen" sections were written by women receiving advanced degrees in Islamic studies at American universities.

18. The disproportionate representation of African American and South Asian American women in the first issue was largely due to the fact that the fashion designer featured in this issue retails South Asian apparel; most of her models represent the latter two ethnic groups. Yet the dominance of African American and South Asian American women in the first issue in no way misrepresents the American *umma*, since these two groups are the largest two ethnic Muslim groups in the United States.

19. *Azizah*'s second issue featured a dissenting response to the premier issue, and some African American women even complained that there were too many fair-complexioned African American models included in that issue.

Part III

Tracing
Muslim Networks

Chapter 9

Ideological & Technological Transformations of Contemporary Sufism

Islam, Ideology, and Sufism

One of the major trends in the development of Islamic religious culture over the past two centuries has been what one may call the Islamization of Islam. With the growing domination of European culture through colonialism, the modern Western concept of religion was applied to categorize what we now familiarly call the religions of the world. "Islam," an Arabic term designating both the individual act of surrender to God and the corporate performance of ritual, became the accepted designation for one religion among many.[1] Nineteenth-century European Orientalist scholarship played a key role in developing this "religionizing" concept of Islam, which excluded many of the intellectual and spiritual dimensions of the tradition; at the same time, colonial policy marginalized and privatized the institutions that had supported and transmitted these aspects of Islamic culture in Muslim countries. Curiously enough, nineteenth-century Muslim thinkers, in part responding to this colonial concept, articulated positions of reform and revivalism that mirrored the Orientalist concept of Islam. In the twentieth century, "Islam" has been increasingly used by fundamentalists as an ideological term for mobilizing mass activism against colonial interests or the secular postcolonial state, and this simple, hard-edged formula of opposition has been uncritically accepted and reproduced by Western media outlets.

Up until now, one major aspect of the contemporary Islamic tradition has been frequently omitted from public discussions: Sufism, or Islamic mysticism. In a recent survey, I have argued that Orientalist scholarship has, since its inception two centuries ago, systematically attempted to exclude Sufism from its definition of Islam.[2] In the nineteenth century and even well into the twentieth century, Sufism was almost invariably defined as the product of "foreign influences," which included anything from Greek philosophy to Buddhism to yoga. The exclusion of Sufism from Islam was paralleled by the new concepts of Islam that were being introduced at the same time by Islamic reformists, forebears of today's fundamentalists. What both Orientalists and fundamentalists failed to acknowledge was the way in which Sufism, broadly defined, had characterized most of the leading Muslim religious thinkers of the premodern period. Certain tropes of hagiography, such as the execution of the Sufi martyr Hallaj (d. 922), were interpreted to mean that Sufism was totally opposed by "orthodox" Islam (however, or by whomever, that was defined). The fact that Muslim scholars from al-Ghazali (d. 1111) to Shah Wali Allah (d. 1762) were saturated with Sufi teachings was an embarrassment to be left out of the history of Islam. Even those figures such as Ibn Taymiyya (d. 1328) who are most often invoked by today's anti-Sufi ideologists were themselves members of Sufi orders, despite their critiques of particular Sufi doctrines and practices. Muslim modernists like Sir Muhammad Iqbal have also tended to reject Sufism as medieval superstition, contributing further to the notion that Sufism is irrelevant to Islam.

It has not been possible to ignore Sufism completely, however. Again, in what conspiracy theorists might call a deep collusion, Orientalists and fundamentalists both conceded that Sufism was once legitimately Islamic, but this concession was tempered by their contention that its legitimacy was limited to a classical golden age in the distant past. One could confidently speak well of Sufi masters who were safely buried centuries ago; Europeans, particularly the Protestant British, agreed with the Wahhabi founders of the Saʿudi regime that dead saints are lifeless dust—in contrast to the vehement pronouncements of Sufis that the saints in their tombs are living conduits to the divine presence. In practice, the Europeans' attitude had the added advantage that it allowed them to safely dismiss contemporary Sufis as the degenerate representatives of a once-great tradition. As far as the study of Sufism is concerned, the golden-age attitude translated into a direct correlation between the relative antiquity of a Sufi and the attention of which he was deemed worthy; consequently, studies of contemporary Sufism, except from a purely political perspective, have been rare until recent times.[3]

Nevertheless, upon closer examination, it turns out that Sufi leaders, Sufi institutions, and Sufi trends of thought have been surprisingly resilient and adaptive to the contested situations of modernity. Nineteenth-century Sufi leaders such as Emir ʿAbd al-Qadir of Algeria were not only active in anticolonial resistance but also were connected with reformist circles. Much the same could be said of Indian Sufis such as the Naqshbandi leader Ahmad Barelwi and the Chishti master Hajji Imdad Allah, the North African shaykh Muhammad ibn Idris al-Shafiʿi, and many others. Today, both in traditionally Muslim countries and in the West, a battle is being waged for control of the symbolic resources of Islam, and in this contest, both fundamentalists and modernists regard Sufism as their chief opponent. In spite of appearances generated by the media, if Sufism is defined broadly to encompass a range of devotional practices including the intercession of saints and reverence for the Prophet Muhammad, it may fairly be said that the majority of Muslims today still adhere to a Sufi perspective on Islam. The aim of this essay is to illustrate how proponents of Sufism and admirers of its cultural products have expressed themselves through the communications media of modern technology and to venture some speculations about the kind of community that is sustained by this technology. In making this analysis, I rely in particular on the insightful observations of Manuel Castells in delineating varied cultural expressions found in the media of print, sound recording, broadcast media, film, and the interactive networking of the Internet (1996, 327–75).

Sufism in Print

In European history, it has become a truism to state that the Protestant Reformation was to a certain extent the child of print; Gutenberg's invention of moveable type made possible the first modern best seller, Martin Luther's German translation of the Bible. In a comparative extension of this topic, Sinologists are now examining the relationship between religion and print in China, where the long history of printing is closely tied to religious texts. Anthropologists and historians of religion alike have focused on the question of the relation between the oral and written aspects of sacred texts. Yet for Islam, perhaps preeminently the "religion of the book," research on the relationship between religion and the technology of print is still in its infancy. Partly this is due to the relatively late introduction of print to Muslim countries; despite the existence of Arabic printing in Europe by 1500, there had been only a few experiments with printing in Muslim countries by the eighteenth century, and it was not until the late nineteenth century that printing became a major factor in the dissemination of Islamic texts.

To date, much of the scholarship on the subject of Islam and print has focused on the phenomena most easily accessible to Europeans, such as the presses established by European Christian missionaries and by governments, whether native or colonial; many other aspects of printing in Muslim countries remain unexplored, however. Orientalists have speculated, often in a condescending way, on the possible causes that hindered the introduction of printing among Muslims until such a late date. Was it an economic threat to the thousands of calligraphers who made their livelihood from copying manuscripts? Was it a problem of capital formation and marketing, due to the difficulty of recouping the large sums required to invest in the machinery of a printing press? Or was it a profound attachment to the oral transmission of the divine word as embodied in the Quran? These questions, and many others, will remain highly debatable as long as the actual history of printing in Muslim countries remains relatively unknown. Clearly, even establishing the outlines of this history will require the labors of scholars working on many different regions and languages, so these large questions remain premature, and may not even be useful. What should be questioned, however, is the degree to which inquiries about Islam and print have been posed from a thoroughly Eurocentric perspective, rather than from the perspective of a comprehensive inquiry into the religious purposes to which Muslims turned the new technology.

To be sure, scholars such as Barbara Metcalf have recognized the important role of print in the Islamic religious academies of nineteenth-century colonial India. Since the 'ulama' (religious scholars) have been the articulators and transmitters of Islamic religious texts, they are certainly a key element to examine for insight into the relation between Islam and print. Yet they are not by any means the only actors to consider. In a provocative essay, Francis Robinson has argued that Islamic religious scholars in India accepted print because, under colonial rule, "without power, they were fearful for Islam" (1993, 240). He also points out that the adoption of print for religious texts had several unexpected results: (1) the rise of "Islamic protestantism," that is, a scripturalist revivalism that rejected many aspects of traditional Islamic practice; (2) the internationalization of the Muslim community; and (3) the democratization of religious knowledge and the consequent erosion of the authority of the 'ulama'. Robinson observes, "Print came to be the main forum in which religious debate was conducted," a generalization that works well even beyond the specific groups he describes.

Another aspect of this topic that has recently claimed the attention of scholars is the use of print (and other means of communication, like the cassette) by twentieth-century Islamist or fundamentalist groups to propagate their ideologies. Certainly the ability of print to fix a text without variants has contributed to the bibliolatry and scriptural literalism that characterizes these groups. But partly because of the way in which these groups have succeeded in monopolizing Islamic symbolism, both in the eyes of foreign journalists and in indigenous forums, those who raise the question of Islam and print have not been impelled to look past these highly visible phenomena. A cynic might call this the closed-feedback loop, in which Western media and scholarship use and are used by twin agendas, that of the fundamentalists and that of the secular governments that they oppose. Once again, those topics of most interest to the West are most prominent in research.

Perhaps the most remarkable aspect of the emergence of Sufism as a topic in the nineteenth and twentieth centuries has been the publicizing of a previously esoteric system of teaching through modern communications media. Today, Sufi orders and shrines in Muslim countries produce a stream of publications aimed at a variety of followers from the ordinary devotee to the scholar. Just as the recording industry democratized the private rituals of *sama*ᶜ (listening to music) for a mass audience (see below), the introduction of print and lithography technology made possible the distribution of Sufi teachings on a scale far beyond what manuscript production could attain. As has been noted of Ibn al-ᶜArabi's Arabic works, which first emerged into print early in the nineteenth century, suddenly a work that had existed in at most a hundred manuscripts around the world (and those difficult to access) was now made easily available at a corner bookstore through print runs of up to a thousand copies (Notcutt 1993).

Evidence is still far from complete, but it has been recently suggested, largely on the basis of Arab and Ottoman evidence, that the main patrons of publishing in Muslim countries in the nineteenth century, aside from governments, were Sufi orders.[4] What was the character and extent of publication by Sufi groups or on Sufism in general? The evidence is still very thin, and it is necessary to tease out Sufism from subject categories that are otherwise defined. What is available, however, is suggestive. For instance, a preliminary survey indicates that there were 112 native presses in various parts of India publishing books in Persian and Urdu during the first half of the nineteenth century and that most of their publications were on religion, poetry, and law (Haider 1981, 230). It is quite likely that many books that fall into the categories of religion and poetry could be described as connected to Sufism. Lists of books published in the early nineteenth century from Bengal include the philosophical encyclopedia of the Brethren of Purity (both in Arabic and in Urdu) and Persian literary classics by Sa'di, Jami, and others (Kesavan 1985, 396, 398–402). The prominence of Persian literary classics in the Indian native presses was also reflected in the presses operated by Europeans in Calcutta in the late eighteenth century.[5] Likewise, books published in Iran since the mid-nineteenth century fall primarily into the categories of classical Persian literature, religious writings, and romantic epics and popular narratives, all of which overlap to some extent with Sufism (Marzolph 2001). The press founded by the Egyptian ruler Muhammad 'Ali Pasha in 1822 published, in addition to a large number of translations of European works on subjects like military science, significant works on religion, ethics, and poetry. Among these were a number of Arabic, Persian, and Turkish Sufi texts by authors such as Sa'di, Rumi, and Ibn al-'Arabi.[6]

The publicization of Sufism occurred at precisely the time when Sufism was becoming an abstract subject, separated from Islam in Orientalist writings and condemned by reformists as a non-Islamic innovation. Some of the Sufi publications in turn responded directly to presentations of Sufism by Orientalists, fundamentalists, and modernists. In this category, one can find not only editions of "classical" Sufi texts in Arabic and Persian (and their Urdu translations) but also writings of contemporary Sufi leaders, including discourses, lectures and essays, biographies, prayer and meditation practices, and manuals for using talismans and charms bearing the names of God (ta'widh). Since all these books were available commercially, the new trend amounted to a mass marketing of Sufism on an unprecedented scale.

Through printed books, today one can also gain access to Sufism through scholarly publications from Western-style universities, learned societies, and cultural centers with government sponsorship. In format and style, these works are very much in the same tradition as European academic Orientalism; European-style punctuation, footnotes, and editorial techniques have been largely adopted in Arabic-script publishing. In contrast, nonacademic Sufi writings tend to preserve the aesthetic form of the manuscript, particularly in lithographs created by trained calligraphers. As opposed to the elite monopoly on culture characteristic of the manuscript, book publication presupposes a mass audience created by public education and sustained by print capitalism. While access to manuscripts in the premodern period was rare and difficult and scribal errors required the comparison of different manuscripts, print makes books easy to acquire and standardizes their texts. Therefore, when a scholar today edits a classical Sufi text, the text does not merely replicate the experience of reading an eleventh-century author for the modern reader. Carrying official authorization as part of "classical" Islamic literature, the printed text now functions in new ways to defend Sufism from the polemics of both fundamentalists and Westernized secularists. In countries like Pakistan, where Arabic and Persian both function as "classical" languages, there has been a concerted effort to translate much of the curriculum of Arabic and Persian Sufi literature into Urdu. Like the classical Greek works of Aristotle and Euripides at Oxford bookstores, the Arabic Sufi works of Sarraj, Qushayri, and Suhrawardi are now to be found in Urdu versions on bookshelves in Lahore. Their eminence and Islamic scholarship makes them powerful allies in the defense of Sufism against ideological opponents.

A striking evidence of the newly specialized situation of Sufism in the early twentieth century is the way Sufi leaders could focus on marketing to their disciples through the publication of serials, a topic that is only beginning to be explored. Probably the first leading Sufi involved in the publication of serials in India was Hasan Nizami, a prolific author and publisher in Urdu from 1908.[7] Arthur Buehler has shown how the modern Naqshbandi teacher Jamaʿat ʿAli Shah (d. 1951) directed his movement through *Anwar al-Sufiyya*, a periodical aimed at Sufi devotees. Mandatory subscriptions for disciples, combined with Jamaʿat ʿAli Shah's rigorous train-travel program, enabled him to use modern technology to keep in touch with a far-flung network of followers.[8] The role of modern communications technology in Pakistani Sufism is also evident in the case of the Chishti master Zauqi Shah (d. 1951). Educated at Aligarh and trained as a journalist in both English and Urdu, he founded a Sufi magazine, *Anwar al-Quds* (The Lights of Holiness), which was published in Bombay from October 1925 to February 1927. He continued to publish in newspapers, including some pieces in *Dawn* (Karachi, 1945–46) and a weekly column in *The People's Voice* (1948–49). While he published some polemical articles on the superiority of Islam in the magazine of Abu'l-Aʿla Mawdudi, *Tarjuman al-Qur'an*, he also wrote essays refuting the claims to authority of the fundamentalist leader of the Jamaʿat-i Islami. In recent years, his successors have published an intermittent English-language journal called *The Sufi Path*. A number of other periodicals devoted to Sufism are currently published in India and Pakistan in Urdu and other languages.[9] There are, likewise, numerous other examples of Sufi periodicals in Egypt and Turkey. Periodicals have the effect of preserving a sense of community among individuals scattered far from the traditional local center.

Sufis were not without ambivalence regarding the use of print for their purposes. Early in the nineteenth century, the Naqshbandi master Shah Ghulam ʿAli was enraged to hear that pictures of saints (evidently printed) were available at the great mosque of Delhi. In a conversation that took place in the 1890s, Haydar ʿAli Shah (a prominent Chishti leader of the Punjab, d. 1908) denounced the production of printed prayer manuals. Affirming the supreme value of oral transmission, he stated that even if a master got the Arabic names of God wrong and taught disciples to say the nonsense words *hajj qajjum* instead of *hayy qayyum* ("the living, the subsistent"), his instruction was to be preferred to an impersonal practice derived from a book. This prejudice did not, however, prevent Haydar ʿAli Shah's disciples from publishing his Persian discourses in 1909. Yet it is striking to see that ritual could be adapted to the new technology, as was the case for documents of initiation. Typically, initiation into a Sufi order in previous times had involved the disciple's learning by heart and then transcribing by hand the family "tree" of the Sufi lineage, inscribing his own name at the end of a line traced back to the Prophet Muhammad. With the availability of print to facilitate this ritual process (as in the mass production of *qawwali*, or recordings), some Sufi groups produced ready-made printed lineage documents, with the "tree" ending in blank spaces for the would-be initiate and the master to inscribe their own names.[10]

The publicizing of Sufism through print (and, more recently, electronic media) has brought about a remarkable shift in the Sufi tradition. Advocates of Sufism have defended their heritage by publishing refutations of fundamentalist or modernist attacks on Sufism. In this sense, the media permit Sufism to be contested and defended in the public sphere as one ideology alongside others. This is very much the case, for instance, in the numerous publications of the Barelvi theological school in South Asia, which over the past century have been used to defend the devotional practices of Sufism against the scripturalist attacks of the Deoband school (Sanyal 1996).[11] Likewise, leaders of Egyptian Sufi groups have responded directly to reformist criticisms posed to them by newspaper editors, claiming that Sufism is at the core of Islam, refuting charges of its foreign origins, and defending Sufi rituals and the master-disciple relationship (Johansen 1996, 169–210). Traditional Sufi genres like biographies and discourses have created an intimate relationship between readers and Sufi masters; through the wider distribution made possible by print, such publications have both served local Sufi networks and at the same time functioned as proclamations that have at least potentially formed part of the public legitimation of Sufism. Through these modern public media, Sufism is no longer just an esoteric community constructed largely through direct contact, ritual interaction, and oral instruction.

Now that Sufism has been publicized through mass printing, what are the changes in personal relationships that the new media entail? As Dale Eickelman has observed, "The intellectual technologies of writing and printing create not only new forms of communication, they also engender new forms of community and authority" (1995, 133). Many questions remain about the number and kinds of books produced on Sufism, the number of copies printed, the audiences they were aimed at, the publishers themselves, and so on, but it is possible to make a few preliminary observations here. Sometimes print is interactive and facilitates the interaction of networks or functions in defense against polemical opponents, but at other times it may be a symbolic or ritual gesture. Simply to publish the writings of a Sufi saint might be considered a pious act that brings blessings with it, and indeed the elaborate poems, dedications, and memorials that conclude many Sufi publications often have a decidedly ritualistic character. As David Gilmartin points out elsewhere in this volume, print as the medium for debate about imagined Muslim community had an ambiguous relation to the networks in Muslim societies. In the case of Sufism, the defenders of strongly local lineages attempted to deflect criticism by claiming to embody the essential teachings of Islam. But there is an inescapably local element to any Sufi tradition or order that is expressed by devotion to particular shaykhs, ritual at certain shrines, and writing in local languages. The very concreteness of local networks exists in tension with universal notions of community; indeed, we cannot speak of any empirical community of Sufis on a global basis. Sufis attempt to trump the systematic ideologies of reformist critics by staking a claim to the key symbolic capital enshrined in the Quran and the Prophet Muhammad. In polemical and academic publications, a universal Sufism aims at capturing "the mantle of the Prophet," in Roy Mottahedeh's apt phrase, but Sufi lineages still depend on face-to-face contact and real communities that are of necessity more limited.

It is my assumption that the extent of publication by contemporary Sufi groups has been underestimated, partly because of the reformist critique mentioned above. But the misreading is also a result of inadequate access to locally distributed publications and of the limited amount of historical research that has been done on printing in Muslim countries. For instance, a knowledgeable British scholar, Graham Shaw, estimated that

Munshi Nawal Kishor, the Hindu founder of the most important Persian/Urdu press in nineteenth-century India, had published around five hundred books by the time of his death in 1895 (1991). But Professor Mohamad Tavakoli-Targhi of Illinois State University a few years ago acquired a complete collection of the publications of the Nawal Kishor press consisting of nearly five thousand volumes! No doubt some of these were printed by Nawal Kishor's successors, but less than one-fourth of the titles are listed in European or American libraries.[12] A great many of these publications were classical Persian poetry (including Sufi poetry), works about Sufism, and Islamic religious texts. The major libraries of Muslim countries doubtless hold a considerable number of volumes on Sufism still unknown in the West, so at the very least the question of Sufism in print provides a charter for further research.

Audio and Film

After the late introduction of print in Muslim countries, the technological pace picked up quickly in the twentieth century with the introduction of mass media, including sound recordings, film, radio, and television. Sufi-related music, which may be found in many countries, soon became available through commercial recordings. These were at first produced both for popular local audiences, as in the case of Indian *qawwali* recordings in the 1920s and 1930s, and for highbrow European ethnomusicologists some years later (Carl Ernst 1999, 189–91, 195–96). In neither case can the recorded music be said to be a product of traditional Sufi *tariqa* organizations; it is, instead, the result of a reconfiguration of which cultural products are available for resale on the mass distribution market (whether one calls these products "pop culture" or not).

In recent years, Sufi music has been the subject of a new appropriation that may be called "remix." On world music albums, at international festivals, and in fusion performances, Sufi music has been performed in contexts never before envisioned. To take but a single example, the *qawwali* music of Pakistani singer Nusrat Fateh 'Ali Khan ("Must Must Qalandar") was remixed by the British trip-hop group Massive Attack in 1990 to become an international dance hit with a strongly reggae flavor. At the same time, performers who were once low-status service professionals catering to the spiritual experience of elite listeners have made the shift to become box office superstars who are regarded as spiritual personalities in their own right. A glance at the top twenty-five hits for a search for the term "Sufi music" on the website of online retailer Amazon.com indicates the remarkable variety and profusion of this music available to the world of consumers today. But such music is best described as a cultural and commercial appropriation of Sufism rather than as the dissemination of Sufi teaching and authority (Qureshi 1992).

Broadcast media in most formerly colonized countries are typically under the control of the state, and so is not surprising to find that films prepared for television distribution in Muslim countries strongly reflect government interests. This political emphasis is obvious in the few documentary films about Sufism that have been produced in non-European countries, particularly when they are contrasted with the cultural focus of the ethnographic films about Sufism made by Western anthropologists. A notable example of an official documentary film on Sufism is *The Lamp in the Niche*, a two-part film directed by Girish Karnad and produced in 1990 by the Ministry of Information of the government of India. This film (winner of a national award for "best non–feature film on social issues") portrays Sufism as a broadly tolerant movement, Islamic in its origins to be sure, but more closely akin to the devotional Bhakti currents of Hinduism than to anything else. Likewise, the secular government of Turkey has produced a film called *Tolerance* devoted to the life and teachings of the thirteenth-century Sufi and poet Jalal al-Din Rumi. Rumi is portrayed in the film as a universal polymath who foreshadows both Turkish nationalism and the secular values of post-Enlightenment modernity, an ironic configuration in a country where the practice of Sufism has been illegal since 1925 (Gerceker 1995). The Foreign Trade Association of the city of Bokhara in Uzbekistan has released *The Beaming One*, a film about the famous fourteenth-century saint Baha'uddin Naqshband. The commercial slant of this film, evidently aimed at encouraging pilgrimage to Uzbekistan from South Asia and Turkey, reveals the curious indecisiveness of post-Soviet societies striving to recapture an Islamic identity; at a loss to explain the mystical charisma of the saint, the narrator ends by comparing him to Gandhi and Tolstoy.[13] Like the occasions when official television broadcasts the ceremonies at annual festivals held at saints' shrines, these official films demonstrate a clumsy attempt to manipulate the symbolism of Sufism for the benefit of the state.

On the Internet

The apparent paradox of publicizing an esoteric tradition is nowhere more apparent than on the Internet, where the open secret of mysticism must be reconfigured in terms of what are basically advertising paradigms. There are today a host of Sufi websites that proclaim themselves to interested Internet surfers, offering everything from detailed textual materials online to boutiques of unusual products. Some of these are related to traditional Sufi orders, such as the Nimatollahi, Naqshbandi, Rifaʿi, and Chishti orders.[14] Sometimes they appear to prolong and perpetuate the authority of the printed text, as one can see from the extensive devotional and spiritual treatises available online in English translation on the elaborate website of the American Naqshbandi order led by Shaykh Hisham Kabbani.[15] This website also features extensive polemics directed against fundamentalist forms of Islam, and the name of the site itself (Sunnah.org) indicates an attempt to appropriate the key symbolic term of the Prophet's moral example (*sunna*). Although many of the Sufi websites do have some interactive features such as e-mail addresses, in terms of their religious message they tend to be largely informational, with a proselytizing touch.

In contrast, the websites associated with Hazrat Inayat Khan in North America play much more fully into the Internet sensibility. Pir Vilayat Khan, Sufi Sam, and other branches of this Sufi tradition have a massive presence that is ramified in a number of parallel but distinct organizations as well as in individual websites. These sites feature numerous interactive features, including discussion groups, travel schedules of leaders, online classes, daily inspirational messages, audio files, and massive collections of links to sites about Sufism and other religions. Discussion groups associated with these sites have free-ranging and sometimes combative debates about topics such as the relationship between Sufism and Islam. This kind of website may truly be said to constitute a "virtual community," which Manuel Castells has defined as "a self-defined electronic network of interactive communication organized around a shared interest or purpose, although sometimes communication becomes the goal in itself" (1996, 361). I shall return to these groups below in connection with the de-emphasis on Islam found in these popular forms of Sufism.

The variation in the kind of Internet presence maintained by different Sufi groups can be understood in terms of some of the fundamental characteristics of modern communications media and technology. As Castells points out, "in a society organized around mass media, the existence of messages that are outside the media is restricted to interpersonal networks, thus disappearing from the collective mind" (336). This new situation constitutes a challenge for groups that were traditionally defined by their access to esoteric teachings reserved for a spiritual elite. Last year, I asked the leader of a South Asian Sufi group whether or not he was interested in setting up a website. (I posed this question on e-mail, since he has access to this technology in his professional capacity as an engineer.) He responded by quoting the words of a twentieth-century Sufi master from his lineage: "We are not vendors who hawk our wares in the bazaar; we are like Mahajans (wholesale merchants)—people come to us." Nevertheless, he indicated that he did find the idea of a website interesting, and it turns out that Malaysian disciples of his order have in fact set up a website where English-language publications by the leading masters of the order are offered for sale.

We should not imagine, however, that Internet representation is completely displacing earlier forms of communications and technology. The history of technology indicates that older cultural forms often persist alongside newly introduced forms of communication. Well after the introduction of writing, and even after the invention of printing, oral forms of culture have persisted up to the present day. The vast majority of participants in the Sufi tradition in Muslim countries are still from social strata that have very little access to the most modern forms of electronic communication, and many are indeed illiterate. Lower-class devotees who attend the festivals of Sufi saints in Egypt and Pakistan are not represented on the web. The effect of the spread of Internet technologies is likely to be "the reinforcement of the culturally dominant social networks, as well as the increase of their cosmopolitanism and globalization" (363). As might be expected, the authors of Sufi websites tend to be members of the cosmopolitan and globalizing classes: either immigrant Sufi leaders establishing new bases in America and Europe, immigrant technocrats who happen to be connected to Sufi lineages, or Euro-American converts to Sufism in one form or other. Outside of America and Europe, the chief locations where Sufi websites are hosted are predictably high-tech areas like Australia, South Africa, and Malaysia. In this respect, the networks of Sufism in the Internet age differ significantly from the locally centered Sufi networks of the time of Ibn Battuta. Now the diasporas based on international business are linked through electronic communications in multiple locations, although it is still possible for Sufi practitioners to return to sacred sites at key times for face-to-face meetings of master and disciple.

Changing Forms of Community

New forms of communications technology have introduced a tension into the internal aspect of religious community associated with Sufism. There is, on the one hand, a continued need for personal mediation and interpretation by the Sufi master and a focus on local shrines combined with the ritual use of texts. On the other hand, texts are published for external audiences—both as printed books and increasingly on the Internet—as invitations to approach the inner teachings. This constitutes, in effect, a kind of Sufi preaching (*da'wa*) that has a self-consciously public posture far more extensive than in previous generations. But the alternative would be a privatization amounting to complete obscurity. Some Sufi websites are tantalizing advertisements of spiritual authority, using sparing amounts of text, graphics, and occasionally photographs to convey the powerful mediating effect of Sufi masters and lineages; their primary interactive goal is to get the viewer into direct personal contact with the Sufi group. Other sites are comprehensive vehicles for virtual communities, loaded with extensive texts and links, where new forms of personal interaction are carried out and mediated by the technology itself. In contrast to the more limited circulation of print, the Internet makes possible the maintenance of networks in a more fluid fashion over any distance. The possibility of a virtual community facilitated by instant communications gives a new significance to the concept of Uwaysi initiation, by which Sufis can enter into contact with masters removed in time or space. Cyberspace becomes a reflection of the unseen spiritual world, though place and physicality are never abandoned.[16]

The spread of new communications media has also had unforeseen effects in that it has allowed popular culture to trump ideology. Muslims who came to the United States after the liberalization of immigration laws in 1965 have tended to be middle-class technical and medical specialists who gravitate toward reformist and fundamentalist forms of Islam. Their children, who are reaching college age today, have been unexpectedly enchanted by the world music phenomenon, and large numbers of them are discovering Sufism through the powerful music of Nusrat Fateh 'Ali Khan and others. In view of the overwhelming anti-Muslim bias in the news media, the stunning popularity of the Sufi poetry of Rumi is another surprising embrace of a manifestation of Islamic culture—although, to be sure, Rumi's Muslim identity is frequently underplayed or elided in favor of a universalist spirituality. Nevertheless, despite the anti-Sufi influence of Saudi-financed forms of fundamentalism, there are increasing signs of interest in Sufi devotionalism in American Muslim communities (particularly among those of South Asian origin, about 45 percent of immigrant Muslims).

Another consequence of the new media is the erosion of textual authority and the social hierarchies associated with religion. The multiple "translations" of poets like Rumi and Hafiz illustrate a very postmodern concept of the poetic text. Almost none of them are by authors conversant with the original language, and while some, like Coleman Barks, are professional poets who work closely with translators and standard editions, there are "versions" of the Sufi poets that have no discernible relationship with any original text. This form of "Sufism in print" sometimes verges on total fantasy, in which the imagined words of the mystic poet become the protean mirror of desire.[17] It is striking, too, that the gender separation and stratification associated with traditional Muslim societies has been ignored in many new Sufi groups in the West. Not only are some groups actually headed by women, but women also join with men in performing ritual music and dance in public (like the *sema* of the Whirling Dervishes). It would be hard to find any precedent for this in traditional Sufi orders.

In addition, Sufism is no longer just for Muslims. The oldest modern presence of Sufism in Europe and America, dating from the early years of the twentieth century, derives from the Indian Sufi master Hazrat Inayat Khan. Faced with anti-Muslim feeling that still dominated the late colonial era, he presented Sufism as a universal form of spirituality beyond any particular religion or creed, despite its acknowledged Islamic roots. Other Sufi teachers who have come to the West, like the Sri Lankan teacher Bawa Muhaiyadeen, have followings comprised of both Muslims and non-Muslims, who dispute the ultimate religious identity of Muhaiyadeen's teachings. While this erosion of Sufism's Islamic identity fulfills the predictions of anti-Sufi fundamentalists, it is balanced by groups that insist upon Sufism as the true essence of Islam. Sufism has become a contested badge of identity that is announced, performed, and disputed through all of the new forms of communication.

Sufism is a form of identity that was partially severed from Islam during the traumatic experience of European colonial domination over most of the rest of the world. It has been defined by Orientalists, maligned by fundamentalists, and condemned as irrelevant by modernists. Yet it has proven to be a highly resilient symbolic system that has endured in local contexts even as it has been appropriated by cosmopolitan elites, both Muslim and non-Muslim. In private networks, publications, pop culture, and virtual communities, it may be expected to continue operating for the formation of identity and community in a variety of situations. And it is safe to say that Sufism will continue to be a formidable issue for Islamic identity in the foreseeable future.[18]

1. The *Oxford English Dictionary* cites Edward Lane's 1842 *Manners and Customs of the Modern Egyptians* as the first published use of the term "Islam" in English. Prior to that, "Mahometanism" was the common designation for this religion. Both terms conveyed the Enlightenment concept of a religion as one of many competitive belief structures. For a fuller discussion, see Carl Ernst 2003, esp. chapter 2.

2. See the evidence discussed in Carl Ernst 1999, esp. chapter 1; see also Carl Ernst 2002a.

3. The critique of "golden-age" approaches to Sufism has been fully developed in Ernst and Lawrence 2002. Although certain major scholars (Louis Massignon, Marshall Hodgson, Ira Lapidus) have recognized the centrality of Sufism in Muslim societies, there has been little attention paid to contemporary Sufism until fairly recently. For brief surveys of nineteenth- and twentieth-century Sufism, see the following articles listed under "Tasawwuf" in Bearman et al. 1999, 313–40: "4. In 19th and 20th-century Egypt" (F. de Jong); "5. In Persia from 1800 onwards" (L. Lewisohn); "6. Amongst the Turks (c) The Ottoman Turkish lands and Republican Turkey in the 19th and 20th centuries" (Th. Zarcone); "7. In Muslim India (b) In the 19th and 20th centuries" (C. Ernst); "8. In Chinese Islam" (J. Aubin); "9. In Africa south of the Maghrib during the 19th and 20th centuries" (J. O. Hunwick).

4. Mahdi 1995, 6–7. Mahdi suggests that the large followings of mystical orders made such publishing economically feasible. Rich evidence from Morocco is supplied by Fawzi Abdulrazak (1990).

5. Examples include *Layli-Majnun* by Hatifi, edited by Sir William Jones (1788); the text and translation of Sa'di's ethical treatise, *Pand nama*, edited by Francis Gladwin (1788); Sa'di's complete works (1791 and 1795); and the poems of Hafiz (1791). See Shaw 1981, nos. 111, 113, 181, 186, 277. See also Storey 1933.

6. Titles include the anonymous *Jawhar al-tawhid* (1825); Sa'di's *Gulistan* (1828 and 1841); 'Attar's *Pand nama* (1828, 1838, and 1842); a Turkish commentary on Hafiz (1835); *Ma'rifat nama*, a Turkish work on mysticism by Ibrahim Haqqi (1836); a three-volume Turkish commentary on Rumi's *Masnavi* by Kefravi (1836); Ibn al-'Arabi's *Fusus al-hikam* (1838); the Ottoman poetry of Shaykh Ghalib (1838); a Sufi Quran commentary by Isma'il Haqqi (1840); the Persian poems of Hafiz (1841); and several Turkish works on Sufism. See Bianchi 1843, 24–61, citing nos. 19, 46, 47, 97, 109, 113, 137, 148, 149, 190, 199, 201, 202, 209, 217.

7. Faruqi 1994, esp. 89–107. See also Ernst and Lawrence 2002, chapter 6.

8. Buehler 1998. Jama'at 'Ali Shah's periodical has recently been revived in English as *Sufi Illuminations* (*Risala-yi Anwar as-Sufiyya* 1, no. 1–2 [1996]), available from the Naqshbandiya Foundation for Islamic Education, P.O. Box 3526, Peoria, IL 61612–3526. Individual subscriptions cost ten dollars a year.

9. The Khanqah Mujibiya in Phulwari Sharif, Bihar, published a journal called *Ma'arif* from the 1950s up to the 1980s (Qadri 1998, 68). American

libraries hold several Sufi periodicals from Pakistan published over the past two decades, including three from Karachi (*Darvish*, *Rumi Digest*, and *Sachal Sa'in*) and one from Quetta (*Dastgir*).

10. Bakhsh 1913; a photograph of the signature page of this document may be seen at ‹http://www.unc.edu/~cernst/chishti.htm›. For other examples of printed *shajara* genealogies, see Qadri 1998, 43 n. 16, and Liebeskind 1998, 219.

11. See the extensive list of Barelvi publications offered for sale in the large (224-page) catalogue *Kitabi Dunya*, offered by Nizami Book Agency of Budaun, Uttar Pradesh (1988–89).

12. The Persian titles from this magnificent collection are in the private collection of Professor Tavakoli-Targhi; the Urdu volumes (about 15 percent of the total) have been purchased by the University of Chicago.

13. Makkhmudov 1993. This film should definitely be viewed in conjunction with *Habiba: A Sufi Saint from Uzbekistan*, a new age film distributed by Mystic Fire Video in its "Women of Power" series (Allione 1997). While this female healer from Uzbekistan quotes the Quran, the Prophet Muhammad, and the Sufi saints, she also makes mysterious references to "the snakes" and "the Goddess" as she leads followers on pilgrimage both to the tomb of Baha'uddin Naqshband and to the tomb of his mother.

14. See a representative listing of 140 sites at ‹http://world.std.com/~habib/sufi.html›.

15. See ‹http://www.sunnah.org›.

16. Jamiluddin Morris Zahuri, letter to the author, March 19, 2001.

17. See the recent recording, *A Gift of Love: Deepak and Friends Present Music Inspired by the Love Poems of Rumi* (compact disc, Tommy Boy Music, 1998), featuring readings by such celebrities as Deepak Chopra, Goldie Hawn, Madonna, Demi Moore, Rosa Parks, Martin Sheen, and Debra Winger.

18. For further reflections on this topic, see Carl Ernst 2002b.

Chapter 10

The Salafi Movement

Violence and the Fragmentation of Community

In the aftermath of September 11, Muslim governments and American policy makers alike swiftly condemned al-Qaeda and attempted to frame Osama bin Laden, Ayman Zawahiri, and other violent Islamists as outliers with little connection to mainstream Islamic interpretations. In some instances, this included the charge that al-Qaeda is constituted by deviant religious usurpers who hijacked religion for immoral aims. President Bush sought to assure the American public that Islam is a peaceful, honorable religion while concurrently demonizing Bin Laden and his supporters as "evil-doers" with little or no grounding in the realities of Islam or the Muslim world. With rhetoric and public pronouncements, the U.S. administration and many world figures (including a number of Muslim leaders) cast al-Qaeda as a nefarious group of zealots isolated from most "good" Muslims. Such distinctions led Western leaders, in particular, to posit the "war on terrorism" as a surgical strike against violent groups rather than a "clash of civilizations" (Huntington 1996).

While the distinction between "good" and "bad" (or evil) Muslims may provide a sense of psychological security and demarcate a distinction between the vast majority of Muslims, who oppose violence, and al-Qaeda, its ethical bifurcation underestimates the spiritual, ideological, and human relationships that connect those who espouse violence against the United States with those of more moderate tendencies in the Muslim world. Rather than acting as an isolated cluster of deviant religious usurpers, the al-Qaeda network represents part of a tendency within a transnational Salafi social movement community. Members of this community believe that over centuries of religious practice, errant Muslims introduced new practices and innovations that corrupted the pure message of Islam. To rectify this condition, Salafis advocate a strict return to the fundamentals of the religion and reject any behavior that was not specifically supported or enjoined by the Prophet Muhammad. Bin Laden and others like him are part of this broad community.

Despite the shared ideological orientation of Salafis, however, there is a dramatic division within the community over the issue of tactics to be used in the promotion and implementation of Salafi doctrine. On the one hand, reformist Salafis argue that violence is religiously prohibited and counterproductive given the realities of the international balance of power. Instead, reformists advocate personal and community religious transformation through lessons, sermons, education, and other instruments of *da'wa* (propagation). "Jihadi" Salafis, on the other hand, believe not only that violent struggle is religiously sanctioned but also that it is an individual obligation and the responsibility of all Muslims. The differences between the two blocs are exacerbated by the decentralized structure of the movement and its lack of central authority, creating centrifugal tendencies toward community fragmentation.

This chapter outlines the basis of the Salafi social movement community and highlights the schism between reformists and jihadis. Rather than perpetuate the rather unhelpful assumption that Bin Laden and al-Qaeda are "outside" Islam, the chapter focuses on the commonalities and conflicts that characterize intra-Salafi relations and networks. It thus offers a more nuanced understanding of violent Islamist contentions by contextualizing the September 11 perpetrators and their al-Qaeda supporters as part of a broader Salafi community that encompasses both violent and nonviolent tendencies.

The Salafi Social Movement Community

Social movement research has long emphasized the importance of formal social movement organizations (SMOs) for contention.[1] SMOs are seen as viable and enduring crucibles for contention, capable of collectivizing what might otherwise remain individualized grievances and ideological orientations. They provide formal institutionalization, leadership, mobilizing structures, and a division of labor through bureaucratic organization. These factors, in turn, make a movement more efficient and effective. While recognizing the role played by social networks and informality, particularly in movement recruitment, most studies focus on movements organized around SMOs.

This emphasis on formality is replicated in the study of Islamic activism. While appreciating the importance of social relationships and networks in Muslim societies, research is characterized by its focus on formal Islamic SMOs. Highly visible and organized movements such as the Muslim Brotherhood, for example, have dominated the study of Islamism. Although rooted in social relationships and community networks, the Muslim Brotherhood and other formally constituted Islamic groups rely extensively upon formal institutions characterized by hierarchy, institutionalized rules for decision making and collective action, and structured leadership. Islamist SMOs include cultural societies, charitable organizations, and political parties. In addition to the creation of Islamist SMOs, formally constituted groups also frequently usurp what Charles Kurzman terms "potential resources"—nonmovement organizational resources that are "captured" rather than produced by the movement itself (1994). Prominent examples include the use of professional syndicates, nonmovement unions, student and faculty associations, and community mosques.

But not all Islamists belong to formal organizations. Many instead rely more extensively upon social networks and informal institutions, including prayer circles, study groups, religious lessons, friendship activities, and so on. Such "micromobilization contexts" foster group identity and solidarity while promoting particular Islamist interpretations and mobilizing contention. These informal settings and their underlying social networks constitute what Stephen Buechler describes as a "social movement community" (SMC)—an organizational pattern "comprised of informal networks of politicized participants who are active in promoting the goals of a social movement outside the boundaries of formal organization" (1993, 61). SMCs are characterized by fluid boundaries between networked individuals permeated by dynamic and shifting patterns of interaction. The formation of an SMC certainly does not mitigate the importance of supportive SMOs; it instead places an emphasis on network-based activism rather than formal institutions. For Islamist groups rooted in SMCs, formal organizations often serve more as forums for networking or instruments for the dissemination of meaning than as authoritative representatives of the entire community.

While some Salafis belong to formal organizations, the movement as a whole is better characterized as an SMC rooted in a particular understanding of religious interpretation. The term "Salafi" derives from the Arabic *salaf*, which means "to precede" and refers to the companions of the Prophet Muhammad, who learned about Islam directly from the messenger of God or those who knew him. Because of the companions' connection to the Prophet and the divine revelations, Salafis believe that these men enjoyed a pure understanding of the religion. Subsequent understandings, Salafis argue, were sullied and distorted by the introduction of innovations (*bid'a*) and the development of schisms in the Muslim community, which pulled the community of the faithful away from the straight path of Islam. Deviations occurred with the passage of time and were reinforced by the syncretic incorporation of local customs as Islam spread to other cultural settings outside the Arabian Peninsula. Popular practices, such as celebrating the Prophet's birthday, visiting the tombs of saints, and various Sufi rituals, are decried by Salafis as un-Islamic deviations that threaten the purity of the message as revealed by the Prophet. The goal of the Salafi movement is to eradicate these innovations by returning to the pure form of Islam practiced by the Prophet and his companions.

As a consequence, the purpose of the movement is not instrumental achievement of materialist or political goals; rather, Salafis seek to promote postmaterialist religious transformation by generating "networks of shared meaning" that connect like-minded Muslims together in a community of true believers.[2] Similar to many new social movements, the Salafis are attempting to build new identities and alternative norms that challenge dominant cultural codes, and in so doing they create an "imagined community" and networks of activists determined to reproduce and expand a particular interpretation of Islam.[3] Such networks—and the formation of a Salafi SMC—bypass traditional rule-making institutions, such as tribes or states, by creating endogenously produced sets of understandings about individual behavior and social interactions. Predicated upon Salafi ideology, the diffusion of these values through expanded networks of shared meaning creates self-motivated individuals who live according to a Salafi *manhaj* (method), at times irrespective of alternative, legally binding sets of rules or laws. This *manhaj* constitutes the ideological moorings that bond Salafis together in a social movement community; it is intended to purify Islam by guiding Muslims to base all their decisions and actions in life on direct evidence from the sources of the religion—the Quran and Sunna (path or traditions of the Prophet Muhammad). The *manhaj* includes several central components shared by all Salafis.[4]

Focus on Authentic Hadiths
Concerned that inaccurate or fabricated hadiths infected the purity of the reported Sunna of the Prophet, Salafis tend to accept only *sahih* (sound) hadiths in which the narrative transmission (*isnad*) of the Prophet's behavior is considered to be unbroken and reliable. Over time, less reliable

hadiths inevitably made their way into mainstream usage, including a large number of forgeries. For Salafis, this state of affairs is unacceptable, since following the lessons from forgeries or inaccurate hadiths is tantamount to following a path other than the straight path of Islam. As a result, some of the best-known Salafi scholars, such as the late Muhammad Nasir al-Din al-Bani (d. 1999) are internationally renowned for their research and efforts in authenticating hadiths. Such a process purifies the religion and supports a true understanding of the prophetic model. Salafis often refer to themselves as *ahl al-hadith* (the people of hadith).

Reverence for Tawhid *and Avoidance of* Shirk

A central component of Salafi ideology is a rigid adherence to *tawhid*—belief in the oneness of God. This includes (1) a belief that God is the only true *rabb*, or lord, (2) a literalist understanding of the attributes of God mentioned in the Quran (though they are beyond the realm of human understanding) as opposed to metaphorical or anthropomorphic interpretations, and (3) a belief that only God can be worshipped. This last belief leads to the rejection of many popular practices, such as praying to saints as intermediaries between Muslims and God, something Salafis argue is blatant *shirk* (ascribing partners to God).

Avoidance of Bidʿa

Salafis argue that because the Quran and Sunna reveal the perfection of Islam, any innovations (*bidʿa*) that deviate from these two sources represent non-Islamic beliefs and practices, and thus heresy. If an action is not enjoined by the Quran or Sunna, then it is considered un-Islamic. As a result, many Salafis adopt particular dress codes, replicating the prophetic model and rejecting the adoption of Western-style clothing. In the more radical manifestation of this attitude (held by only a small minority), Salafis reject modernity itself. Since the Quran is silent about many contemporary issues, Salafis tend to rely more extensively upon the Sunna as a model for avoiding innovations.

Rejection of Madhhabs

For Salafis, there is only one correct understanding of Islam—that which was revealed through the Quran and Sunna. These immutable and perfect sources of religion represent *the* straight path of Islam. As a result, the division of Islamic jurisprudence into separate schools or methods (*madhhabs*) is unacceptable to Salafis. If God perfected religion through the divine revelations of the Quran and the example of the Prophet, there can be only one correct interpretation of Islam. From a Salafi perspective, following a *madhhab* without searching for direct evidence constitutes blind adherence (*taqlid*), which leads Muslims astray. Despite their rejection of *madhhabs*, however, the literalist nature of Salafi ideology tends to make the Salafi movement resemble the Hanbali *madhhab*.

Rather than relying upon SMOs to reproduce their *manhaj* and expand the Salafi network of shared meaning, Salafis have created a broad social movement community predicated upon an assortment of mechanisms for the transmission of knowledge. The dominant instrument for this transmission is the student-teacher relationship, which represents the most important social tie in the Salafi community. Because the Salafi movement is based upon the sponsorship and dissemination of a particular *manhaj*, student-teacher ties are a primary conduit for the movement message and a nexus between different individuals and groups. This relationship is also a source of network expansion. As more students are incorporated into lessons, meetings, and informal interactions with teachers, they learn more about the *manhaj*, and the network of shared meaning expands. Other common informal mechanisms include study circles formed to discuss publications by various Salafi scholars, *khutbas* (sermons), and informal meetings. Where Salafi SMOs are active, they are typically devoted to "cultural" activities intended to promote the Salafi *manhaj*, especially to publication offerings. Salafi organizations are decentralized and usually represent clusters of individuals operating at the local level (though there are some instances of larger, more broadly based organizations). As a result, they do not function as authoritative decision-making centers intended to direct the entire movement. Formal SMOs can help reproduce the movement message, but networks of shared meaning are predominantly created through personal interactions and in informal settings where interpretive codes are transmitted.

Intramovement Conflict

Social movements are not monolithic entities. They are represented by a variety of actors and perspectives, none of which are coterminous with the entire movement. While cooperation among these actors is common, so too is conflict. Though there is usually a consensus about the general basics of the movement's ideology or other such relevant issues, there are frequent disagreements about specifics and plans of action, creating diversity and multivocality. As Mayer Zald and John McCarthy argue, "Whether we study revolutionary movements, broad or narrow social reform movements, or religious movements, we find a variety of SMOs or groups, linked to various segments of supporting constituencies (both institutional and individual), competing among themselves for resources and symbolic leadership, sharing facilities and resources at other times, developing stable and differentiated functions, occasionally merging into ad hoc coalitions, and occasionally engaging in all-out war against each other" (1987, 161).

The Salafi movement reflects the pattern of differentiation that Zald and McCarthy describe. Within the community, there is a shared consensus about the *manhaj* that produces a certain degree of "cognitive closure," whereby core beliefs are no longer subject to questioning (Gerlach and Hine 1970, 161). However, the segmented, reticulated, and multiheaded structure of the community has engendered multiple sources of authority with differing perspectives about the "correct" Salafi understanding of religious practice and behavior. Unlike in formal movements, such as the Muslim Brotherhood, leadership and authority in an SMC are not predicated upon institutional positions and roles. There is no organizational president or spiritual guide. Instead, recognition of a scholar or leader is informally bestowed by groups of Salafis within the community as the individual develops a reputation through lessons, religious rulings, and social interactions.

The process of recognition, however, is a subjective process of individual assessment and reputation formation that leads to the emergence of multiple sources of authority. Individual Salafis do not agree as to a hierarchy of scholars, and in many instances they shift allegiances from one scholar to another. This creates a degree of competition among scholars—each seeking to gain a broader audience and a stronger reputation—that frequently manifests itself in polemics and personal attacks intended to undermine the legitimacy of others. These interactions take on heightened religious sensitivity, because Salafis believe that there is only one accurate religious truth as revealed by the Prophet Muhammad. As a result, in disagreements, only one scholar (if any) can be judged to have the "correct" understanding. The lack of centralized leadership in the Salafi movement thus creates a fluid dynamic vulnerable to fragmentation and intramovement disagreements.

In movements whose various actors share a common ideological perspective such as the Salafi movement, intramovement competition often occurs over tactical considerations.[5] Motivated by a common ideology, movement actors frequently diverge over how to achieve group objectives and social transformation. There are many possible solutions to any given movement concern, and the multiplicity of choices creates the possibility of tactical differentiation and fragmentation within the movement. This frequently takes the form of splits between "moderates," who seek gradual change through nonviolent means, and a smaller group of "militants," who espouse violence as a mechanism for rapid success.

Among Salafis, the most prevalent intramovement conflict is a debate about the use of violence as a tactic for religious transformation, and this debate has fragmented the Salafi community into two major groupings.[6] Jihadis, such as Bin Laden, believe in waging a jihad against the United States (as well as Muslim governments viewed as "un-Islamic"), and they consciously implement the Salafi *manhaj* by locating religious evidence to legitimize particular conflicts, actions, and decisions.[7] In contrast, reformist Salafis prioritize less violent tactics of reform such as preaching, publication, and lessons. Tactical differences between these two groups have engendered a vitriolic conflict over the permissibility of jihad that has fractured the movement since the conclusion of the war against the Soviet Union in Afghanistan. The Afghan experience radicalized Arab Salafi *mujahidin* (holy fighters), who attempted to export the religious justification for war to new contexts and enemies. Reform-oriented Salafis, on the other hand, mobilized to condemn broader military actions by Muslim fighters. Reformists propose instead that a focused effort to promote Salafi thought needs be made before launching a jihad, which would become appropriate only at a much later point.

The members of the two Salafi groups repeatedly denounce one another and challenge the Salafi "credentials" of their opponents within the movement. Through the Internet, an assortment of publications, and public pronouncements, jihadis and reformists lash out at one another and charge their opponents with deviations from the straight path of Islam. Reformists frequently call the jihadis "modern Kharijites" (the Kharijites were the earliest Islamic sect) and "Qutubis" (followers of Sayyid Qutb) in an attempt to delegitimize jihadi Salafi interpretations.[8] Such delegitimations also frequently include challenges to the scholarly credentials of jihadi leaders, who are declared ignorant and unknowledgeable. In an interview with the author, for example, the prominent reformist scholar Salim al-Hilali adamantly dismissed the relevance of Abu Qatadah, the radical jihadi shaykh considered to be one of the most important scholars of the al-Qaeda network (Amman, Jordan, April 2, 1997). Based in London, Abu Qatadah served as a prominent spiritual leader of the Armed Islamic Group in Algeria until the outbreak of civilian massacres in the mid- and late 1990s, and his influence has reached a number of radical

Salafis throughout the world. Hilali's dismissal was based upon his rejection of Abu Qatadah's interpretation of jihad, which Hilali considers to be an ignorant misreading of the religious sources.

Jihadis themselves often denounce reformist opponents as the "shaykhs of authority," implying an insidious connection between regime sponsorship or largesse and reformist opposition to violence. Reformists are often framed as regime instruments, bought to protect immoral regimes from the wrath of true Muslims. Jihadis have also charged that prominent reformists, including al-Bani, are ignorant of current affairs and thus ill equipped to issue edicts and judge the permissibility of jihad, even if they hold respectable understandings of the religion in general. At least a few jihadis have even gone so far as to decry senior Saudi Salafis as traitors and apostates.

As Salafis act to promote a network of shared meaning, there is profound disagreement over interpretations of tactics and jihad. This disagreement—and the resulting fragmentation—is exacerbated by the decentralized nature of network-based activism, since there is no coordinated authority capable of imposing interpretations or standards. Individual scholars enjoy their own followings, and because they hold that there is only one correct understanding on any given point, each frequently believes his interpretation represents the straight path while all others reflect ignorance and a lack of religious knowledge. As a result, the community speaks with multiple voices, especially when it comes to violence.

Salafis and the Afghan Experience

Prior to the war in Afghanistan, there was very little discussion in the Muslim world about the contemporary use of violence and jihad in Islam. Certainly, small radical groups such as Islamic Jihad produced material that justified assassination and other forms of violence, but these justifications were rejected by most Islamists, and they remained limited in number and reach.[9] The war in Afghanistan, however, led both states (for example, Saudi Arabia) and individual Islamists to focus more extensively on finding a religious justification for a contemporary war that could both facilitate Muslim support and mobilize volunteers to combat the Soviet Union.

During the initial stages of the war, the small Arab contingent that went to fight encountered difficulty soliciting volunteers from the Middle East. At least in part, the reluctance to volunteer was due to many Arab

Muslims' strong belief that any military efforts should be directed toward combating the Israeli presence in the Palestinian territories and Jerusalem. Radicals, moreover, wanted to first focus on fighting incumbent Arab regimes. The difficulty of finding volunteers was compounded by the fact that, because classical Muslim debates on warfare had predominantly focused on *jus in bello* (legitimate means in warfare) rather than *jus ad bellum* (grounds for warfare), there were few recent publications about the appropriate religious justifications for a contemporary war such as the one in Afghanistan.

The call to "join the caravan" in Afghanistan, however, grew with the financial support of Gulf countries and the efforts of "Arab Afghans," who believed the war was a religious obligation. Organizations based in Saudi Arabia and Kuwait, in particular, championed the call to arms and funded an array of *madrasas* (religious schools) and training camps in Pakistan for Arab volunteers. Their backing also included support for local organizations such as Ahl-i-Hadith in Pakistan and Afghanistan, which set up an array of Salafi-oriented *madrasas* and actively recruited Salafi fighters from Gulf countries. These local spiritual and military training centers helped sponsor the spread of the Salafi *manhaj* among newly recruited Arab volunteers; these socializing institutions heavily influenced the religious understanding of thousands of Arab volunteers from non-Gulf countries, especially Algeria and Egypt, who eventually returned to their homes indoctrinated in Salafi thought and determined to lead Muslim uprisings against Arab regimes.[10] The spread of Salafi thought through local religious institutions was reinforced by the participation of Saudi-based Salafi *mujahidin*, who comprised the largest national grouping of Arab fighters in the war.[11] Salafi organizations and groups such as Abu Sayyaf and Jama'at al-Da'wa used their ideological affinity with Gulf contributors to raise millions of dollars for Salafi operations.[12]

The underlying religious justification for Arab participation in the war was constructed by 'Abdullah 'Azzam, a Palestinian graduate of al-Azhar University who resurrected the call to jihad that attracted thousands of volunteers from the Middle East. Salafi jihadis view Azzam as a cornerstone of the contemporary jihad movement, and his writings have heavily influenced conceptions of *jus ad bellum* and the obligations of jihad among Salafis. His ideational influence was supported by his strategic location in the international networks that supported the *mujahidin*, a position that was augmented by his leadership at the Islamic Coordination Council in Peshawar, which provided social services for the *mujahidin* and served as the dispatcher for Arab volunteers. ʿAzzam was eventually assassinated by a car bomb in Peshawar in 1989 and is considered a martyr in the jihad movement.

In his legitimation for a jihad in Afghanistan, ʿAzzam outlined two kinds of jihads against the unbelievers. The first is an offensive attack made in enemy territory when the enemy is not gathering to attack Muslims; it has the minimum goal of establishing strong borders and occasionally sending armies to harass the unbelievers. According to ʿAzzam, this type of jihad is a collective responsibility (*fard kifaya*), meaning that if any one group performs the task, other Muslims are absolved of the responsibility of carrying it out. The second type of jihad against unbelievers is a defensive jihad to protect Muslim territory and populations. The religious obligation for such a jihad is an individual obligation (*fard ʿayn*) that is incumbent upon all Muslims and equal to other religious duties such as the five pillars of the faith. The obligation initially falls to those Muslims who are nearest to the enemy. If that group cannot effectively defeat the enemy, then the obligation expands to the next closest group of Muslims. The geographic proximity for obligatory participation expands as it becomes clear that the enemy cannot be effectively defeated under current conditions. If too few Muslims participate in the jihad to repel the enemy, then the entire Muslim community is in sin. The jihad in Afghanistan was clearly delineated by Azzam as an invasion of Muslim territory by a force of unbelievers, and thus it resonated with many Muslims in the Arab world as a just jihad.[13]

Azzam's legitimation of Muslim participation in the Afghan war enjoyed broad support in Muslim countries, where leaders and Islamic activists alike condoned the argument for jihad. Radical Islamists, in particular, rejoiced at the opportunity to resurrect jihad as an essential component of religious duty. This sentiment is encapsulated in a statement made by Omar Abdul Rahman, a Salafi spiritual leader currently serving a life sentence in the United States for his involvement in the 1993 World Trade Center bombing: "When the Afghans rose and declared a jihad—and jihad had been dead for the longest time—I can't tell you how proud I was" (Rubin 1995, 187). Azzam's call for jihad informs current Salafi jihadi arguments and structures understandings about the obligation of jihad.

Transnationalizing Jihad beyond Afghanistan

The call for a defensive jihad to protect Muslim populations continued to resonate with Salafi jihadis long after the Soviets withdrew from Afghanistan, and the Salafi Arab Afghans searched for new venues of combat. They argued that despite the liberation of Afghanistan from the Soviet Union, war in defense of Islam still remained an individual obligation because Muslim populations remained oppressed by unbelievers around the globe, even in the Middle East. Jihad was thus viewed as an ongoing process of Muslim liberation on a global level, what could be called an obligatory "nomadic jihad" (Roy 1999).

Shortly after the fall of Kabul in the war in Afghanistan, Arab Salafis considered waging a jihad in the Philippines or Kashmir as part of the individual responsibility to protect Muslim countries and populations, but the sense of urgency produced by ethnic cleansing in Bosnia in 1992–95 redirected efforts toward the former Yugoslav republic. Abu ʿAbd al-ʿAziz (nicknamed Barbarossa because of his red beard) consulted with famous Salafi scholars, including Muhammad Nasir al-Din al-Bani, ʿAbd al-ʿAziz bin Baz, and Muhammad bin ʿUthman, who agreed that the war in Bosnia had become an individual obligation. Al-ʿAziz led a new group of Salafi fighters into Bosnia that was initially comprised of nomadic jihadis based in Afghanistan and Pakistan. As Arab regimes increased their repression of radical Islamists, especially in Egypt and Algeria, the nomadic jihadis were joined by other radical Salafis who sought to escape domestic intelligence services. Still others joined the fight to enhance and practice their combat skills before returning to the Middle East.

The new jihad was supported by Salafi missionary work, funded primarily by Saudi Arabia and other Gulf countries; the missionary funding included assistance for local religious centers to promote Salafi publications and ideology. The Travnik Islamic Center, in particular, received funding and Islamic books and eventually recommended a booklet to its visitors titled *Ideas We Have to Correct* that was published by the Salafi missionary Committee for Bosnia-Herzegovina of the Kuwait Organization for the Rebirth of the Islamic Tradition.[14]

The next battle in the nomadic jihad took place in Chechnya, embroiling the Russians in combat against Bin Laden's associates and others in the Salafi global network. Although the uprising in Chechnya initially adopted an Islamic identity as a way of unifying against the Russians (similar to the Algerian strategy of mobilization in the revolution against the French), Salafis soon joined the war and attempted to promote their stricter variant of Islam. Chechnya quickly became a beacon for Salafis seeking to continue the defensive jihad, and battle-hardened Arab detachments from Afghanistan, Bosnia, Pakistan, and elsewhere joined the fighting in the mid-1990s.

The rapid influx of Arab fighters challenged the hegemony of local religious leaders and created friction among different Muslim groups in

Chechnya, especially as the fighting diminished. In a region where Sufi practices predominate, the Salafi ideology of the Arab *mujahidin* directly contradicted local understandings of Islam and fomented tensions between Chechens and their Arab allies. Ahmad Khadzhu Kadryov, the mufti of Chechnay-Ichkeria, explains: "Detachments of Wahhabi [Salafi] volunteers from Arab countries came to us during the war in Chechnya. These detachments were very well armed, and for this reason our Chechens also readily joined them. Many of them [Chechens] were introduced to this teaching and began to attempt to teach us, maintaining that we were distorting Islam."[15] Dialogue between the Chechen religious leaders and the Salafi fighters was unsuccessful, leading to factional clashes and internal conflict.

The forced Russian withdrawal from Chechnya further emboldened Salafi jihadis, who exported the revolution to neighboring Dagestan. Reports of a Salafi presence in Dagestan had begun to emerge as early as the beginning of perestroika, when preachers from the Arab world first came to the area. This early presence was reinforced by the influx of young Dagestanis educated in Salafi-controlled *madrasas*, who were given cash incentives and encouraged to return to Dagestan. Groups of Salafis from Dagestan who had fought in Chechnya returned to their homes in 1996 and made it clear that they intended to create an Islamic state. One young Salafi from Dagestan defiantly commented: "The Chechens defeated the Russians. It is now our turn to fight for an Islamic State."[16] The fight was supported by Mullah Bagauddin, the spiritual leader of the Salafi movement in Dagestan, who initially announced that Dagestan would remain in Russia, but only if Russia became an Islamic state. Growing nationalist sentiments prompted increased Russian intervention, and Salafis mobilized for jihad under the leadership of a Jordanian Arab Afghan named Khattab, who had been instrumental in the war in Chechnya. After the war, he built blood relations with Dagestanis by marrying a woman from the mountain village of Karamacki, which subsequently became a center for Salafi activity and proclaimed itself an independent imamate in 1998.[17] Over a number of years, Khattab and radical Salafis established a Salafi base in the central region of Dagestan that came to be widely known as "Little Chechnya."[18]

The nomadic jihad was expanded to a variety of other countries and regions as well, including Uzbekistan, Tajikistan, the Philippines, Macedonia, western China, and Kosovo. In effect, wherever Salafis identified an oppressed Muslim population, the jihad became an individual obligation. There were certainly priorities, such as Bosnia and Chechnya, but the Salafi jihadi movement spawned myriad radical groups intent on defending the Muslim community through violence in multiple geographic locations. Azzam's original call to defend the Muslim community in Afghanistan was used to extend the jihad indefinitely, moving the nomadic jihad into new countries to face infidel oppression. This movement, in turn, created a vast international network of Salafi jihadis, many of whom joined Bin Laden and al-Qaeda.

Jihad at Home

While large contingents of Salafis joined the nomadic jihad, a substantial portion of Arab Afghans returned to their home countries in the 1990s to lead Islamic revolutions against regimes in the Middle East. But unlike the resilient support among Salafis for a defensive jihad against the Soviet invasion, support for such radical endeavors was more ambiguous, since it constituted uprisings against regimes that many Muslims accepted as at least nominally Islamic. Since Islam explicitly rejects rebellion against Muslim leaders, Salafi jihadis faced a potential theological obstacle in legitimating violent actions at home.

Given this prohibition, Salafis had to construct a discourse that demonstrated that Arab leaders and regimes were no longer Muslim, thus opening possibilities for the jihad. To do so, they drew upon the writings of the medieval scholar Taqi al-Din Ahmad Ibn Taymiyya, whose unique contribution to Salafi thought was his elaboration of the concept of jihad (Voll 1991, 353–54). He lived during the Crusades and the Mongol invasions, and it was the latter experience that shaped his interpretation of jihad. As the Mongols conquered Muslim societies, they were exposed to Islam and eventually converted. The dilemma faced by Islamic scholars when the Mongols converted was whether the war against them could still be considered a jihad or whether it had become a war between two Muslim entities, in which case it was no longer a jihad. In his fatwa about the Mongols, Ibn Taymiyya recognized that the Mongols practiced the pillars of the faith but questioned whether this made them true Muslims. The dominant interpretation was that the shari'a (Islamic law) considered such groups Muslim, regardless of their actions, because they fulfilled the basic Muslim obligations. Ibn Taymiyya introduced a new criterion for evaluating the question. He argued that, regardless of whether a person follows the basics of the faith, if an individual fails to uphold any aspect of the shari'a, that person is no longer to be considered a Muslim. Such people became *kafirs* (unbelievers), because they embraced Islam but through their actions left the faith.[19]

The act of declaring Middle Eastern regimes heretical frames their leaders as un-Islamic rulers who enforce their power and control over Muslim societies, and thus it plays to defensive understandings of jihad. Jihadi discourse goes even further and argues that Western influence over Arab governments through foreign assistance, International Monetary Fund loans, military connections, and political alignments renders these governments "puppets" of the West and its "Zionist" allies in the Middle East. Arab regimes are thus considered to be the functional equivalent of foreign occupiers, and this perspective legitimates a jihad against them in defense of Islam. In Algeria, for example, Islamist rebels went to considerable effort to frame the government as a French surrogate intent on preventing society from fully realizing its Islamic potential. The military hierarchy, in particular, was singled out as *hizb Faransa* (the party of France). Radical Salafis decry other rulers as well, including those in Egypt and Saudi Arabia, as instruments of Western imperialism who are determined to undermine Muslim society. Saudi Arabia's decision to allow American troops into the kingdom during the Gulf War is considered evidence of such connections. Even the Yemeni government, which had for a long time distanced itself from strong relations with the West, was charged with acting as a tool of American interests when it allowed U.S. forces to operate in Yemen in the 1990s.

In issuing such serious charges, jihadi Salafis have decentralized *takfir* (the act of declaring someone an apostate). Whereas in the past, decisions about whether someone had left Islam were predominantly made centrally by religious authorities and shariʿa courts often tied to the state, radical Salafis have adopted *takfir* as a flexible weapon to use against an assortment of individuals, institutions, and regimes deemed un-Islamic by Salafi standards. The ambiguity in such standards is that it is unclear where the threshold for jihad lies. Some radical groups argue that any single transgression can constitute apostasy, and thus they employ *takfir* with reckless abandon, even while Salafis themselves struggle to emulate the pristine model of the Prophet. Under such circumstances, *takfir* becomes a weapon selectively wielded to legitimize attacks against those deemed to be obstacles to Salafi thought and activism. In addition, individual Salafi groups, some with little expertise in the study of the Hadith, have adapted the defensive legitimation of jihad without the sufficient evidence demanded by the Salafi *manhaj*.

The decentralization of *takfir* and its violent consequences became readily apparent during the civil war that plagued Algeria in the 1990s.[20] The initial call to jihad was launched in response to the cancellation of election results in January 1992, when the Islamic Salvation Front (FIS) was poised to control parliament. The subsequent crackdown on the Islamic movement and the concomitant repression of Islamist leaders and grassroots activities were framed by the Salafis as a war against Islam waged by a French surrogate in Algeria, and various groups and tendencies within the movement mobilized for what was viewed as a defensive jihad directed against the incumbent regime.

The shared understanding about legitimate targets, however, quickly disintegrated with the emergence of the Armed Islamic Group (GIA), which distinguished itself from other Islamic groups through its willingness to use extreme forms of violence. While the GIA initially included both jihadi Salafis and Algerianists (members of more nationalist-oriented Islamic groups) in an attempt to foster a unified front against the regime, cooperation soon disintegrated over doctrinal issues. In 1994, Salafis in the GIA moved against the Algerianists, killing 140, including prominent Islamist figures such as Muhammad al-Said and ʿAbd al-Razzak Radjam. The carnage consolidated the dominance of the Salafi tendency within the loose organizational structure of the GIA, which was in reality an amalgamation of Salafi groups with varying levels of doctrinal adherence.[21]

The decentralization of *takfir* led a number of GIA groups to frame civilian populations as legitimate targets in the jihad, leading to massacres during the mid-1990s. In 1996, Antar Zouabri became the emir of the GIA and inaugurated his new leadership with a fatwa that condemned anyone who did not directly assist the GIA. In a distorted adoption of the "defensive" jihad argument, Zouabri claimed that ordinary villagers were tacitly supporting the regime and thus were on the offensive against Islam. The GIA argued that such behavior made the citizens apostates and thus shariʿa-sanctioned targets of jihad. Ibn Taymiyya's argument was in this way extended to include jihad as defense against a population viewed as un-Islamic because it did not actively rise up in support of the GIA. Oftentimes, GIA factions killed the populations of entire villages with machetes and other handheld weapons; they are estimated to have killed tens of thousands of innocent civilians in the massacres.[22]

Other civilian targets of the GIA jihad included the media, schools, and foreign nationals. The media was framed as merely an extension of the regime and thus an offensive tool for the repression of Islam. In a communiqué issued in 1995, the GIA clearly articulated this view: "The rot-ten apostate regime did not stop using the mercenary media to cover its crimes and rationalize its aggression. This has turned all written, seen, and heard media outlets into a tool of aggression spreading lies and rumors."[23] Similar criteria were used to justify attacks against schools. Since most schools in Algeria are controlled by the state, the GIA reasoned that they were un-Islamic institutions designed to support an unbeliever regime. The GIA claimed that "according to the sharia, one is not allowed to work in establishments which belong to the government or its allies," especially in schools where the curriculum is "contrary to Islam."[24] In the last two months of 1994, 30 schoolteachers and school directors were killed and 538 schools suffered arson attacks. By the end of 1994, GIA factions had assassinated 142 teachers. Foreign nationals were viewed as agents sent to undermine the jihad and Islam. Missionaries were killed by GIA factions, including 7 French Trappist monks who were beheaded in 1996 in a brutal display of violence. In all of these cases, GIA factions paid lip service to the defensive legitimation as it had been adapted from the call to arms in Afghanistan.

Despite condemnations from other Salafi jihadis, who charged that factions of the GIA had transgressed and misapplied Islamic principles in massacring civilian populations, the decentralization of *takfir* led ultraviolent GIA factions to continue their reign of terror. Omar Abu Qatadah (a former spiritual guide for the GIA living in the United Kingdom), Muhammad Mustafa al-Muqri' (identified as the leading candidate to succeed Omar 'Abd al-Rahman as spiritual leader of the Gamiyya Islamiyya in Egypt), and other jihadi Salafi personalities withdrew their support for the group once the scope of the violence became clear (Qatadah associate, interview by the author, Amman, Jordan, 1996). Even Osama bin Laden allegedly decried the GIA's actions, preferring instead to support a new Salafi movement founded by former GIA commander Hasan Hattab and called "the Salafi Group for Call and Combat." In May 1998, Bin Laden gave Qamar al-Din Kharban, leader of the Algerian Afghans, funds to mobilize support for al-Qaeda through the European networks. Testifying in a trial in Tizi Ouzou, Muhammad Barashid, an emir close to Hattab, claimed that Bin Laden promised logistical and financial support for the new movement because he felt that the GIA had "strayed," and it is rumored that Bin Laden suggested the name for the new Salafi group.[25]

Differences among Salafi jihadis in Algeria over the issues of *takfir* and proper conduct in warfare accelerated at the end of the 1990s, leading to the creation of spin-off movements and splinter groups. Disagreements about the permissibility of killing civilians, in particular, led to serious intra-Salafi clashes, with various groups charging others with heresy. *Takfir* was thus utilized even within the Salafi movement to decry groups with divergent views of jihad. In addition to Hattab's new movement, other Salafi-based groups emerged to combat the GIA and brand them as heretics, including the "Islamic Movement for Spreading the Faith and Holy War" and the "Faithful to the Oath." These groups promised to continue a legitimate defensive jihad against the regime while concurrently combating the GIA and its atrocities. The jihad at home, initially a unified assault on the regime, was derailed by the decentralization of *takfir*, leading to violence against broader publics and within the Salafi jihadi community itself.

Although the Algerian civil war provides a stark case study of Salafi violence and the decentralization of *takfir*, it is certainly not the only example of a "jihad at home." In Yemen, for example, Salafis operating in Aden launched a violent struggle against the regime and "un-Islamic behaviors" in society. This assault included an attempt to impose control over the city and an attack on shrines at the Hashemite mosque in 1994 as well as an assortment of other violent clashes with government troops, many in 1998.[26] Former Arab Afghan fighters announced the formation of the Militant Islamic Group, allegedly a Salafi-based group operating in the northeastern and northwestern parts of Libya that reportedly clashed with Qaddafi's forces during the 1990s. In Jordan, several violent Salafi groups emerged in the late 1980s and the 1990s, including groups linked to internationally renowned jihadi Salafis such as Osama bin Laden, Abu Qatadah, and Abu Muhammad al-Maqdisi, a Palestinian living in Jordan who served as a spiritual inspiration for the November 1995 bombing in Riyadh, Saudi Arabia, that killed five Americans and two Indian nationals.[27] And in Egypt, the Salafi-inspired Gamiyya Islamiyya waged a low-intensity conflict against the Mubarak regime throughout the 1990s that claimed more than thirteen hundred lives.

The Reformist Counterdiscourse on Jihad

Despite the increasing popularity of rhetoric condoning a nomadic jihad or a jihad at home against un-Islamic regimes, the transnational Salafi movement is not unified in its view of violence. Within the Salafi community, there are strong dissenting voices that represent a counterdiscourse about jihad that is related to jihadi thought in its sources of inspiration but differs in emphasis and interpretation. These differences represent an internal battle about the discourse of jihad and legitimate warfare, as each side mobilizes rhetoric, evidence, and scholars on behalf of its cause.

For reformist Salafis, there is great concern that the Muslim community is not ready to engage in jihad against either incumbent Arab regimes or the United States. It is not that jihad is rejected as a tactic of religious transformation; rather, reformists believe that several prior phases need to be passed through before a jihad is permissible.[28] The central contention of the reformist counterdiscourse on jihad is that unless Muslims follow the straight path of Islam and the Salafi *manhaj*, they will be unable to engage in a successful jihad, since God rewards only the true believers. A lack of effective Salafi propagation and concomitant divisions within the Muslim community creates weakness that will prevent a successful jihad against Western countries, particularly the United States. Any premature movement toward the use of violence is therefore doomed to fail. In fact, a few well-known reformists have recently used Afghanistan as an example of failure, not success. They argue that after the Soviets were expelled, the Muslims fell into disarray and experienced factional clashes and rifts in a civil war that reflected divisions and a lack of unity in the Salafi *manhaj*. Afghanistan's Muslims, the reformists conclude, were spiritually unprepared to engage in a jihad.[29]

The Salafis' weakness and inability to engage in an effective jihad is perceived to stem from several sources. First, reformist Salafis believe that the Muslim community remains divided, weak, and astray from the Salafi *manhaj*. As a result, it cannot prepare for jihad properly, because it lacks the spiritual preparation. In a debate between Muhammad Nasir al-Din al-Bani, one of the most well-known and respected reformist Salafis, and a member of the Egyptian Islamic Jihad, al-Bani complained, "We notice the mujahids [those who actively take part in a jihad] call for whatever of the Muslims to join the fight, and when they go to fight they find disagreements among themselves in matters of their faith and the basics of Islam. How do these people get ready for jihad when they are yet to understand what is obligatory on them of aqida [articles of faith]?!"[30] Reformists believe that only when Muslims agree on the true faith, as understood in Salafi doctrine, will unity in jihad endure and Muslims remain united. It is only at such a point that triumph will become an inevitable reward from God for the community of the faithful.

Given the current context of unbelief, deviant religious practices, and weakness, the reformists believe that the first necessary stage on the path to righteous jihad involves *tarbiya* (education and cultivation to encourage proper Muslim practices) and *tasfiya* (purification). Change thus begins at the level of individual and personal transformation without the use of violence. The hope is that religious change will transform society through individuals who adopt the Salafi *manhaj*. As ʿAli Hasan al-Halabi, a former student of al-Bani, argues: "If the Muslims desire good, unity, and establishment upon the earth, then they should make their manners and behaviors like that of the Salaf of this *Ummah* and begin by changing themselves. However, he who is unable to change even himself, will not be able to change his family, not to mention changing the *Ummah*" (1995b, 16).

The reformists draw analogies to the early stages of divine revelation, when the focus of the Islamic mission was propagation rather than jihad. Today's society is likened to the early community of Muslims, who were surrounded by remnants of the *jahiliyya* (period of ignorance). During this initial period, Muhammad spent most of his time in preaching and *daʿwa* (calling people to Islam), rather than fighting. As al-Bani argues: "History repeats itself. Everybody claims that the Prophet is their role model. Our Prophet spent the first half of his message making daʿwa, and he did not start it with jihad."[31] Instead of waging war, reformists argue, Muslims should use the early model of the Prophet "and train the people to understand the correct Salafi doctrine, which is void of myths and heresies, and . . . teach them good morals, so that [they] can emerge with a broad base that embellishes this religion for human beings."[32] Jihad is thus viewed as the final stage of development that can be reached only after the Muslim community is unified and strong, certainly not the conditions that prevail today.

A second source of opposition to the use of violence among reformists derives from the belief that a premature jihad launched before the purification of the Muslim community is complete will engender harsh responses that could make even basic propagation difficult, a condition that is considered *haram* (religiously forbidden) by many Muslims. The necessity of engaging in actions that produce more good than harm derives from a general acceptance of the medieval Salafi scholar Ibn Qayyim al-Jawziyya's four levels of forbidding evil. According to al-Jawziyya, there are four possible consequences of any action: (1) the evil is replaced with something good, (2) the evil is diminished without ending completely, (3) the evil is replaced by an equivalent evil, and (4) the evil is replaced by an even greater evil. The first two are considered to be religiously acceptable, the third involves *ijtihad* (the exercise of independent judgment), and the fourth is forbidden (Halabi 1995a, 18–19). Reformist Salafis believe that the use of violence will prompt a pernicious response from state authorities, who would limit the capacity of the movement to promote its *manhaj*. As Salim al-Hilali, an internationally renowned reformist Salafi, argues, Muslims "should not say the state is un-Islamic and change it with force. Otherwise the mosques would be closed and scholars would be put in prison. Change in Islam must be for the better" (interview by the author, Amman, Jordan, April 2, 1997). Another Salafi scholar argues that "if you cannot achieve your objectives through jihad, then it is *haram*" (interview by the author, Amman, Jordan, 1997).

It is not that the reformist Salafis reject jihad; quite the contrary. They argue that in certain contexts it is a religious obligation, but that the time is not yet right, and the movement must focus first on more basic stages of religious propagation and purification. As a result, reformists have vehemently denounced the use of violence. The Saudi Salafi scholar Muhammad al-ʿUthaymin decries the use of unrest: "Let those who riot know that they only serve the enemies of Islam; the matter cannot be handled by uprising and excitement, but rather by wisdom" (quoted in Halabi 1995a, 2). Muhammad Nasir al-Din al-Bani warns: "The way to salvation is not, as some people imagine, to rise with arms against the rulers, and to conduct military coups. In addition to being among contemporary *bidʿas* (innovations), such actions disregard texts of Islam, among which is the command to change ourselves. Furthermore, it is imperative to establish the basis upon which the building will stand" (2). ʿAli Hasan al-Halabi adds: "Anyone who examines the past and present of *Islam* would clearly see that excessiveness has brought for the *Ummah* disasters, bloodshed, eviction, and harm that cannot be known to the full extent except by Allah. It suffices in this regard to remember the turmoils of the Khawaarij [Kharijites] and the advocates of *Takfir* from past to present" (3–4). The reference to the Kharijites, a sect that fomented rebellion and assassinated important leaders during the early years of Islam, is intended to equate the jihadis with what is generally viewed by many Muslims to have been a heretical group that undermined the stability of the Muslim world.

The reformists are well represented within Salafi communities in a variety of countries, creating transnational linkages. In Yemen, for example, Shaykh Muqbil Bin-Hadi al-Wadi'i runs an assortment of reform-oriented institutions and organizations designed to promote the Salafi *manhaj*. Al-Wadi'i studied Salafi thought for fifteen years while in Saudi Arabia before being deported to Yemen in the early 1980s for his alleged links to the radical Islamists who seized the Grand Mosque in 1979. He currently supervises major Salafi missionary centers in Sanaʿa, including the Damaj Center, Maaber Center, Mareb Center, al-Hudeida Center, and al-Khair

Mosque, all officially supported by the Holy Mosque Establishment, a charitable organization in Saudi Arabia (*Yemen Times*, July 17–21, 2000).

While there have been some rumors about a connection with Bin Laden,[33] al-Wadi'i has adamantly opposed the use of violence. In particular, he actively condemns the use of violence by the Islamic Army of Aden-Abayan, which is responsible for attacks on the government and society and is rumored to have connections to attacks against U.S. forces in Yemen, including the attack against the USS *Cole*. In 2000, al-Wadi'i publicly distanced himself from such actions: "We have even condemned these groups and called it the movements of corruption, not jihad. We always disapprove of any violent actions to spread Islam. Islam is a religion of peace and harmony, and such violence should never be thought of as part of Islam" (*Yemen Times*, July 24–30, 2000). Thousands of Salafi students flock to Yemen every year from a variety of countries (including Western countries) to learn about Salafi thought at the institutions Wadi'i supervises (*Yemen Times*, July 17–21, 2000). His reformist orientation has attracted more than one hundred thousand students over the past twenty years, but he has also incurred the wrath of the jihadis, who have allegedly attempted to assassinate him several times.

Reformists are active in other Middle Eastern countries as well. In Jordan, prominent reformists such as Muhammad Abu Shaqra, ʿAli Hasan al-Halabi, Salim al-Hilali, and Mashhur Hasan Salman enjoy substantial followings in the Salafi community. Despite the emergence of more radical Salafi groups in the 1980s and 1990s such as the "Reformation and Challenge Group," the "Oath of Loyalty to the Imam," and an informal network of radicals affiliated with Bin Laden who were tried for attempted bombings during millennium celebrations, the reformists dominate the landscape of discursive contention. These high-profile Salafis consistently condemn violence and have successfully directed most Jordanian Salafis away from the course of jihad. Prominent reformist Salafis also operate in Kuwait and Saudi Arabia, where they staff the state religious hierarchy.

In some cases, reformist Salafis have even participated in democratic elections, indicating a strong inclination to work within the system. In Kuwait, in particular, a number of Salafis from the Society for the Revival of Islamic Heritage hold seats in parliament, and the movement has shown strong support for participation in political life. In Egypt, jihadis-turned-reformists from the Gamiyya Islamiyya and Islamic Jihad formed the Shariʿa Party and the Islah Party to remold the movement for jihad into a movement that operates through party politics. Although the regime has not issued a permit for the parties and the Gamiyya Islamiyya leadership called for an election boycott, Shaykh Muhammad ʿAli Sulaiman from the Gamiyya Islamiyya ran for parliament in 2000 (*Al-Ahram Weekly*, October 12–18, 2000). And in Jordan, a few Salafis indicated their intention to run for parliament, and one successfully won a seat in the Chamber of Deputies in 1997. While most reformists continue to condemn democracy as antithetical to Islam, at least a few have expressed interest in working for reform through democratic institutions.

Despite the appeal of the jihadis to wage war against un-Islamic Arab regimes and those that oppress Muslim populations, the ubiquity of the reformist Salafis and their message of religious transformation has had a transnational impact. Members of the GIA in Algeria, for example, have claimed that their surrender was strongly influenced by prominent reformists who argued that the jihad in Algeria was no longer a true jihad. While this influence was largely due to the work of the Algerian reformist al-ʿla Cherifi (alias Abu ʿAbd al-Bari), who has encouraged widespread defections and surrenders through informal contacts, cassettes, discussions with Salafi fighters, and lectures at the University of Algiers and Fath al-Imam Mosque, internationally recognized figures outside Algeria have also had an impact. One Salafi fighter recalled the influence that a prominent reformist Salafi's words had on him: "I was sitting in the mountain and warplanes were dropping their bombs but that did not move me. At the time, I was leaning against something with my weapon beside me and I was listening to a tape by Shaykh Muhammad al-Salih Bin al-ʿUthaymin. When I heard him say that this is not jihad, that did to me a great deal more than a bomb dropping from the sky." The power of the ideational influences of reputable scholars is echoed by a nineteen-year-old from the GIA, who summarized his decision to surrender as follows: "By God, I did not return because of the use of force of arms but because of the words of the clergymen and religious conviction."[34] The resonance of such reformist messages is reflected in the agitation they produced among the GIA leadership, which decried ʿUthaymin and other reformists as traitors.

With a similar effect, the reform-oriented statements issued by the former leaders of the Gamiyya Islamiyya from the Turah Prison in Egypt on July 5, 1997, helped provide the foundations for a cease-fire initiated in the late 1990s. The turning point in the low-intensity conflict between the Gamiyya Islamiyya and the Mubarak regime occurred on November 17, 1997, when, with the approval of the military leaders abroad and Rifaʿi Ahmad Taha, a faction of al-Shahid Talʿat Hamam (the military wing of the Gamiyya Islamiyya) massacred fifty-eight tourists and four Egyptians outside the Queen Hatshepsut Temple in Luxor, raising the specter of an Algerian-style conflict. The Egyptian public was stunned by the actions, and condemnations were swift; leaders in the Gamiyya Islamiyya denounced the attack and attempted to distance themselves from the atrocities. The massacres hardly looked like a defensive jihad, and the imprisoned Gamiyya Islamiyya leaders accelerated its new direction toward reform by once again calling for a cease-fire and a reevaluation of the group's strategies. It took until March 1999 for the movement's military leadership abroad, which has direct ties to Bin Laden and al-Qaeda, to finally agree to support the initiative. This included the support of top al-Qaeda lieutenants from Egypt, such as Ayman Zawahiri and Rifa'i Ahmad Taha. The impact of the new, more reform-oriented argument can be seen in the virtual disappearance of Islamist-sponsored violence from Egypt after 1997.

It is not clear whether such influences are systematic, but the Algerian and Egyptian cases and interviews by the author with both reformist and jihadi Salafis in Jordan indicate that reformist influence can have a substantial impact on perceptions about the legitimacy of violence in particular contexts. The ability of reformists to mobilize symbolic and material resources to combat jihadi arguments represents an alternative understanding that emphasizes the fragmentation of the Salafi social movement community.

Conclusion

The difference between the jihadi and reformist factions of the transnational Salafi movement is not due to a disagreement over whether jihad is needed but rather to a disagreement about the appropriate timing for any struggle. Even prominent Salafi reformists such as the late Muhammad Nasir al-Din al-Bani have agreed that current conditions make jihad an individual obligation. But the factions disagree as to whether that obligation must be fulfilled immediately or only after a great deal of spiritual preparation. Reformists argue that Salafis must first build the base of religious understanding before the *umma* (Muslim community) will be prepared to wage jihad. When reformists do sanction jihad, it is only under extreme circumstances, such as the Soviet invasion of Afghanistan or the massacre of Muslims in Bosnia. On the other hand, jihadis believe that Salafis should pursue all options at once. Propagation is important, they argue, but it should temporally coincide with jihad, which must be waged wherever Muslims are oppressed. Given the similarity of these two perspectives, both rooted in the Salafi *manhaj* and perceptions of current conditions, al-Qaeda and violent Salafis should not be viewed as un-Islamic outliers who have little relation to other Muslim communities. As this chapter has noted, they instead constitute an important tendency within a broad Salafi social movement community.

In Salafi circles, the shared ideological basis of the community means that there is a great deal of reformist appreciation for arguments that legitimate an attack against the United States. Even though reformists may disagree with civilian targeting, there is a shared understanding about the defensive nature of jihad, rooted in the earlier Afghan experience, that seems pertinent today to many Salafis; in fatwas and various public statements, jihadis are careful to couch the jihad as a defense of Islam in the face of American aggression. In an interview with *Nida'ul Islam*, for example, Bin Laden clearly took this position: "The evidence overwhelmingly shows America and Israel killing the weaker men, women, and children in the Muslim world and elsewhere." This argument is common in other statements Bin Laden has made as well, and the supposed unwillingness of the United States to distinguish between civilians and military targets is considered by Bin Laden to justify a proportional response against American civilians. Bin Laden cites several pieces of "evidence" of this "state terrorism," including the use of atomic bombs in Japan; massacres carried out in Lebanon by Israel (an arm of the United States); the deaths of hundreds of thousands of Iraqis due to sanctions and military operations; the withholding of arms from Muslims in Bosnia, rendering Bosnians vulnerable to Serbian rapes and massacres; and "the occupation of the two sacred mosques in Saudi Arabia."[35] It is this last action that has driven Bin Laden's jihad against the United States since the Gulf War, when he began agitating against the decision to allow American troops into the holy land. For Bin Laden, this affront alone constitutes grounds for jihad. But he has been careful to accumulate a list of aggressions that justify a defensive jihad and to garner broader support among other Salafis and the Muslim world in general.[36]

Bin Laden's careful construction of a justification for jihad and his use of the Salafi *manhaj* reflect the fact that al-Qaeda and its supporters are not religious deviants, as reprehensible as their tactics are. By contextualizing these violent individuals and groups as part of a broad Salafi social movement community, this chapter has attempted to depict radicals as embedded within a broader movement and network. This broader movement is based upon common ideological roots, yet fragmented by divergences over tactics.

1. See, for example, Zald and McCarthy 1987.

2. For "networks of shared meaning," see Melucci 1989.

3. For the concept of "imagined community," see Benedict Anderson 1983.

4. See Wiktorowicz 2001b, 111–20.

5. See Benford and Zurcher 1990.

6. See Wiktorowicz 2001b and Doran 2002.

7. In his 1996 "Declaration of War" against the United States, for example, Bin Laden carefully constructed his legitimation of violence using the Quran and authentic hadiths, citing pieces of evidence according to the Salafi *manhaj* and praising publications by other well-known Salafis such as Safar al-Hawali, a Saudi religious scholar known for his opposition to the U.S. military presence in Saudi Arabia. Such careful presentation of evidence is ubiquitous in jihadi Salafi publications and statements, and jihadis proudly identify themselves using well-known Salafi labels such as *ahl al-hadith* (people of hadith), *ta'ifat al-mansura* (the aided group), *al-firqa al-najiyya* (the saved sect), and "those who follow the creed or way of the Sunna and Jama'a." "Declaration of War" available at ‹http://www.pbs.org/newshour/terrorism/international/fatwa_1996 .html›.

8. See, for example, ‹http://www.salafipublications.com/›.

9. See Faraj 1982, Kepel 1993, and Jansen 1985.

10. Certainly not all Arabs who fought in the war were "converted" to Salafi thought, but most of the returnees known as "Arab Afghans" are considered now to be part of the Salafi movement.

11. While not all Arab volunteers saw combat, estimates indicate that the Arab Afghans included 5,000 Saudis, 3,000 Yemenis, 2,000 Egyptians, 2,800 Algerians, 400 Tunisians, 370 Iraqis, 200 Libyans, and a number of Jordanians. For more details, see Bruce 1995.

12. For more details, see Rubin 1995.

13. 'Abdullah 'Azzam, *Join the Caravan* and *Defense of Muslim Lands*. Both these sources were initially available through ‹http://www.azzam.com/›. Since the terrorist attacks against the United States, however, this and other jihadi-related websites have been shut down, either by those running them or through state intervention. The sources can now be found at ‹http://www.islamistwatch .org/›.

14. *Sarajevo Dani*, June 8–22, 1998, in Foreign Broadcast Information Service (hereafter FBIS) EEU-98-198.

15. *Nezavisimaya Gazeta*, August 11, 1998, in FBIS-SOV-98-229.

16. Ibid., February 12, 1998, FBIS-SOV-98-054.

17. *Moscow Segodnya*, September 3, 1998, FBIS-SOV-98-252.

18. "The Situation in Dagestan," briefing for the Commission on Security and Cooperation in Europe, September 21, 1999, 6. Available at ‹http://www .csce.gov/›.

19. For Ibn Taymiyya's interpretation of jihad, see ‹http://www.salafi publications.com/›.

20. For details about the civil war and Islamists in Algeria, see Martinez 2000, Willis 1997, Hafez 2000, and Wiktorowicz 2001a.

21. While GIA factions viewed themselves as Salafis, there were, in practice, many groups that operated more like criminal gangs than as an ideological vanguard. The entire tenor of the legitimation for violence, however, was rooted in Salafi thought, even if it was unevenly applied by the various component groups of the GIA.

22. Armed Islamic Group, communiqué issued January 16, 1995. Originally posted by the American Islamic Group on the MSAnews listserv. No longer available.

23. See, for example, Amnesty International 1997a, Amnesty International 1997b, United Nations 1998. While most blame the GIA for the massacres, there is some evidence that the Algerian military may have been responsible in some instances. See the confession and observations of former officer Habib Souaida (2001).

24. AFP, August 6, 1994, in *Joint Publication Research Service*-TOT-94-034-L.

25. *Al-Majallah*, June 20–26, 1999, 1, 23, in FBIS-NES-1999-0627.

26. *Mideast Mirror* 8, no. 170 (September 5, 1994); *Al-Hayah*, June 1, 1998, in FBIS-NES-98-152; *Al-Watan al-ʿArabi*, March 20, 1998, in FBIS-TOT-98-081.

27. *Jordan Times*, August 18, 1997. See also the interview with al-Maqdisi in *Al-Hayah*, July 20, 1996.

28. Within the reformist faction, there are variations on this theme. The members of at least a few groups believe that violence is only rarely justified, but most reformists accept the need for jihad at a later date when the Muslim community is more prepared for it both spiritually and militarily.

29. See *Fatwa al-Banni*, transcript at ‹http://www.allaahuakbar.net/scholars/ albaani/albaani_on_jihad.htm›.

30. *Munatharah maʾ Tantheem al-Jjihad al-Islami*, audio cassettes, no date, transcript posted at ‹http://www.allaahuakbar.net/scholars/albaani/debate_on_ jihad.htm›.

31. Ibid.

32. ʿUsamah Siddiq ʿAli Ayyub, an Egyptian Salafi who gained political asylum in Germany in 1999, quoted in *Al-Sharq al-Awsat*, October 12, 1999, in FBIS-NES-1999-1013. Ayyub is considered one of the most wanted Salafis in Egypt.

33. *Al-Watan al-ʿArabi*, March 20, 1998, in FBIS-TOT-98-081.

34. *Al-Sharq al-Awsat*, February 13, 2000, in FBIS-NES-2000-0214.

35. *Nidaʾul Islam*, October–November 1996; Osama bin Laden, interview by John Miller, ABC News, May 28, 1998; Bin Laden, "Declaration of War," ‹http:// www.pbs.org/newshour/terrorism/international/fatwa_1996.html›.

36. For a more detailed analysis of Bin Laden's argument, as presented in the 1998 fatwa against American military and civilian targets, see Ranstorp 1998.

Chapter 11

Defining Islamic Interconnectivity

Whether digital cartography of Islamic cyberspace would produce a map that reproduces the real-world phenomena of Muslim networks is open to question. Such a map would bear little relation to the contemporary projections of the Muslim worlds or to the classic charts of early Islamic mapmaking. Its patterns and masses would shift from minute to minute in response to the seismic digital shifts in cyber-tectonic plates. Any analysis of an online *dar al-Islam* (however that might be defined to incorporate Islam's global reach) would require consideration of appropriate methodological approaches and frameworks for study.

The focus for this chapter's map is on jihad elements following 9/11, a microelement of a much wider—and more benign and complex—Muslim networking phenomenon. The September 11, 2001, attacks on the United States and the subsequent military campaigns in Afghanistan and Iraq transformed cyberspace as well as real space. Investigating jihad elements on the Internet in the period surrounding 9/11 provides a snapshot of a cyber Islamic environment in a formative phase, prior to a substantial expansion of sites and content.[1]

Defining the Internet has become less of a necessity than it was several years ago. Briefly, for this chapter, the term "Internet" means the connected network of computers and other electronic communications tools through which diverse forms of electronic communications and media sharing can be facilitated. The term "Web," or World Wide Web, can possess a general meaning, but for our purposes its meaning is "the global web of interlinked files that can be located using the http protocol." The term "cyberspace" is regularly utilized but rarely defined in discussions of the Internet; it is used here to depict the electronic and amorphous territory that can be navigated, or "surfed," by the use of a browser. The term "cyber

Islamic environments" stresses how Islamic conceptual frameworks and expressions are integrated and facilitated on the Internet. Whilst recognizing the significance of related tools, the focus here is on the World Wide Web, whose content, or Web pages, may have to be accessed, read, and interpreted in a very different way from other sources, particularly from traditional Islamic sources. The content of the Web may be focused upon reaching a particular sector of the Muslim constituency that is not necessarily as "wired" to traditional Islamic discourse. The application of the term "traditional" in this context relates to oral, memorized, written, and printed materials and dialogues. (For a full discussion of these distinctions, see Jon Anderson's essay in this volume.)

The mediation of cyber Islamic environments involves diverse media and interfaces that change and evolve rapidly in reaction to contemporary events and influences; this fact was never more evident than after September 11, 2001. The lack of a fixed form in cyber Islamic environments, combined with the need to develop new readings of conventional materials, means that approaches toward sources of knowledge about Islam have to be reevaluated both by their readers and by academics studying the phenomena of Islam and cyberspace. Websites rarely come with clear labels, commentaries, or explanations explicitly indicating the religious, political, social, and cultural values of their authors, although it is possible to track down details about authors through a number of channels. Determining what makes a site "Islamic" is perhaps a matter best left to the individual reader, as the definition can incorporate a number of factors. Does the term mean a site that includes specific symbols of Islam, including images of the Quran or Mecca? Or does it mean a site presenting religious authority from a specific spiritual or religious leader? Questions arise as to whether the online opinions of such men and the creation of new forms of online Muslim authority have the potential to transcend and transform conventional understandings of Muslim networks and communities both within academic frameworks and across Muslim societies.

It can be particularly difficult to position an Internet site on a real-world map and to determine the location of its authors (if revealed) together with the social, political, cultural, and/or religious dimensions that may influence its selection as a subject of study. Also, the content of sites can change on a regular basis, making the assembly of data difficult. There can be problems in determining the provenance of a site. Information gathering and "fieldwork" may require e-mail interviews with authors, sponsors, creators, and designers who do not necessarily wish to reveal their identities (if they wish to dialogue with academic researchers at all). Information can be deduced from analyzing the "about us" section of a site or even by exploring the encoding of a page to determine the intended keywords and themes. There are generic tools available to track down an ISP (Internet service provider) and other data related to a site's origins and ownership, including Astilbe Revealer and SamSpade.org, that can be applied to build a basic profile of site identity and affiliations.[2] There is evidence that governmental agencies have access to more sophisticated tools beyond the reach of this writer, although how effectively these tools have been applied is open to question.[3] Sites that have been closed or forced to migrate to other ISPs—perhaps under local pressure or because of hacking—can also be tracked through analysis of related websites' link pages, "chatter" in Web forums, news feeds, news from e-mail listings, and Web logs from diverse perspectives, including those vehemently opposed to particular interpretations of Islam and those with a security agenda.

Especially since 9/11, the continued expansion of the Internet has meant an inevitable proportional increase in Islam-related websites. It heightens the need to analyze, research, and record online developments within and between cyber Islamic environments. But is it appropriate, necessary, or indeed possible for all of these developments to be recorded and analyzed? Such an undertaking would require the efforts of many subject specialists from diverse related disciplines in order to construct a holistic and scientific analysis of Islam in cyberspace. Sites would have to be recorded and stored, as the "evidence" changes rapidly, and old versions of pages are rarely archived for public use by their authors or service providers. Other archives, such as the Internet Archive Wayback Machine, only harvest (gather and digitally archive) a portion of the Internet—and it should be noted that a number of jihadi platforms have been removed from the database. Search engine caches, such as that provided by Google, have some application for recently harvested sites but are more problematic when data and networks have to be tracked back in time.[4]

Cyber Islamic Networks after 9/11

The Internet (in particular, the World Wide Web) is one arena in which it was possible to observe some of the networking between and within diverse Muslim perspectives after 9/11, as well as the reconfiguration of relationships and ideologies. After 9/11, online Islamic themes were often subsumed or integrated into dialogues about 9/11 and the changing world order, marginalizing significant Islam-related issues altogether. New affiliations emerged (at least in cyberspace), enhancing the connec-

tivity between campaigns and conceptual frameworks of Islamic understanding. Attention should be drawn to the fact that Muslim networks,
groups, and individuals who were not aligned with or supportive of al-
Qaeda used the medium in order to demonstrate their antipathy toward
Bin Laden and their sympathy toward the 9/11 victims. Such expressions
were sometimes couched in terms of the wider picture in relation to Islam,
the Muslim worlds, and the West by means of commentary and explanations of why the events of 9/11 occurred. Some of these statements might
be described as reflexive, apologetic, and defensive in nature, attempting as
they did to shore up the position of Muslim communities in minority contexts that were stigmatized for the actions of Bin Laden. A prominent example of this phenomenon is the Muslims against Terrorism pages, which
used Quranic interpretive frameworks to condemn the 9/11 attacks (Bunt
2003b, 112–23). These pages, part of the more broadly focused Islam for
Today pages, included statements from Quran and Hadith sources juxta-
posed with photos of the attacks.[5]

The interpretations available on the Internet reflect a spectrum of understanding, rather than a monochrome picture, and the Internet indicates
the nuances of understanding in regard to the place of Islam in contemporary societies. It is possible to obtain a broad range of fatwas online associated with the aftermath of 9/11, some justifying the attacks, others un-
equivocally condemning them, and others at points in between these poles
(67–134). Fatwa-Online, Islam Q&A, and Ask the Imam are examples of
sites that addressed aspects of the post–9/11 situation to varying degrees.[6]
Fatwa-Online reproduced an *Arab News* story about fatwas issued by the
Saudi Arabian Grand Council of Scholars that condemned suicide bombings and the "abuse" of the concept of jihad.[7] Some prominent, populist
interpreters and authorities such as the Qatar-based Egyptian scholar and
media personality Yusuf al-Qaradawi denounced both al-Qaeda's attacks
and U.S. policies associated with the Middle East. These statements were
published on websites closely affiliated with al-Qaradawi, such as Islam
Online.[8] It should be stressed that juristic opinions and fatwas are not necessarily representative of the interests of all Muslims and that the Net is
also a source of criticism of these perspectives from other Muslim channels.[9]

Naturally, online attention was focused on Osama bin Laden, the Taliban, and the al-Qaeda configurations, though these groups are not representative of mainstream opinion. Supporters of al-Qaeda used the Internet
to disseminate statements from Bin Laden and others in the organization
representing al-Qaeda's influence in (aspects of) jihadi networks in vari-

ous locations, including Chechnya, Palestine, the Maghrib, Sudan, Iran, Afghanistan, South and Central Asia, and a variety of Muslim-minority Western contexts. The connections between various campaigns were emphasized online, suggesting the global and cellular nature of al-Qaeda.[10] This dissemination drew on the representation of campaigns and statements through websites as well as chat rooms and e-mail listings.

There is evidence that such online activism drew recruits and finance into al-Qaeda and its affiliated platforms. The Al-Neda website, which broadly represented al-Qaeda opinion, became one focus of such activities. Heightened awareness of al-Qaeda after 9/11, coupled with censorship and other pressures, forced the site away from conventional ISPs. Al-Neda's online tactics evolved, and its owners at times resorted to parasitically placing content on other sites. The URLs were then publicized by e-mail to various websites and listings. Al-Neda's webmaster, Yusuf Bin-Salih al-Ayiri, was killed in a June 2003 gun battle with Saudi forces.[11]

Al-Qaeda's ideology and associated supportive perspectives continued to appear online in a variety of languages.[12] Whilst the dissemination usually took the form of text, there has been an increase in the use of increasingly sophisticated multimedia. A *du'a* (invocation) sound recording in Arabic by Shaykh Muhammad Al Mohaisany was the soundtrack for a Macromedia Flash presentation of a slide show containing images of the Muslim victims of conflict, the activities of *mujahidin*, and photos of al-Aqsa Mosque (in Jerusalem/Al-Quds), Mecca, and the "enemies" of Islam. It also contained photos from September 11, 2001, and of American soldiers (drawn from *Al-Jazeera*) captured in Iraq during 2003.

The *du'a* was recorded in the Masjid al-Haram, Mecca, during Ramadan 2001, and shortly after its recording, Saudi authorities arrested Al Mohaisany.[13] The *du'a* itself was delivered in highly emotive language to an appreciative audience in the sacred precincts of Mecca, and its online incarnations included a subtitled English version. The invocation had a wide circulation on the Internet in textual and audio-only formats, but the multimedia file was significant in its ability to reinforce the controversial speech with what were perceived as contextual and Quranic references.[14] Al Mohaisany himself may have been unaware of how this *du'a* was edited for online presentation.

The presence of al-Qaeda and its affiliates remained expansive on the Net during 2003, including its presence on revived, "official" Al-Neda sites. The Internet continued to be an integral part of al-Qaeda's media propagation and logistics network, linking autonomous nodes of the network together. Its support ranged from the publication of content justifying campaigns (including bin Laden's videos) to the circulation of a film showing *Wall Street Journal* reporter Daniel Pearl's murder. Shortly after 9/11, a site named after Osama bin Laden's mentor (and assassination victim), Abdullah Azzam, appearing under the headline "The Monumental Struggle of Good versus Evil," presented a statement from Osama bin Laden disclaiming responsibility for 9/11.[15] Al-Qaeda supporters created a number of online forums to discuss issues, including one called "Clearguidance" that provided a thematic listing of regularly updated chat strands about campaigns and contemporary issues. Following the conviction of the "Bali bombers" (see below), the following statement appeared on Clearguidance, accompanied by a photo and blessings: "These are the brothers who were responsible for last year's attacks in Bali, Indonesia celebrating 'Eid ul-Fitr today in jail. They've each been given death (i.e. shahaadah) sentences, fakallaahu 'asrahum. Subhaan-Allaah, look at the noor [spiritual light] on their faces."[16]

As in the real world, the lines between al-Qaeda's online networking manifestations and identities can blur. Al-Qaeda was associated with a group of Kurdish Islamists operating primarily in North Iraq under al-Ansar al-Islam's banner. Its Cihad.net was a typical one-stop shop for al-Qaeda data, with regular updates on all global campaigns, including the 2003 Riyadh and Istanbul bombings. The site featured a multimedia montage of the Muslim child victims of war along with images of Chechen jihadis on maneuvers. The chosen images included Osama bin Laden, Camp X-Ray prisoners, Shaykh Omar Abdul Rahman (imprisoned for instigating the first attack on the World Trade Center in 1993), a 9/11 attacks montage, and a burning American flag. These images were accompanied by a *nashid* (a type of religious music) and viewed through an animated, bullet-shaped window. The video libraries feature clips of substantial length from various campaigns in Kurdistan, Iraq, Afghanistan, Kashmir, and Chechnya interlaced with iconic imagery of "martyrs" and Islamic symbols.[17]

The use of multimedia has been a critical adjunct to al-Qaeda's propagation (or *da'wa*) strategies. In addition to reproducing conventional video film, specific online presentations have been created in the form of photograph or film-clip montages accompanied by *nashids*, recitation, or speech-sermons (for example, by Osama bin Laden). These presentations use Flash-style software and animation software and draw upon other media, such as videotapes produced by the sites' media arms for circulation by supporters. The writer has seen content in Chechen-oriented videos subsequently appear online in edited form. The existence of such videos online provides a wider global audience for the material, which it is not always safe or easy to circulate in hard-copy video format.

The editing and juxtaposition of emotive content (for example, images of child victims of conflict) with the message of al-Qaeda, which often draws upon interpretations of the Quran, indicates a sophisticated approach toward the propagation of the al-Qaeda message. Specific motifs also appear online: the image of an Arabian horse, in silhouette or in animated form, is part of the Al-Neda "brand."[18] Osama bin Laden's statements, edited from other broadcasts and placed against an "Islamic" backdrop, are also a dynamic feature of the compiled presentations. Examples studied by this writer also incorporate images of the 9/11 attacks and of their instigators with soundtracks and quotations that are meant to justify the men's actions.

Palestinian-oriented presentations feature images of IDF soldiers confronting children. These are sequenced alongside images of the victims of suicide bombings and of a Kalashnikov resting on a grave with the Quran. The sequence concludes with the image of Osama bin Laden. Such presentations circulate rapidly around the Internet, publicized through chat rooms, e-mail listings, and other sites. However, their location usually shifts quickly from one site to another as they evade censorship and ISP crackdowns.

Al-Faroq presented itself as a "gateway to jihad." This site reappeared in December 2003 with a comprehensive selection of jihadi content, campaign posters, links to related chat rooms and sites, and statements supporting various ideological concepts surrounding al-Qaeda. There were also links to compressed zip files offering other multimedia content. The multimedia elements included several Flash presentations drawn from diverse sources, with another set of images presenting photos of "martyrs" and ideologues.[19]

It should be noted that Taliban sites, too, retained a position online after 9/11. American ISPs unwittingly hosted some pro-Taliban sites owned by people claiming to have addresses in New York.[20] Although Mullah Omar continued to evade the Americans during 2003, statements apparently from him were reproduced on the Web. The Taliban used the Web to publicize the cost of weaponry and military equipment together with bank account details. Even when the organization had gone to ground in the real world, in virtual space it continued its networking activities.

Variations on anti-Israeli, anti-Zionist, and anti-Jewish sentiments can be found on jihadi sites. After 9/11, Hamas pages suggested that Israeli interests were behind the attacks.[21] This theory has continued to appear frequently elsewhere in cyberspace. The fact that the Hamas site existed in a (relatively) sanitized version for English speakers and in a hard-core version for Arabic speakers is an interesting contrast that needs to be explored further.

Careful consideration goes into jihadi site content; the sites incorporate a broad range of perspectives that are not always mutually supportive and reflect different approaches toward some of the militaristic interpretations of "jihad."[22] A site may be tailored for existing supporters or may seek to broaden support for campaigns from other Muslims or from non-Muslims or both. Some sites provide content for supporters only (complete with password protection and subscription systems). Jihad is marketed to various audiences in different ways. These have included the online marketing of a pro-Hizbullah "Special Force" computer game under the banner "Special Force game will render you a partner of the resistance."[23] Hizbullah's extensive media operations have incorporated several websites in different formats and languages.

The concept of the online martyr gallery has emerged in a number of contexts associated with jihad campaigns. The wills and photos of 9/11 hijackers were featured widely on the Internet. Images of the Chechens responsible for the attacks on the Moscow Theatre in 2002 also circulated widely. Chechen platforms have developed their media strategy to promote their causes, providing video of attacks on Russian troops.[24] The notion of embedded reporting entered Islamic cyberspace with the "reality" coverage of jihad online, such as films of attacks on American vehicles in Iraq during 2003 and 2004.[25] The Palestinian Kataeb Ezzeldeen Brigades' Ezzedeen.net provided detailed accounts of "martyrdom operations." These were illustrated with highly stylized photos of youthful jihad participants posing with weapons in front of Islamic backdrops. Such images quickly appeared online after "successful" operations.[26]

Some sites presented a complex array of messages under the banner of their interpretation of Islam, interlinking diverse global campaigns. In December 2003, Al-Intashar was located on free Web space from an American ISP, using a top-level ".tk" domain from the Pacific atolls of Tokeau.[27] Al-Intashar ("the Spread") described itself as "an Islamic movement from the soon to be Islamic region of Egypt." Al-Intashar expressed support for the 2002 Bali bombings, posting photos of the destroyed nightclub. Quotes and photos from the trial of the bombings' instigator, Amrozi bin Nurhasyim, were placed adjacent to a hyperlinked listing of Indonesian nightclubs, presumably for further targeting. The same site condemned suicide operations in Turkey and Saudi Arabia as "cowardly" and "un-

Islamic." Al-Intashar's inherent complexity is indicated in its support of aspects of Orthodox Judaism, its opposition to Wahhabism, and its promotion of Sipahe Sahabah's anti-Shia campaigns. (Ramzi Yousef, a key World Trade Center bomber in 1993, was associated with Sipahe Sahabah.) Al-Intashar condemned Muslims attending demonstrations against the war in Iraq in 2003 (for being "like westerners") and castigated Turkish women in *hijab* "who think they are Muslim but are truly just western pigs with cloths on their head." The Al-Intashar site incorporated many elements that might be deemed stereotypical of jihad sites and was one of several sites that have been accused on other jihad sites of being a CIA or FBI "sting" designed to acquire information about site visitors.[28]

Whether such sites can—or should—be shut down is no doubt a subject for debate. The same technology that fosters them also allows opinions and discussion to be circulated on subjects that could not be aired in other forms of media, such as criticisms of "human rights abuses" in various Muslim contexts. Sites that are banned by governments or ISPs—or hacked by opponents—are rarely down for long. There are mirror copies of many jihad sites and enough enthusiasts to reproduce sites should their original authors be unavoidably detained from putting them back online.

E-Mujahidin *Networks*

If the prismatic, militaristic interpretations of jihad extend into cyberspace, then their advocates could be styled "e-*mujahidin*." These Net-head protagonists are hidden from view and their identities shielded, although the shouts of their alter egos are as strident and devout as those of any fighter at Badr. Their image bears little resemblance to the warriors described in traditional Muslim historical sources. However, it may be that these unseen online fighters are as significant as other fractured expressions of jihad. Consideration of unconventional electronic networking must include questions about how e-mail has been applied as a mobilizing and radicalizing tool and about the type of operational intelligence that has been derived from the Net, two significant factors. The application of encryption to hide strategic information in apparently innocuous images or to cloak e-mail also requires exploration. There has been a hint of future major network disruptions (and attendant catastrophes) insofar as computer training has become part of the portfolio of skills of the graduates of al-Qaeda training camps.[29] Concerns regarding jihad and the Internet were heightened when investigators considered the role of the Merkezi Internet café in Bingöl in eastern Turkey. It was used by members of Kurdish Hizbullah, allegedly responsible for the 2003 suicide bombings in Istanbul.

The long-term online conflict between supporters of Muslim factions in Palestine and pro-Israeli interests has involved Web and e-mail campaigning as well as hacking and cracking activities in which sites on all sides have been defaced or "adjusted." A notable victim of such activities was a site promoting Ariel Sharon, which was subtly altered to suggest Sharon's complicity in terrorism. An American Jewish organization's site was compromised to reveal the credit card details of its members. The people responsible for anti-Israeli attacks in these types of cases may be enthusiastic hackers, or "script kiddies," but they provide an indicator of the potential damage that could be done by more professional hits. The disruptive activities have led religious authorities to deliver fatwas encouraging or condemning such behavior.

The expressions of "hacktivists" manifested themselves on all sides following 9/11. In some cases, anti-Muslim hackers attacked anything that resembled a cyber Islamic environment with network vulnerabilities, regardless of its worldview. (In this way, perhaps, they mirrored the actions and prejudices of those in the "real" world.) However, it could be said that such a lack of discernment was pronounced in other forms of hacking activity on all sides. There was evidence of intra-Muslim hacking, too. Networks of Muslim hackers supportive of al-Qaeda were proactive in attacking other Muslim sites, although the alarmist concerns of some commentators that this "cyber-war" would lead to a collapse of the World Wide Web were unjustified, at least in the two years following 9/11. In some cases, such concerns led to improvements in computer network security. Technological advances present both new ways of accessing information in contexts where restrictions are evident and new ways for authorities to censor and restrict surfers.

The phenomenon of so-called "electronic jihad" (or "e-jihad," alternatively described as an "inter-fada") was highlighted in a "virtual conflict" in cyberspace between Palestinian and Israeli interests.[30] Digital activism is not a new phenomenon, although its association with religion became more pronounced in this case, as religion formed one theme of the conflict. Could hacking be justifiably interpreted as an "Islamic" activity? What kinds of issues emerged with this kind of campaigning, and were they truly significant and influential in terms of Muslim worldviews and opinion? Finding answers to such questions might, in some contexts, require recourse to legal scholarship focusing on notions of analogical reasoning, given that cases of e-jihad have no precedents in Islamic jurisprudence or conventional Muslim sources of knowledge. IslamOnline produced an on-line fatwa that stated that Israeli banks in the occupied territories were legitimate targets. It also proclaimed that visiting secular and "Zionist" websites was permissible for Muslim surfers as an information-gathering exercise.[31] In March 2001, visitors to a Hamas site were diverted (by anti-Hamas hackers) to a "Hot Motel Horny Sex Sluts" site. The Hamas leader, Shaykh Ahmad Yassin, classified this hack as an attack on Islam and responded angrily. He had been quoted as saying in 2000, "We will use whatever tools we can—e-mail, the Internet—to facilitate jihad."[32]

His comment can be linked to a 2000 fatwa from the grand mufti of Saudi Arabia, Shaykh Abdul Aziz Al Alshaikh (a member of the Saudi Arabian Grand Council of Scholars), that supported hacking-related activity. It was written in response to the question, "If there were websites on the internet that are hostile to Islam, and broadcasting immoral materials. Is it permissible for me to send it viruses to disable and destroy these websites?" Al Alshaikh declared: "If these websites are hostile to Islam and you could encounter its evilness with goodness; And to respond to it, refute its falsehood, and show its void content; that would be the best option. But if you are unable to respond to it, and you wanted to destroy it and you have the ability to do so, its OK to destroy it because it is an evil website."[33] The fatwa may have contributed to a general upsurge in e-jihad activities, particularly in relation to Palestine.

E-jihad activities, particularly those related to the conflict between Palestinians and Israelis, were intensifying even before 9/11. The application of the term "jihad" is itself significant, given its association in English with other forms of activism.[34] In the context of cyberspace, the traditional concept of jihad as an inner Muslim spiritual striving has frequently been negated in favor of a digital sword striking at a broad selection of targets. The term is used descriptively, and it is particularly applied to the hacking of Israeli sites, although it should be stressed that hackers do not always have an overtly Muslim identity and are not always Palestinian. E-jihad may be a useful description rather than an accurate definition of hackers' activities.

The results of such hacking and cracking (on both sides) were varied but included e-mail overload, system failure, "defacement" of Web content, database acquisition, and dysfunctional and crashed sites. Similar hacking resources were available on pro-Israeli and pro-Palestinian sites as well as on generic, neutral sites, from which many of the tools were drawn. Hacking technology improved during the conflict as special applications were created by both sides to be used as weapons. E-jihad extended to dominate cyber Islamic environments in the period following 9/11, with thousands of sites being compromised on all sides and groups of Muslim hackers networking to disrupt a variety of targets. Hacking is subject to constant refinement, and it could have a greater impact in future "campaigns" than the defacement and disruption of sites. In recording and evaluating the macro- and micro-impacts of such developments on activities undertaken in the name of Islam, in time we may be able to draw the networking connections together—perhaps with the aid of digital cartographers.

The Future of Muslim Networks in a Virtual World

The above examples of electronic connectivity between aspects of Muslim movements and networks should not detract from the more mundane applications of the Internet found in other areas of Islamic cyberspace, which are also of significance (and have been discussed by this writer elsewhere). Those living in environments hostile to their religious worldview may find comfort, advice, and inspiration through the content of Web pages, whilst others might appreciate the perspectives of other dimensions of interpretation and understanding. The influence of scholars, and of others giving advice based on Islamic principles, can be extended from their own (micro-) communities to a global audience. The analysis, observation, and recording of developments such as the online fatwa in cyber Islamic environments, where "real-world" decision making is informed through Internet discussion, represents a significant new research area in Islamic studies.[35]

Although it is difficult to quantify, the extension of Internet access seems to have led to a growth in Arabic- and other Islamic-language content online, which includes diverse perspectives on Islam and Muslim issues. This is a technical trend, rather than a result of 9/11. The consequences of 9/11 dominated discourse on a number of sites and (re-)emphasized for some observers (and Muslim organizations) the importance and potential of the Web as a networking medium as they jostled for position both among themselves and between themselves and other media providers (such as local and international news sources) that offer multimedia content. Those who had an infrastructure already in place were well positioned to disseminate their opinions, including fatwas and other forms of advice.

The capacity of the Web to act as a conduit through which Muslim organizations and individuals exchange and obtain information was highlighted during the Afghanistan and Iraq campaigns. The role of the Internet was extended from news coverage to blogging (Web logging), the growth of which has created a significant channel for expanded networking and dissemination. Blogging provides an opportunity for diverse perspectives on Islam to be presented, it links communities and individuals together, and it is certainly an area of cyberspace that will require further study in relation to Islam and Muslims.

A couple of examples indicate its relevance, especially in a post–9/11 context. During the Iraq campaign, personal diaries published online from within Iraq presented the opinions of "ordinary" Iraqis. In some cases, these blogs were regularly updated, offering insights that were unavailable in traditional media. The blog of Iraqi "Salam Pax"—entitled "Where is Raed?"—obtained a substantial following. Pax was a twenty-nine-year-old architect whose blogging (in English) drew a substantial international audience, leading him to write a column for the *Guardian* newspaper and eventually a book drawn from the blog (2003).

Salam Pax understandably retained his anonymity in order to guarantee his personal security as he wrote about life in Baghdad and presented his opinions about the various factions and parties associated with the Iraq campaign. His writing included his perspectives on the Baath Party and the Iraqi Mukhabbarat (Intelligence Service), as well as his thoughts about the United States, the CIA, politicians, some of his e-mail correspondents, and various Islamist parties. He wrote about a number of subjects, including sexuality, popular music, and culture. Salam Pax also referred to Islam in Iraq, discussing the use of religious rhetoric by various parties. His is certainly a significant online contribution from a Muslim milieu, linking into wider historical and contemporary discourse in the Muslim worlds while maintaining a substantial international audience at a critical time in Iraqi history.[36]

Subject to Net access (and to a censorship-free environment), blogging allows for relatively easy and immediate online publication of individual thoughts, diaries, and journals. Key future elements to observe in relation to cyber Islamic environments will be the publication of blogs from diverse Muslim perspectives; for example, Iranian blogging (from within the Islamic Republic and from the wider diaspora) became a phenomenon that Iranian authorities sought to restrict.[37]

There is evidence that blogging is growing in popularity in other Muslim contexts: some Muslim women have engaged in it, including those in *hijab* who have seen blogging as an appropriate way to engage with a wider world. A good example of this is "Veiled4Allah," part of the wider Al-Muhajabah series of blogs and sub-blogs; Al-Muhajabah also includes "A Quranic Journal" (incorporating commentary and Arabic script), a technical area about creating a blog, and the "Niqabi Paralegal," which discusses "legal issues facing Muslims in the United States."[38] The tens of thousands of Muslim blogs that have emerged represent a substantial area for discourse and networking (including networking in relation to fatwas and e-jihad); the extent to which they reflect historical patterns or engender new elements or both is a question for future consideration.

Blogging is an example of a technological leap (in terms of the creation of, and the growth in the popularity of, blogging software) that has taken place in a relatively compressed time period in a variety of languages and cultural contexts; it is indicative of the continually evolving nature of the Internet. There continue to be substantial growths in Net access in Muslim-majority contexts that reflect technological advances such as improved telecommunications infrastructures and cheaper computers, which must influence how Web content (including material about Islam) is distributed (Bunt 2003a). This is not to suggest, nor to imply, that Islamic materials are necessarily the main focus for readers in Muslim-majority contexts.

Conclusion

The presence both of materials written by Muslims on a variety of subjects that are colored by their experiences as Muslims and of a growing readership for these materials surely affects global knowledge about Islam and Muslim societies, even if only a relatively small (but influential) proportion of the world's Muslim population can access them. The media through which these materials are accessed extends from traditional home-based computers to the interfaces that are becoming more popular for Web access; the expansion of Internet cafés, the development of mobile computing devices (including WAP phones), and the creation of satellite television channels (including proposed Islamic channels) that incorporate online Islamic content in their output are just some examples of the changes taking place in information access.[39]

The speed and immediacy of the transformation within cyber Muslim networks post–9/11 highlights the need to record, analyze, and provide initial interpretations of developments at this crucial period in Islamic discourse and expression. While there are substantial 9/11 archives representing the attacks and their aftermath from various U.S. perspectives, the broad range of Islamic reactions is not formally archived at present, and many Islamic websites and pages have disappeared without being archived.[40] At the time of writing, in close proximity to the events of September 11, 2001, and their consequences, it is clear that cyberspace has become a critical component of the mapping of Islam and Muslim networks in the twenty-first century.

NOTES

1. Site URLs were correct in May 2004 unless otherwise stated. Updated links to the sites discussed in this chapter can be found on the writer's website, Virtually Islamic, ‹http://www.virtuallyislamic.com›.

2. Astilbe Revealer, ‹http://www.dataphone.se/~astilbe/cgi-bin/netcheck/reveal.cgi›.

3. For a perspective on perceived U.S. governmental security responsibilities in relation to cyberspace, see Verton 2003, 17–30.

4. Internet Archive Wayback Machine, ‹http://www.archive.org›.

5. Bunt 2003b, 113–15; Muslims against Terrorism, ‹http://www.islamforto day.com›.

6. Fatwa-Online, ‹http://www.fatwa-online.com›; Islam Q&A, ‹http://www.islam-qa.com›; Ask the Imam, ‹http://www.ask-imam.com›.

7. "Council of Senior Scholars Back Government Crackdown on Terrorists," *Arab News*, August 17, 2003, posted by Fatwa-Online, ‹http://www.fatwa-on line.com/news/0030817.htm›.

8. For a discussion of a broad range of "scholarly" opinions issued post–9/11 condemning the attacks, see IslamOnline, "Islamic Scholars Refute Al-Qaeda's 9/11 Justifications," September 15, 2003, ‹http://www.islam-online.net/English/News/2002–09/15/article15.shtml›.

9. See Jon Anderson's essay in this volume. Also see Bunt 2003b, 156–60.

10. There have been a number of journalistic and academic analyses of al-Qaeda's structure and global activities. The links between various regional campaigns and organizations are discussed in Bodansky 1999. Also see Gunuratna 2002, Reeve 1999.

11. Muhamad Al-Shafi'i, article in *Al-Sharq al-Awsat*, picked up by BBC Monitoring Middle East, edited and reproduced in "Sharia Watch," June 5, 2003, ‹http://groups.yahoo.com/group/shariawatch/message/55›.

12. This fact opens up a debate about censorship and control of the Internet that is beyond the scope of this chapter. What can be said is that such sites offer security services an opportunity to monitor various jihadi sites' readers and their opinions, but that efforts are made by some of these readers to cloak their identities (with varying degrees of success).

13. An English-language transcript of the slide show appeared on a Malaysian site based in Terengganu, Trianungkite.net. "Du'a of Sheikh Al Mohaisany," ‹http://www.tranungkite.net/c04/jiwa10.htm›.

14. For example, this file appeared on CityLink Computers, a London company's site, but was subsequently deleted: ‹http://www.citylinkcomputers.com/duafull.swf› (May 2003). It also appeared on JihadFiles, ‹http://www.geocities.com/jihadfiles/flash.html›. It was additionally circulated on various pro-Israeli

sites. The original source of the file was difficult to determine at the time of writing.

15. Azzam Publications, ‹http://www.azzam.com› (September 19, 2001; link deleted).

16. Clearguidance, "Pics of the Bali Bombers Celebrating 'Eid Today," November 25, 2003, ‹http://www.clearguidance.com›. This quotation reproduces the post's spellings and definition of a "death sentence."

17. Cihad, ‹http://cihad.net›.

18. This choice may be drawn from Osama bin Laden's videotaped statement, broadcast on December 13, 2001, and transcribed for the Pentagon: "When people see a strong horse and a weak horse, by nature, they will like the strong horse. This is only one goal; those who want people to worship the lord of the people, without following that doctrine, will be following the doctrine of Muhammad, peace be upon him." Reproduced on C-Net News, December 13, 2001, ‹http://news.com.com/2009-1023-276989.html?legacy=cnet›.

19. Al-Faroq, ‹http://members.lycos.co.uk/alfaroq› (December 9, 2003; link deleted).

20. For example, Halal Flowers in New York controlled Taliban-News.com (one of several sites), according to a search of the Whois registration database (Bunt 2003b, 69–70; Whois, ‹http://www.whois.com›).

21. Palestine Info, ‹http://www.palestine-info.com› (September 13, 2001; link deleted); Bunt 2003b, 91.

22. Discussed in detail in Bunt 2003b, 25–34.

23. Special Force, ‹http://download.specialforce.net› (link deleted).

24. Kavkaz Centre, ‹http://www.kavkaz.org.uk› (December 2003).

25. Islam Today, ‹http://www.islamtoday.net› (December 2003; link deleted).

26. Kataeb Ezzeldeen Brigades, ‹http://ezzedeen.net› (link deleted). Similar images were found on sites such as Palestine Way (‹http://www.palestineway.com›) and Qudsway (‹http://www.qudsway.com›), which incorporated detailed statements and illustrated commentaries on specific operations.

27. DotTK, ‹http://www.dot.tk›; Al-Intashar, ‹http://www.al-intashar.tk›.

28. Al-Intashar, ‹http://www.al-intashar.tk›.

29. See Bunt 2003b, 56–62; Gunaratna 2002; and Verton 2003, 80–114.

30. For an expanded definition of "e-jihad," see Bunt 2003b.

31. The Internet extends the questions and challenges articulated by critics associated with notions of Islamic authority. The area of self-proclaimed online authority is discussed in Bunt 2000, 104–31, and 2003b, 184–204.

32. Pramit Pai Chaudhuri, "What are Islamic Fundamentalists Doing in Porn Sites? The CIA Tells You," *Hindustan Times Online*, February 18, 2001, ‹http://www.hvk.org/articles/0201/92.html›.

33. Shaykh Abdul Aziz Al Alshaikh, untitled fatwa, *Al-Daawa Magazine*, May 11, 2000. Reproduced in Saudi Information Agency, "Exclusive: Saudi Grand Mufti OK's Cyber Terrorism," December 2, 2002, ‹http://www.arabia news.org/english/article.cfm?qid=19+sid=6› (link deleted). The Saudi In-

formation Agency is a reform-centered organization based in Washington. A translated copy of the fatwa, together with a brief discussion, was found at Atlanta Independent Media Center, "Open Communications," ‹http://atlanta .indymedia.org/newswire/display/24146/index.php›.

34. One example is Queer Jihad, initially a response by British gay activists to al-Muhajiroun, the U.K. "back to the caliphate" group that frequently articulated a militaristic and aggressive approach to the term "jihad," especially when pronouncing on "appropriate" treatment for homosexuals. A separate "Muslim" gay and lesbian group online later adopted the term "queer jihad." See Bunt 2000, 118.

35. See Bunt 2003b, 124–204, for a discussion of these issues.

36. Salam Pax, "Where is Raed?," ‹http://dear_raed.blogspot.com›.

37. BBC News, "Iranian Bloggers Rally against Censorship," December 11, 2003; World Summit on Information Society, ‹http://dailysummit.net›. For a listing of Iranian blogs, see Hossein Derakhshan's comprehensive listing, ‹http: //www.hoder.com/weblog›.

38. "Veiled4Allah" and "A Quranic Journal," both at ‹http://www .muhajabah.com/islamicblog›; "Niqabi Paralegal," ‹http://www.niqabi paralegal.com›.

39. This issue is also discussed in Bunt 2004.

40. For example, see September 11 Digital Archive, ‹http://911digitalarchive .org›.

Chapter 12

Wiring Up

The Internet Difference for Muslim Networks

The Internet is changing the face of Muslim networks. In little more than a decade, and less than two, a growing sample of the actual diversity of the Muslim world, Muslim interests, and Muslim spiritual and social projects have found or brought their voices to the postmodern information age's diagnostic medium. All manner of organized expression, shades of opinion, and positions on subjects both theological and pragmatic can now be found there. The sample is skewed, but not just in favor of spreading a message. It is affected by the character of the medium, its modes of access and of production, and its location in a transnational social space that eliminates some asymmetries while introducing others. This social space involves more than a new medium: it involves its population, in an active sense; who participates in it and in what capacities; who came online first; and responses to those people's actions, as the Internet has developed from humble beginnings to public prominence to reshape the public sphere of Islam.

Teasing apart this process—actually, multiple intersecting processes— can be devilishly hard. The story is still unfolding, experiments are proceeding, and the evolving interactivity of the Internet as new technologies come online provides an unusual level of responsiveness to the religious "market" for Islamic messages, discourse, and networking, which coevolve with the wider world that they address and in which they are cast. Some of the story has already disappeared, quite literally gone off-line, as both the Internet and the world have moved on from an initial phase of bringing religion online in pious acts of witness to a more complex one of enacting officializing strategies in a world of multiple, contested, and contesting authorities. While contest and multiplicity have drawn the most attention to the Internet realm of Islam (Bunt 2000, Mandaville 2001), a more comprehensive perspective requires a fuller account to be made of how such moves unfold in relation to each other, are rooted in practices, and convey authority.

The concept of "officializing strategies" is one of several that Pierre Bourdieu advanced to refocus social theory on wider ranges of practice than does the moot structuralist concept of fully socialized actors (1977). Bourdieu's idea bears some resemblance to venerable concepts such as "legitimation," but like others in his lexicon, it was aimed at upending presumptions of the priority over action of values, intentions, even knowledge, and reconceptualizing those internal concepts as practices—not just as regulations or conceptualizations—of social life, uncognized as well as cognized. Bourdieu expressed deep skepticism toward accounts for actions as accounting for actions, and thus toward meaning-giving moves such as legitimation that left representations on a field of sublime transcendence, apart from action but also definitive of it. He saw representations— myth and ritual in the anthropologists' "primitive" societies, rationalization in literate and bureaucratic ones—instead as a type of action, a type of discursive practice, as moves in a larger field of practice. Such attempts to "regularize," he argued, are merely a category of officializing practices, whose objective feature "is to transmute 'egoistic,' private, particular interests (notions definable only within the relationship between a social unit and the encompassing social unit at a higher level) into disinterested, collective, publically available, legitimate interests" (1977, 40). To define this transmutation as a social and practical process instead of its detached ideational double, Bourdieu assigned the process to contexts where, absent violence, "political action proper can be exercised only by the effect of officialization and thus presupposes the *competence* . . . required in order to manipulate the collective definition of the situation in such a way as to bring it closer to the official definition of the situation and thereby to win the means of mobilizing the largest possible group, the opposite strategy tending to reduce the same situation to a merely private affair" (40, emphasis in the original).

Clearly, the reference to "competence" implies limitation to what is valuable as well as to what is doable by sheer force or by material means alone. At the same time, the stress Bourdieu places on "competence" puts actions accomplished by material means on the same level as those accomplished by force. Its focus is compliance, not consensus. The process Bourdieu addresses with his concept of officializing strategies is not one of making interpretations more sublime; like so many of his other concepts, this one presupposes a situation fundamentally of contest and resources, but contest of a particular sort, which he calls "the dialectic of the official and the useful" (41). This is a familiar tension in religious discourse, as are the desired outcomes—that private reasons become shared ones, or that the support of the largest possible public be drawn to these reasons.

Online Islam displays several such dialectics, not just between competence in religion and practices of the Internet but also between competences in each and between practices in each. The particular boundlessness of the Internet and its malleability allow it to facilitate such dialectics of synthesis and transference. It does so not just by providing a new medium, arena, or ground—although it does that—but also by drawing in what Dale Eickelman (1992) has called alternative "intellectual technologies," or, more modestly, rhetorical techniques and analytical strategies that a generation-long rise in mass education, particularly in mass higher education, in Muslim countries has introduced into popular religious discourse across the Muslim world. Although varying from country to country, the overall trend has been a marked expansion in secular schooling since Muslim nations won their independence, which, Eickelman observes, shapes discussion of Islam not guided by traditional hermeneutics of the 'ulama' and contributes to an ongoing "Islamic Reformation" of alternative interpretations that implicitly, in becoming public, as well as often explicitly, in their content, contest conventional authority (1998). The Islamic Reformation has not only moved online from the print domain, where a vigorous increase in Islamic publication also developed in the same period (Eickelman and Anderson 1997; Gonzalez-Quijano 1998), the Internet also originates in this world of secular education and contributes its specific practices as well as shared features of modern scientific-technical education and its underlying analytic philosophy to extending the space, scope, and content of Islamic discourse, interlocutors, and authorities.

The Internet intersects the contemporary revival of Islamic discourse at this popular, secularized level. Eickelman locates its techniques in the rise in Muslim countries of mass education, and particularly of mass higher education, which supplies those techniques along with confidence to use them, at a particular point: in the diaspora of Muslims into the most advanced sectors of Western industrial societies. While now known in its most popular, most public manifestations as an information tool, the Internet originated as a communications appliance in the world of engineering and applied science; it conveys the values of this world and has consistently favored new users most like its existing users. Engineers and applied scientists built the Internet as a tool for their own work and extended it both through new uses and to new users who took up and extended those uses. The Internet combined technologies at hand to create interactive, multiuser, multimedia, and networking functions that in the 1960s put computers on the desks and in the laboratories of scientists and engineers and fit computing to their work habits as well as their workplaces. What became the Internet first extended the existing technologies through programming that gave different systems the ability to communicate with each other, eventually transparently; for its engineers, the Internet has always been software as well as a tool, less a thing than a service implemented by programming left in the users' own hands.[1]

The Internet grew in two ways. To communication with distant and disparate machines was quickly added communication between their operators: e-mail was added in 1971 and electronic mailing lists in 1973, and new uses brought new users, along with connections to commercial data networks in 1974 and electronic conferencing, or bulletin boards, by 1980. In social terms, the Internet expands not only who but what is online. The process of expansion was built into the Internet by its engineers, who designed it around their own work habits and values: quick and open access, free flow of information, a decentralized model of administration, and a participatory model of contribution. It grew as other scientists, other academics, and the professionals they trained were attracted to it and added their interests to its design, and also as the interests of its original operators expanded beyond their vocations to include hobbies, politics, and religion.

In this context, Islam was brought online in the 1980s, initially by students from Muslim countries who studied and worked in some of the high-tech institutes where the technology was being developed or extended. These students were among the best and brightest; they went overseas for advanced training not available at home in new disciplines, from computer science to materials engineering, as well as in other applied sciences that were making use of the Internet revolution, from computerized graphics to business and public administration. Much as their counterparts in these fields were bringing avocational interests online, they brought interests in Islam online as pious acts of witness in the new medium of their work; in doing this, they exploited two technologies of the Internet at the time, file archives and electronic discussion groups, that were its most advanced forms of technology.

What they brought online were digitized texts of the holy Quran and the Hadith of the Prophet Muhammad, which modern Islamists from Salafis onward had elevated to sources of the religion. Some were undoubtedly

FIGURE 12.1.
Haroon Internet Café on University Street in Irbid, Jordan, 1999. University Street reputedly has the most Internet cafés of any street in the world. (Photograph by Jon W. Anderson)

scanned from translations in university libraries, others borrowed from digital library experiments like Project Gutenberg that computerized public domain texts. They also created electronic discussion groups that mixed debate about religion with questions about applying the texts to contemporary life and to issues of Muslim life in the diaspora that ranged from where to find places of worship, Muslim bookstores, and halal butchers to news about home, cheap flights, and even matrimonials. Student pioneers were followed by professionals and others in the diaspora who expanded the online forms to include digital newsletters, which were often addressed to particular national populations or focused on Muslim populations in particular Western countries.

What emerged was an often creolized discourse (Jon Anderson 1995) conducted almost entirely in English (reflecting the sites of participants' occupations), though sometimes in French and ad hoc transliterations of Arabic, Persian, or other languages, that applied to religious interpretations the intellectual techniques drawn from educations such as those that Eickelman (1992, 1998) has associated with the spread of mass education. Broadly, a population of persons tracked early into science and mathematics and turning or returning to religion in young adulthood applied techniques acquired in their educations to interpreting texts, techniques that did not include the traditional textual hermeneutics of *madrasa* training. In other words, what these early technological adepts brought online were both the texts—without their surrounding interpretive contexts of *'ulamid* learning—and discussion rooted in diaspora life that drew on resources available in their special segment of it. Theirs was a direct engagement that circumvented, sometimes by design but often just in practice, the continuous interpretive traditions of specifically Islamic learning. Hence Eickelman's characterization of an "Islamic Reformation," that it depended on direct interaction with and interpretation of scripture broadly based in the wider Islamic world, is clearly at work here in the essentially diasporic world that initially brought Islam online.

The creolization mentioned above operated at several levels. On the intellectual level was the application to religious texts of analytical reason and systematization characteristic of modern science education, a pattern that extends back at least to interpretive pioneers of Islamic revival such as Muhammad 'Abduh and Maulana Abu'l-A'la Mawdudi, who opened the space that could hold both science and religion. Equally important as this intermediate ground on which meet members of communities that themselves do not overlap is the intermediate sociological context of diaspora life, which was reflected in the growth of sites that included practical information for leading a Muslim life in non-Muslim-majority societies of North America and Europe. With the advent of the World Wide Web, these came to include sites for national Islamic organizations in North American and in Europe. Such sites replaced with more organized expression the distinctly personal efforts—such as the early website of "Selim the Cybermuslim," which provided primers on Islam in a catchy, youthful idiom of the "*Masjed* of the Ether"—created by students and others who had mastered the technology but were not religious specialists.

As suggested above, the initial phase was followed by another, whose overriding characteristic came to be its restoration of contexts missing or underdeveloped in the initial phase. The first phase was dominated by technological adepts, including pious as well as critical Muslims and some sectarian partisans, but few people with professional religious training or, it often seemed, much religious training beyond elementary levels; their efforts were tied to initial social and technical phases of the Internet that grew in worlds of research and higher education and were limited to those who inhabited them until the invention of the World Wide Web in 1990 opened the Internet to a much wider public. With that opening—and very quickly—more institutional spokesmen for Islam were attracted both to this medium and by the Islam already online, spokesmen with deeper Islamic credentials to represent the religion in more collective terms. What ensued were multiple attempts, strategies, and projects to "correct" what was represented as having been elided, reduced, or misrepresented.

Addressing the elided, reduced, or misrepresented aspects of Islam online as part of a larger problem, two broad sorts of officializing strategies came into play on the Internet. One proceeded from established institutional perspectives and spokespersons, such as those based in traditional *da'wa* organizations; it deployed established apologetics and was devoted to outreach. Sites that represented this strategy were not produced directly by *'ulama'* but by spokespersons from within Muslim-majority societies, and they were not a product of the anxieties of the diaspora. An early example was a website from the embassy of Saudi Arabia in Washington, D.C., on which the embassy's brochures about Islam and texts manifesting the Saudi state's claim to act as a protector of Islam were posted. Others were created by established *da'wa* organizations that provided conventional apologetics and justifications of faith, partly for an already-Muslim audience and partly as outreach to seekers. Few came from schools or other training institutes, although, tellingly, one of the first such sites was created by the missionizing Tablighi Jama'at in Pakistan, which had established a website by the mid-1990s.

The other officializing strategy was more oppositional in tone, substance, and address. It was associated with "political" Islam, or "Islamism," as it came to be called in the 1990s. Sites that represented this strategy spoke not in the language of *da'wa*, rooted as it is in traditional justifications of faith, but with a pointed religious critique of national and traditional religious authority—particularly authorities in Muslim countries— that drew on social experience and language. In a comparative study of Muslim preaching, P. D. Gaffney has provocatively characterized this as the "warrior" style, distinguishable from both scholarly and spiritual styles by a this-worldly focus that draws on practical knowledge and "heavily on scientific and medical allusion" (1994, 43). Some early examples of this style on the Internet were represented in the fashion of movements pressing Islamic critique of regimes in Arab nations, but they employed a political language. Among them were early websites representing positions of the FIS (Islamic Salvation Front) in Algeria and the Movement for Islamic Reform (MIRA) in Saudi Arabia (which aimed at the Saudi government), both based overseas and both of which moved onto the Internet from using fax machines and other small media to spread their messages (see Fandy 1999). Their websites were largely individual efforts or were produced by small groups, not by oppositional organizations such as the Muslim Brotherhood, based in Egypt, or the Shiite Hizbullah movement in Lebanon, although those organizations, too, came online by the later 1990s.

As different as the two approaches described above are in orientation, they are united as officializing strategies that aim to bring online discourse about Islam into line with wider (albeit competitive), more collective authenticity. But the migration brings the familiar "transmutations," to use

Bourdieu's term, into contact with other dynamics—some embedded in the technology, some in diaspora-homeland relations, and some linking them—that reshape Muslim networks in additional, subtle ways.

By the later 1990s, most individual efforts to represent Islam on the Internet had given way to the more institutionally based efforts of movements, schools, and publishing houses, taking forms from static informational websites to the latest interactive portals in multiple languages. Contemporary examples range from Islam101.com, sponsored by a pious foundation that offers instructional material, lesson plans, and exams online as well as topical essays expounding Islamic views about settings of modern life, to Islamworld.net, also directed at non-Muslims but more focused on rites and rights, on the conventional topics and discursive content of *da'wa*, and linked to a full-service Muslim school in the Washington, D.C., suburbs. Even those sites focused on individuals or ostensibly provided by individuals have adopted institutional forms, formats, and connections to religious authorities. Bouti.com offers religious rulings, books, lectures, and sermons by Syria's famous television shaykh and grand mufti, Ramadan Al-Bouti, in Arabic as well as French and English as an online arm of the Dar Al-Fikr publishing house, whose offerings range from encyclopedias of religious knowledge to books for children. The more conservative (Salafi, it would appear from the content) Islamtoday.net presents itself as a collective effort "to present Islam according to the prophetic methodology and stay free from all forms of innovation and corruption" but features its supervising shaykh, Salman bin Fahd al-Oudah, with a traditional *ijaza* of shaykhs he studied with, works he committed to memory, and books he has written, which are available from the site's library along with categorized and searchable fatwas. Both sites are multilingual.

At the discursive level, the gap between diaspora and homeland experiences and concerns blurs not just with the advent online of authoritative spokesmen and the evocation of their institutional authorities; it is also blurred by appropriation of the—likewise institutional, although differently originating—forms of lesson plans for schools offered on Islam101 .com, by the Muslim summer camps offered through Islamworld.net, and by the searchable databases of fatwas and ask-the-Shaykh features on Bouti .com and Islamtoday.net. In similar fashion, oppositional discourse extended its critiques to include additional formats of human rights and social justice (Fandy 1999, Mandaville 2001).

The technology of the World Wide Web underwrites such crossovers. Web technology not only made the Internet more public but also more effectively a publication medium. It shifted the Internet balance from the early models of archive and bulletin board in favor of the later "content providers," an Internet term that distinguishes the conception of the Internet as a tool for delivering content from the more technically-minded construction of it as a platform for providing "services." In the early days of the Web, material was simply transposed from other media—particularly from print—much of it already prepared, such as on the websites mentioned above. Thus, more institutional voices replaced less institutional ones and did not include the more down-market reaches populated by posters, pamphlets, and chapbooks (see Starrett 1995). So, while the Internet initially appeared to be a haven for alternative, noninstitutional voices, it actually came to favor institutions, and particularly media, in its guise as the Web. The reason is that the technology is dynamic, pushed by those it attracts as well as pulling them. The technological possibilities of the Web, and possibilities of showing them off, exert a pressure toward a middle market that also (and increasingly) comes to the Web for work and leisure, as did the pioneering tech adepts. One of the more prominent Islamic sites, IslamOnline.net, which features the most famous Sunni preacher today, Shaykh Yusuf Al-Qaradawi, moved beyond the basic Web technology of hyperlinks to presenting prepared material and then to embracing the more dynamic portal format, with multiple offerings and interactive features from online polls to searchable databases. The latter include not only fatwas but also psychological advice about social relations; they discuss in-laws, non-Muslim coworkers, interfaith marriages, separations for work or schooling, and child rearing, and they provide material on the religious instruction of children, entertainment, health, and contemporary issues as well as continuously updated news of interest to Muslims. IslamOnline's model is shared with news portals, such as the English-Arabic Albawaba.com, which also use newer Web technologies, from searchable databases to user-configurable interfaces, to fit their materials to multiple profiles, interests, and languages.[2] Standardization of Arabic text-processing technology makes it possible to address the same material and extend the same capabilities to homeland audiences, which are broader than those that can be reached with English alone.

At the multiple intersections of these two dynamics of standardization and arabization, technological appropriation and social transmission blur some boundaries and sharpen others. Boundaries between diaspora and homeland populations are blurred, while those between the Internet's favored demographic of middle-class professionals and others sharpen. As boundaries sharpen online, other domains are affected—for instance, *da'wa* flows into lesson plans and teaching materials for schools, into alternative sites for socialization such as summer camps and online lessons, and into alternative types of socialization such as soliciting a fatwa or researching databases of fatwas to find a congenial shaykh. Thus, Islamic universities come online in much the same formats and with much the same ways of organizing information as secular ones, effectively announcing their intention to compete in and to be compared with secular universities in the context of a transnational bourgeois world.

At one point, the global reach of the Internet was thought to comport with a proliferation of alternatives, and superficially that seems to be the case, as the real diversity of the Muslim world is increasingly on display on the Internet, suggesting that Muslim networking takes on the characteristics of a marketplace. But there are reasons to believe otherwise. In drawing up his conceptualization of "officializing strategies," Bourdieu seems to have stressed individuals' recasting of self-interested, highly situated actions in more collective terms. But his evocation of the "competence" to do that as parallel to power (even in place of power) and in place of a language of rights points in another direction. It points to institutional frames and to institutional resources that are shared but not divided. It further suggests that the mobilization of these institutional frames and resources is what distinguishes officializing strategies from mere legitimation moves that are confined to a mental-conceptual level, such as the legitimation of values.

On a more substantive level, online Islam draws on a prior proliferation already set in motion by the spread of mass education in Muslim countries following independence. That education is the setting of dual competences in discourses about Islam, from the texts-as-sources model to political Islam, and in the information technologies that are a subset, or privileged corner, of that education. Somewhat oversimply, Islam had already escaped the *madrasa* and *madrasa* formula, not into the infinite diversity of "local," popular Islams but into the more finite diversity of a debate lodged in (and to some extent between) the middle classes and middle-class struggles over how to lead a Muslim life—what the religion required—in a modern world. Officializing strategies make connections both between *madrasas* and local Islams and between *madrasas* and the middle-class religious debate, and online they make them in both directions, with both—or with multiple—competences. A competency that the Internet brings to Muslim networking is its match with what Manuel Castells calls "the new social morphology of our societies" (1996, 469), by which he suggests that such technologies as the Internet correspond to the material base of a mode of production. At a minimum, the field this opens is a middle or intermediate ground between "elite" Islam tied to *madrasas* and their networks and "folk" Islam tied to places and their networks, and the intermediacy of this ground is reflected in creolization. A segment of this ground is the Internet, substantively composed of the people who populate it and their practices, characterized in the early stage by creolized discourses and more recently by a broader sort of creolized practices.

Finally, it matters how the Internet is conceived. Framing it as a medium tends to focus attention on the multiplication of senders that distinguishes it from prior mass media, which provide the template. And this framing emphasizes a political dimension that intersects with the contemporary Islamic revival's more critical sides and its extensions of the competences of religion as critical political discourse. But the Internet is also technology, and as technology it involves a different set of actors and competences, from finance to engineering, arts to administration, whose habits—competences—come to the fore in making online Islam fit their measures, needs, and resources. The Internet difference does not seem to be that it provides a haven for alternatives but rather that it sustains officializing strategies through the capabilities, resources, and habits that it conveys to them. Those first restore a moderating center to expressions of Islam on the Internet and then expand with its competences and practices the intermediate ground missing in both older dichotomies of elite and folk and newer ones of radical and traditional Islam.

NOTES

This essay draws on several research projects and collaborations, including a conference on print Islam organized at the Rockefeller Foundation's Bellagio Center by Dale F. Eickelman and a comparative study of Internet innovators in four Arab countries supported by grants from the United States Institute of Peace (in collaboration with Michael C. Hudson) and from the American Center of Oriental Research in Amman, Jordan. Earlier versions of this essay were presented at Duke University, at a summer institute on public spheres and Muslim identities at Dartmouth College supported by the Alexander von Humboldt Foundation, and at a meeting of the Islamic Area Studies Project in Japan. I am grateful to Bruce Lawrence and Carl Ernst for their comments and encouragement to sharpen the argument here.

1. The best actual history of the Internet is by Janet Abbate (1999), who makes clear the bricolage of its "invention," its roots in engineering, and engineers' understanding of it fundamentally as software that appropriates hardware

resources. For an account by the principals in the creation of the Internet and cast in terms of software written and decisions taken, compare Leiner et al. (1997).

2. The connection is more than metaphoric. The software company that designed and produces IslamOnline.net also produced the website for Al-Jazeera satellite television, using the same technology.

Chapter 13

A New Research Agenda

Exploring the Transglobal Hip Hop *Umma*

Alim: When did you come into your Islamic knowledge?

Mos Def: I took my *shahada* four years ago.

A: I noticed in "Fear Not of Man" you opened up with "*Bismillah Al-Rahman Al-Rahim*." Was that important for the album?

M: Well, I had been advised that when you do works that go out to the public—written works or spoken works—that you should bless them like that, you know. It makes sense to me. The spiritual level just puts the seal on it. Like I'm making a effort to reach Allah with this. And, *Insha'Allah*, my efforts will be accepted.

MOS DEF, interview by the author, quoted in part in Alim 2001b

"I believe that there is no God but Allah, and I believe that Muhammad is his Messenger." These are the words that rappers Mos Def, Beanie Sigel, Freeway, Common, Chuck D, Napoleon of the Outlawz, and the Rza, along with over one billion other Muslims around the world, proclaimed upon accepting the Islamic faith. Implicit in these words is a commitment to a way of life that is governed, regulated, and mediated by the precepts of Islam, by which Muslims are taught to "fear not of man," but to fear Allah alone (as Brooklyn rapper Mos Def makes clear above). Despite the fact that Islam has been a normative practice in African America since slavery, the full story of African American Muslim movements remains untold. In particular, despite journalist Harry Allen's description of Islam as hip hop's "official religion," Islam's dynamic presence and central role in the hip hop nation have been largely unexplored.

In this exploratory final chapter of *Muslim Networks from Hajj to Hip*

Hop, I will be raising a number of issues and questions for further exploration in our ongoing attempt to gain an understanding of what I am calling the "transglobal hip hop *umma*" within a borderless Islamic nation. That is, the Prophet Muhammad did not speak of an "Islamic Iraq" or of a "Muslim Senegal"; he imagined a transglobal Muslim community, an *umma* where citizenship was based on faith rather than on contemporary nation-state distinctions, or rather, on how colonizing cartographers cut up the global landscape. The original goal of the *umma* was to be a network that was fixed in faith but mobile in all its parts.

We can begin with general questions: How much do we know about the relationship between "hip hop" and "Islam"? Do we even see these two communities as compatible? We can further problematize the notion of "Islamic hip hop" by reconsidering what it means to be an "Islamic artist" more generally, as Judith Ernst asked us to do in her chapter. And we can delve deeper into the history of the hip hop cultural movement and ask questions like the following: Given the fact that Islamic civilization has been at once "transnational" and "connective" (as cooke and Lawrence write in their introduction), how has this transnational connectivity been manifested within the hip hop cultural movement?[1] Further, given the transglobal nature of the hip hop cultural movement, which developed at least two decades ago in the movement's early period (Spady and Eure 1991; Mitchell 2001)—what Perkins (1996) referred to as "youth's global village" and Osumare (2002) as the "Hip Hop Global 'Hood"—how has this cultural nation without traditional borders served the purposes of spreading Islamic knowledge, values, teachings, ideas, and ideals?

Before we can consider the transglobal hip hop *umma*, we need to explore the hidden historics of African American Muslim movements in the hip hop nation. As Spady (2002) argues, "It is helpful to examine the current spread of Hip Hop Culture throughout Algeria and other African countries within the historical context of the Pan African, Pan Islamic and PanBanegritude movements of the 20th century."[2] Through the use of primary sources, namely oral histories and life history narratives, we can begin to develop a deeper understanding of the social, political, and cultural consciousness that is central to the philosophy of the hip hop cultural movement. At the same time, my research draws upon ethnographic techniques and demands direct engagement with hip hop artists wherever hip hop is practiced, that is, from the stadiums to the streets.

"Islam" needs to be broadly conceived, encompassing a spectrum of ideologies and schools of thought. I will focus on the three most dominant forms of Islam in the hip hop nation in the United States—the Nation of Islam, the Nation of Gods and Earths (or the Five Percent Nation of Islam), and the Sunni Muslim community. While there are theological and terminological differences between these communities, all view Islam as a transformative force in the lives of its practitioners, and the data reveal similarities among the views of their adherents. For example, the belief in Allah and the revelation of the Quran through the Prophet Muhammad is a tenet of all Muslim communities. These similarities are revealed through discussions with hip hop artists about the various creative processes involved in their craft.

Hip Hop Texts and the Quranic Text: Structural and Symbolic Similarities

Just as Mecca remains the metaphoric center of the global Muslim network, so do the concepts of the Quran and its revelation to the Prophet Muhammad remain at the core of Muslim beliefs. Members of the hip hop nation who represent the three African American Muslim movements I mentioned above have independently observed that the very means by which the Quran was revealed to the Prophet—that is, orally and, in large part, through rhymed prose—exhibits parallels to the linguistic and literary mode of delivery found in hip hop lyrical production. The African American oral tradition has rarely been interpreted in this way, yet Muslim artists have creatively conceptualized links between their mode of production and their Islamic faith. Through dozens of ethnographic interviews with hip hop artists in the United States, it became clear to me that Muslim hip hop artists were making new connections between hip hop lyrical production and the method and means by which Allah revealed the Quran to the Prophet. They were forging a new transnational network even while acknowledging and privileging its historical antecedents.

Engaged in a conversation about how black youth, often as early as preschool, are familiar with "rap language," rapper Wise Intelligent (a member of the Nation of Gods and Earths and of the rap group Poor Righteous Teachers) claimed: "You have to understand that the potency of the melanin in the black man makes him naturally rhythmic. So when he hears anything that has that rhythm he's going to become a part of that instantly. Anything that rhymes. Many of our ancestors were poets. Imhotep, who built the first step pyramid. The pharaoh Akhenaton, he was a poet. The Prophet Muhammad even wrote poetry. This is our blood" (Spady and Eure 1991, 74). Rapper Mos Def, who is a member of the Sunni Muslim community, discussed the reasons why he believes hip hop lyrics can be an effective medium in educational practice. In the midst of his animated description, he drew a bridge between hip hop poetics and the Quranic text as forms of poetry, each possessing a rhyme scheme and an ability to transmit "vital information" in a relatively short amount of time. His knowledge of the Quran and the Arabic language through which it was revealed were evident in his comments:

> Alim: What do you feel the larger relationship between hip hop and education could be?
>
> Mos Def: I mean, hip hop could be *phenomenal*. Hip hop's relationship to education could be phenomenal. It could be extremely phenomenal, in the sense that hip hop is a medium where you can get a lot of information into a very small space. And make it hold fast to people's memory. It's just a very radical form of information transferal.
>
> A: So, you see it as being a vehicle for transferring information?
>
> M: Oh, hell, yeah! I mean, do you know how much information— vital information—you could get across in three minutes?! You know, and make it so that . . . I mean, the Quran is like that. The reason that people are able to be *hafiz* [one who memorizes the entire Quran through constant repetition and study] is because the entire Quran rhymes. [Mos Def begins reciting Islamic verses from the Quran.] *"Bismillah Al-Rahman Al-Rahim. Al-hamdulillahi Rabb Al-Alameen."* Like everything . . . Like, you see what I'm saying? I mean, it's any *surah* that I could name. *"Qul huwa Allahu ahad, Allahu samud. Lam yalid wa lam yulad wa lam yakun lahu kufwan ahad."* It's all like that. Like, you don't even notice it. *"Idha ja'a nasru Allahi wal fath. Wa ra'aita al-nas yadkhuluna fi dini Allahi afwajan. Fa sabbih bi hamdi rabbika wa istaghfirhu innahu kana tawwab."* Like, there's a rhyme scheme in all of it. You see what I'm saying? And it holds fast to your memory. And then you start to have a deeper relationship with it on recitation. Like, you know, you learn *Surat Al-Ikhlas*, right. You learn *Al-Fatiha*. And you learn it and you recite it. And you learn it and you recite it. Then one day you're reciting it, and you start to understand! You really have a deeper relationship with what you're reciting. *"A'udhu billahi min al-shaitan al-rajim. . . ."* You be like, "Wow!" You understand what I'm saying? Hip Hop has the ability to do that—on a poetic level. (interview by the author, quoted in part in Alim 2001b)

Bay Area rapper JT the Bigga Figga, a registered member of the Nation of Islam, also refers to the literary similarities between what young African Americans are doing with language (see Alim 2002, 2003, 2004) and the purposeful use of creative language by Allah as a pedagogical tool to reach the hearts and minds of humankind. In a discussion of the relationship between the "language of the streets" and the "language of hip hop," JT drew on his knowledge of the Quran and linked it to his Bay Area comrade rapper E-40's inventive and metaphorical use of language:

Alim: How does he [E-40] come up with all this different stuff, man?

JT: Just hangin out and just different people talkin. And, you know, "fo sheezy, off da heezy!" Me and you, what we doin right now, to him, it's called marinatin.

A: Yeah, I hear him say that.

J: Marinatin. We marinatin right now. We goin over . . . Like, it's almost like with Allah how he'll describe his prophets as moonlight. He'll describe his word that he speaks in a metaphoric phrasing. Where he'll say the clouds and when they swell up heavy and the water goes back to the earth, distilling back to the earth. The water's heavier than gravity so it distills back to the earth on dry land, producing vegetation and herbs comin up out the ground, you feel me? And results is happening, you feel me? And the Disbelievers, how they dry land and the sun's scorching it. . . .

A: So he's describing the Believers when things start growing, right.

J: Yeah, yeah. He describe the different conditions, you know what I'm saying? And it can be related to nature, you feel me? *Nature*. And what we see, how we conduct ourself, can be related to some aspect of nature. . . . And that's kinda like what E-40 do when he take something and take a word and apply it, you feel me? (interview by the author)

Whether engaged in conversations about young black children's familiarity with "rap language," the pedagogical potential of hip hop music, or the inventive and innovative use of language by specific artists within the hip hop nation, these hip hop artists invoke Islamic knowledge to accomplish diverse tasks. For Wise Intelligent, it makes sense that young black children would be so attentive to "rap language," because their ancestry (as he describes it), including the Prophet Muhammad, has always been attentive to poetry, and to rhyme in particular. For Mos Def, hip hop's ability to function as what he calls a "radical form of information transferal" is similar to the poetic and pedagogical means by which Allah revealed the Quran to humankind through the Prophet Muhammad. Finally, JT the Bigga Figga refers to Allah's use of metaphoric phrasing in order to clarify his description of E-40's lexical innovation and semantic expansion. Muslim hip hop artists' descriptions of their craft often recalls the function of the Quran. In many of my interviews, I heard Islamic knowledge being invoked spontaneously in the flow of conversation (as often occurs in Muslim-Muslim conversations), pointing to the fact that members of the hip hop nation are studying and applying Islam in their everyday lives.

The Agents of the Transglobal Hip Hop Umma: Some Thoughts for Future Research

Hip hop music has been an active vehicle for social protest in the United States. Its targets have been racism, discrimination, police brutality, miseducation, and other social ills (Rose 1994). Many of the artists involved in the global manifestations of the hip hop cultural movement—in places like France, Canada, Japan, Italy, South Africa, and Palestine—resist the multifarious forms of oppression in global societies. When hip hop pioneer Afrika Bambaataa launched the Muslim-influenced Zulu Nation in the United States in the 1970s and expanded the movement globally in places like France in the early 1980s (Prévos 2001), he was networking to help spread socially and politically conscious ideas and ideals, to build a community of people who would actively resist social, political, and economic subordination. Exploring what he refers to as the "transglobal Islamic underground" and commenting in particular on England's Fun-Da-Mental and France's IAM, Ted Swedenburg writes: "In both countries Muslims are attempting to construct cultural, social and political spaces for themselves as ethnic groups (of sorts), and are massively involved in antiracist mobilizations against white supremacy. Hip-hop activism has been an important arena for anti-Islamophobic mobilization for both French and British Muslims" (2002, 16).

These brief but remarkable examples of anti-imperial, antiracist activities offer a range of sites for us to explore a fundamental question: How do the Muslim members of the hip hop cultural movement make the move from discursive to practical consciousness? In other words, how do these agents go from, as some hip hoppers would say, "*talkin* about it, to *bein* about it"? What is it that makes Public Enemy's Chuck D "try to do some of the things that he talks about" (Spady and Eure 1991, 191)? When San Francisco's JT the Bigga Figga states, "I could sit here and talk to you and tell you what I think I'm seeing, but to really know that in your heart mean you gon *act* on it now, even in a bigger way," what is mediating the move to an active, practical nation-consciousness? Clearly, from these narratives, we can see that such moves are predicated upon faith. JT continues, "And have faith in yourself and in the God who brought you into existence to know that, 'I'm behind you. Do the inspiring thing'" (interview by the author).

My research reveals that not only are these artists studying Islam (as demonstrated by their ability to quote and vividly describe Quranic passages) and applying it to their everyday lives, they are also operationalizing Islam, that is, acting upon what they have learned in order to help build a nation. Mos Def not only raps about issues like consciousness and justice, he lives them. His Islamic consciousness moved him and partner Talib Kweli to rescue Nkiru Bookstore, a black-owned bookstore in his home community of Brooklyn, from having to shut down. It guided him to actively participate in the creation of a hip hop album (*Hip Hop for Respect*) dedicated to obtaining justice for police brutality victims and the immoral murder of Amadou Diallo, a Muslim immigrant from Guinea who was killed by officers of the New York Police Department in 1999. Mos paraphrased the Quran and expressed his faith in Allah at a public rally against the acquittal of the officers who fired forty-one shots at the brother: "To people who seek justice, to the Amadou Diallo family, and to everyone who speaks against oppression, I say, *fear not*, Allah is the best of judges."

Similarly, Public Enemy front man Chuck D's Islamic consciousness moved him from giving live performances in concert halls to giving talks about nation building in the streets, prisons, and schools of black communities. It is what moved him to become perhaps the most well-known advocate for "cutting out the middle man" in the hip hop record industry by circumventing major record labels and distributors, building independent labels, and engaging in e-commerce. JT the Bigga Figga not only realized that he "had a bigger work to do through this music," but he has also helped to revitalize his local communities of Fillmore and Bay's View–Hunter's Point through filling speaking engagements and providing business classes to youth. He not only actively supported and attended the Million Man March and the Million Family March, as well as the many Nation of Islam–sponsored Hip-Hop Summits that have been organized since 1997, he has also assembled a group of young blacks, Latinos, and Pacific Islanders into a national cooperative business venture named Black Wall Street (in commemoration of the United States government's bombing of Oklahoma's Black Wall Street in 1934), thereby providing networking and economic growth opportunities to those traditionally excluded from such enterprises.

I am currently conducting research to uncover more of these Islamic nation-building activities within the hip hop nation. More attention needs to be directed, however, at exploring the role of Muslim female artists who are covering in the name of Allah. What do we know about Philadelphia rapper Eve's struggle and search for inner peace in a male-dominated recording industry? As she reminds us, "Heaven Only Knows." But we can start by engaging Eve and other Muslim female artists in informal conversation. Eve, who opened up the liner notes on her album *Eve of Destruction* with "All Praise Is Due To Allah," speaks about her relationship with Islam: "It's not strong like it should be. I'm striving. When I get to the point where I'm stable I definitely want to cover and go to the *masjid*. But now it's hard. It is really hard. But it definitely has a grip on me. I pray to Allah every night, every morning, all during the day, know what I'm saying? If it wasn't for him I wouldn't be blessed" (interview by the author, quoted in part in Spady, Lee, and Alim 1999). What do we know about New York City's Egyptian female rapper Mutamassik (meaning "tenacious" in Arabic)? What are her personal struggles, and how has she contributed to nation-building activities through and beyond her music (see Swedenburg 2001)?

International Context

What is the relationship between African American Muslim movements in the hip hop cultural movement and the global Islamic world? What kinds of nation-building activities are occurring when Wu-Tang Clan's Rza visits with his Muslim brethren in Egypt, or when the Sunz of Man meet up with IAM in France? What happens when Palestinian rhymer and graffiti artist Masari writes a graff on a San Francisco city wall reading "Liberate Palestine," then spits out these lines on the concrete streets of the United States to note that "back in Ramallah, my brothers are straight strugglin" (interview by the author, 2001):

Those gone souls are in my soul
So now my mission's to be plottin
Let the evil rot in . . .
And our people live forever, cuz souls are not to be forgotten.

What are we to make of the many sons and daughters of Muslim immigrants to the United States who have been hiphopitized by this African American cultural movement? Will academic centers like Duke University's Center for the Study of Muslim Networks begin examining the role that hip hop has played in networking Muslims around the globe, from South Asia to South Philly, from South Africa to South Carolina? These are issues and questions for future research.

Researchers are needed to study the trilingual (Arabic, Hebrew, and English) rappers in Palestine as they rail against what they perceive to be the tyranny of the Israeli state, to explore the struggles of Muslim rappers in Algeria as they wage war on what they believe are corrupt regimes (rappers with African American–inspired names like Ole Dirty Shame, MC Ghosto, and Killa Dox), and to examine how Muslim artists in South Africa are critiquing what they perceive as the hypocrisy of their nation's "new democracy." How are these groups networked? How are they communicating with each other and the world? How has the Internet helped network Muslim artists and practitioners in the hip hop cultural movement? How are newsgroups such as Yahoo's "Muslims in Hip Hop" contributing to nation-building activities within the transglobal hip hop *umma*?

Conclusion

In conclusion, the hip hop cultural movement needs to be examined with a seriousness of purpose and a methodology that considers the networked nature of Islam in order to reveal the hidden aspects of this highly misunderstood transglobal phenomenon, a cultural movement whose practitioners represent, arguably, some of the most cutting-edge conveyors of contemporary Islam. What will the new knowledge that is revealed mean for Islamic scholars who teach courses on *fiqh* (jurisprudence), Quranic exegesis, Islamic civilization, or Islam and modernity? Will it transform our view of the impact of popular culture, particularly hip hop culture, in constructing an Islam appropriate to the needs of contemporary society? Further, will imams revise their pedagogies in efforts to engage Muslim youth who are living in this postmodern hip hop world?

There will undoubtedly be many changes in the way that hip hop culture is studied in the academy within the next five to ten years. Hip hop culture's global impact has helped to transform public opinion (including opinion within the academy) of the art form. Only a decade ago, hip hop culture occupied a shunned pariah status in the academy; today, universities like Stanford, Harvard, Berkeley, Duke, and the University of Pennsylvania are offering hip hop courses in departments as diverse as linguistics, religious studies, philosophy, and African American studies. Hip hop culture is being widely recognized as the most recent instantiation of an African American oral tradition that has "gone global," become syncretized with other world cultures and musics as new manifestations of hip hop form worldwide (see Egyptian singer Hakim's latest offering, *Tamenny Alaik*, which combines French and Spanish-language rap with contemporary Egyptian *sha'abi* music), and galvanized an entire generation of youth to become more involved in social and political causes.

Many questions remain for what Jamillah Karim calls the "American *umma*." Will hip hop culture's profound impact on Muslim immigrants to the United States, and their sons and daughters, help to reduce the current divide between the African American Muslim communities and immigrant Muslim communities? Will hip hop culture be the vehicle that helps unite the "American *umma*"? Or will the transformative, resistive power of hip hop culture be undercut by its widely gained acceptance and co-optation by some of the very institutions it was created to resist? For now, we will continue to document the nation-building activities that are occurring around a world that is more and more tightly networked by these two seemingly contradictory communities—Islam and the hip hop nation—or, as we have conceived it here, the transglobal hip hop *umma*.

NOTES

1. Hip hop culture is sometimes defined as having four major elements: MCing (rapping), DJing (spinning records), break dancing (also known as "street dancing," an array of acrobatic dances associated with the hip hop cultural domain), and graffiti art (also known as "writing" or "tagging" by its practitioners). To these, pioneering hip hop artist KRS-One adds knowledge and Afrika Bambaata, founder of the hip hop cultural movement, adds "overstanding," a word used frequently by Rastafarians to mean more than a cursory understanding, an ability to read between the lines to arrive at a deeper, sometimes hidden, meaning. Even with six elements, this definition of hip hop culture is quite limited in scope. It is useful to distinguish between the terms "hip hop" and "rap." Rapping, one aspect of hip hop culture, consists of the aesthetic placement of verbal rhymes over musical beats. "Hip hop culture" refers not only to the various elements listed above but also to the entire range of cultural activity and modes of being that encompass the hip hop culture-world. This is why Bloods say, "Hip hop ain't just music, it's a whole way of life!"

2. "PanBanegritude" is an anticolonial movement that had its origins among francophone Africans and Asians in France and Belgium during the 1920s. Kojo Touvalou Houenou, a Dahomean lawyer trained at the University of Bordeaux in France and a leader of the Universal Negro Improvement Association organized by Marcus Garvey, was a forerunner of the Pan African movement who claimed his negritude a decade before the literary negritude movement organized by Leopold Senghor, Leon Damas, and Aime Cesaire. Houenou's Ligue

Universelle de la Défense de la Race Noire (Universal League for the Defense of the Black Race) and Ho Chi Minh's organization, Union Internationale, contributed to PanBanegritude unity. The Asian African caucus, founded at the inaugural conference of the League against Imperialism held in Brussels, Belgium, in 1927, predated the better-known Bandung Conference of Asians and Africans held in Indonesia by nearly three decades.

Afterword

Raymond Williams would have called this volume a subjunctive, not an indicative, text. Whereas indicative texts indicate happenings, subjunctive texts offer radical perspectives that move beyond socially and politically observable phenomena. Subjunctive texts attempt "to lift certain pressures, to push back certain limits; and all the same, in a fully extended production, bearing the full weight of the pressures and limits, in which the simple forms, the simple contents, of mere ideological reproduction can never achieve" (1986, 16). The category of network functions like a subjunctive text, compelling us to rethink Muslim cultures and societies. It is not enough to describe these societies; we must open theory to that which theory cannot synthesize.

Muslim Networks from Hajj to Hip Hop displaces traditional ways of conceiving Islam and Islamic phenomena that fix Islam and Muslims in the Orient while mapping Muslim culture onto Oriental Muslim territory. Instead, our gaze is shifted to the image of travel. We encounter the idea of Islam on the move. We face again and again, wherever we look, whatever we imagine, the heterogeneity of Islam and the imbrication of Muslims with various non-Muslim others across the globe and throughout history. The essays that comprise *Muslim Networks* also travel. They breach disciplinary boundaries. They deploy strategies and modes of thinking derived from the multifaceted concept "network" to reflect upon various aspects of Islam. They mark a paradigmatic shift in the study of Islam and Muslims. Islamic history becomes much more than a chronological unfolding of events since the Prophet Muhammad's revelation in seventh-century Arabia. The history of Islam itself changes, at once producing and reflecting on myriad spatial and temporal interactions between people, events, and ideas.

The contributors perceive history as disruptive rather than continuous. History disrupts homogeneous time. Multiplying links between different levels of analysis, the contributors generate nonlinear modes of thought. They also subvert hierarchical relations, whether social or mental. Deploying the tropological construct of network, they problematize monocausal, top-down ways of thinking. History is neither given nor fixed. History is neither directly accessible nor analytically unproblematic. History, rather, becomes a critical discourse that appropriates the past for present purposes. The study of Islam has as much to do with pragmatics and contingencies as it does with theology and metaphysics, and precisely because the latter has been so much stressed, the present volume restores a measure of balance by accenting the former.

The contributors construct history echoing Jacques Derrida's "concept." They acknowledge complicity with an eschatological and teleological metaphysics yet do not remain bound by its weight. Like Derrida, they attempt to reinscribe history as a holistic enterprise "by writing histories that set up supplementary figures whose logic simultaneously invokes and works against historical totalities" (Derrida 1978, 291). Both editors and contributors to *Muslim Networks* talk about the "spatial rhythm" of Islamic history, marking Mecca as the "defining node for a worldwide community of believers." The role played by Mecca across history confers on this spiritual capital of Islam a dimension that exceeds its existence as mere location. The Mecca of the "ordinary believer" and her imagination is as real as the Mecca of the Arab rulers who fought for its physical control and inclusion in their territorial domains.

Closely bound up with this revisionist perspective on history is a perspective on culture that goes against the grain. Culture is not an all-encompassing phenomenon, a cosmos within which individuals act. What individuals do with their lives is more than a localized cultural fact. In Theodor Adorno's sense of the phantasmagoric, the local conceals as much as it reveals; it is always and everywhere a contingent configuration structured by transnational networks. The here is shaped by the elsewhere, and culture, once reconceived through the image of networks, becomes inseparable from travel. Too often Ibn Battuta's *rihla* has been seen as an exceptional voyager's travelogue, but in this volume it becomes what it is most suited to be: "a template for understanding Muslim networks." Travel was integral to the constitution of Muslim networks; movement from place to place, and also reflection on travel as an exemplary, anticipated activity, affected trade, language, and scholarship.

And more: travel shaped the core of Muslim identity. Because it is the basis for shared values that are specifically marked as Muslim, travel is of particular interest for the study of Islam. We find Muslim intellectuals conceptualizing scholarship as a site of travel at the same time that they perceive uprootedness to be inextricably linked to dissent. When legal schools were founded in fourteenth-century Morocco, Shaykh Abili objected to their creation on the ground that they were likely to tie scholars to particular places and to make them dependent on their patrons (Wansharisi 1981, vol. 2). As men whose mission is exhortation for the good and dissuasion from the evil (*al-amr bi al-ma'ruf wa al-nahy 'an al-munkar*), Islamic scholars gained from the autonomy that travel offered them. However, dissent was not the only reason why these scholars preferred movement. Many enjoyed the generosity of the various rulers they served and for whose rule they provided an ideological cover. Travel allowed these scholars to participate in an exclusive interpretive community at the same time that they shaped a broad discursive tradition.

Networks free individuals. They are more affiliative than filiative. They involve a measure of choice that implies agency. A networked approach to Islam reveals Islamic identity as a crossroads rather than an island, a construction rather than an essence. Nowhere is this more evident than in the perception of the Islamic *umma*. Traditionally perceived as a unified, homogeneous community, the notion of *umma* has always occluded rifts and contradictions and has been unlinked from any idea of travel and movement. This conservative view of the *umma* is undermined by the various contributors, who perceive the *umma* as mobile and malleable, as the context for Muslim networks, not their antithesis.

A number of contemporary Muslim scholars share this perspective on the *umma*, projecting it as at once heterogeneous and conflict-ridden. Abdelkebir Khatibi, one of the most thought-provoking cultural critics in Morocco, rejects as theological the notion of unity deployed as "a community principle" within one country or as a means of "rallying all Moslems in the framework of an Umma" (1993, 9). Khatibi has urged the necessity of internationalizing research and of opening it up to different methodologies. Rejecting sterile rootedness, Khatibi advocates approaching the study of Islam as a hybrid discursive space.

But how does the study of Islam become a hybrid discursive space? For the contributors to this volume, the necessary first step is to deploy network as a metaphorical methodology. This metaphorical move, at work throughout *Muslim Networks*, has important antecedents in critical European thinking as well as in some circles of Muslim revisionism. In "The Retrait of Metaphor," Derrida problematizes the relation between metaphor and concept, on the one hand, and between dead and live metaphors, on the other hand. He does so in order to show how words are above all polyvalent; they cannot be restricted to the sense attached to them in conventional theory. Roland Barthes goes further, considering "historical discourse" to be "a fudged up performative, in which what appears as a statement (and description) is in fact no more than the signifier of the speech act as an act of authority." For Barthes, "the real" in history is merely an "unformulated signified, sheltering behind the apparently all-powerful referent" (1981, 17). To challenge the constructedness of "the real," in Barthes's view, requires a double subversion, subverting the linear movement from the past to the present but also subverting the univocal, unidirectional relation between context and text.

If "Muslim networks" conjures a single image, it is the Internet, even though both the novelty and the transformative value of the Internet become problematized as soon as one puts it within the broad framework of networks advocated by contributors to this volume. While the emergence of the Internet does allow new modes of networking, this technological change should not be interpreted as necessarily enabling the marginalized or promoting a democratic means of connectivity. The Internet constitutes a site of struggle between various subject positions, all of which seek to reclaim Islam. Often they have not just disparate but also incompatible goals. Some Islamist groups, for instance, deploy the Internet to facilitate a kind of virtual *umma*, one where the members, disembedded from their "original" nations, try to rebuild what they deem to be a singular Islamic society, at once pure and uncontaminated. Some Muslim women, on the other hand, appropriate the Net in order to constitute a subaltern public sphere that empowers them to subvert male dominance, beginning with an alternative narrative of Muslim loyalty and legitimacy.

Women's voices on the Net, while important, do not exhaust the transformative potential of women's voices in contemporary Muslim society. Sometimes, as in the case of Iraqi women refugees after the first Gulf War, there must be a painful re-membering of past ordeals in order to make sense of them. Ritual lamentations serve as a kind of anamnesis, the psychoanalytic procedure that allows patients "to elaborate their current problems by freely associating apparently inconsequential details with past situations—allowing them to uncover hidden meanings in their lives and behavior" (Lyotard 1992, 93). The stories of Iraqi Shiite women in exile seal these women's relations with their brothers and sisters at home, their sisters away from home, and, paradoxically, with their oppressors. These women live in what Barbara Adam calls a "multitude of times"

(1995, 12), in memory, in consciousness, and in narrative. Temporal displacement occurs each time these women organize their *majlis al-qiraya*: through interconnective networking, they escape the tyranny of standardized temporality that reckons them only by their physical condition and not by their imaginative resources of self-definition and historical engagement.

An even starker contrast to traditional male-dominated spheres is presented in both the Islamization of Egyptian elite women through salons and the politicization of middle-class American women through an activist magazine. In both cases, these women's reinterpretations of texts and appropriations of space indicate how Islam has become a site of struggle due to aggressive networking. "Muslim women are demanding equal access to scriptural truth at a time when Islamic discourse is on the rise," miriam cooke has written (2001, xi). Who are these publicly engaged but often invisible Muslim women? They are Islamic feminists who "are inventing ways to navigate between forced changes necessary for survival, a critique of globalized modernity, and a viable means of self-projection that retains dignity, modernity, and integrity. In this balancing act, women are gaining symbolic importance" (xix).

Muslim women activists use print, but they do so recognizing it as one, but only one, means of injecting themselves into a broadened public sphere. While the use of print helps to instrumentalize modernity on behalf of an Islamic feminist agency, other Muslim groups have deployed print, audio, and film, as well as the new computer-mediated communication technologies, to promote their agendas. Many of the contributors to *Muslim Networks* ponder the scope of what has been dubbed "the information revolution." The new global arrangements have been marked, above all, by the transformative impact of technology, giving rise to what Manuel Castells calls "the network society," "the networking form of organization," and also to "powerful expressions of collective identity that challenge globalization and cosmopolitanism on behalf of cultural singularity and people's control over their lives and environment" (1997, 1–2). The various political contenders in the new global order/disorder are aware that "globalizing capitalism and the ubiquitous computing that it depends upon mean that networks of interconnectivity are set to deepen and widen, spreading its temporality across more and more realms of life. Email, mobile telephony, SMS text messaging, interactive digital television, Personal Digital Assistants (PDAs), pagers, mobile computing, Bluetooth and WAP-enabled applications, and the Internet itself, are building into the thicket of interconnectivity that constitutes the technological framework for network time" (Hassan 2003, 234). Not only political activists but also Sufi leaders use "the new, powerful technological media, such as worldwide, interactive, telecommunication networks" (Castells 1997, 1–2). In a new situation in which Sufism is no longer confined to Muslims, Sufis are coping with the tensions between the internal aspect of the Sufi religious community and its externalization through the publication of Sufi texts for foreign consumption. Sufis, far from submitting to the marginalizing strategies of their numerous detractors, have actively engaged in a successful politics of identity.

One must also address identity politics as itself a new social movement. The traditional social movement paradigm emphasized economic growth, the distribution of wealth, social security, and social control, and it was primarily based on class. The multilevel character of social movements is constituted by their networks of informal interactions between unaffiliated individuals, groups, and formal organizations engaged in social conflict on the basis of a collective identity. The collective identity explored in this volume is a Salafi one premised on the view that a return to the fundamentals of Islam is not only desirable but necessary. Yet "collective identity does not imply homogeneity of ideas and orientation within social groups" (Diani 1992, 9). As Alain Touraine, Alberto Melucci, and Charles Tilly have argued, schism is a defining characteristic of social movements. To the extent that Salafis are schismatics who continue to interact with parts of the *umma*, Bin Laden and al-Qaeda are not "outside" Islam. The Islamic *umma*, in their view, has become a monolith collapsed into the new age of ignorance, or *jahiliyya*, akin to that which prevailed prior to the advent of Islam. Rather than relying on formal organizations, which are liable to be co-opted by the surveillant state, they construct informal networks that are "decentralized" and less bound by national or international regulations. In sum, Salafism projects both a conflict-ridden community and a network-based activism.

No less subject to interconnectivity and networking activism are "cyber Islamic environments." Virtual Islam is in constant flux and thus requires continuous reassessment from an interdisciplinary perspective. The crucial, recurrent question is: What determines an Islamic site? Is it the symbols and the images on the site, or is it the religious authority it has? Similar questions need to be asked of Islamic art. It too reflects a shifting set of traits, marked as hybrid rather than predictive. Islam is not naturally and automatically inscribed in either a website or an art object. Indeed, the Islamic character of both forms of representation—on the Web and in the studio—remains open to contestation. New forms of circulation of Islamic knowledge threaten to undermine the power of traditional centers of authority and to empower individuals and groups in their search for alternative interpretations. Islamic activists, like Islamic artists, instrumentalize modern information technology to interconnect within the framework of the network.

It is fascinating to chart how the Internet has changed Muslim networks. Online Islam during the 1980s emerged as a creolized discourse, and to the present, the Internet remains a site for alternative, radical, or folk voices opposed to traditional or elite voices. Yet to the extent that the Internet favors institutions, it remains conservative, privileging those who have frequent access to it over occasional users or nonusers. But even among the privileged, there has occurred a blurring of the boundaries between diaspora and homeland populations and a sharpening of the boundaries between "the Internet's favored demographic of middle-class professionals and others."

Islamic individuals as well as groups try to appropriate information technology and to imbricate it in modernity and globalization dynamics. Muslim identities are not fixed along clearly demarcated lines that disallow negotiations, ambivalence, hybridity, and vernacular cosmopolitanisms. Muslims try to reinvent and reinterpret their traditions and their communities through the adoption of network technologies, even when the modernity that promotes these technologies is made the object of attack.

Focus on the "cyber *umma*" toward the end of this volume complements the other essays in *Muslim Networks* that focus on the "historical *umma*." In both cases, what is emphasized is the network as a framework for understanding Islamic connectivity across history. This has allowed the thinking of distinctions within the Islamic polity in terms of connections, but at the same time it draws our attention to the necessity of reflecting on networking not merely as a utopia but also as a major site of conflict.

Muslim Networks allows a return to the past, but it is not a unidirectional return. The volume frames the past as an engagement with the present, evoking a presentist pressure that questions the past even while shedding light on its continuing importance. The contributors have engaged in a Foucauldian history of the ambiguous present. Their several essays enable a mode of thinking about the past as present, and the present as past, that moves away from the deep-laid essentializing assumptions about Islam. Other critical models, inspired mainly by the revisionist work of Edward Said, have facilitated a critique of homogenizing perspectives of Islam, but what seems most innovative in *Muslim Networks* is its movement away from the simple binarism and totalitarianism associated with the critique of the Orientalist perspective. Even though the category "network" may evoke images of solidary utopianism, all contributors are aware of the fact that networks can also be alienating. As Jeremy Rifkin points out in his discussion of digital networks, such networks can "relentlessly constitute and reconstitute us as 'focus groups,' 'niche markets,' 'demographics,' 'zones,' 'customer profiles' and so on, to be classified, bought sold just like any other commodity" (2000, 55). This "multivalence" of the term "network" makes it an ideal tool to engage with "Muslim," the other term of the title of this work that is equally complex and multivalent. Muslim networks becomes an appropriate means to complicate the reductive views of Islam that have proliferated since 9/11, and so *Muslim Networks* is not a simple celebration of postmodern nomadic travel theory but a critique of the interpretive matrices by which Islam has been perceived as a homogeneous, discrete, object-like phenomenon occupying the Orient.

Just as Muslim networks require travel, so this volume needs to travel. It needs to travel into many domains of thought and labor. It needs to engage both Muslims and non-Muslims about the future—which is inseparable from the past and present—of Islam and Muslim networks.

Abbate, Janet. 1999. *Inventing the Internet*. Cambridge, Mass.: MIT Press.

Abdo, Geneive. 2000. *No God but God: Egypt and the Triumph of Islam*. New York: Oxford University Press.

Abdulrazak, Fawzi. 1990. "The Kingdom of the Book: The History of Printing as an Agency of Change in Morocco between 1865 and 1912." Ph.D. diss., Harvard University. Translated into Arabic by Khalid Bin al-Saghir as *Mamlakat al-kitab: Tarikh al-tibaʿh fi al-Maghrib, 1865–1912*. Rabat, Morocco: Jamiʿat Muhammad al-Khamis, Kulliyyat al-Adab wa-al-ʿUlum al-Insaniyya, 1996.

Abu-Lughod, Janet. 1989. *Before European Hegemony: The World System, A.D. 1250–1350*. New York: Oxford University Press.

Abu-Lughod, Lila. 1985. "Honour and the Sentiments of Loss in a Bedouin Society." *American Ethnologist* 12(2): 245–61.

———. 1993. "Islam and the Gendered Discourses of Death." *International Journal of Middle East Studies* 25(2): 187–205.

Adam, Barbara. 1995. *Timewatch*. Cambridge: Polity Press.

Adelkhan, Fariba. 2000. *Being Modern in Iran*. New York: Columbia University Press.

Ahmed, Durre. N.d. "Notes toward the Construction of a Pathology of Interpretation: A Postmodern Postmortem." Unpublished paper.

Ahmed, Leila. 1992. *Women and Gender in Islam: Historical Roots of a Modern Debate*. New Haven, Conn.: Yale University Press.

Akhavi, Shahrough. 1980. *Religion and Politics in Contemporary Iran: Clergy-State Relations in the Pahlavi Period*. Albany: State University of New York Press.

Alam, Muzaffar. 1998. "The Pursuit of Persian: Language in Mughal Politics." *Modern Asian Studies* 32(2): 317–49.

Algar, Hamid. 1983. *The Roots of the Islamic Revolution*. London: Open Press.

Ali, Lorraine. 2002. "A Magazine of Their Own." *Newsweek*, 26 May.

Ali, Nadje Sadiq Al-. 2000. *Secularism, Gender, and the State in the Middle East: The Egyptian Women's Movement*. Cambridge: Cambridge University Press.

Alim, H. Samy, ed. 2001a. "Hip Hop Culture: Language, Literature, Literacy and the Lives of Black Youth." Special issue, *Black Arts Quarterly* 6(2).

———. 2001b. "Three-X-Black: Mos Def, Mr. Nigga (Nigga, Nigga) and Big Black Afrika X-amine Hip Hop's Cultural Consciousness." In "Hip Hop

Culture: Language, Literature, Literacy and the Lives of Black Youth," edited by H. Samy Alim. Special issue, *Black Arts Quarterly* 6(2): 6–9.

———. 2002. "Street Conscious Copula Variation in the Hip Hop Nation." *American Speech* 77(3): 288–301.

———. 2003. "On Some Serious Next Millennium Rap Ishhh: Pharoahe Monch, Hip Hop Poetics, and the Internal Rhymes of Internal Affairs." *Journal of English Linguistics* 31(1).

———. 2004. "Rap and Hip Hop." In *Language in the USA: Themes for the Twenty-First Century*, edited by Edward Finnegan and John R. Rickford. New York: Cambridge University Press.

Aljeffri, Sharifah Zuriah. 1993. "Bosnian Series Art Statement." Privately published for distribution at the NGO Forum, United Nations Conference on Human Rights, Vienna, Austria, June.

Allione, Costanzo, dir. 1997. *Habiba: A Sufi Saint from Uzbekistan*. VHS. New York: Mystic Fire Video.

Amili, A. al-. 1992. *Al-Bakauun al-khamsa*. Beirut: Matbaa Dar al-Funun.

Amin, Betty Hasan. 2001. "Hajj in a Wheelchair." *Azizah*, Winter.

Amnesty International. 1997a. *Algeria: Civilian Population Caught in a Spiral of Violence*. New York: Amnesty International.

———. 1997b. *Algeria: Civilians Caught between Two Fires*. New York: Amnesty International.

Anderson, Benedict. 1991. *Imagined Communities: Reflections on the Origin and Spread of Nationalism*. London: Verso.

Anderson, Jon W. 1995. "'Cybarites,' Knowledge Workers and New Creoles on the Superhighway." *Anthropology Today* 11(4): 13–15.

———. 1999. "The Internet and Islam's New Interpreters." In *New Media in the Muslim World: The Emerging Public Sphere*, edited by Dale F. Eickelman and Jon W. Anderson, 41–56. Bloomington: Indiana University Press.

———. 2002. "New Media in the Arab Middle East and Diaspora." Address to the First World Congress for Middle Eastern Studies, Mainz, Germany, September.

Aqqad, M. al-. 1997. "Al-azza al-Husayni" [The Husaynid Lament]. *Al-Nur Magazine* 76:44–50.

Arberry, A. J., trans. 1975. *Discourses of Rumi*. London: J. Murray.

Arjomand, Said Amir. 1984. "Traditionalism in Twentieth-Century Iran." In *From Nationalism to Revolutionary Islam*, edited by Said Amir Arjomand, 195–232. Albany: State University of New York Press.

———. 1996. "The Crisis of the Imamate and the Institution of Occultation in Twelver Shi'ism: A Sociohistorical Perspective." *International Journal of Middle East Studies* 28(4): 491–515.

Arquilla, John, and David Ronfeldt. 1996. *The Advent of Netwar*. Santa Monica, Calif.: Rand.

Asad, Talal. 1986. *The Idea of an Anthropology of Islam*. Washington, D.C.: Center for Contemporary Arab Studies.

Asnad-i Inqilab-i Islami [Documents from the Islamic Revolution]. 1990–96. 5 vols. Tehran: Markaz-i Asnad-i Inqilab-i Islami.

Badr, Hoda. 2000. "Al-Noor Mosque: Strength through Unity." In *Religion and the New Immigrants: Continuities and Adaptations in Immigrant Congregations*, edited by Helen Rose Ebaugh and Janet Saltzman Chafetz, 193–227. Walnut Creek, Calif.: AltaMira Press.

Badran, Margot. 1995. *Feminists, Islam, and Nation*. Princeton, N.J.: Princeton University Press.

Badran, Margot, and miriam cooke, eds. 1990. *Opening the Gates: A Century of Arab Feminist Writing*. Bloomington: Indiana University Press.

Bagby, Ihsan, Paul M. Perl, and Bryan T. Froehle. 2001. *The Mosque in America: A National Portrait; A Report from the Mosque Study Project*. Washington, D.C.: Council on American-Islamic Relations.

Bakhash, Shaul. 1984. "Sermons, Revolutionary Pamphleteering and Mobilisation: Iran, 1978." In *From Nationalism to Revolutionary Islam*, edited by Said Amir Arjomand. Albany: State University of New York Press.

Bakhsh, Hajji Makhdum, ed. 1913. *Silsila-i ʿaliyya-i Chishtiyya Nizamiyya Fakhriyya Sulaymaniyya Lutfiyya*. Lucknow, India: Nawal Kishor.

Baqillani, Abu Bakr ibn al-Tayyib al-. 1987. *Kitab tamhid al-awaʾil wa talkhis al-dalaʾil* [Book of Principles and Guides]. Edited by ʿImad al-Din Ahmad Haydar. Beirut: Muʾassasat al-Kutub al-Thaqafiyah.

Barthes, Roland. 1981. "The Discourse of History." Translated by Stephen Bann. *Comparative Criticism* 3: 7–20.

Batalvi, ʿAshiq Husain. 1969. *Iqbal ke akhari du sal*. Lahore, Pakistan: Iqbal Akadimi.

Bautze, Joachim K. 1998. *Interaction of Cultures: Indian and Western Painting, 1780–1910*. Alexandria, Va.: Art Services International.

Bearman, P. J., T. Bianquis, C. E. Bosworth, E. J. van Donzel, and W. P. Heinrichs. 1999. Volume 10, *Encyclopaedia of Islam, New Edition*. Leiden, Netherlands: Brill.

Behn, Wolfgang. 1984. *Iranian Opposition to the Shah*. Zug, Switzerland: Inter Documentation.

Benford, Robert D., and Louis Zurcher. 1990. "Instrumental and Symbolic Competition among Peace Movement Organizations." In *Peace Action in the Eighties: Social Science Perspectives*, edited by San Marullo and John Lofland, 125–39. New Brunswick, N.J.: Rutgers University Press.

Berkey, Jonathan P. 2003. *The Formation of Islam: Religion and Society in the Near East, 600–1800*. New York: Cambridge University Press.

Bianchi, T. X. 1843. "Catalogue général des livres arabes, persans et turcs, imprimés à Boulac en Égypte depuis l'introduction de l'imprimerie dans ce pays." *Journal Asiatique* (July–August): 24–61.

Binder, Leonard. 1979. "Revolution in Iran: Red, White, Blue or Black?" *Bulletin of the Atomic Scientists* 35(1): 48–54.

Blank, Jonah. 2001. *Mullahs on the Mainframe: Islam and Modernity among the Daudi Bohras*. Chicago: University of Chicago Press.

Bloch, Marc. 1953. *The Historian's Craft*. Translated by Michael Putnam. New York: Vintage.

Bloom, Jonathan, and Sheila Blair. 1997. *Islamic Arts*. London: Phaidon.

Bodansky, Yossef. 1999. *Bin Laden: The Man Who Declared War on America*. Roseville, Calif.: Prima.

Bonner, Jay. Forthcoming. *Islamic Geometric Patterns: Their Historical Development and Traditional Methods of Derivation*. Ashland, Ore.: White Cloud Press.

Bourdieu, Pierre. 1977. *Outline of a Theory of Practice*. Translated by Richard Nice. London: Cambridge University Press.

Braswell, George W., Jr. 1975. "A Mosaic of Mullahs and Mosques: Religion and Politics in Iranian Shiʿah Islam." Ph.D. diss., University of North Carolina at Chapel Hill.

Bruce, James. 1995. "The Azzam Brigades: Arab Veterans of the Afghan War." *Jane's Intelligence Review* 7(4): 175–79.

Buechler, Stephen. 1993. *Women's Movements in the United States: Woman Suffrage, Equal Rights, and Beyond*. New Brunswick, N.J.: Rutgers University Press.

Buehler, Arthur F. 1998. *Sufi Heirs of the Prophet: The Indian Naqshbandiyya and the Rise of the Mediating Sufi Shaykh*. Columbia: University of South Carolina Press.

Bulliet, Richard W. 1972. *The Patricians of Nishapur: A Study in Medieval Islamic Social History*. Cambridge, Mass.: Harvard University Press.

Bunt, Gary. 2000. *Virtually Islamic: Computer-Mediated Communication and Cyber-Islamic Environments*. Cardiff: University of Wales Press.

———. 2003a. "Islam Interactive: Mediterranean Islamic Expression on the World Wide Web." In *Shaping the Current Islamic Reformation*, edited by B. A. Roberson, 164–86. London: Frank Cass.

———. 2003b. *Islam in the Digital Age: E-Jihad, Online Fatwas, and Cyber Islamic Environments*. London: Pluto Press.

———. 2004. "Rip.Burn.Pray: Islamic Expression Online." In *Religion Online: Finding Faith on the Internet*, edited by Douglas E. Cowen and Lorne L. Dawson, 123–34. New York: Routledge.

Cannadine, David. 2001. *Ornamentalism: How the British Saw Their Empire*. Oxford: Oxford University Press.

Castells, Manuel. 1996. *The Information Age: Economy, Society and Culture*. Vol. 1, *The Rise of the Network Society*. Malden, Mass.: Blackwell.

———. 1997. *The Power of Identity*. Malden, Mass.: Blackwell.

———. 2000. *The Information Age: Economy, Society, and Culture*. Malden, Mass.: Blackwell.

Chakrabarty, Dipesh. 2000. *Provincializing Europe: Postcolonial Thought and Historical Difference*. Princeton, N.J.: Princeton University Press.

Chatty, Dawn, and Annika Rabo, eds. 1997. *Organizing Women: Formal and Informal Groups in the Middle East*. Oxford: Berg.

Clark, Janine Astrid. 2003. *Faith, Networks, and Charity: Islamic Welfare Activ-*

ism and the Middle Class in Egypt, Yemen, and Jordan. Bloomington: Indiana
University Press.

Cohn, Bernard. 1983. "Representing Authority in Victorian India." In *The Invention of Tradition*, edited by Eric J. Hobsbawm and Terence O. Ranger,
165–210. Cambridge: Cambridge University Press.

———. 1985. "The Command of Language and the Language of Command."
In *Subaltern Studies: Writings on South Asian History and Society*, vol. 4,
edited by Ranajit Guha, 276–329. Delhi: Oxford University Press.

Conrad, Lawrence I. 1996a. "Through the Thin Veil: On the Question of Communication and the Socialization of Knowledge in *Hayy ibn Yaqzan*." In *The
World of Ibn Tufayl: Interdisciplinary Studies on "Hayy ibn Yaqzan,"* edited by
Lawrence I. Conrad, 238–66. Leiden, Netherlands: Brill.

———, ed. 1996b. *The World of Ibn Tufayl: Interdisciplinary Studies on "Hayy ibn
Yaqzan."* Leiden, Netherlands: Brill.

Cook, Michael. 2000. *Commanding Right and Forbidding Wrong in Islamic
Thought*. New York: Cambridge University Press.

cooke, miriam. 1988. *War's Other Voices: Women Writers on the Lebanese Civil
War*. Cambridge: Cambridge University Press.

———. 1997. *Women and the War Story*. Berkeley and Los Angeles: University
of California Press.

———. 2001. *Women Claim Islam: Creating Islamic Feminism through Literature*. New York: Routledge.

Cornell, Vincent J. 1998. *Realm of the Saint: Power and Authority in Moroccan
Sufism*. Austin: Texas University Press.

———. 1999. "Faqih versus Faqir in Marinid Morocco: Epistemological Dimensions of a Polemic." In *Islamic Mysticism Contested: Thirteen Centuries of
Controversies and Polemics*, edited by Frederick De Jong and Bernd Radtke,
207–24. Leiden, Netherlands: Brill.

Dar-barah-yi qiyam-i hamasah-afarinan-i Qum va Tabriz [On the Epic Uprising
of Qum and Tabriz]. 1978. 3 vols. Tehran: Nahzat-i Azadi-yi Iran.

Davani, 'Ali. 1998. *Nahzat-i ruhaniyun-i Iran* [The Movement of the Clerics in
Iran]. 10 vols. Reprint edition. Tehran: Bunyad-i Farhang-i Imam Riza.

Deftari, Fereshteh. 2002. "Another Modernism: An Iranian Perspective." In
Picturing Iran: Art, Society and Revolution, edited by Shiva Balaghi and Lynn
Gumpert, 39–87. London: I. B. Tauris.

Denny, Frederick Mathewson. 1995. "The Umma in North America: Muslim
'Melting Pot' or Ethnic 'Mosaic'?" In *Christian-Muslim Encounters*, edited
by Yvonne Yazbeck Haddad and Wadi Zaidan Haddad, 342–56. Gainesville:
University Press of Florida.

Denoeux, Guilain. 1993. *Urban Unrest in the Middle East: A Comparative Study
of Informal Networks in Egypt, Iran, and Lebanon*. Albany: State University of
New York Press.

Derrida, Jacques. 1978. *Writing and Difference*. Translated by Alan Bass. London: Routledge and Kegan Paul.

Desai, Vishakha N. 2001a. "Engaging 'Tradition' in the Twentieth-Century Arts of India and Pakistan." In *Conversations with Traditions: Nilima Sheikh and Shahzia Sikander*, 4–17. New York: Asia Society. ‹http://www.asiasociety.org/arts/convoessay.html›.

———. 2001b. "Vishakha N. Desai Interviews Nilima Sheikh and Shahzia Sikander." In *Conversations with Traditions: Nilima Sheikh and Shahzia Sikander*, 64–77. New York: Asia Society. ‹http://www.asiasociety.org/arts/convointerview.html›.

Diani, Mario. 1992. "The Concept of Social Movement." *Sociological Review* 40(1): 1–25.

Diani, Mario, and Doug McAdam. 2003. *Social Movements and Networks: Relational Approaches to Collective Action*. Oxford: Oxford University Press.

Diouf, Mamadou. 2000. "The Senegalese Murid Trade Diaspora and the Making of a Vernacular Cosmopolitanism." Translated by Steven Rendall. *Public Culture* 12(3): 679–702.

Doran, Michael Scott. 2002. "Somebody Else's War." *Foreign Affairs* 81(1): 22–42.

Du Bois, W. E. B. 1989. *The Souls of Black Folk*. New York: Penguin.

Dunn, Ross. 1986. *The Adventures of Ibn Battuta: A Muslim Traveler of the Fourteenth Century*. Paperback edition, 1989. Berkeley and Los Angeles: University of California Press.

Eickelman, Dale F. 1992. "Mass Higher Education and the Religious Imagination in Contemporary Arab Societies." In "Imagining Identities: Nation, Culture, and the Past." Special issue, *American Ethnologist* 19(4): 643–55.

———. 1995. "Introduction: Print, Writing, and the Politics of Religious Identity in the Middle East." *Anthropological Quarterly* 68(3): 133–38.

———. 1998. "Inside the Islamic Reformation." *Wilson Quarterly*, Winter.

Eickelman, Dale F., and Jon W. Anderson. 1997. "Print, Islam and the Prospects for Civic Pluralism: New Religious Writings and their Audiences." *Journal of Islamic Studies* 8(1): 43–62.

———, eds. 1999. *New Media in the Muslim World: The Emerging Public Sphere*. Bloomington: Indiana University Press.

Eickelman, Dale F., and James Piscatori. 1996. *Muslim Politics*. Princeton, N.J.: Princeton University Press.

Engineer, Asghar Ali, ed. 1987. *The Shah Bano Controversy*. Bombay: Orient Longman.

Ernst, Carl W. 1999. *The Shambala Guide to Sufism*. Boulder, Colo.: Shambala Books.

———. 2002a. "Between Orientalism and Fundamentalism: Problematizing the Teaching of Sufism." In *Teaching Islam*, edited by Brannon Wheeler, 108–23. Oxford: Oxford University Press.

———. 2002b. "Sufism, Islam, and Globalization in the Contemporary World: Methodological Reflections on a Changing Field of Study." Paper presented at the conference "The Role of Sufism and Muslim Brotherhoods in Contemporary Islam: An Alternative to Political Islam?," Edoardo Agnelli Foundation, Turin, Italy, November 19–21.

————. 2003. *Following Muhammad: Rethinking Islam in the Contemporary World*. Chapel Hill: University of North Carolina Press.

Ernst, Carl W., and Bruce B. Lawrence. 2002. *Sufi Martyrs of Love: The Chishti Order in South Asia and Beyond*. New York: Palgrave.

Ernst, Judith. 1995. *The Golden Goose King: A Tale Told by the Buddha*. Chapel Hill, N.C.: Parvardigar.

Euben, Roxanne L. 1999. *Enemy in the Mirror: Islamic Fundamentalism and the Limits of Modern Rationalism; A Work of Comparative Political Theory*. Princeton, N.J.: Princeton University Press.

Fadlallah, M. 1997. "Al-ʿazza al-husayniyya fi al-manfa" [The Husaynid Lament in Exile]. *Al-Nur Magazine* 75:42–50.

Fandy, Mamoun. 1999. "CyberResistance: Saudi Opposition between Globalization and Localization." *Comparative Studies in Society and History* 41(1): 124–47.

Faraj, Muhammad ʿAbd al-Salam. 1982. *Al jihad: Al-farida al-ghaʿiba* [Jihad: The Neglected Duty]. Jerusalem: Maktabat al-Batal ʿIzz al-Din al-Qassam.

Faraz'ha'i az tarikh-i inqilab bih ravayat-i asnad-i SAVAK va Amrika [High Points of the History of the Revolution according to the Documents of SAVAK and America]. 1989. Tehran: Ravabit-i ʿUmumi-yi Vizarat-i Ittilaʿat.

Faruqi, Nithar Ahmad, ed. 1994. *Khwaja Hasan Nizami*. New Delhi: Mahnama Kitab-numa.

Fattah, Hala. 1998. "Representations of Self and the Other in Two Iraqi Travelogues of the Ottoman Period." *International Journal of Middle East Studies* 30(1): 51–76.

Ferhat, Halima. 1993. *Sabta des origines au xivème siècle*. Rabat, Morocco: Ministère des Affaires Culturelles.

Fernea, Elisabeth. 1998. *In Search of Islamic Feminism: One Woman's Global Journey*. New York: Doubleday.

Festival of India in the United States, 1985–1986. 1985. New York: Harry N. Abrams.

Fidirasiyun-i Muhasilin va Danishjuyan-i Irani dar Faransih [Federation of Iranian Pupils and University Students in France]. 1978. "The Bloody Uprising of Tabriz." Translated by S. Azad. *Review of Iranian Political Economy and History* 2(2): 75–92.

Freitag, Sandria. 1988. "The Roots of Muslim Separatism in South Asia: Personal Practice and Public Structures in Kanpur and Bombay." In *Islam, Politics, and Social Movements*, edited by Edmund Burke III and Ira M. Lapidus. Berkeley and Los Angeles: University of California Press.

Gaffney, P. D. 1994. *The Prophet's Pulpit: Islamic Preaching in Contemporary Egypt*. Berkeley and Los Angeles: University of California Press.

García-Arenal, Mercedes. 1978. "The Revolution of Fes in 869/1465 and the Death of Sultan ʿAbd al-Haqq al-Marini." *Bulletin of the School of Oriental and African Studies* 41(1): 43–66.

Gendler, Everett. 2003. "Ancient Visions, Future Hopes: Rabbi Aaron Samuel Tamaret's Objection to Zionism as We Know It." *Tikkun* 18(4).

Gerceker, Fehmi, dir. 1995. *Tolerance: Dedicated to Mawlana Jalal-Al-Din Rumi*. VHS. Falls Church, Va.: Landmark Films.

Gerlach, Luther P., and Virginia H. Hine. 1970. *People, Power, Change: Movements of Social Transformation*. Indianapolis: Bobbs-Merrill.

Ghazali, Abu Hamid Muhammad al-. N.d. *Ihya' 'ulum al-din* [Resuscitation of the Religious Sciences]. 5 vols. Beirut: Dar al-Ma'arif.

Gibb, H. A. R., trans. 1958–2000. *The Travels of Ibn Battuta, A.D. 1325–1354*. 5 vols. Edited by C. Defrémery and B. R. Sanguinetti. Index by A. D. H. Bivar. Cambridge and London: Cambridge University Press / Hakluyt Society.

Gilmartin, David. "The Shahidganj Mosque Incident: A Prelude to Pakistan." In *Islam, Politics, and Social Movements*, edited by Edmund Burke III and Ira M. Lapidus, 146–68. Berkeley and Los Angeles: University of California Press.

Gonzalez-Quijano, Y. 1998. *Les gens du livre: Champ intellectual et édition dans l'Egypte républicaine*. Paris: CNRS Éditions.

Goodman, Lenn Evan, trans. 1972. *Ibn Tufayl's "Hayy Ibn Yaqzan."* New York: Twayne.

Gunuratna, Rohan. 2002. *Inside Al Qaeda: Global Network of Terror*. London: Hurst.

Haddad, Yvonne Yazbeck, ed. 1991. *The Muslims of America*. New York: Oxford University Press.

Haddad, Yvonne Yazbeck, and John L. Esposito, eds. 1998. *Muslims on the Americanization Path?* Atlanta: Scholars Press.

Haddad, Yvonne Yazbeck, and Adair T. Lummis, eds. 1987. *Islamic Values in the United States: A Comparative Study*. New York: Oxford University Press.

Haeri, Shahla. 1989. *Law of Desire: Temporary Marriage in Shi'i Iran*. Syracuse, N.Y.: Syracuse University Press.

Hafez, Muhammad M. 2000. "Armed Islamist Movements and Political Violence in Algeria." *Middle East Journal* 54(4): 572–91.

Hafiz. 1988. *Hafez: Dance of Life*. Translated by Michael Boylan. Illuminated by Hossein Zenderoudi. Washington, D.C.: Mage.

Haider, Syed Jalaluddin. 1981. "Munshi Nawal Kishore (1836–1895): Mirror of Urdu Printing in British India." *Libri* (Copenhagen, Denmark) 31:227–37.

Halabi, Ali Hasan al-. 1995a. *Fundamentals of Commanding Good and Forbidding Evil according to Shaykh Ul-Islam Ibn Taymiyya*. Cincinnati: Al-Quran al-Sunnah Society of North America.

———. 1995b. "Tarbiyah: The Key to Victory." *Al-Ibaanah* 2(August): 15–19.

Hardy, Peter. 1971. *Partners in Freedom—and True Muslims: The Political Thought of Some Muslim Scholars in British India, 1912–1949*. Lund, Sweden: Scandinavian Institute of Asian Studies.

Hasan, Mushirul. 1997. *Legacy of a Divided Nation: India's Muslims since Independence*. Boulder, Colo.: Westview Press.

Hasan, Zoya. 1998. "Gender Politics, Legal Reform, and the Muslim Community in India." In *Appropriating Gender: Women's Activism and Politicized*

Religion in South Asia, edited by Patricia Jeffery and Amrita Basu. New York: Routledge.

Hassan, Robert. 2003. "Network Time and the New Knowledge Epoch." *Time and Society* 12(2/3).

Haydar ʿAli Shah, [Sayyid], of Jalalpur Sharif. 1909. *Nafahat al-mahbub* [Perfume of the Beloved]. Sadhura, Pakistan: Bilali Steam Press. Translated from Persian to Urdu by ʿAbd al-Ghani as *Malfuzat-i Haydari*. Lahore, Pakistan, 1983–84.

Haydari, Ibrahim al-. 1999. *Trajidia Karbala': Susyulujiya al-khitab al-Shiʿi.* Beirut: Dar al-Saqi.

Herman, Judith Lewis. 1992. *Trauma and Recovery*. New York: Basic Books.

Hodgson, Marshall G. S. 1974. *The Venture of Islam: Conscience and History in a World Civilization*. 3 vols. Chicago: University of Chicago Press.

Hoffman-Ladd, Valerie. 1992. "Devotion to the Prophet and His Family in Egyptian Sufism." *International Journal of Middle East Studies* 24(3): 615–37.

Hourani, Albert H. 1991. *A History of the Arab Peoples.* Cambridge, Mass.: Harvard University Press, Belknap Press.

Huntington, Samuel P. 1996. *The Clash of Civilizations and the Remaking of World Order*. New York: Simon and Schuster.

Husain, Marjorie. 1994. Preface to *A Selection of Contemporary Paintings from Pakistan*. Pasadena, Calif.: Pacific Asia Museum.

Ibn Battuta. 1997. *Rihlat Ibn Battuta*. Beirut: Dar al-nafa'is.

Ibn Maja al-Qazwini, Abu ʿAbdallah Muhammad. N.d. *Sunan*. Edited by Mahmud Fu'ad ʿAbd al-Baqi. 2 vols. Beirut.

Ibrahim, Saad Eddin. 1996. "Egypt's Landed Bourgeoisie." In *Egypt, Islam and Democracy: Twelve Critical Essays*, edited by Saad Eddin Ibrahim, 123–30. Cairo: American University of Cairo Press.

Ifrani, Muhammad al-Saghir al-. [1970s?]. *Nuzhat al-hadi bi-akhbar muluk al-qarn al-hadi*. Edited by Octave Victor Houdas. Reprint of 1888 Paris edition. Rabat, Morocco: Maktabat al-Talib.

Ignatius, David. "A Netwar Clash." *Washington Post*, October 7, 2001.

Inqilab-i Islami bih ravayat-i asnad-i SAVAK [The Islamic Revolution according to SAVAK Documents]. 1997–99. 4 vols. Tehran: Surush; Markaz-i Barrasi-yi Asnad-i Tarikhi-yi Vizarat-i Ittilaʿat.

Irfani, Suroosh. 1997. "Between Brick and Glass." In *The Herald Annual*. Karachi.

Itzkowitz, Norman. 1972. *Ottoman Empire and Islamic Tradition*. Chicago: University of Chicago Press.

Izutsu, Toshihiko. 1983. *Sufism and Taoism: A Comparative Study of Key Philosophical Concepts*. Berkeley and Los Angeles: University of California Press.

Jackson, Peter. 1999. *The Delhi Sultanate: A Political and Military History*. Cambridge: Cambridge University Press.

Jalal, Ayesha. 1985. *The Sole Spokesman: Jinnah, the Muslim League, and the Demand for Pakistan*. Cambridge: Cambridge University Press.

————. 1990. *The State of Martial Rule: The Origins of Pakistan's Political Economy of Defense*. Cambridge: Cambridge University Press.

Jansen, Johannes J. G. 1985. *The Neglected Duty: The Creed of Sadat's Assassins and the Islamic Resurgence in the Middle East*. New York: Macmillan.

Johansen, Julian. 1996. *Sufism and Islamic Reform in Egypt: The Battle for Islamic Tradition*. Oxford: Clarendon Press.

Jones, Kenneth W., ed. 1992. *Religious Controversy in British India: Dialogues in South Asian Languages*. Albany: State University of New York Press.

Kahera, Zainab. 2001. "Sisters in the Game." *Azizah*, Summer.

Karnad, Girish, dir. 1990. *The Lamp in the Niche*. VHS. Ministry of Information, Government of India.

Kepel, Gilles. 1993. *Muslim Extremism in Egypt: The Prophet and the Pharaoh*. Berkeley and Los Angeles: University of California Press.

————. 2002. *Jihad*. Cambridge, Mass.: Harvard University Press.

Kesavan, B. S. 1985. *History of Printing and Publishing in India: A Story of Cultural Re-awakening*. New Delhi: National Book Trust.

Khabar-namah [The Newsletter]. 1977–78. Tehran: Jibhah-yi Milli-yi Iran.

Khalid, Kaubab, and Qadira Yamini. 2001. "The Art of Making Art." *Azizah*, Summer.

Khalkhali, ʿAli Rabbani. 1982–83. *Shuhada-yi ruhaniyat-i Shiʿah dar yak-sad salih-i akhir* [Martyrs of the Shii Clergy in the Past Century]. 2 vols. Qum, Iran: Intisharat-i Maktab-al-Husayn.

Khan, Shahnaz. 2000. *Muslim Women: Crafting a North American Identity*. Gainesville: University Press of Florida.

Khatibi, Abdelkebir. 1993. *Penser le Maghreb*. Rabat, Morocco: Société marocaine des éditeurs réunis.

Khomeini, Ruhollah. 1981. *Islam and Revolution: Writings and Declarations of Imam Khomeini*. Translated by Hamid Algar. Berkeley: Mizan Press.

————. 1982. *Majmuʾahʾi az maktubat, sukhanraniʾha, payamʾha va fatavi-yi Imam Khomeini* [A Collection of Letters, Speeches, Messages, and Opinions of Imam Khomeini]. Edited by M. Dihnavi. Tehran: Intisharat-i Chapkhass.

Khosrokhavar, Farhad. 1979. "Le Comité dans la Révolution Iranienne: Cas d'une ville moyenne; Hamadan" [The Committee in the Iranian Revolution: The Case of a Midsized City, Hamadan]. *Peuples Mediterranéens* [Mediterranean Peoples] 9:85–100.

Kugle, Scott. 2001. "Framed, Blamed, and Renamed: The Recasting of Islamic Jurisprudence in Colonial South Asia." *Journal of Modern Asian Studies* 35(2): 257–313.

Kurzman, Charles. 1994. "A Dynamic View of Resources: Evidence from the Iranian Revolution." *Research in Social Movements, Conflicts and Change* 17:53–84.

————, ed. 1998a. *Liberal Islam: A Sourcebook*. New York: Oxford University Press.

————. 1998b. "Organizational Opportunity and Social Movement Mobi-

lization: A Comparative Analysis of Four Religious Social Movements."
Mobilization 3(1): 23–49.

———, ed. 2002. *Modernist Islam: A Sourcebook, 1840–1940*. New York: Oxford University Press.

———. 2004. *The "Unthinkable" Revolution in Iran*. Cambridge, Mass.: Harvard University Press.

Laffan, Michael Francis. 2002. *Islamic Nationhood and Colonial Indonesia: The Umma below the Winds*. London: RoutledgeCurzon.

Lapidus, Ira M. 1975. "Hierarchies and Networks: A Comparison of Chinese and Islamic Societies." In *Conflict and Control in Late Imperial China*, edited by Frederic Wakeman Jr. and Carolyn Grant, 26–42. Berkeley and Los Angeles: University of California Press.

Lawrence, Bruce B. 1989. *Defenders of God: The Fundamentalist Revolt against the Modern Age*. San Francisco: Harper and Row.

———. 1998. *Shattering the Myth: Islam beyond Violence*. Princeton, N.J.: Princeton University Press.

Legander-Mourcy, Basimah. 2001. "How Inclusive of the Disabled Is the Muslim Community?" *Azizah*, Winter.

Leiner, Barry M., Vinton G. Cerf, David D. Clark, Robert E. Kahn, Leonard Kleinrock, Daniel C. Lynch, Jon Postel, Larry G. Roberts, and Stephen Wolff. 1997. *A Brief History of the Internet*. ‹http://www.isoc.org/internet-history›.

Liebeskind, Claudia. 1998. *Piety on Its Knees: Three Sufi Traditions in South Asia in Modern Times*. Delhi: Oxford University Press.

Lincoln, C. Eric. 1997. "The Muslim Mission in the Context of American Social History." In *African-American Religion*, edited by Timothy E. Fulop and Albert J. Raboteau, 277–94. New York: Routledge.

Lyotard, Jean François. 1992. *The Postmodern Explained to Children: Correspondence, 1982–1985*. Edited by Julian Pefanis and Morgan Thomas. Sydney: Power Publications.

Maalouf, Amin. 1994. *Leo Africanus*. Translated by Peter Sluglett. Lanham, Md.: New Amsterdam Books.

———. 2001. *In the Name of Identity: Violence and the Need to Belong*. Translated by Barbara Bray. New York: Arcade.

MacIntyre, Alasdair. 1984. *After Virtue: A Study in Moral Theory*. Notre Dame, Ind.: University of Notre Dame Press.

———. 1987. "Relativism, Power, and Philosophy." In *After Philosophy: End or Transformation?*, edited by Kenneth Baynes, James Bohman, and Thomas McCarthy, 385–411. Cambridge, Mass.: MIT Press.

———. 1988. *Whose Justice? Which Rationality?* Notre Dame, Ind.: University of Notre Dame Press.

———. 1998. *A Short History of Ethics: A History of Moral Philosophy from the Homeric Age to the Twentieth Century*. Notre Dame, Ind.: University of Notre Dame Press.

Macleod, Arlene Elow. 1991. *Accommodating Protest: Working Women, the New Veiling, and Change in Cairo*. New York: Columbia University Press.

Mahdi, Muhsin. 1995. "From the Manuscript Age to the Age of Printed Books." In *The Book in the Islamic World: The Written Word and Communication in the Middle East*, edited by George N. Atiyeh, 1–15. Albany: State University of New York Press.

Majeed, Hadayai S. 2001. "Muslim Safe Houses: Body and Soul Shelters." *Azizah*, Spring.

Makdisi, George. 1981. *The Rise of Colleges: Institutions of Learning in Islam and the West*. Edinburgh: Edinburgh University Press.

Makkhmudov, Shuukhrat, dir. 1993. *The Beaming One*. VHS. Bokhara, Uzbekistan: Ozma Productions.

Mandaville, Peter. 2001. *Transnational Muslim Publics: Reimagining the Umma*. New York: Routledge.

Marmura, Michael E. 1983. "The Islamic Philosophers' Conception of Islam." In *Islam's Understanding of Itself*, edited by R. G. Hovannisian and S. Vryonis, 87–102. Malibu, Calif.: Undena Publications.

Martinez, Luis. 2000. *The Algerian Civil War, 1990–1998*. Translated by Jonathan Derrick. New York: Columbia University Press.

Marzolph, Ulrich. 2001. *Narrative Illustration in Persian Lithographed Books*. Leiden, Netherlands: Brill.

McCloud, Aminah Beverly. 1995. *African American Islam*. New York: Routledge.

Mediano, Fernando. 1995. *Familias de Fez (ss. XV–XVII)*. Madrid: Consejo Superior de Investigaciones Científicas.

Melucci, Alberto. 1989. *Nomads of the Present: Social Movements and Individual Needs in Contemporary Society*. Edited by John Keane and Paul Mier. Philadelphia: Temple University Press.

Menocal, María Rosa. 1987. *The Arabic Role in Medieval Literary History: A Forgotten Heritage*. Philadelphia: University of Pennsylvania Press.

Mernissi, Fatima. 1991. *The Veil and the Male Elite: A Feminist Interpretation of Women's Rights in Islam*. Translated by Mary Jo Lakeland. New York: Addison-Wesley.

Messick, Brinkley. 1993. *The Calligraphic State: Textual Domination and History in a Muslim Society*. Berkeley and Los Angeles: University of California Press.

Metcalf, Barbara D. 1982. *Islamic Revival in British India: Deoband, 1860–1900*. Princeton, N.J.: Princeton University Press.

———. 1990. *Perfecting Women: Maulana Ashraf Ali Thanawi's "Bishti Zewar"; A Partial Translation with Commentary*. Berkeley and Los Angeles: University of California Press.

Minault, Gail. 1982. *The Khilafat Movement: Religious Symbolism and Political Mobilization in India*. New York: Columbia University Press.

Mitchell, Tony, ed. 2001. *Global Noise: Rap and Hip-Hop Outside the USA*. Middletown, Conn.: Wesleyan University Press.

Mohammadi, Ali, ed. 2002. *Islam Encountering Globalization*. London: Rout-ledgeCurzon.

Mohanty, Chandra Talpade. 1988. "Under Western Eyes: Feminist Scholarship and Colonial Discourses." *Feminist Review* 30.

Mossavar-Rahmani, Shahin. 1987. "The Iranian Revolution and Its Theoretical Implications." Ph.D. diss., University of Pennsylvania.

Moussavi, Ahmad Kazemi. 1985. "The Establishment of the Position of Mar-ja'iyyat-i Taqlid in the Twelver-Shi'i Community." *Iranian Studies* 18(1): 35–51.

Muhammad, Ruqayyah Kamillah, and Tayyibah Taylor. 2001. "Reality Check: Addressing the Media's Portrayal of Muslim Women." *Azizah*, Fall.

Murad'hasali-Khamanah, A'zam. 2001. *Tabriz dar khun* [Tabriz in Blood]. Tehran: Intisharat-i Markaz-i Asnad-i Inqilab-i Islami.

Muzafar, M. al-. 1999. *Aqa'id al-imamiya*. Cairo: Matbaa al-Qahira.

Nabard-i tudah'ha: Chand guzarish az Iran [The Struggle of the Masses: Several Reports from Iran]. 1978. Frankfurt: Ittihadiyah-yi Danishjuyan-i Irani dar Alman [Union of Iranian Students in Germany].

Nadwi, Abu'l-Hasan 'Ali. 1983–97. *Karwan-i zindagi*. 7 vols. Karachi, Pakistan: Majlis-i nashriyyat-i Islam; Lucknow, India: Maktaba-i Islam.

Nahavandi, Houchang. 1981. *Iran: Deux rêves brisés* [Iran: Two Broken Dreams]. Paris: Albin Michel.

National Security Archive. 1989. *Iran: The Making of U.S. Policy, 1977–1980*. Edited by Eric J. Hooglund. Alexandria, Va.: Chadwyck-Healey; Washington, D.C.: National Security Archive.

Nivedita, Sister, and Ananda Coomaraswamy. 1914. *Myths of the Hindus and Buddhists*. Illustrations under the direction of Abanindranath Tagore. New York: Henry Holt.

Notcutt, Martin. 1993. "Ibn 'Arabi in Print." In *Muhyiddin Ibn 'Arabi: A Commemorative Volume*, edited by Stephen Hirtenstein, 328–39. Rockport, Mass.: Element.

Nyang, Sulayman S. 1994. "The Honorable Elijah Muhammad and the Black Quest for Identity in the U.S." In *Elijah Muhammad and the Ideological Foundation of the Nation of Islam*, edited by Adib Rashad [James Miller]. Newport News, Va.: U.B. and U.S. Communications Systems.

Oberschall, Anthony. 1973. *Social Conflict and Social Movements*. Englewood Cliffs, N.J.: Prentice-Hall.

Omar, Manal. 2002. "Global Sisterhood: Rhetoric or Reality?" *Azizah*, Spring.

Osumare, Halifu. 2002. "Troping Blackness in the Hip Hop Global 'Hood." In "Black Culture's Global Impact," edited by H. Samy Alim. Special issue, *Black Arts Quarterly* 7(1): 24–26.

Pamuk, Orhan. 2002. *My Name is Red*. Translated by Erdag M. Goknar. New York: Vintage.

Parsa, Misagh. 1989. *The Social Origins of the Iranian Revolution*. New Brunswick, N.J.: Rutgers University Press.

Patriotic Muslim Students of Tabriz University. 1978. "Report on the Tabriz

Uprising." Translated by S. Azad. *Review of Iranian Political Economy and History*.

Pax, Salam. 2003. *The Baghdad Blog*. London: Guardian Books.

Perkins, William Eric, ed. 1996. *Droppin' Science: Critical Essays on Rap Music and Hip Hop Culture*. Philadelphia: Temple University Press.

Petry, Carl F. 1981. *The Civilian Elite of Cairo in the Later Middle Ages*. Princeton, N.J.: Princeton University Press.

Pishtazan-i shahadat dar inqilab-i sivvum [The Front Ranks of Martyrdom in the Third Revolution]. 1981. Qum, Iran: Daftar-i Intisharat-i Islami.

Pliskin, Karen L. 1980. "Camouflage, Conspiracy, and Collaborators: Rumors of the Revolution." *Iranian Studies* 13(1–4): 55–81.

Portelli, Alessandro. 1991. "What Makes Oral History Different." In *The Death of Luigi Trastulli and Other Stories: Form and Meaning in Oral History*. Albany: State University of New York Press.

Prévos, André J. M. 2001. "Postcolonial Popular Music in France: Rap Music and Popular Culture in the 1980s and 1990s." In *Global Noise: Rap and Hip-Hop Outside the USA*, edited by Tony Mitchell. Middletown, Conn.: Wesleyan University Press.

Putnam, Robert D. 1993. *Making Democracy Work: Civic Traditions in Modern Italy*. Princeton, N.J.: Princeton University Press.

———. 2000. *Bowling Alone: The Collapse and Revival of American Community*. New York: Simon and Schuster.

Puzo, Mario. 1996. *The Last Don*. New York: Random House.

Qadri, Fozail Ahmad. 1998. *The Celebrated Garden: A Study of Phulwari Sharif Family of Muslim Divines*. Shillong, India: North-Eastern Hill University Publications.

Qaradawi, Yusuf al-. 2000a. *Al-muslimun wa'l-'awlama* [Muslims and Globalization]. Cairo: Dar al-tawzi' wa'l-nashr al-islamiyya.

———. 2000b. *Al-siyasa al-shar'iyya fi daw' nusus al-shari'a wa maqasidiha* [Juridicial Politics in Light of the Law and Its Goals]. Beirut: Mu'assassat al-risala.

———. 2001a. *Kayfa nata'amal ma'a'l-turath wa'l-tamadhhub wa'l-ikhtilaf* [How to Interact with Tradition, Religion, and Diversity]. Cairo: Maktabat wahba.

———. 2001b. *Al-Shaykh Abu'l-Hasan 'Ali al-Nadwi kama 'araftuhu* [Shaykh Abu'l-Hasan 'Ali al-Nadwi as I Knew Him]. Damascus, Syria: Dar al-qalam.

Quraishi, Asifa. 2001. "The Plurality of Islamic Law." *Azizah*, Summer.

Qureshi, Regula. 1992. "'Muslim Devotional': Popular Religious Music and Muslim Identity under British, Indian and Pakistani Hegemony." *Asian Music* 24(1): 111–21.

Radley, Alan. 1990. "Artefacts, Memory, and a Sense of the Past." In *Collective Remembering*, edited by David Middelton and Derek Edwards, 46–59. London: Sage Publications.

Rahimi, Parvaneh, trans. 1995. *Manifestation of Feeling: A Selection of Painting by Iranian Female Artists*. Tehran: Iran Visual Arts Association, with the cooperation of the Center for Visual Arts, Ministry of Culture and Islamic Guidance.

Raja'i-Khurasani, Sa'id [Tabriz University instructor and Islamic activist]. 1984. Interview by Zia Sedghi. New York. December 21. Harvard Iranian Oral History Collection.

Ranstorp, Magnus. 1998. "Interpreting the Broader Context and Meaning of Bin-Laden's Fatwa." *Studies in Conflict and Terrorism* 21(4): 321–30.

Rawls, John. 1999. *A Theory of Justice*. Cambridge, Mass.: Harvard University Press, Belknap Press.

Reeve, Simon. 1999. *The New Jackals: Ramzi Yousef, Osama bin Laden and the Future of Terrorism*. London: André Deutsche.

Renard, John. 1996. *Seven Doors to Islam: Spirituality and the Religious Life of Muslims*. Berkeley and Los Angeles: University of California Press.

Rifkin, Jeremy. 2000. *The Age of Access*. London: Penguin.

Roberson, Barbara Allen, ed. 2003. *Shaping the Current Islamic Reformation*. London: Frank Cass.

Robinson, Francis. 1993. "Technology and Religious Change: Islam and the Impact of Print." In "How Social, Political and Cultural Information is Collected, Defined, Used and Analyzed," edited by Gordon Johnson. Special issue, *Modern Asian Studies* 27(1): 229–521. Revised as Robinson 1996.

———. 1996. "Islam and the Impact of Print in South Asia." In *The Transmission of Knowledge in South Asia: Essays on Education, Religion, History, and Politics*, edited by Nigel Crook, 62–97. New Delhi: Oxford University Press.

———. 1997. "Ottomans—Safavids—Mughals: Shared Knowledge and Connective Systems." *Journal of Islamic Studies* 8(2): 151–184.

Rose, Tricia. 1994. *Black Noise: Rap Music and Black Culture in Contemporary America*. Middletown, Conn.: Wesleyan University Press.

Roy, Olivier. 1999. "The Radicalization of Sunni Conservative Fundamentalism." *ISIM Newsletter* 2(March): 7.

———. 2002. *L'islam mondialisé*. Paris: Le Seuil.

Rubin, Barnett R. 1995. *The Fragmentation of Afghanistan: State Formation and Collapse in the International System*. New Haven, Conn.: Yale University Press.

Rugh, Andrea B. 1986. *Reveal and Conceal: Dress in Contemporary Egypt*. Syracuse, N.Y.: Syracuse University Press.

Ruhani, Hamid [Hamid Ziyarati]. 1982. *Shari'at-Madari dar dadgah-i tarikh* [Shari'at-Madari in the Court of History]. Qum, Iran: Daftar-i Intisharat-i Islami.

Rustaveli, Shota. 1986. *The Knight in the Panther's Skin*. Translated by Venera Urushadze. Tbilisi, Georgia: Sabchota Sakartvelo. Reprint, Huntington, N.Y.: Nova Science, 1999.

Ruz-shumar-i Inqilab-i Islami [Chronology of the Islamic Revolution]. 1997–99. 3 vols. Tehran: Howzah-yi Hunari-yi Daftar-i Adabiyat-i Inqilab-i Islami.

Sabir, Nadirah Z. 2001. "America's First Muslimah Judge." *Azizah*, Winter.

Saduqi, Muhammad. 1983. *Majmu'ah-yi ittila'iyah'ha-yi sivvumin-i shahid-i mihrab hazrat Ayatullah Saduqi* [The Third Collection of Pronouncements of the Holy Martyr, the Honorable Ayatullah Saduqi]. Tehran: Vizarat-i Irshad-i Islami.

Safi, Omid, ed. 2003. *Progressive Muslims on Gender, Justice and Pluralism.* Oxford: Oneworld.

Salehi, M. M. 1988. *Insurgency through Culture and Religion: The Islamic Revolution of Iran.* New York: Praeger.

Salvatore, Armando. 1997. *Islam and the Political Discourse of Modernity.* Reading, U.K.: Ithaca.

Sanyal, Usha. 1996. *Devotional Islam and Politics in British India: Ahmad Riza Khan Barelwi and His Movement, 1870–1920.* Delhi: Oxford University Press.

Sassen, Saskia, ed. 1999. *Globalization and Its Discontents: Essays on the New Mobility of People and Money.* New York: New Press.

SAVAK va ruhaniyat: Bulitin'ha-yi nubah-yi SAVAK az tarikh-i 49/12/25 ta 57/6/30 [SAVAK and the Religious Scholars: Periodic SAVAK Bulletins from March 16, 1971, to September 19, 1978]. 1992. Tehran: Howzah-yi Hunari-yi Sazman-i Tablighat-i Islami; Daftar-i Adabiyat-i Inqilab-i Islami; Markaz-i Asnad-i Vizarat-i Ittila'at.

Sayyad, Nezar al-, and Manuel Castells, eds. 2002. *Muslim Europe or Euro-Islam: Politics, Culture, and Citizenship in the Age of Globalization.* Lanham, Md.: Lexington Books.

Schubel, Vernon James. 1993. *Religious Performance in Contemporary Islam: Shi'i Devotional Rituals in South Asia.* Columbia: University of South Carolina Press.

Shaheed, Farida. 1995. "Networking for Change: The Role of Women's Groups in Initiating Dialogue on Women's Issues." In *Faith and Freedom: Women's Human Rights in the Muslim World,* edited by Mahnaz Afkhami, 78–103. Syracuse, N.Y.: Syracuse University Press.

Shahidi digar az ruhaniyat [Another Martyr from the Clergy]. 1978. Najaf, Iraq: Ruhaniyat-i Mubariz-i Irani, Kharij az Kishvar, Najaf-i Ashraf.

Shaikh, Farzana. 1989. *Community and Consensus in Islam: Muslim Representation in Colonial India, 1860–1947.* Cambridge: Cambridge University Press.

Shams al-Din, M. 1985. *The Rising of al-Husayn: Its Impact on the Consciousness of Muslim Society.* Translated by I. K. A. Howard. London: Muhammadi Trust.

Shaw, Graham. 1981. *Printing in Calcutta to 1800: A Description and Checklist of Printing in Late Eighteenth-Century Calcutta.* London: Bibliographical Society.

———. 1991. "Matba'a [Printing]. 4. In Muslim India." In Volume 6, *Encyclopaedia of Islam, New Edition,* edited by C. E. Bosworth, E. van Donzel, and C. Pellat, 806. Leiden, Netherlands: Brill.

Shelf, Dana. 1998. "Shahzia Sikander: Drawings and Miniatures." Catalog essay. Kansas City, Mo.: Kemper Museum of Contemporary Art. ‹http://www.kemperart.org/exhibits/CatalogEssays/sikandershahzia.asp›.

Shibli Nu'mani, Muhammad. N.d. *Safarnama-i Rum wa Misr wa Sham.* Lucknow, India: Anwar al-matabi'.

Shirkhani, 'Ali. 1998. *Hamasah-yi 19 Day* [The Uprising of 9 January (1978)]. Tehran: Intisharat-i Markaz-i Asnad-i Inqilab-i Islami.

———. 1999. *Hamasah-yi 29 Bahman-i Tabriz* [The Tabriz Uprising of 18 February (1978)]. Tehran: Intisharat-i Markaz-i Asnad-i Inqilab-i Islami.

Singerman, Diane. 1995. *Avenues of Participation: Family, Politics, and Networks in Urban Quarters of Cairo*. Princeton, N.J.: Princeton University Press.

Smith, Jane. 1999. *Islam in America*. New York: Columbia University Press.

Souaida, Habib. 2001. *La sale guerre*. Paris: La Découverte.

Spady, James G. 2001. "Moving in Silence: Motion, Movement and Music in a Hip Hop Centered Cultural Universe." In "Hip Hop Culture: Language, Literature, Literacy and the Lives of Black Youth," edited by H. Samy Alim. Special issue, *Black Arts Quarterly* 6(2): 28–31.

Spady, James G., and Joseph Eure. 1991. *Nation Conscious Rap: The Hip Hop Vision*. Philadelphia: Black History Museum.

Spady, James G., Charles G. Lee, and H. Samy Alim. 1999. *Street Conscious Rap*. Philadelphia: Black History Museum Umum / Loh.

Starrett, Gregory. 1995. "The Political Economy of Religious Commodities in Cairo." *American Anthropologist* n.s. 97(1): 51–68.

Stempel, John D. 1981. *Inside the Iranian Revolution*. Bloomington: Indiana University Press.

Storey, C. A. 1933. "The Beginning of Persian Printing in India." In *Oriental Studies in Honour of Cursetji Erachji Pavry*, edited by Jal Dastur Cursetji Pavry, 457–61. London: Oxford University Press.

Sullivan, Earl. 1986. *Women in Egyptian Public Life*. Syracuse, N.Y.: Syracuse University Press.

Swedenburg, Ted. 2001. "Islamic Hip-Hop versus Islamophobia." In *Global Noise: Rap and Hip-Hop Outside the USA*, edited by Tony Mitchell. Middletown, Conn.: Wesleyan University Press.

———. 2002. "Hip Hop Music in the Transglobal Islamic Underground." In "Black Culture's Global Impact," edited by H. Samy Alim. Special issue, *Black Arts Quarterly* 7(1): 16–18.

Tadili, Abu Ya'qub Yusuf ibn al-Zayyat al-. 1984. *Al-tashawwuf ila rijal al-tasawwuf wa akhbar Abu'l-'Abbas al-Sabti* [Anticipating the Sufis and News of Abu'l-'Abbas al-Sabti]. Edited by Ahmad Toufiq. Rabat, Morocco: Université Mohamed V.

Talbot, I. A. 1980. "The 1946 Punjab Elections." *Modern Asian Studies* 14(1): 65–91.

Taylor, Mark C. 2002. *Moment of Complexity: Emerging Network Culture*. Chicago: University of Chicago Press.

Taylor, Tayyibah. 2001. "Female Scholars in America: Changing the Patriarchal Shape of Islamic Thought." *Azizah*, Spring.

Tehranian, Majid. 1980. "Communication and Revolution in Iran: The Passing of a Paradigm." *Iranian Studies* 13(1–4): 5–30.

Telhami, Ghada Hashem. 1996. *The Mobilization of Muslim Women in Egypt*. Gainesville: University Press of Florida.

Thursby, G. R. 1975. *Hindu-Muslim Relations in British India*. Leiden, Netherlands: Brill.

Tilly, Charles. 1978. *From Mobilization to Revolution*. Reading, Mass.: Addison-Wesley.

———. 1985. "War Making and State Making as Organized Crime." In *Bringing the State Back In*, edited by Peter Evans, Dietrich Rueschemeyer, and Theda Skocpol, 169–91. Cambridge: Cambridge University Press.

Troll, Christian W. 1997. "Muhammad Shibli Nu'mani (1857–1914) and the Reform of Muslim Religious Education." In *Madrasa: La transmission du savoir dans le monde musulman*, edited by Nicole Grandin and Marc Gaborieau, 145–57. Paris: Editions Arguments.

Turner, Richard. 1997. *Islam in the African-American Experience*. Bloomington: Indiana University Press.

Tusi, Nasir al-Din. 1964. *The Nasirean Ethics*. Translated by G. M. Wickens. London: Allen and Unwin.

Union des Étudiants Iraniens en France. 1978. *Iran: Vagues d'offensive populaire dans plus de 50 villes* [Iran: Wave of Popular Offensive in More Than Fifty Cities]. Paris: Union des Étudiants Iraniens en France.

United Nations. Department of Public Information. 1998. *Algeria: Report of Eminent Panel, July–August 1998*. New York: United Nations.

United Nations Development Programme. 2000. *Human Development Report 2000*. Oxford: Oxford University Press.

Varisco, Daniel M. 2002. "September 11: Participant Webservation of the 'War on Terrorism.'" *American Anthropologist* 104(3): 934–38.

Verton, Dan. 2003. *Black Ice: The Invisible Threat of Cyber-Terrorism*. Emeryville, Calif.: McGraw-Hill / Osborne.

Virilio, Paul. 2000. *The Information Bomb*. New York: Verso.

Voll, John O. 1991. "Fundamentalism in the Sunni Arab World: Egypt and the Sudan." In *Fundamentalisms Observed*, edited by Martin E. Marty and R. Scott Appleby. Chicago: University of Chicago Press.

Waili, A. al-. 1997. "Al-'azza al-husayniyya wa al-khitab al-dini" [The Husaynid Lament and Religious Discourse]. *Al-Nur Magazine* 77:48–50.

Wansharisi, Ahmad ibn Yahya. 1981. *Al-mi'yar al-mu'rib wa al-jami' al-mughrib 'an fatawa ahl Ifriqiyya wa al-Andalus wa al-Maghrib* [Legal Opinions from Africa, Andalusia, and the Maghrib]. 13 vols. Rabat, Morocco: Wizarat al-Awqaf wa-al-Shu'un al-Islamiya lil-Mamlaka al-Maghribiya.

Wasserman, Stanley, and Katherine Faust. 1994. *Social Network Analysis: Methods and Applications*. Cambridge: Cambridge University Press.

Weaver, Mary Anne. 1999. *A Portrait of Egypt: A Journey through the World of Militant Islam*. New York: Farrar, Strauss and Giroux.

Weiss, Bernard. 1992. *The Search for God's Law: Islamic Jurisprudence in the Writings of Sayf al-Din al-Amidi*. Salt Lake City: University of Utah Press.

Wiktorowicz, Quintan. 2001a. "Centrifugal Tendencies in the Algerian Civil War." *Arab Studies Quarterly* 23(3): 65–82.

———. 2001b. *The Management of Islamic Activism: Salafis, the Muslim Brother-hood, and State Power in Jordan*. Albany: State University of New York Press.

———, ed. 2003. *Islamic Activism: A Social Movement Theory Approach*. Bloom-ington: Indiana University Press.

Williams, Raymond. 1986. "Forms of Fiction in 1948." In *Literature, Politics, and Theory: Papers from the Essex Conference, 1976–84*, edited by Francis Barker et al. London: Methuen.

Willis, Michael. *The Islamist Challenge in Algeria: A Political History*. New York: New York University Press, 1997.

Wright, E. M. 1995. *Empedocles, The Extant Fragments*. London: Bristol Classical Press.

Yamani, Mai, ed. 1996. *Islam and Feminism*. New York: New York University Press.

Yaran-i imam bih ravayat-i asnad-i SAVAK [Friends of the Imam according to the Documents of SAVAK]. 1998–99. 12 vols. Tehran: Markaz-i Barrasi-yi Asnad-i Tarikhi-yi Vizarat-i Ittila'at.

Yuan, Yuan. 2003. "Muslim Networks in China and Imperial Patronage Prior to Qing Dynasty." Unpublished paper.

Zald, Mayer N., and John D. McCarthy, eds. 1987. *Social Movements in Organi-zational Society*. New Brunswick, N.J.: Transaction.

Zaman, Muhammad Qasim. 1998a. "Arabic, the Arab Middle East, and the Definition of Muslim Identity in Twentieth Century India." *Journal of the Royal Asiatic Society*, ser. 3, 8(1): 59–81.

———. 1998b. "Sectarianism in Pakistan: The Radicalization of Shi'i and Sunni Identities." *Modern Asian Studies* 32(3): 689–716.

———. 2002. *The Ulama in Contemporary Islam: Custodians of Change*. Prince-ton, N.J.: Princeton University Press.

———. [2004]. "The 'Ulama of Contemporary Islam and Their Conceptions of the Common Good." In *Public Islam and the Common Good*, edited by Dale F. Eickelman and Armando Salvatore, 129–55. Leiden, Netherlands: Brill.

Zamimah-yi Khabar-namah [Supplement to the Newsletter]. 1977–78. Tehran: Jibhah-yi Milli-yi Iran.

Zebiri, Kate. 1993. *Mahmud Shaltut and Islamic Modernism*. Oxford: Clarendon Press.

Zeghal, Malika. 1995. *Gardiens de l'Islam: Les oulémas d'Al Azhar dans l'Egypte contemporaine*. Paris: Presses de la Fondation nationale des sciences poli-tiques.

———. 1999. "Religion and Politics in Egypt: The *Ulema* of al-Azhar, Radical Islam, and the State (1952–94)." *International Journal of Middle East Studies* 31(3): 401–27.

Zuhur, Sherifa. 1992. *Revealing Reveiling: Islamist Gender Ideology in Contempo-rary Egypt*. Albany: State University of New York Press.

H. SAMY ALIM
  is assistant professor of linguistics at the University of California, Berkeley.
  He is a specialist in the language of hip hop. His publications include
  Language, Education, and Social Change in African America and Beyond
  (forthcoming).

JON W. ANDERSON
  is professor of anthropology at Catholic University of America. He is a
  specialist in Afghan and Pakistani tribalism and Islamic cosmology. His
  current work focuses on new media in the Middle East. His publications
  include *Arabizing the Internet* (1998) and *New Media in the Muslim World*
  (co-edited with Dale F. Eickelman, 1999).

TAIEB BELGHAZI
  is professor of English literature at the Université Mohamed V, Rabat
  (Morocco). His publications include *Actions collectives: De la mobilisation des
  ressources à la prisède parole* (co-authored with Muhammad Madani, 2001)
  and *Local/Global Cultures and Sustainable Development* (co-edited with
  Lahcen Haddad, 2001).

GARY BUNT
  is lecturer in Islamic studies at the University of Wales, Lampeter.
  His publications include *Islam in the Digital Age: E-jihad, Online Fatwas,
  and Cyber Islamic Environments* (2003) and *Virtually Islamic: Computer-
  Mediated Communication and Cyber Islamic Environments* (2000),
  ‹www.virtuallyislamic.com›.

miriam cooke
  is professor of Arabic literature at Duke University and author of several
  monographs, including *War's Other Voices: Women Writers on the Lebanese
  Civil War* (1988); *Women and the War Story* (1997); and *Women Claim Islam:
  Creating Islamic Feminism through Literature* (2001). She has co-edited
  several volumes, including *Opening the Gates: A Century of Arab Feminist
  Writing* (1990); *Gendering War Talk* (1993); and *Blood into Ink: South Asian
  and Middle Eastern Women Write War* (1994).

VINCENT J. CORNELL

is professor of history and director of the King Fahd Center for Middle East and Islamic Studies at the University of Arkansas. He is a specialist in Sufism, Islamic theology and philosophy, and Islamic intellectual history. His works include *Realm of the Saint: Power and Authority in Moroccan Sufism* (1998) and *The Way of Abu Madyan* (1996).

CARL W. ERNST

is Zachary Smith Professor of Religious Studies at the University of North Carolina at Chapel Hill. He is a specialist in Islamic studies with a focus on West and South Asia. His recent publications include *Following Muhammad: Rethinking Islam in the Contemporary World* (2003) and *Sufi Martyrs of Love: Chishti Sufism in South Asia and Beyond* (co-authored with Bruce Lawrence, 2002).

JUDITH ERNST

is a painter, ceramic artist, and writer. Her *Song of Songs: Erotic Love Poetry* (2003) presents an illuminated version of this biblical classic. In 1996 her illustrated Buddhist story, *The Golden Goose King*, won the Skipping Stones Honor Award.

DAVID GILMARTIN

is professor of history at North Carolina State University. He is a specialist in the history of the Indian subcontinent (especially in the nineteenth and twentieth centuries). His publications include *Empire and Islam: Punjab and the Making of Pakistan* (1988) and *Beyond Turk and Hindi* (co-authored with Bruce Lawrence, 2001).

JAMILLAH KARIM

is assistant professor of religion at Spelman College. She obtained her Ph.D. in Islamic studies at Duke University. She specializes in Islam in America, women and Islam, African American Islam, and Islam and culture.

CHARLES KURZMAN

is associate professor of sociology at the University of North Carolina at Chapel Hill and author of *The Unthinkable Revolution in Iran* (2004). He is editor of *Liberal Islam and Modernist Islam, 1840–1940* (1998 and 2002) and co-editor of *An Islamic Reformation?* (2004).

BRUCE B. LAWRENCE

is Nancy and Jeffrey Marcus Professor of the Humanities and Professor of Islamic Studies at Duke University. A comparative medievalist, he has also written extensively on contemporary religious movements, including *Defenders of God: The Fundamentalist Revolt against the Modern Age* (1989); *Shattering the Myth: Islam beyond Violence* (1998); and *New Faiths, Old Fears: Muslims and Other Asian Immigrants in American Religious Life* (2002).

SAMIA SERAGELDIN

is a writer, editor, and columnist. Her novel, *The Cairo House*, traces political events in Egypt over the second half of the twentieth century. She served as consulting editor and contributed essays to *In the Name of Osama Bin Laden: Globalization and the Bin Laden Brotherhood* (2002).

TAYBA HASSAN AL KHALIFA SHARIF

completed her doctoral dissertation, "Resistance and Remembrance: History-Telling of Iraqi Shiite Refugee Women and Their Families in the Netherlands," for the University of Amsterdam in 2003. She is currently an officer in the United Nations High Commission for Refugees, and she has worked in South Asia and the Middle East.

QUINTAN WIKTOROWICZ

is assistant professor of international studies and J. S. Seidman Research Fellow at Rhodes College. He is the editor of *Islamic Activism: A Social Movement Theory Approach* (2004) and author of *The Management of Islamic Activism* (2001) and *Radical Islam Rising: Al-Muhajiroun and High Risk Activism* (forthcoming).

MUHAMMAD QASIM ZAMAN

is associate professor of religious studies at Brown University. His research interests include religious authority, institutions and traditions of learning in Islam, Islamic law, and contemporary religious and political movements in the Muslim world. He is the author of *The Ulama in Contemporary Islam* (2002) and *Religion and Politics under the Early Abbasids* (1997).

Bin Baz, 'Abd al-Aziz, 219
Bin Laden, Osama: as founder of al-Qaeda, 25; Bush on evil of, 208; and Salafi movement, 209, 215, 219, 221, 225, 280; and funds for al-Qaeda, 224; and GIA, 224; and al-Wadi'i, 229; and Gamiyya Islamiyya, 231; and justification of jihad against United States, 232, 233 (n. 7); and Internet, 238, 240, 241, 250 (n. 18). *See also* Al-Qaeda
Bin Nurhasyim, Amrozi, 242
Bin Uthman, Muhammad, 219
Black Wall Street, 270
Blair, Sheila, 128
Bloch, Marc, 14
Blogging, 246–48
Bloom, Jonathan, 128
Bohras, 23
Bonner, Jay, 108–12, 121–22, 128
Bosnia, 123, 124, 219, 221, 231, 232
Boulet, Susan Seddon, 125
Bourdieu, Pierre, 253–54, 259, 261
Bouti, Ramadan Al-, 259
Bouti.com, 259
Boylan, Michael, 113
Brethren of Purity, 196
British colonialism, 55–63, 94–95
Buechler, Stephen, 210
Buehler, Arthur, 197
Bunt, Gary, 21, 23, 25, 27
Burqa, 169, 186 (n. 2)
Burujirdi, Ayatullah Husayn, 75
Bush, George, 208
Butt, Rasheed, 111

Cairo University, 156, 164
Canada, 269
Cannadine, David, 67 (n. 2)
Castells, Manuel, 21, 193, 202, 261–62, 279
Cesaire, Aime, 273 (n. 2)
Charity and charitable organizations, 7, 157–58
Chechnya, 219–20, 221, 239, 240, 242

Cherifi, al-'la, 230
China: and Silk Road, 5; Western view of as classical, 17; root metaphors for, 52, 53; Ibn Battuta in, 85, 88–89; religion and print in, 193; jihad in, 220
Chishti order of Sufism, 193, 198, 202
Chuck D, 264, 269, 270
Chughtai, Abdul Rahman, 118–19, 123
CIA, 243, 247
Cihad.net, 240
Citizenship, 32, 54
CNN, 162
Cohn, Bernard, 94–95
Collective identity, 280
Colonialism, 16–19, 25. *See also* India; Neocolonialism
Color of Paradise, 119
Common (rapper), 264
Competence, 253–55, 261–62
cooke, miriam, 151, 170, 171, 181–82, 265
Coomaraswamy, Ananda, 118
Cornell, Vincent J., 4, 5, 54, 65, 67 (n. 1)
Cosmopolitan, 175
Cosmopolitanism, 84–89, 94
Creolization, 256–57, 262, 281
Cybercafes, 13, 243–44, 248, 256
"Cyberoptics," 1
Cyberspace, 235. *See also* Internet
Cyber-war, 51, 244

Dagestan, 220
Damas, Leon, 273 (n. 2)
Dar al-aman (abode of safety), 14
Dar Al-Fikr publishing house, 259
Dar al-harb (abode of war), 14
Dar al-Islam (abode of Islam), 4, 8, 13, 14, 235
Dar al-mu'ahada (abode of covenant), 14
Dar al-'Ulum, 95
Darbars, 56, 67 (n. 2)

Data Darbar Shrine, 109
Daudi Bohras, 92
Da'wa (preaching), 204, 209, 227, 240, 258, 259, 260–61
Dawn, 197
Deftari, Fereshteh, 115–16, 130–31 (n. 6)
Deobandi *'ulama'*, 57–60, 63–64, 67 (n. 3), 198
Derrida, Jacques, 276, 277–78
Desai, Vishakha N., 116, 117
Diallo, Amadou, 270
Dikaiosune (justice), 36
Diouf, Mamadou, 16
Disabilities, 184–85
Discourse. *See* Language
Distributive justice, 36–37
Diversity. *See* Ethnic diversity
Divorce, 91, 160, 166–67
Du'a (invocation), 239
Du Bois, W. E. B., 187 (n. 16)
Duke University Center for the Study of Muslim Networks, 271
Dunn, Ross, 7, 8, 28 (n. 2), 47

E-40 (rapper), 268
Education: and *madrasas*, 7, 43–44, 93, 95, 217, 220, 256, 261, 262; and Muslim networks, 17; of *'ulama'*, 43–44; *usul*-based education, 43–44; of women in Islamic studies at American universities, 188 (n. 17); mass education in Muslim countries, 254, 256, 261; Islamic universities on Internet, 261
Egypt: Islamic salons in, 12, 155–68, 279; *'ulama'* in, 96–97; al-Azhar in, 96–97, 98; Muslim Brotherhood in, 97, 210, 214, 258; Islamization of, 155–57, 160–61, 163, 279; veiling of women in, 156, 161, 163–65; women at mosques and *zawias* in, 157, 159; charitable organizations in, 157–58; social mobility in, 161; televangelists in,

163; family law reform in, 165–67; publishing in, 196, 197; Sufism in, 197, 198; and war in Afghanistan, 217; repression of radical Islamists in, 219; and Salafi movement, 222, 225, 229–31; Gamiyya Islamiyya in, 225, 229–31; Islah Party in, 229; Shari'a Party in, 229; violence in, 230–31
Eickelman, Dale, 199, 254, 257
E-ijtihads (interpretations of foundational texts), 22, 23, 24
E-jihad (struggle or war), 23, 25, 233 (n. 13), 235, 238–46
Empedocles, 43, 49–50 (n. 12)
E-mujahidin networks, 243–46
England. *See* British colonialism
England, Catherine, 178, 185, 186
English language, 17, 94, 95–96, 104 (n. 15), 256
Enlightenment, 15, 17, 49 (n. 2)
Ernst, Carl W., 19–20
Ernst, Judith, 13–14, 265
Ethics, proportional, 37–38
Ethnic diversity: in *Azizah* magazine, 172, 176, 177–78, 185–86, 188 (nn. 18–19); of Muslims in United States, 185, 186–87 (nn. 3–4)
Ethnic mosque, 172, 186 (n. 4)
Ethnic nationalism, 18
Euben, Roxanne, 93
Eunus, Muhammad, 119–20
Euripides, 197
Eve (rapper), 271
Ezzedeen.net, 242

Faisal, King, 91
Family law reform in Egypt, 165–67
Fard 'ayn (individual obligation), 218
Fard kifaya (collective responsibility), 218
Fateh 'Ali Khan, Nusrat, 200, 204
Fatima, Sayyida, 135
Fatwa-Online, 238
FBI, 243

strategies, 253–62; engineers and applied scientists' use of, 254–55; and competence, 254–55, 261–62; growth of, 255; and creolization, 256–57, 262, 281; institutional perspectives and spokespersons on, 257–61, 281; and Islamism, 258; and diaspora-homeland relations, 259; and content providers, 260

Internet Archive Wayback Machine, 237

Internet cafes, 13, 243–44, 248, 256

Iqbal, Muhammad, 67 (n. 12–13), 192

Iran: Islamic Republic of, 19, 45; revolution (1978–79) in, 19, 70–83; and Seljuqs in eleventh century, 48; mosque network in, 69–83; SAVAK in, 72, 74, 76, 81; student protests in, 72, 77–79; Society of Qum Seminary Instructors in, 75, 82; Revolutionary Council in, 82; Society of Struggling Religious Scholars in, 82; modernism in, 130–31 (n. 6); and Iran-Iraq War, 150, 151; publishing in, 196; and jihad, 239

Iranian Revolution (1978–79), 19, 70–83

Iraq: Gulf War (1991) in, 12, 133, 143, 150–52, 222, 232, 278; U.S. war against (2003), 23, 150–51, 162, 239, 242, 243, 247; Saddam Hussein in, 133, 136, 141, 143, 145, 151, 152; persecution of Shiite women in, 133, 146–47; uprising of 1991 in, 133, 150; prohibition of Shiite mourning rituals in, 137–38, 143, 146–47; and Iran-Iraq War, 150, 151; Kurdish Islamists in, 240

Iraqi Shiite women: as refugees in Netherlands, 12–13, 132–34, 139, 143, 145–47, 151, 153; as refugees in Saudi Arabia, 12–13, 132–34, 151, 153; mourning and remembrance rituals by, 12–13, 132–54,

278–79; and *mullaya*, 13, 132, 139, 141–45, 147–48; persecution of in Iraq, 133, 146–47; and healing at shrines, 137–38; and prohibition of Shiite mourning rituals in Iraq, 137–38, 143, 146–47; and remembrance and mourning rites of Zaynab, 140–49; and Gulf War, 143, 150–52, 278; personal stories and therapeutic narratives of, 145–53; nonverbal communication by, 149, 152; and silence, 152

Isabella, Queen, 4

Islah al-dakhil (internal reform), 100–101

Islah Party, 229

Islam: diversity within, 2, 23; and submission to the One, 7; and trust, 7, 13, 16; Western view of, 17; in colonial India, 17, 55–64; and nation-states, 18; straight path as metaphor of, 26–27; guideposts of, 27; network metaphor for, 52–55, 66; worldview of, 53; Egypt's Islamization, 155–57, 160–61, 163, 279; fundamentalists in, 192, 193, 195, 196, 202; and print publications, 193–94; first published use of term in English, 206 (n. 1); in United States, 265–66. *See also* Muhammad, Prophet; Muslim networks; Quran; Shari'a; Sufism

Islamic Army of Aden-Abayan, 229

Islamic art: problem of Muslim-ness of, 13–14, 107–30, 280; characteristics of, 53; definition of, 107; and virtual travel, 108; patrons of, 108, 121–22; Bonner's architecture, 108–12, 121–22, 128; Sliding Domes project in Medina, 109–11; pan-Islamic art, 110–12, 122, 128; Ernst's art, 112, 114–15, 122–23; botanical and bird paintings from India, 112–13; Zenderoudi's art, 113–16, 123; and Sagha-Khaneh

Magazines: *Azizah*, 11–12, 169–88; *Sisters*, 174, 179, 180, 183; Sufi magazines, 197–98, 206–7 (nn. 8–9)

Maghreb Collectif, 18

Maghrib, 239

Maghribi, Jamal al-Din al-, 45–46

Mahdi, Imam al-, 154 (n. 8)

Mahdi, Muhsin, 206 (n. 4)

Mahmud, 'Adb al-Halim, 98

Majlis al-qiraya (mourning ritual), 133–54, 278–79

Makarim, Nasir, 75

Malabar Coast, 88

Maldives, 31, 85–87, 88

Maliki jurisprudence, 8, 31, 44, 45, 48, 84, 86, 88–89

Mamluks (slave-soldiers), 33

Manhaj (method), 211–14, 217, 222, 226–28, 231, 232, 233 (n. 7)

Maqdisi, Abu Muhammad al-, 225

Maraji'-i taqlid (sources of imitation), 71

Ma'rifat nama (Haqqi), 206 (n. 6)

Marriage, 166–67. *See also* Divorce

Masalla (women's prayer spaces), 173

Masari (rapper), 271

Maslaha (public interest), 97

Masnavi (Rumi), 206 (n. 6)

Massignon, Louis, 206 (n. 3)

Massive Attack (music group), 200

Ma'sum (immune from error), 135

Ma'tam (lamentation for the dead), 144

Matisse, Henri, 125

Mawdudi, Abu'l-A'la, 95, 197, 257

McCarthy, John, 213–14

McCloud, Aminah, 184

MC Ghosto, 272

Mecca: as birthplace of Prophet Muhammad, 1; Hajj to, 1, 3, 12, 20, 165, 168 (n. 3), 184–85; as geographic node of Muslim networks, 2, 3–4, 276; Ibn Battuta in, 8; Great Mosque in, 108; 'Umra to, 158, 168 (n. 3)

Medina, 4, 33, 41, 108–11, 158

Melucci, Alberto, 280

Merchants, 42–43, 47, 50 (n. 12)

Mernissi, Fatima, 24

Meta-cities, 21

Metcalf, Barbara, 194

Militant Islamic Group, 225

Military in medieval Muslim state, 42, 43, 46, 50 (n. 12)

Million Family March, 270

Million Man March, 270

Missionaries, 224

Modernists: and *'ulama'*, 98; definition of, 103–4 (n. 10); in Iran, 130–31 (n. 6)

Mohanty, Chandra, 170–71

Mongols, 221

Morocco, 45, 206 (n. 4), 277

Morris, William, 118

Mos Def, 264, 266–67, 268, 270

Mosque network in Iran: structure of, 70–71, 75; contested nodes of, 71–73; disrupted spokes in, 73–75; overturned structure of, 75–81; and radicals' tactics, 76–80; and lessons about Muslim networks, 81–83; male-only leadership in, 183

Mosques: in Iran, 71; Egyptian women in, 157, 159; ethnic mosque, 172, 186 (n. 4); U.S. women in, 173, 183, 187 (n. 5); occupation of in Saudi Arabia, 232

Mottahedeh, Roy, 199

Mourning and remembrance rituals, 12–13, 132–54, 278–79

Movement for Islamic Reform (MIRA), 258

Mu'awiya, 153–54 (n. 5)

Mubarak, Susan, 166

Mughals and Mughal culture, 15, 104 (n. 18), 118, 122, 123

Mugtama'at sayyidat (women-only gatherings), 160

Muhaiyadeen, Bawa, 205

Muhammad, Prophet: death of, 5;

daughter and granddaughter of, 12, 13, 135; proselytizing and trading networks of, 14; on women, 24; state established by in Medina, 41; on *'ulama'*, 42; sayings of, 49 (n. 8); defamation of in *Rangila Rasul*, 61, 66; and imams, 76; Muslim philosophers on, 93–94; normative example of, 103 (n. 4); and Sunni Muslims, 134; and Shiites, 134–35; as descendant of Ibrahim, 135; companions of, 210–11; and *umma*, 265; and Quran, 266

Muhammad, Sabirah, 186

Mujahidin (holy fighters), 215, 217–18, 220, 239. *See also* E-*mujahidin* networks; Jihad

Mujawir, 8

Mullaya (woman religious leader), 13, 132, 139, 141–45, 147–48

Al-Muntada Al-Islami, 178

Muntaziri, Ayatullah Hussein-'Ali, 74

Muqri', Muhammad Mustafa al-, 224

Murid brotherhood, 16

Mushatara (sharing in proportionate measure), 38

Music and Sufism, 195, 200–201, 204

Muslim: definition of, 1; negative stereotypes of, 17, 208

Muslim Brotherhood, 97, 210, 214, 258

Muslim League, 55, 62–64

Muslim networks: definition of, 1; and *umma*, 2; men as privileged in, 2–3; as medium and method, 2–10; and trade networks, 5; and scholarship, 5, 6–7; and Sufism, 5, 7, 191–205; and reciprocity and hierarchy, 5–6; as metaphor, 10–15, 52–55, 66, 277–78; and *Azizah* magazine in United States, 11–12, 169–88; Islamic salons in Egypt, 12, 155–68, 279; and Iraqi Shiite women, 12–13, 132–54, 278–79;

and Islamic art, 13–14, 107–30, 280; history of, 15–19; and Pakistan formation, 17, 22, 55–66; and colonialism, 17–19; and Iranian Revolution (1978–79), 19, 70–83; and information revolution, 19–24; rivalry between, 22; and globalization, 24–26; as episteme, 25; and Salafi movement, 25, 208–34, 280; and hip hop, 26, 264–73; conclusions on, 26–28, 275–82; lessons about from mosque network in Iran, 81–83. *See also* Internet; Women's networks; *and specific networks*

Muslim Personal Law (MPL), 18, 166–67, 168

Muslims against Terrorism, 238

Muslim Student Association, 22

Muslim women: participation of in Hajj, 3, 12, 165, 184–85; mourning rituals of Iraqi Shiite women, 12–13, 132–54, 278–79; and MPL, 18, 166–67, 168; and *ijtihad*, 24; rights for, 24, 165–67; in Afghanistan, 26; Ibn Battuta on, 31; as artists, 112, 114–15, 122–23, 125–29; veiling of, 156, 161, 163–65, 169–72, 176, 178–81, 186 (n. 2), 243, 247; at mosques and *zawias* in Egypt, 157, 159; and charitable organizations, 157–58; in Saudi Arabia, 160, 172–73; literacy of in Egypt, 167; burqa worn by, 169, 186 (n. 2); and imageness, 170–71; stereotypes and third-world image of, 170–72, 187–88 (nn. 12–13); at mosques in United States, 173, 187 (n. 5); and Islamic feminism, 181–83, 187 (n. 15), 279; with disabilities, 184–85; and Sufism, 205; and blogging, 247; and hip hop, 270–71. *See also* Women's networks

Mut'a (temporary marriage for payment), 89

Mutahhari, Ayatullah Murtaza, 74
Mutamassik (rapper), 271
Mutanabbi, al-, 9
Muwatta, 88–89
Mysticism. *See* Sufism

Nadwat al-'Ulama,' 90, 91, 95
Nadwi, Abu'l-Hasan 'Ali, 6, 90–92,
　95–96, 102
Najaf, 137, 154 (n. 6)
Najafi-Mar'ashi, Ayatullah Shiha-
　buddin, 78
Nameen, Narges Rasoulzadeh, 125,
　128
Napoleon of the Outlawz, 264
Naqshband, Baha'uddin, 201, 207
　(n. 13)
Naqshbandi order of Sufism, 198, 202
Naqshbandiya, 16
Nashid (religious music), 240
Nassef, Malak Hifni, 157
Nasser, Gamal Abdel, 90, 96, 162
Nasserism, 90
Nationalism, ethnic, 18
Nationhood, 32
Nation of Gods and Earths, 266
Nation of Islam, 265–66, 267, 270
Nation-states, 18, 32, 48, 54, 65, 66
Nawal Kishor, Munshi, 200
Al-Neda website, 239, 241
Neocolonialism, 100. *See also* Colo-
　nialism
Netherlands: Shiite women in, 12–13,
　132–34, 139, 143, 145–47, 151, 153
Network analysis, 69–70
Networks: definition of, 1; and "net-
　war," 51, 244; scholarly interest
　in, 51–52, 69; nodes of, 69, 82; in
　social science, 69–70; structure of,
　69–70, 82; building and rebuilding
　of, 82; purposes of, 82; and reifi-
　cation, 82–83. *See also* Muslim
　networks; Women's networks;
　and specific networks
New Bengal Movement, 118, 119

Newsweek magazine, 169
Nida'ul Islam, 232
Nimatollahi order of Sufism, 202
9/11 attacks, 51, 52, 66, 208, 209, 235,
　238, 239, 240, 241, 246, 248
Niqab (face covering), 164
Nizami, Hasan, 197
Nkiru Bookstore, 270
Nomadic jihad, 218–21

Officializing strategies, 253–62
Oikumene, 15
Ole Dirty Shame, 272
Omar, Manal, 177
Omar, Mullah, 241
One and a Half (Ahmed), 125, 129
Opposite Direction, 20
Orientalists, 191, 192, 194, 196, 205,
　282
Osumare, Halifu, 265
Ottoman *khalifa* (caliph), 61–62
Oudah, Salman bin Fahd al-, 259

Pakistan: Muslim networks and
　formation of, 17, 22, 55–66, 67
　(n. 10); Afghan refugees in, 26;
　establishment of, 55; nation-state
　of, 65; society of, 65; Data Darbar
　Shrine in, 109; Sufism in, 197, 207
　(n. 9); and war in Afghanistan,
　217; Tablighi Jama'at in, 258
Palestine (Alsaie), 125, 126
Palestine and Palestinians, 162, 217,
　241, 244–45, 269, 271, 272
Palestine Way, 250 (n. 26)
Pan African movement, 265, 273
　(n. 2)
Pan-Arab nationalism, 90
PanBanegritude movement, 265,
　273–74 (n. 2)
Pan-Islamic art, 110–12, 122, 128
Pan Islamic movement, 265
Pascal, Blaise, 21
Pearl, Daniel, 240
People's Voice, 197

Periodicals. *See* Magazines

Perkins, William Eric, 265

Persian language, 5–6, 17, 90, 104 (n. 18), 195–96, 197, 256

Philippines, 220

Pir Vilayat Khan, 202

Polygyny, 173

Poor Righteous Teachers, 266

Portelli, Alessandro, 151

Postmodernism, 125, 127

Printing and print publications: Gutenberg's printing press, 21, 193; in India, 58–61, 67 (n. 4), 194–95, 197, 200; in China, 193; and Protestant Reformation, 193; and Islam, 193–94; and Sufism, 193–200, 204, 206 (nn. 5–6); and fundamentalist groups, 195

Project Gutenberg, 256

Proportional ethics, 37–38

Protestant Reformation, 193

Public Enemy, 269, 270

Publishing. *See* Printing and print publications

Puzo, Mario, 32, 33, 39

Qaddafi, Omar, 225

Qadi, qudat (judges), 8, 84, 85–87, 103 (n. 5)

Qadi al-jamaʿa (chief justice), 44, 47

Qadir, Emir ʿAbd al-, 193

Al-Qaeda: Bin Laden as founder of, 25; Bush on evil of, 208; and Salafi movement, 209, 215, 221, 232, 280; funds for, 224; and Gamiyya Islamiyya, 231; and Internet, 238–41, 243, 244. *See also* Bin Laden, Osama

Qaradawi, Yusuf al-, 6, 91, 96–102, 238, 260

Qatar, 20, 238

Qawwali (recordings), 198, 200–201

Qayrawani, ʿAbd al-ʿAziz al-, 48

Qudsway, 250 (n. 26)

Queer Jihad, 251 (n. 34)

Qumi, Ayatullah Hasan, 81

Quraishi, Asifa, 177, 184

Quran: online versions of, 22, 255–56; and Salafi movement, 25, 211, 212; as guidepost of Islam, 27; straight path as metaphor in, 27; egalitarian principles of, 33; on justice, 38; as basis of legal decisions, 44; on divorce, 91, 160; anti-hermeneutical stance toward, 93; Zenderoudi's illustrations for, 113, 131 (n. 7); Christ in, 122; apocalyptic *surahs* in, 123; and Shiites, 134; and Sunni Muslims, 134; study circles on, 157, 159, 160; women's interpretation of, 177, 184; women reciters of, 187 (n. 9); and condemnation of 9/11 attacks, 238; and Prophet Muhammad, 266; and hip hop texts, 266–70

Qushayri, 197

Qutb, Sayyid, 95

Qutb Minar, 108

Racketeering, 33–40

Radjam, ʿAbd al-Razzak, 223

Radley, Alan, 140

Rahman, Omar Abdul, 218, 224, 240

Raʾiya, al- (flock), 33

Ramadan, 157, 158–59, 239

Rand Corporation, 51

Rangila Rasul, 61, 66

Rap, 273 (n. 1). *See also* Hip hop

Rasch, Bodo, 109

Rawls, John, 49 (n. 2)

Raza Khan, Maulana Ahmad, 60

Reciprocity, 5–7, 34–36

Reconquista, 4

Refugees: Iraqi Shiite women as, 12–13, 132–54, 278–79; Afghan refugees in Pakistan, 26

Revolutionary Association of the Women of Afghanistan (RAWA), 26

Revolutionary Council (Iran), 82

Rifa'i order of Sufism, 202
Rifkin, Jeremy, 282
Rihla (travel memoir), 3, 4, 9, 31, 40, 276
Rihlat Ibn Battuta (Ibn Juzayy), 3, 40, 84, 85
Rijal al-'ilm (men of knowledge), 41
Riyadh bombing (1995), 225, 240
Robinson, Francis, 194–95
Roumani, Rhonda, 182
Ruhaniyat (religious scholars), 71
Rumi, Jalal al-Din, 41, 49 (n. 8), 119, 196, 201, 204, 205, 206 (n. 6)
Rushdie, Salman, 66
Rustaveli, Shota, 118
Rza (rapper), 264, 271

Sabir, Nadirah, 183, 185
Sabo, Sarah, 180, 187 (n. 14)
Sabti, Abu al-'Abbas al-, 37–38
Sadat, Anwar, 166, 168 (n. 7)
Sadat, Jihan, 166
Sa'di, Muhammad al-Sheikh al-, 48, 196 (nn. 5–6)
Sadra, Mulla, 15
Saduqi, Ayatullah Muhammad, 79–80
Saeed, Ayesha Lorenz Al-, 175–76, 187 (n. 10)
Safavid empire, 15
Sagha-Khaneh movement, 115–16
Said, Edward, 281–82
Said, Muhammad al-, 223
Salaf (to precede), 210
Salafi movement: and jihad, 25, 209, 215–32; and Quran, 25, 211, 212; and Algerian civil war, 25, 222, 223–25; goal and beliefs of, 208–9, 211–14, 226; intramovement conflict in, 209, 213–16; reformist counterdiscourse on jihad, 209, 215–16, 225–32, 234 (n. 28); as social movement community, 209–13; origin of name of, 210–11; avoidance of *bid'a* by, 211, 212;

and focus on authentic hadiths, 211–12; rejection of *madhhabs* by, 212–13; reverence for *tawhid* and avoidance of *shirk* by, 212; and Internet, 215; and war in Afghanistan, 215, 216–19, 226, 231, 233 (nn. 10–11); and nomadic jihad, 218–21; and jihad against Middle Eastern regimes, 221–25; and *takfir*, 222–25, 228; conclusions on, 231–32; as schismatic, 280
Salahuddin, Amidah, 185
Salam Pax, 247
Salman, Mashhur Hasan, 229
Salons. *See* Islamic salons in Egypt
Samara, 137, 154 (n. 8)
SamSpade.org, 237
Sanusi, Sanusi Lamido, 24
Sarraj, 197
Sassen, Saskia, 19, 21
Satanic Verses (Rushdie), 66
Satellite television, 20, 162, 248, 263 (n. 2)
Saudi Arabia: Iraqi Shiite women in, 12–13, 132–34, 151, 153; Awal-Net in, 20; and HADI-sponsored website, 23; King Faisal in, 91; sex segregation in, 160, 172–73; and war in Afghanistan, 216, 217; and nomadic jihad, 219; and Salafi movement, 222, 229; U.S. military presence in, 222, 233 (n. 7); bombing in Riyadh (1995), 225, 240; occupation of mosques in, 232; suicide operations in, 242–43; MIRA in, 258; website from embassy of in United States, 258
Saudi Arabian Grand Council of Scholars, 238, 245
Saudi Information Agency, 250–51 (n. 33)
SAVAK (security police), 72, 74, 76, 81
Seattle's Islamic Sisterhood (SIS), 172, 173, 174

195, 200–201, 204; translation of Sufi literature, 197; and periodical publishing, 197–98, 206–7 (nn. 8–9); initiation into, 198; and Islamic identity, 205; and women, 205

Suhrawardi, 197

Suhur, 158, 159

Sulaiman, Shaykh Muhammad 'Ali, 230

Sultanate, 33–40, 45–47, 87–88. *See also specific sultans*

Sumatra, 88

Sunna (Prophet's moral example), 202, 211, 212, 233 (n. 7)

Sunnah.org, 202

Sunni Muslims: jurisprudence of, 8, 88; Internet and Sunni women, 14; academic networks of, 16; in eleventh century, 34; on state and its corruption, 41; compared with Shiites, 134–35; in United States, 266

Sunz of Man, 271

Swedenburg, Ted, 269

Syria, 259

Tablighi Jama'at, 258

Tagore, Rabindranath, 118

Taha, Rifa'i Ahmad, 230–31

Tahari, Ayatullah Jalaluddin, 81

Tajikistan, 220

Takfir (declaring apostate), 222–25, 228

Taliban, 26, 57, 169, 170, 241

Taliban-News.com, 250 (n. 20)

Taliqani, Ayatullah Mahmud, 74

Tamar, 118

Taqlid (blind adherence), 213

Tarjuman al-Qur'an, 197

Taskhir (reciprocity), 5–6, 35–36, 38, 49 (n. 4)

Tavakoli-Targhi, Mohamad, 200, 207 (n. 12)

Tawhid (belief in oneness of God), 212

Taylor, Tayyibah, 172–80, 182–84

"Tele-presence," 20

Television, 20, 162, 200, 201, 248, 259, 263 (n. 2)

Terrorism, 23, 51, 208. *See also specific terrorist acts*

Thomas Aquinas, 15

Thumali, Abu Hamza al-, 149

Tile Pond (Nameen), 125, 128

Tilly, Charles, 33, 34, 280

Time magazine, 169, 170

Tolerance, 201

Touraine, Alain, 280

Trade networks, 5

Travel writings, 3–5, 9, 31, 40, 84, 85, 88, 276

Treaty of Versailles (1919), 18

Trust, 7, 13, 16, 22

Turkey, 197–98, 201, 242, 243

Tusi, Nasir al-Din at-, 42–43, 50 (n. 12)

Ul Akhlaq, Zahoor, 116–17

'Ulama' (scholars): travel by, 3–5, 7–10, 277; as protectors of moral values of Islam, 6–7, 27, 40–49, 54; and *ijtihad*, 23; jurists as, 41–45; Muhammad on, 42; position of in social hierarchy, 42–43; education of, 43–44, 57; mistrust of state by, 44–46, 63; torture and execution of, 46–47; political and social agendas of, 47–48; Deobandi *'ulama'*, 57–60, 63–64, 67 (n. 3), 198; in India, 57–60, 63–64, 91–92, 194–95; publications by, 58–60, 67 (n. 4); Barelvi *'ulama'*, 60, 198; and Pakistan movement, 63–64; scope and limits of Islamic cosmopolitanism of, 84–89; discursive language of, 85, 89–102; in Egypt, 96–97; and Muslim modernists, 98; and new media, 101–2; and print publications, 194–95; traditional hermeneutics of, 254